FROM THE LIBRARY

EUROPE INFO
Verzeichnis der Netzwerke und
anderen Informationsquellen der Europäischen Union

EUROPE INFO
Directory of networks and other
European Union information sources

EUROPE INFO
Répertoire des réseaux
et autres sources d'information de l'Union Européenne

Bibliographische Daten befinden sich am Ende der Veröffentlichung
Cataloguing data can be found at the end of this publication
Une fiche bibliographique figure à la fin de l'ouvrage.

Luxemburg: Amt für amtliche Veröffentlichungen der Europäischen Gemeinschaften, 1994
Luxembourg: Office for Official Publications of the European Communities, 1994
Luxembourg: Office des publications officielles des Communautés européennes, 1994

ISBN: 92-827-4950-9

Printed in The Netherlands

Gemeinsame Veröffentlichung von:
Joint publication by:
Publication coéditée par:

GD X   "Information, Kommunikation, Kultur, Audiovisuelle Medien"
           Referat "Informationsrelais und -netze"
DG X   "Information, Communication, Culture, Audiovisual"
           Unit "Information Relays and Networks"
DG X   "Information, Communication, Culture, Audiovisuel"
           Unité "Relais et Réseaux d'information"

KEG, CEC, CCE rue de la Loi, 200, B-1049 Bruxelles

EUR-OP: Abteilung "Verkauf"
           Gruppe Marketing, Öffentlichkeitsarbeit, Information
           Sales Department
           Group Marketing, Public Relations, Information
           Département "Vente"
           Groupe Marketing, Relations Publiques, Information

           2, rue Mercier, L - 2985 Luxembourg

3

Vorwort

Aufgrund ihrer Tätigkeit in vielen Bereichen wirkt die Gemeinschaft immer stärker in den Alltag der Bürger hinein, die deshalb laufend allgemeine und besondere Informationen über die Union benötigen. Daher hat es sich die Europäische Kommission zur Aufgabe gemacht, ihre Arbeitsweise überschaubarer zu gestalten und einen Dialog mit der Öffentlichkeit einzuleiten, der ihr ein besseres Verständnis für die Anliegen, Fragen und Hoffnungen der Bürger ermöglichen soll. Außerdem kann sie den Bürgern so auch die großen Aufgaben der Union erläutern und die Gründe für ihre Beschlüsse vermitteln. Die Union muß ihre Bürger besser informieren, damit diese sich eine eigene Meinung zum europäischen Einigungswerk bilden können. Die Frage ist daher, was geschehen muß, damit diese Informationen alle gesellschaftlichen Gruppen in ihrer eigenen Umwelt erreichen.

Um diesem Ziel näher zu kommen, richtete die Kommission in den Mitgliedstaaten und in einer Reihe von Drittländern schrittweise Verbindungsstellen und Informationsnetze ein, die als Informationsvermittler von größtem Nutzen sind. Sie leisten eine bürgernahe, bedarfsorientierte und somit besonders gute Informationsarbeit. Außerdem versetzen ihre Berichte die Kommission in die Lage, bei ihrer Arbeit die Gegebenheiten jedes Landes zu berücksichtigen und auf die Anliegen seiner Bürger einzugehen.

Das Bemühen, die Information zum Bürger zu bringen, reicht indes nicht aus. Es bedarf auch einer Orientierungshilfe, damit potentielle Informationsnutzer in dem reichhaltigen Angebot das Gesuchte finden können. Daher soll dieses Verzeichnis der Verbindungsstellen und Informationsnetze, das nach sachlichen, aber auch nach räumlichen Gesichtspunkten geeignete Informationsquellen nennt, als Wegweiser dienen.

Die zahlreichen Informationsstellen sind nicht als Einrichtungen gedacht, die getrennt voneinander tätig sind. Die Kommission ist gemäß ihrer Strategie, die europabezogenen Informationsstellen auszubauen, bestrebt, ein gewisses Maß an Abstimmung und eine regional ausgewogene Streuung zu fördern. Sie ermuntert die Einrichtungen zur Zusammenarbeit bzw. zum Auf- und Ausbau partnerschaftlicher Beziehungen mit nationalen, regionalen und lokalen Stellen der betreffenden Länder.

Marcelino Oreja
Mitglied der Kommission

Preface

The various Community policies are having an ever growing impact on the daily life of individuals who are constantly having to ask for information, both general and specialized, about the Union. The European Commission's objective is to ensure transparency in its procedures, communicate with the general public in order to understand its concerns, wishes and aspirations, and at the same time make sure that citizens have a better grasp of the issues at stake and the reasons for its decisions. Better information for the people of Europe is vital if they are to make up their minds sensibly about where European integration should be heading. The next question then comes automatically: how to bring information about Europe to the various sectors of society in accordance with their specific needs?

The gradual establishment of information relays and networks in the Member States and non-Union countries was one of the Commission's answers to this question. The relays and networks are invaluable distribution instruments since they bring our information activities to the citizen by making them accessible (by virtue of their proximity), better adjusted to their requirements, and thus in the long run more effective. Through feedback they enable us to maintain permanent contact with the various local situations and to be aware of the public's concerns.

Although the effort to bring information to every individual is worthwhile in itself, potential users must be able to navigate through the vast range of existing networks. This is the raison d'être for this directory. It is designed to help users select the most appropriate source of information in the light of their specific needs or precise location. The directory lists the characteristics and special features of each network and the precise location of the centres making up the network.

This wealth of information sources available to users is far from fixed. Applying a clearly defined development strategy, the Commission is continuing its work in the field. It is particularly concerned to make sure there is consistency between centres and to ensure regional balance in their distribution. It encourages centres to cooperate in their information activities, and to seek and develop partnerships with national, regional and local institutions.

Marcelino Oreja
Member of the Commission

Préface

Les différentes politiques communautaires ont de plus en plus d'incidence sur le quotidien des citoyens qui sont sans cesse amenés à solliciter une information, tantôt généraliste, tantôt spécialisée sur l'Union. Parallèlement, la Commission européenne s'est donné pour objectif de travailler en toute transparence, de communiquer avec le grand public afin de mieux comprendre ses préoccupations, ses demandes, ses espoirs, et de permettre aux citoyens de mieux saisir les enjeux, les raisons d'être des décisions. Il s'agit de mieux informer nos peuples, condition essentielle à la formation d'une opinion argumentée sur l'évolution de la construction européenne. Dans ce cas, une question s'impose de manière naturelle: comment faire parvenir l'information sur l'Europe aux différents secteurs de la société en fonction de leur propre réalité?

La création progressive de relais et de réseaux d'information dans les Etats membres comme dans les pays tiers, a été l'une des solutions apportées par la Commission à cette interrogation. En effet, les relais et réseaux sont des instruments de diffusion d'une valeur inégalable puisqu'ils rapprochent nos activités d'information du citoyen en les rendant (du fait même de leur proximité) accessibles, mieux adaptées à ses demandes et donc, en définitive, plus efficaces. Ils nous permettent, en outre, par un phénomène de feedback, de rester en contact permanent avec les diverses réalités locales et d'être à l'écoute des préoccupations du citoyen.

Mais si l'effort de rapprocher l'information de tout un chacun est en soi méritoire, encore faut-il que l'utilisateur potentiel voie clair face au vaste éventail de réseaux existants. C'est là toute la raison d'être de ce répertoire, conçu pour aider à choisir la source d'information la plus appropriée en fonction de besoins spécifiques ou de l'endroit précis où l'on se trouve.
Le présent répertoire indique les caractéristiques et les particularités de chaque réseau ainsi que le lieu d'implantation des relais qui composent le réseau.

Ce riche patrimoine de sources d'information dont nous disposons est loin d'être figé. Appliquant une stratégie de développement clairement définie, la Commission poursuit ses efforts en la matière. Elle reste particulièrement attentive à ce qu'il existe une cohérence entre tous ces centres de même qu'elle veille à l'équilibre régional dans leur répartition. Elle les stimule, en outre, à collaborer les uns avec les autres dans leurs activités d'information, et à rechercher et développer les relations en partenariat, tant avec des institutions nationales que régionales ou locales.

Marcelino OREJA
Membre de la Commission

Inhalt

9

Dritter Teil

Vierter Teil

Fünfter Teil

11

Vertretungen der Kommission und
Informationsbüros des Europäischen Parlaments
in den Mitgliedstaaten

Table of Contents

13

Part Three

The Office for official publications

14

Table des matières

16

Troisième Partie

17

1

ZENTREN FÜR INFORMATIONEN ÜBER EUROPA

Die Zentren für Informationen über Europa werden aus einer gemeinsamen Initiative der Europäischen Kommission und der Regierung eines Mitgliedstaats ins Leben gerufen, die ein Partnerschaftsabkommen abschließen, dem sich gegebenenfalls andere Organismen anschließen können. Das erste Zentrum dieser Art wurde 1992 in Paris eröffnet: "Sources d'Europe"; das Jacques-Delors-Zentrum wurde vor kurzem in Lissabon gegründet und Zentren in anderen Ländern sind in der Planung.

➤ **Ziele**
Die Zentren sollen folgendes gewährleisten:
- Unterrichtung der breiten Öffentlichkeit über die Unionspolitik
- Bearbeitung von Einzelanfragen
- Ausbildung von Verantwortlichen für Information auf lokaler und regionaler Ebene
- Betreuung der bestehenden Netze
- Bildung eines Treffpunkts für Debatten über Europa.

➤ **Verfügbare Information**
Die Zentren für Informationen über Europa verfügen sowohl über alle offiziellen Dokumente sowie über alle Veröffentlichungen der europäischen Institutionen in schriftlicher, audiovisueller EDV-Form und über nationale Dokumentationen europäischen Charakters, Nachschlagewerke, internationale Presse.
Sie haben auch Zugang zu bestimmten EG-Datenbanken (Info 92, Celex, Rapid,...).
Die Zentren erfassen das gesamte europäische Informationsspektrum, von einfachen, allgemein gehaltenen Informationen bis hin zu fachspezifischen Informationen, so daß alle Erwartungshaltungen erfüllt werden: dies reicht von der einfachen Auskunft, über den Studenten mit Fragen zu seiner Doktorarbeit bis hin zum politischen Entscheidungsträger.

➤ **Aktionen**
- Sammlung, Präsentation und Verbreitung von Informationen über Europa
- Veranstaltung von Treffen und Seminaren für institutionelle und lokale Betreuer zur Vermittlung einer Ausbildung für die Verbreitung der europäischen Informationen
- Organisation von Ausstellungen zur Förderung des kulturellen Lebens in Europa
- Erstellung von hauseigener Dokumentation (Fachdossiers, Mitteilungsblätter, Artikel)

➤ **Mittel**
Die Centres d'information sur l'Europe verfügen über sehr große Räumlichkeiten, einschließlich einer Mediathek (Multimedia-Saal nur für EG-Dokumentationen), Konferenzsäle, Ausstellungsräume, eine Buchhandlung sowie Verkaufsstellen, (Promotion-Schaufenster, Boutique mit Gegenständen in den Europa-Farben ...).

➤ Europäische Kommission
Generaldirektion X
Referat X/A/4 - Informationsrelais und -netze
200 Rue de la Loi
B - 1049 Brüssel
Tel. (32.2) 299 94 25/299 90 65

EUROPEAN INFORMATION CENTRES ON EUROPE

The Information Centres on Europe were set up at the joint initiative of the European Commission and the Government of a Member State who between them concluded a partnership agreement to which other organisations can be associated if need be.
The first centre of this kind was opened in Paris in 1992: "European Sources"; the Jacques Delors centre was just set up in Lisbon, other centres are under study in a number of countries.

➤ **Objectives**

The Information Centres on Europe must provide:
* information for the general public on Union policies;
* prompt response to requests for information;
* training for those responsible for information at local and regional levels;
* animation of existing systems;
* setting up a place for meetings and discussions on Europe.

➤ **Available Information**

The Information Centres on Europe have available all the official documents as well as other publications of the European Institutions, in written, audiovisual or computerised data form, national documentation relative to Europe, works of reference and the international press.
They also have access to certain Community databases (Info 92, Celex, Rapid,...).
The Centres cover the whole spectrum of European information, from the simplest and most general information to the most specific and technical, so as to be able to respond to peoples' various needs: from the person who wants a simple clarification, the political decision-maker, to the PhD student preparing his thesis.

➤ **Actions**

* collection, presentation and dissemination of information on Europe;
* organisation of meetings and seminars for the benefit of local and institutional animators in order to ensure training for those who disseminate European information;
* staging exhibitions for the promotion of European cultural life;
* creation of own documentation (thematic files, bulletins, articles...).

➤ **Means**

The Information Centres on Europe have available to them a very large area comprising a media library (with a multimedia room devoted exclusively to Community documentation), conference and exhibition halls, a bookshop, as well as sales outlets (promotional window, a shop with articles in European colours, ...).

➤ European Commission
Directorate-General X
Unit X/A/4 - Information relays and networks
200 rue de la Loi
B - 1049 Brussels
Tel.: (32.2) 299.94.25/299.90.65

CENTRES D'INFORMATION
SUR L'EUROPE

Les Centres d'information sur l'Europe sont créés à l'initiative conjointe de la Commission européenne et du Gouvernement d'un Etat membre qui concluent entre eux un accord de partenariat auquel d'autres organismes peuvent s'adjoindre, le cas échéant.
Le premier centre de ce type a été ouvert à Paris en 1992: "Sources d'Europe"; le centre Jacques Delors vient d'être créé à Lisbonne; d'autres centres sont en projet dans certains pays.

> **Objectifs**
Les Centres d'information sur l'Europe doivent assurer:
- l'information du grand public sur les politiques de l'Union;
- le traitement des demandes d'information ponctuelles;
- la formation des responsables de l'information au niveau local et régional;
- l'animation des réseaux existants;
- la création d'un lieu de rencontres et de débats sur l'Europe.

> **Information disponible**
Les Centres d'information sur l'Europe disposent à la fois de tous les documents officiels ainsi que des autres publications des Institutions européennes, sous forme écrite, audiovisuelle ou informatique, et de la documentation nationale à caractère européen, des ouvrages de référence, de la presse internationale.Ils ont aussi accès à certaines bases de données communautaires (Info 92, Celex, Rapid,...).
Les Centres balaient tout le spectre de l'information européenne, de l'information la plus simple et généraliste à l'information la plus spécifique et technique, de façon à pouvoir répondre à l'attente de tous les types de publics: de la personne qui veut un simple éclaircissement à l'étudiant en thèse de doctorat, en passant par le décideur politique.

> **Activités**
- collecte, présentation et diffusion de l'information sur l'Europe;
- organisation de rencontres et de séminaires au profit des animateurs institutionnels et locaux afin d'assurer une formation à ceux qui diffusent l'information européenne;
- réalisation d'expositions susceptibles de promouvoir la vie culturelle en Europe;
- création de documentation propre (dossiers thématiques, bulletins, articles...).

> **Moyens**
Les Centres d'information sur l'Europe disposent d'un très grand espace comprenant une médiathèque (salle multimédia entièrement consacrée à la documentation communautaire), des salles de conférence, d'exposition, une librairie, ainsi que des comptoirs (vitrine de promotion, boutique d'objets aux couleurs de l'Europe, ...).

> Commission européenne
Direction générale X
Unité X/A/4 - Relais et réseaux d'information
200 rue de la Loi
B - 1049 Bruxelles
Tél.: (32.2) 299.94.25/299.90.65

SOURCES D'EUROPE
Centre d'information sur l'Europe
Socle de la Grande Arche
F - 92054 PARIS LA DEFENSE
FRANCE

CENTRO EUROPEU DE INFORMACAO
JACQUES DELORS
Centro cultural de Belem
P - 1000 LISBOA
PORTUGAL

24

(¹) Im Jahr 1993 wurde in Rom ANIDE gegründet (Associazione Nazionale per
Informazione e la Documentazione Europea) deren Hauptaufgaben aus der
Veröffentlichung von ANIDE-Informationsbroschüren und Konzeptpapierenn
der ANIDE, der Organisation von Debatten und Seminaren über Themen der EG und
aus Ermittlungen und Studien über europäische Fragen bestehen. Zu einem
späteren Zeitpunkt soll ANIDE ein Zentrum für Informationen über Europa werden.

(²) In 1993, ANIDE (Associazione Nazionale per Informazione e la Documentazione
Europea) was created in Rome. Its main activities are: the publication of ANIDE
dossiers and notebooks , the organisation of debates and seminars on Community
subjects and research and study of European questions. When fully established,
ANIDE will become an Information Centre on Europe.

(³) En 1993 a été créée à Rome l'ANIDE (Associazione Nazionale per l'Informazione
e la Documentazione Europea) dont les principales activités sont: la publication
des dossiers de l'ANIDE et des cahiers de l'ANIDE, l'organisation de débats et de
séminaires sur des thèmes communautaires, et la recherche et l'étude sur
les questions européennes. A terme, l'ANIDE devrait se constituer en Centre
d'Information sur l'Europe.

ANIDE
Via Veneto, 96
I-00187 Roma
Tel: 06/48903167 - Fax: 06/4741778

INFO-POINTS EUROPE

➤ **Akronym**

I P E

➤ **Trägerorganisation**

Die IPE werden innerhalb einer Struktur mit starkem Publikumsverkehr gegründet. Es handelt sich hier um: Gebietskörperschaften, öffentliche Bibliotheken ...

➤ **Zielgruppe**

Breite Öffentlichkeit

➤ **Wirkungsweise**

32 Zentren sind in Betrieb und andere werden bald in den Unionsländern eröffnet.

➤ **Ziele**

- Bereitstellung von allgemeinen Informationen über die Europäische Union und die Gemeinschaftspolitik
- Weiterleitung von fachspezifischen Anfragen zu den geeigneten Quellen.

➤ **Aktionen**

- Verbreitung von Veröffentlichungen allgemeinen Interesses über die Gemeinschaftspolitik
- Bearbeitung von allgemeinen Anfragen
- Konsultationsmöglichkeit bestimmter offizieller Veröffentlichungen (Amtsblatt der Europäischen Gemeinschaften, Reihe L und C sowie Nachschlagewerke)
- Präsentation von Videos über die Gemeinschaftspolitik
- in bestimmten Fällen wird ein Frage-Antwort-Dienst eingerichtet.

➤ **Betreuung des Netzes und Kommunikationstechnik**

- Ausbildung der Verantwortlichen
- regionale Sitzungen der verschiedenen EG-Informationsstellen.

➤ Europäische Kommission
Generaldirektion X
Referat X/A/4 - Informationsrelais und -netze
200 Rue de la Loi
B - 1049 Brüssel
Tel. (32.2) 299 94 25/299 90 65

EURO INFO-POINTS

> **Acronym**

E I P

> **Host structure**

The EIPs are set up within facilities which are visited frequently:
national or local community facilities, public libraries...

> **Target public**

The general public

> **Community coverage**

32 centres in operation and others being opened in the countries
of the Union.

> **Objectives**

- the provision of general information on the European Union and
  Community policies;
- direct specific requests to the appropriate sources.

> **Actions**

- distribution of publications of general interest concerning all
  Community policies
- dealing with requests for general information;
- make available for consultation various official publications
  (Official Journal of the European Communities, series L and C
  and work of reference);
- presentation of videos on Community policies;
- in certain cases, a question and answer service is provided.

> **Network animation and methods of communication**

- training of those involved
- regional meetings of different Community information relays.

> European Commission
Directorate-General X
Unit X/A/4 - Information relays and networks
200 rue de la Loi
B - 1049 Brussels
Tel.: (32.2) 299.94.25/299.90.65

INFO-POINTS EUROPE

➢ **Acronyme**

I.P.E.

➢ **Structure hôte**

Les IPE sont créés au sein d'une structure ayant un important taux de fréquentation.
Il s'agit de: collectivités territoriales ou locales, bibliothèques publiques...

➢ **Public cible**

Le grand public

➢ **Rayonnement communautaire**

32 centres en fonctionnement et d'autres en voie d'ouverture dans les Pays de l'Union.

➢ **Objectifs**

- Fournir des informations d'ordre général sur l'Union européenne et les politiques communautaires;
- orienter les demandes spécialisées vers les sources appropriées.

➢ **Actions**

- Diffusion de publications d'intérêt général concernant toutes les politiques communautaires
- traitement des demandes d'information générale;
- mise en consultation de certaines publications officielles (Journal Officiel des Communautés européennes, séries L et C et ouvrages de référence);
- présentation de vidéos sur la politique de la Communauté;
- dans certains cas, un service questions/réponses est organisé.

➢ **Animation du réseau et techniques de communication**

- Formation des responsables
- réunions régionales des différents relais d'information communautaire.

➢ Commission européenne
Direction générale X
Unité X/A/4 - Relais et réseaux d'information
200 rue de la Loi
B - 1049 Bruxelles
Tél.: (32.2) 299.94.25/299.90.65

BELGIQUE-BELGIË

INFO-POINT EUROPE
Commission européenne
R.P. Schuman, 12
1049 BRUXELLES
BELGIQUE-BELGIË
Tel: 32/2 296 99 24 - 32/2 295 66 28
Fax: 32/2 296 54 00

DEUTSCHLAND

EU Informationsstelle
Bundesministerium für Wirtschaft (BMWI)
Scharnhorstr., 36
D - 10115 BERLIN
DEUTSCHLAND
Tel : 49/30 234 1992
Fax : 49/30 201 47045

Informationsstelle der Europäischen Kommission
Bertha von Suttner Platz , 2-4
D - 53111 BONN
DEUTSCHLAND
Tel : 49/228 63 86 48
Fax : 49/228 63 03 43

EU Informationsstelle
Wissenschaftliche Allgemeinbibliothek
Domplatz, 1
D - 99084 ERFURT
DEUTSCHLAND
Tel : 49/361 562 4876
Fax: 49/361 562 6329

EU Informationsstelle
Haus der Kunste
Lindenallee, 6 -8
D - 15230 FRANKFURT (ODER)
DEUTSCHLAND
Tel: 49/335 22393

EU Informationsstelle
Georg Schumann Platz 5
D - 06110 HALLE/SAALE
DEUTSCHLAND
Tel: 49/228 63 86 48
Fax: 49/228 63 03 53

28

EU Informationsstelle
Europa-Haus Leipzig
Wilhelm Leuschner-Platz, 1
D - 04107 LEIPZIG
DEUTSCHLAND
Tel: 49/341 960 1977 - 49/341 211 0744
Fax: 49/341 960 1490

EU -Umwelt-Informationszentrum
Umwelt-Center der Stadt SUHL
Bahnhofstr., 20
D - 98527 SUHL
DEUTSCHLAND
Tel: 49/3681 22195
Fax: 49/3681 22057

INFO-POINT EUROPE
EU Informationsstelle
Lagerstrasse, 26
18055 ROSTOCK
DEUTSCHLAND
Tel: 49/381 37014 - 49/381 454395
Fax: 49/381 31222

ELLAS

GRAFEIO ENIMEROSIS tou POLITI tis EYROPAIKIS ENOSIS
(Bureau d'information du citoyen de l'UE)
7, Rue XENOFONDOS
10557 ATHINAI
ELLAS
Tel: 30/1 32 55 550

GRAFEIO ENIMEROSIS tou EYROPAIOU POLITI tis EYROPAIKIS ENOSIS
(Bureau d'information du citoyen de l'UE)
KAROLOU NTIL ,29
54623 THESSALONIKI
ELLAS
Tel: 30/31 22 34 28
Fax: 30/31 22 31 92

ESPAÑA

INFO-POINT-EUROPE
Oficina Europea de la Joventut
Calabria , 147
08029 BARCELONA
ESPAÑA
Tel: 34/3 483 8409
Fax: 34/3 483 8300

INFO-POINT-EUROPE
Universitat de Barcelona
Balmes , 21
08007 BARCELONA
ESPAÑA
Tel: 34/3 412 42 25
Fax: 34/3 412 38 97

INFO-POINT EUROPE
Diputación Provincial de La Coruña
c/ Alférez Provisional, s/n
15006 LA CORUÑA
Tel: 34/81 18 33 00
Fax: 34/81 18 33 02

INFO-POINT EUROPE
Ayuntamiento de Lleida
Plaza Paeria s/n
25007 LLEIDA
ESPAÑA
Tel: 34/73 22 28 22
Fax: 34/73 22 28 77

FRANCE

INFO-POINT EUROPE
Place St. Sernin, 21
31000 TOULOUSE
FRANCE
Tel: 33/61 12 34 34
Fax: 33/61 13 70 22

IRELAND

INFO-POINT EUROPE
Athlone Chamber of Commerce
Jolly Mariner Marina
Athlone
Co. Westmeath
IRELAND
Tel: 353/902 73173
Fax: 353/902 73326

INFO-POINT EUROPE
Dundalk RTC
DUNDALK
Co Louth
IRELAND
Tel: 353/42 34 785
Fax: 353/42 38 313

INFO-POINT EUROPE
Mullingar Chamber of Commerce
MULLINGAR
Co. Westmeath
IRELAND
Tel: 353/44 41414
Fax: 353/44 41078

ITALIA

INFO-POINT EUROPE
Piazza Amendola, 5
74100 SALERNO
ITALIA

LUXEMBOURG

INFO-POINT EUROPE
Grand-rue, 22
L - 1660 LUXEMBOURG
LUXEMBOURG
Tel: 352/46 62 56
Fax: 352/46 90 49

INFO-POINT EUROPE
Office des Publications officielles des CE
2, rue Mercier
2985 LUXEMBOURG
LUXEMBOURG
Tel: 352/49 92 81

NEDERLAND

KIOSK 'EUROPA IN HET KLEIN'
Gravenstraat., 15
NL - 1012 AMSTERDAM
NEDERLAND
Tel: 31/20 627 38 78

ÖSTERREICH

INFO-POINT EUROPE
Rathaus
Landhausgasse, 2
8000- GRAZ
ÖSTERREICH
Tel: 43/316 83 17 81
Fax: 43/316 872 5602

29

EU-Informationsstelle
Spittelwiese, 4
4020 - LINZ
ÖSTERREICH
Tel: 43/732 7720 5620
Fax: 43/732 7720 4022

EU Informationsstelle
Bürgerbüro der Salzbürger
Landesregierung
Kaigasse, 39
5020- SALZBURG
ÖSTERREICH
Tel: 43/662 8042 2035
Fax: 43/662 8042 3070

PORTUGAL

CENTRO DE INFORMACAO EUROPEIA
Mediateca da Caixa Geral de Depositos
Avenida João XXI, N¤ 63 - 1¤
P - 1000 LISBOA
PORTUGAL
Tel: 351/1 795 30 00 - 351/1 790 50 46
Fax: 351/1 790 52 86

INFO-POINT EUROPE
Commisão de Coordenação de Região do
Algarve
Praça da Liberdade
8000 FARO
PORTUGAL
Tel: 351/89 80 24 01 - 351/89 80 24 02
Fax: 351/89 80 35 91

INFO-POINT EUROPE
Associação Industrial do Minho
Av. Dr. Francisco Pines Gonçalves
4701 BRAGA
PORTUGAL
Tel: 351/53 61 33 57
Fax: 351/53 76 601

SVERIGE

INFO-POINT EUROPE
Norrmalmstorg 4, BV
111 46 STOCKHOLM
SVERIGE
Tel: 46/8 678 45 10
Fax: 46/8 678 88 11

UNITED KINGDOM

WALES INFO-POINT EUROPE
EUROPEAN COMMISSION
Cathedral Road, 4
UK - CARDIFF CF1 9SG
UNITED KINGDOM
Tel: 44/222 39 54 89
Fax: 44/222 39 54 89

INFO-POINT EUROPE
EUROPEAN COMMISSION OFFICE IN THE
UNITED KINGDOM
Jean Monnet House
Storey's gate, 8
SW1P 3AT LONDON
UNITED KINGDOM
Tel: 44/71 973 1992 - 44/71 973 1979
Fax: 44/171 973 1900

EUROPÄISCHE DOKUMENTATIONSZENTREN

➤ **Akronym**

E D Z (frz.: CDE)

➤ **Trägerorganisation**

Die 1963 gegründeten EDZ sind den Hochschuleinrichtungen angeschlossen, die Studien und Forschung im EG-Bereich fördern und konsolidieren.

➤ **Zielgruppe**

Hochschulmilieu (Professoren, Studenten, Forscher), aber auch universitätsexternes Publikum.

➤ **Wirkungskreis**

299 Zentren in der Gemeinschaft
110 Zentren in Drittländern.

➤ **Ziele**

- Unterstützung der Hochschuleinrichtungen bei der Konsolidierung von Unterricht und Forschung im Bereich der europäischen Integration durch Bereitstellung von notwendigen Informationsquellen
- Sensibilisierung aller europäischer Bürger für die Politik der Union, in Synergie mit anderen Stellen
- Zugänglichkeit der von der Europäischen Union erstellten Dokumente
- Teilnahme an der Debatte über die Europäische Union, gegebenenfalls mit anderen europäischen Stellen und Informationsnetzen.

➤ **Ihnen zur Verfügung stehende Informationen**

Die EDZ erhalten die gesamte EG-Dokumentation, die vom Parlament, der Kommission und anderen Gemeinschaftsinstitutionen erstellt wird. Sie haben einen bevorrechtigten Zugang zu den EG-Datenbanken. Bestimmte - sogenannte spezialisierte - EDZ erhalten je nach Bedarf fachspezifische Dokumentationen.

➤ Europäische Kommission
Generaldirektion X
Referat X/A/4 - Informationsrelais und -netze
200 Rue de la Loi
B - 1049 Brüssel
Tel. (32.2) 299 94 25/299 92 72

EUROPEAN DOCUMENTATION CENTRES

➤ **Acronym**

E.D.C.

➤ **Host structure**

The EDCs, set up in 1963, are assigned to the universities promoting and consolidating studies and research in Community matters.

➤ **Target public**

The university community (lecturers, students, researchers), but also the non-university public.

➤ **Community coverage**

299 centres in the Community;
110 centres in non-EC countries.

➤ **Objectives**
- help universities to consolidate teaching and research on European integration in providing them with the sources of information which they require;
- contribute to making the policies of the Union known to all European citizens, in working together with the other relays;
- make the documents produced by the European Union accessible;
- participate in discussions on the European Union, if need be in liaison with the other European relays and information networks.

➤ **Information which they have available**

The EDCs receive all the Community documentation produced by the Parliament, the Commission and the other Community Institutions; they have privileged access to the Community databases.
Some EDCs, those which are specialised, receive documentation selected in relation to their needs.

➤ European Commission
Directorate-General X
Unit X/A/4 - Information relays and networks
200 rue de la Loi
B - 1049 Brussels
Tel.: (32.2) 299.94.25/299.92.72

CENTRES DE DOCUMENTATION EUROPÉENNE

> **Acronyme**

C.D.E.

> **Structure hôte**

Les CDE, nés en 1963, sont attribués aux institutions universitaires promouvant et consolidant les études et la recherche en matière communautaire.

> **Public cible**

Le milieu universitaire (professeurs, étudiants, chercheurs), mais aussi le public non-universitaire.

> **Rayonnement communautaire**

299 centres dans la Communauté;
110 centres dans les pays tiers.

> **Objectifs**

- Aider les Institutions universitaires à consolider l'enseignement et la recherche sur l'intégration européenne en leur fournissant les sources d'information dont elles ont besoin;
- contribuer à faire connaître à l'ensemble des citoyens européens les politiques de l'Union, en synergie avec les autres relais;
- rendre accessibles les documents produits par l'Union européenne;
- participer au débat sur l'Union européenne, le cas échéant en liaison avec les autres relais et réseaux d'information européens.

> **Informations dont ils disposent**

Les CDE reçoivent l'ensemble de la documentation produite par le Parlement, la Commission et les autres Institutions communautaires; - ils ont un accès privilégié aux bases de données communautaires. Certains CDE, dits spécialisés, reçoivent une documentation sélectionnée en fonction de leurs besoins.

> Commission européenne
Direction générale X
Unité X/A/4 - Relais et réseaux d'information
200 rue de la Loi
B - 1049 Bruxelles
Tél.: (32.2) 299.94.25/299.92.72

BELGIQUE-BELGIË

ANTWERPEN

Universiteit Antwerpen (UFSIA)
Bibliotheek
Prinsstraat 93
2000 Antwerpen
Belgique/België
tel. (32-3) 220 49 96
fax (32-3) 220 44 37

BRUGGE

Collège d'Europe
Bibliothèque
Dijver 11
8000 Brugge
Belgique/België
tel. (32-50) 33 53 34

BRUXELLES

Centre for European Policy Studies
Library
Place du Congrés, 1
1000 Bruxelles
Belgique/België
tel. (32-2) 218 22 47
fax (32-2) 219 41 51

Université Libre de Bruxelles
Institut d'Etudes Européennes
Avenue F. D. Roosevelt 39
1050 Bruxelles
Belgique/België
tel. (32-2) 650 30 73
fax.(32-2) 650 30 68

Vrije Universiteit Brussel
Faculteit der Rechtgeleerd ,
Heid Seminaire Europees Recht
Pleinlaan 2
1050 Bruxelles
Belgique/België
tel. (32-2) 641 26 31
fax (32-2) 641 36 33

GEEL

Hoger Instituut der Kempen
Campus Westelijke Ring
2440 Geel
Belgique/België

GENT

Rijksuniversiteit Gent
Dienst voor Europees Recht
Universiteitstraat 4
9000 Gent
Belgique/België
tel. (32-91) 264 0 906, 264 691

LEUVEN

Katholieke Universiteit Leuven
Universiteitsbibliotheek
Mgr. Ladeuzeplein 21
3000 Leuven
Belgique/België
tel. (32-16) 28 46 18

LIEGE

Université de Liège
Faculté de Droit, Institut d'Etudes
Juridiques Sart Tilman
boulevard du Rectorat 7
4000 Liège
Belgique/België
tel. (32-41) 56 30 24

LOUVAIN-LA-NEUVE

Université Catholique de Louvain
Institut d'Etudes Européennes
place des Doyens, 1
1348 Louvain-la-neuve
Belgique/België
tel. (32-10) 47 85 50
fax (32-10) 47 85 49

NAMUR

Université Notre Dame de la Paix.
Bibliothèque Universitaire Moretus Plantin
rue Grandgagnage 19
5000 Namur
Belgique/België
tel. (32-81) 22 90 61

DANMARK

AALBORG

Aalborg Universitets Bibliotek ,
International Publications
P.B. 8200
9220 Aalborg oest
Danmark
tel. (45) 98 15 85 22 ext. 2604

34

AARHUS

Statsbiblioteket
Sektion for Internationale Organisationers
Publikationer Universitetsparken
8000 Aarhus C
Danmark
tel. (45) 86 12 20 22

Handelshojskolen I Aarhus V
Biblioteket
Fuglesang alle 4
8210 Aarhus V
Danmark
tel. (45) 86 15 55 88
fax (45) 86 15 01 88

ESBJERG

Sydjysk Universitets Center
Bibliotek
Glentvej, 7
6705 Esbjerg
Danmark
tel. (85) 79 14 11 11
fax (85) 79 14 11 30

KOBENHAVEN

Handelshøjskolens
Bibliotek
Rosenørns allé 31
Kobenhavn
Danmark
tel. (45) 38 15 36 66
fax (45) 38 15 36 63

Kobenhavns Universitet
Institut for International Ret Og Europaret
Studiestraade 6 -1
1455 Kobenhavn K
Danmark
tel. (45) 35 32 31 30
fax (45) 35 32 32 03

ODENSE

Odense Universitets
Bibliotek
Campusvej 55
5230 Odense M
Danmark
tel. (45) 66 15 86 00

ROSKILDE

Roskilde Universitets
Bibliotek
PO Box 260
DK 4000 Roskilde
Danmark
tel (45) 46 757711
fax (45) 46756102

DEUTSCHLAND

AACHEN

Aachener Zentrum für Europäische Studien RWTH
Theaterstr. 67
52062 Aachen
Deutschland
tel. (49-241) 345 64
fax (49-241) 40 29 17

AUGSBURG

Universität Augsburg
Universitätsbibliothek
Eichleitnerstr. 30
86135 Augsburg
Deutschland
tel. (49-821) 59 83 42 / 59 84 79

BAMBERG

Universität Bamberg
Universitätsbibliothek
Postfach 1549, Feldkirchenstr. 21
96045 Bamberg
Deutschland
tel. (49-951) 863 84 39
fax (49-951) 863 15 65

BAYREUTH

Universität Bayreuth
Bibliothek
Universitätsstr, 30 Postfach 10 12 51
95440 Bayreuth
Deutschland
tel. (49-921)55 34 20

35

BERLIN

Freie Universität Berlin
Universitätsbibliothek
Garystr. 39
14195 Berlin
Deutschland
tel. (49 30) 838 23 99
fax (49 30) 838 37 38

Europäische Akademie Berlin
Bibliothek
Bismarckallee 46-48
14193 Berlin
Deutschland
tel. (49-30) 826 20 95

BIELEFELD

Universität Bielefeld
Universitätsbibliothek
Universitätsstr. 25
33615-1 Bielefeld
Deutschland
tel. (49-521) 106 38 06
fax (49-521) 106 41 06

BOCHUM

Ruhr-Universität Bochum ,
Universitätsbibliothek
Universitätsstr. 150
44801 Bochum
Deutschland
tel. (49-234) 700 69 45
fax. (49-234) 700 62 69

BONN

Gesellschaft für Auswärtige Politik E.V.
Bibliothek
Adenauerallee 131
53113 Bonn
Deutschland
tel. (49-228) 267 51 26
fax (49-228) 267 51 73

Universitäts und Landesbibliothek Bonn
Adenauerallee 33
53000-1 Bonn
Deutschland
tel. (49-228) 73 79 91
fax (49-228) 73 75 46

BREMEN

Universität Bremen
Zentrum für Europäische Rechtspolitik
(ZERP)
Universitätsallee gw 1
28359 Bremen
Deutschland
tel. (49-421) 218 22 47 / 218 32 14
fax. (49-421) 34 03

DARMSTAD

Technisches Hochschule Darmstadt
Residenzschoss, 21, 216 - Makplatz, 15
64283 Darmstadt
Deutschland
tel. (49-6151) 16 21 42

DRESDEN

**Akademische Zentralbibliothek für
Geisteswissenschaften**
Sächsische Landesbibliothek
Marienallee 12
01099 Dresden
Deutschland
tel. (49-351) 526 77
fax (49-351) 532 21

DUISBURG

Gerhard-Mercator-Universität
Gesamthochschule Duisburg,
Universitätsbibliothek
Lotharstr. 65
41001 Duisburg
Deutschland
tel. (49-203) 379 20 83
fax (49-203) 379 33 33

EBENHAUSEN

Stiftung Wissenschaft und Politik
Forschungsinstitut F. Int. Politik
Haus Eggenberg
82067 Ebenhausen
Deutschland
tel. (49-8178) 703 00
fax.(49-8178) 703 12

ERLANGEN

**Universität Erlangen- Nürnberg
Jurist. Institut Bibliothek**
Schillerstr. 1
91054 Erlangen
Deutschland
tel.(49-9131) 85 2817, 85 22 40
fax. (49-9131) 85 24 81

FRANKFURT AM MAIN

Universität Frankfurt/Main
Institut für Ausländisches und
Internationales Wirtschaftsrecht
Senckenberganlage 31 - Postfach 11 19 32
60054 Frankfurt am Main
Deutschland
tel. (49-69) 798 31 93
fax.(49-69) 798 84 66

FRANKFURT ODER

Europa Universität Viadrina
Postfach 776 - Grosse Scharrnstr. 59
15207 Frankfurt Oder
Deutschland

FREIBURG

Universität Freiburg
Institut für Öffentliches Recht
Europa platz 1 -Kollengiengebäude, II
79085 Freiburg
Deutschland
tel. (49-761) 203 35 13
fax (49-761) 203 31 89

FULDA

Fachhochschule Fulda
Marquardstrasse 35
36039 Fulda
Deutschland
tel: 06 61 96400 ext. 108
fax: 06 61 40 199

GIESEN

Justus-Liebig-Universität
Fachbereich Rechtswissenschaften
Licher str. 76   Haus 2
35394 Gießen
Deutschland
tel. (49-641) 702 50 301
fax.(49-641) 702 50 97

GÖTTINGEN

Universität Göttingen
Bibliothek der Wirtschafts und Sozial
Wissenschaftlichen
Platz der Göttinger Sieben 3
37073 Göttingen
Deutschland
tel. (49-551) 39 72 52
fax (49-551) 39 96 47

HAGEN

Fernuniversität   GHS
Universitätsbibliothek Tausch und
Geschenkstelle Feithstraße 152
58097 Hagen
Deutschland
tel. (49-2331) 987 28 92
fax (49-2331) 98 73 13

HALLE

Martin-Luther Universität
Max-Planck-Gesellschaft
Franckeplatz, 1- Haus 42
06132 Halle (Saale)
Deutschland
tel. (49-345) 29 852
fax (49-345) 29 853

HAMBURG

HWWA Institut für
Wirtschaftforschung Abteilung
Neuer Jungferstieg 21
20347 Hamburg
Deutschland
tel. (49-40) 356 22 19
fax. (49-40) 35 19 00

Universität Hamburg
Abteilung Europarecht
Schlusterstr.28/111
20146 Hamburg
Deutschland
tel. (49-40) 41 23 30 31, 30-29
fax. (49-40) 41 23 62 52

HANNOVER

Niedersächsische Landebibliothek
Wunstorferstr. , 14
30453-91 Hannover
Deutschland
tel. (49-511) 762 55 98

HEIDELBERG

Heidelberg Universität
Max-Planck Institut für Ausländisches
Öffentliches und Völkerrecht
Berliner str. 48
69120 Heidelberg
Deutschland
tel. (49-6221) 48 22 24
fax. (49-6221) 48 22 88

37

JENA

Universität Jena,
Rechtswissenschaftliche Fakultat
Friederich Schiller
Leutragraben 1 23
07743 Jena
Deutschland
tel. (49-3641) 82 24 119, 83
fax.(49-3641) 82 24 167

KEHL

Fachhochschule für Öffentliche
Verwaltung
Institut für Regional Zusammenarbeit und
Europäische Verwaltung
Kinzigallee, 1
77675 Kehl
Deutschland
tel. (49-7851) 894 13
fax (49-7851) 894 74

KIEL

Universität Kiel
Bibliothek
Düsternbrookerweg 120
24100-1 Kiel
Deutschland
tel. (49-431) 88 141
fax (49-431) 85 853

KÖLN

Universitäts-und-Stadtbibliothek Köln
Universitätsstr. 33
50931 Köln
Deutschland
tel. (49-221) 470 33 12, 08
fax (49-221) 470 51 66

Universität Köln
Institut für das Recht der E.U.
Albertus Magnus- platz
50931-41 Köln
Deutschland
tel. (49-221) 470 38 23/62
fax (49-221) 470 38 41

KONSTANZ

Universität Konstanz
Bibliothek
Universitätsstr., 10
78461 Konstanz
Deutschland
tel. (49-7531) 88 28 45
fax.(49-7531)88 30 82

LEIPZIG

Universität Leipzig
Zentrum für Internationale
Wirtschaftsbeziehungen Hauptgebäude,
Raum 2-33/36 Augustusplatz 10, 11 -
Postfach 9 20
0-7010 Leipzig
Deutschland
tel. (49-341) 719 22 68/85
fax (49-341) 719 22 86

MAINZ

Universität Mainz Institut für
Politikwissenschaften FB
Saarstr. 21, Haus Bamberger
55099 Mainz
Deutschland
tel. (49-6131) 39 21 50, 39 46 33
fax.(49-6131) 39 46 35

MANNHEIM

Universität Mannheim
L 15, 16
68131 Mannheim
Deutschland
tel. (49-621) 292 53 71
fax (49-621) 292 84 35

MARBURG LAHN

Philipps-Universität Marburg
Bibliothek
Wilhelm-Röpke-str. 6 - Block b
35032 Marburg/Lahn
Deutschland
tel. (49-6421) 28 43 79

MÜNCHEN

Universität München
Institut für International Recht
europäisches und internationales
Wirtschaftsrecht
Ludwigstr. 29/III
80539 München
Deutschland
tel. (49-89) 21 80 32 68
fax (49-89) 21 80 29 04

MÜNSTER

Westfälische Wilhelms Universität
Institut für Politikwissenschaft
Scharnhorststr. 100
48151 Münster
Deutschland
tel. (49-251) 83 43 77/71
fax (49-251) 83 43 72

NÜRNBERG

Universität Erlangen Nürnberg
Fachbereich Wirtschafts und
Sozialwissenschaft
Lange Gasse 20
90403 Nürnberg
Deutschland
tel: (49-911) 530 23 56

OSNABRUCK

Universität Osnabrück
Institut für Europarecht
Martinistraße 8
49034 Osnabruck
Deutschland
tel. (49-541) 969 45 05
fax (49-541) 969 4 482

PASSAU

Universität Passau
Lehrstuhl für Staats- und Verwaltungsrecht
Völkerrecht und Europarecht
Innstr. 25 - Postfach 25 44/ pl 249030
94032 Passau
Deutschland
tel. (49-851) 50 93 13/92 36
fax. (49-851) 50 95 09

REGENSBURG

Universität Regensburg
Universitätsbibliothek
Universitätstr. 31-33
93053-1 Regensburg
Deutschland
tel. (49-941) 943 26 51
fax (49-941) 943 32 85

ROSTOCK

Universität Rostock
Gebäude der jur. Fakultät
Möllnerstr. 9 - Postfach 999
25-18109 Rostock
Deutschland
tel. (49-361) 37 59 12 19

SAARBRÜCKEN

Universität des Saarlandes
Reichtswissenschaftliche Fakulteit, Europa
Institut
Am Stadtwald
66123 Saarbrücken
Deutschland
tel. (49-681) 302 25 43/03

**Saarländische Universitäts und
Landesbibliothek**
Postfach 15 11 41
66123 Saarbrücken
Deutschland
tel. (49-681) 302 20 73
fax (49-681) 302 27 96

SIEGEN

Universität Gesamthochschule Siegen
Universitätsbibliothek
Adolph-Reichwein-Straße 2
57076-21 Siegen
Deutschland
tel. (49-271) 740 42 92
fax (49-271) 740 23 30

SPEYER

**Hochschule für
Verwaltungswissenschaften**
Lehrstuhl F. Öffentliches Recht , Völker u.
Europarecht
Freiherr-von-Stein-Str. 2
67324 Speyer
Deutschland
tel. (49-6232) 6540, 6548
fax (49-6232) 654 208

STUTTGART

Universität Hohenheim
Institut für Agrarpolitik und
Landwirtschaftliche Marktlehre
Postfach 70 05 62 Schloß Osthof
7000 Stuttgart 70
Deutschland
tel. (49-711) 459 26 34

TRIER

Universität Trier
Universitätsbibliothek
Universitätsring 15
54286 Trier
Deutschland
tel. (49-651) 201 24 55
fax (49-651) 251 35

39

TÜBINGEN

Universität Tübingen
Universitätsbibliothek
Wilhelmstr. 32
72016 Tübingen
Deutschland
tel. (49-7071) 29 25 77, 29 31 23

WÜRZBURG

Universität Würzburg
Institut für Völkerrecht Europarecht und
Internationalesrecht
Domerschulstr. 16
97070 Würzburg
Deutschland
tel. (49-931) 313 5 fax.(49-931) 57 047

ELLAS

ATHENS

Spoudastirio Diethnon Spoudon
Kentro Europaikis Tekmiriossis
14 rue Sina
106 72 Athens
Ellas
tel. (30-1) 361 58 12

**Athens University of Economics and
Business**
Department of international and european
economic studies
76 Patission street
104 34 Athens
Ellas
tel. (30-1) 822 14 56
fax (30-1) 89 22 62 04

**Panteion University of Social and
Political Sciences**
Section of International Institutions
176, Syngrou avenue
176 71 Athens
Ellas
tel. (30) 19225055

KALAMARIA

**Centre of International and European
economic law**
b.p. 14
551 02 Thesaloniki , Kalamaria
Ellas
tel. (30-31) 473 403

KOMOTINI

**Université Demokritos de Thrace
Faculté de Droit**
r. Rukoloran Zoidon, 79
69100 Komotini
Ellas
tel. (30-531) 26101
fax. (30) 351 272 65

PIRAEUS

**University of Piraeus Department of
business administration**
80 Karaoli and Dimitriou str.
185 34 Piraeus
Ellas
tel. (30-1) 41146 30
fax (30-1) 41 20653

ESPAÑA

ALICANTE

Universidad de Alicante
c/ Gravina, 4, entr.
03003 Alicante
España
tel. (34-6) 514 43 66/96
fax (34-6) 521 31 40

BADAJOZ

**Centro de Documentación e
Información Europea**
Universidad de Extremadura
av. de Europa, 4
06004 Badajoz
España
tel. (34-24) 24 13 01
fax. 924- 24 38 53

BARCELONA

**Escuela Superior de Administración y
Dirección de Empresas (ESADE)**
Biblioteca calle Marqués de Mulhacén, 40, 42
08034 Barcelona
España
tel. (34-3) 280 61 62 (ext. 367/339)
fax (34-3) 204 81 05

40

Universidad Autónoma de Barcelona
Facultad de Económicas
Edificio E1 campus universitario
08193 Bellaterra (Barcelona)
España
tel. (34-3) 581 16 81
fax (34-3) 581 30 63

BILBAO

Universidad del País Vasco (UPV-EHU)
Facultad de Ciencias Económicas
Av. Lehendakari Agirre,83
48015 Bilbao
España
tel. (34-4) 447 35 62 / 447 28 00 (ext. 351)
fax (34-4) 447 35 66

Universidad de Deusto
Instituto de Estudios Europeos
Av. de las Universidades, s/n apartado 1
48080 Bilbao
España
tel. (34-4) 445 31 00/50, ext. 2316
fax (34-4) 445 06 00

CASTELLON

Universidad Jaume I
Campus del Carrer - Herrero
2005 Castellón
España
tel. (34-64) 34 58 01
fax (34-64) 34 56 45

CORDOBA

Universidad de Córdoba
Facultad de Derecho
Puerta Nueva, s/n 2 planta
14002 Córdoba
España
tel. (34-57) 25 49 62
fax.(34-57) 26 11 20

GIRONA

Universitat de Girona,
Facultat de Dret
Rambla Xavier Cugat, 1,
17071 Girona
España
tel (34-72) 22 71 00
fax (34-72) 22 70 04

GRANADA

Centro de Documentación Europea de Granada
Palacio de los Condes de Gabia
plaza de los Girones, 1
18001 Granada
España
tel. (34-58) 22 40 80
faax (34-58) 22 40 80

LA CORUÑA

Centro de Información, Documentación y Estudios Comunitarios de la Coruña (CIDEC)
Universidad de La Coruña
c/ Alameda, 30-32, 3
15003 La Coruña
España
tel.(34-81) 22 21 33

LLEIDA

Universitat de Lleida
Escola Técnica Superior d'Enginyeria
Agrària
av. Alcade Rovira Roure, 177
25006 Lleida
España
tel. (34-73) 75 25 16/70 25 17
fax (34-73) 23 82 64

MADRID

Universidad Autónoma de Madrid
Facultad de Ciencias Económicas
Canto Blanco
28049 Madrid
España
tel. (34-1) 397 47 97
fax (34-1) 885 40 95

Universidad Complutense de Madrid
Facultad de Derecho, Instituto de Estudios
Europeos
Ciudad Universitaria
28040 Madrid
España
tel. (34-1) 394 54 67
fax.(34-1) 549 28 84

Universidad Carlos III
Biblioteca
av. de Madrid, 126-128
28903 Getafe (Madrid)
España
tel. (34-1) 624 97 94
fax (34-1) 624 97 83

41

**Centro de Estudios y Documentación
Europea de Somosaguas (CEDES)**
Universidad Complutense de Madrid
Facultad de Ciencias Económicas y
Empresariales
edificio de Biblioteca
28023 Madrid
España
tel./fax (34-1) 394 26 01

Universidad de Alcalá de Henares
Colegio San Ildefonso
Plaza de San Diego, s/n   Alcalá de Henares
28801 Madrid
España
tel. (34-1) 885 41 93/94
fax (34-1) 885 40 95

**Universidad Nacional de Educación a
Distancia (UNED)**
calle Senda del Rey s/n
28040 Madrid
España
tel. (34-1) 398 78 88
fax (34-1) 398 78 89

**Centro de Estudios y Documentación
Europeos (CEYDE)**
Universidad Politécnica de Madrid
Paseo Juan XXIII, 11, 2ª planta
28040 Madrid
España
tel. (34-1) 336 62 40/336 79 87
fax (34-1) 336 62 58

Universidad San Pablo CEU
calle Julián Romea, 22
28003 Madrid
España
tel. (34-1) 536 02 85
fax (34-1) 554 84 96

MURCIA

Universidad de Murcia
Facultad de Ciencias Económicas y
Empresariales
Instituto Regional de Cooperación Europea
(IRCE)
Ronda de Levante, 10
3008 Murcia
España
tel (34-68) 63 30 15
fax (34-68) 36 37 59

OVIEDO

Universidad de Oviedo
c/ Gil de Jaz 10, 4
33004 Oviedo (Asturias)
España
tel. (34-85) 23 65 84
fax (34-85) 27 15 57

PALMA DE MALLORCA

**Consorcio Centro de Documentación
Islas Baleares**
c/ Patronato Obrero, n¤ 30
07006 Palma de Mallorca
España
tel. (34-71) 46 10 02, 46 14 12
fax.(971) 46 30 70

NAVARRA

Universidad de Navarra
Facultad de Derecho y Económicas
Campus Universitario
 31080 Pamplona
España
tel. (34-48) 10 56 00
fax (34-48) 10 56 22

REUS

Universitat Rovira i Virgili
Facultat de Ciéncies Económiques i
Empresarials Passeig Misericòrdia, s/n
43205 Reus
España
tel. (34-77) 32 33 43
fax (34-77) 32 11 59

SALAMANCA

Universidad de Salamanca
Plaza de los Sexmeros, 2 , apartado 726
37001 Salamanca
España
tel. (34-23) 27 81 00 ext. 110
fax (34-23) 27 81 08

SAN SEBASTIAN

**Fundación Centro de Estudios
Europeos**
P¤ Ramón María Lilí , 6,5¤
20002 San Sebastián
España
tel. (34-43) 29 18 77/67
fax (34-43) 29 16 63

42

SANTANDER

Universidad de Cantabria
Facultad de Ciencias Económicas y
Empresariales avda. de los Castros s/n
 39005 Santander
España
tel. (34-42) 27 47 27 / 20 16 19
fax.(942) 201 603

SANTIAGO DE COMPOSTELA

Universidad de Santiago
Facultad de Ciencias Económicas y
Empresariales
Juan XXIII s/n
15705 Santiago de Compostela
España
tel. (34-81) 56 39 90
fax (34-81) 57 33 35

SEVILLA

Universidad de Sevilla
c/ San Fernando 4
41004 Sevilla
España
tel. (34-54)   421 34 30 - 455 11
58/59/60/61
fax (34-54) 421 06 23

TENERIFE

Universidad de La Laguna
Facultad de Derecho
camino de La Hornera s/n
38071 La Laguna (Tenerife)
España
tel./fax (34-922) 60 39 04

TOLEDO

Universidad de Castilla La Mancha
Palacio Universitario Cardenal Lorenzana,
s/n
45002 Toledo
España
tel 925 226350

VALENCIA

Universidad de Valencia
Facultad de Ciencias Económicas y
Empresariales
avda de Blasco Ibañez 30
46010 Valencia
España
tel. (34-6) 96 386 47 83
fax (34-6) 96 3864783

VALLADOLID

Universidad de Valladolid
Facultad de Derecho
Calle Librería s/n
47002 Valladolid
España
tel. (34-83) 423009
fax. 983 - 423012

ZARAGOZA

Universidad de Zaragoza
Facultad de Derecho
c/ Pedro Cerbuna, 12
50009 Zaragoza
España
tel. (34-76) 35 22 94
fax (34-76) 55 00 80

FRANCE

AIX-EN-PROVENCE

Service de Documentation CERIC
Université d'Aix-Marseille III
Faculté de Droit et de Sciences Politiques
Pavillon de Canfat, 346 , Route des Alpes
13100 Aix-en-Provence cedex 1
France
tel. (33) 42 96 98 36
fax (33) 42 23 09 71

AMIENS

Centre de Documentation et de
Recherches Européennes
Université de Picardie Jules Verne   Faculté
d'Économie et de Gestion
Chemin du Thil
80000 Amiens cedex 1
France
tel. (33) 22 82 74 40
fax.(33) 22 827412

ANGERS

Université d'Angers
Bibliotheque, Section Droit et Sciences
Économiques
5 rue Lenotre
49045 Angers cedex
France
tel. (33) 41 35 21 00/35
fax (33) 41 35 21 05

43

BAYONNE

Université de Bayonne
Faculté pluridisciplinaire de
Bayonne/Anglet/Biarritz
29-31 Cours du Comte de Cabarrus
64100 Bayonne
France
tel. (33) 59 63 31 77/99
fax (33) 59 63 07 77

BESANÇON

**Centre de Documentation et de
Recherche Européennes**
Université de Besançon UER Droit
Avenue de l'Observatoire, La Bouloie
25030 Besançon cedex
France
tel. (33) 81 50 34 88

BORDEAUX

**Centre de Recherches et
Documentation Européennes**
Université de Bordeaux
Faculté de Droit et Sciences Économiques
Av. Léon Duguit
33604 Pessac
France
tel. (33) 56 84 85 48
fax (33) 563 700 25

BREST

**Centre de Documentation et
Recherche Européennes**
Université de Bretagne occidentale
Faculté de Droit et des Sciences Économiques
b.p. 331 - 12, rue de Kergoat
29273 Brest cedex
France
tel. (33) 98 31 60 33 / 98 47 63 62
fax (33) 91 31 65 90

CAEN

Université de Caen
Faculté de Droit et de Sciences Politique
Esplanade de la Paix
14032 Caen cedex
France
tel. (33) 31 45 55 00
fax.(33-31) 455 970

CLERMONT-FERRAND

Université de Clermont-Ferrand
Faculté de Droit
41 boulevard Gergovia b.p. 54
 63002 Clermont-Ferrand cedex
France
tel. (33) 73 43 42 23 / 73 93 84 20
fax.(33) 73935707

CORSE

Université de Corse
avenue Jean Nicoli b.p. 52
20250 Corte
France
tel. (33) 95 45 30 10
fax (33) 95 46 03 21

DIJON

**Centre de Documentation et
Recherche Européennes**
Université de Dijon Faculté de Droit et
Sciences Politiques
4 bld Gabriel
21000 Dijon
France
tel. (33) 80 39 53 29/83
fax (33) 80 39 56 48

ECULLY

**Groupe Ecole Supérieure de Commerce
de Lyon**
23 avenue Guy de Collongue b.p. 174
69132 Ecully cedex
France
tel. (33) 78 33 78 00
fax (33) 78 33 61 69

FONTAINEBLEAU

**Institut Européen d'Administration
des Affaires (INSEAD)**
Bibliothèque
Boulevard de Constance
77305 Fontainebleau
France
tel. (33-1) 60 72 40 48
fax.(33-1) 60 72 42 42

44

GRENOBLE

Université de Sciences Sociales Pierre Mendès France Grenoble II
Centre Universitaire de Recherche
Européenne et Internationale
b.p. 47
38040 Grenoble cedex
France
tel. (33) 76 82 58 44/55 93
fax (33) 76 82 56 64

Université de Sciences Sociales Pierre Mendes France de Grenoble I
Institut d'Etudes Politiques de Grenoble
(IEPG)
b.p. 45
38402 St Martin d'Hères cedex
France
tel. (33) 76 82 60 00
fax (33) 76 82 60 70

GUADELOUPE

Université des Antilles et de la Guyane
UER des Sciences Juridiques et
Economiques de la Guadeloupe
b.p. 810 Campus de Fouillole
97174 Pointe-á-Pitre cedex
Guadeloupe

LE MANS

Université du Maine Bibliothèque
Route de Laval
72017 Le Mans cedex
France
tel. (33) 43 83 30 65
fax.(33) 43 83 35 37

LILLE

Centre de Recherche et de Documentation Européennes (C.R.D.E.)
Université de Droit et Santé Lille II
Faculté de Sciences Juridiques et
Politiques,
Institut de Recherches Internationales
Européennes et de Défense (I.R.I.E.D.)
BP 169
59653 Villeneuve d'Ascq cedex
France
tel. (33) 20 05 74 82
fax (33) 20 05 74 03

Université de Sciences et Technique Lille I
Faculté de Sciences Economiques et
Sociales
bât. sh2 - USTL - Cite Scientifique b.p. 36
59655 Villeneuve d'Ascq cx
France
tel. (33) 20436 727
fax. 20436655

LIMOGES

Université de Limoges
Bibliothèque Universitaire
39 rue Camille Guerin 5
87031 Limoges cedex
France
tel. (33) 55 01 38 71
fax (33) 55 50 93 14

LYON

Centre Etudes Science Politiques et Documentation Européenne (CESPEDE) Université de Lyon II Institute d'Etudes politiques
1 rue Raulin
69365 Lyon cedex 07
France
tel. (33) 78 697 276
fax.(33) 78 69 7093

Centre de Documentation et Recherche Européennes
Université Jean Moulin Lyon III
b.p. 0638 , 15, Quai Claude Bernard
69239 Lyon cedex 2
France
tel. (33) 72 72 20 61
fax.(33) 727 22 050

MARSEILLE

Université d'Aix-Marseille III
Faculté des Sciences Economiques
rue Puvis de Chavannes
13001 Marseille
France
tel. (33) 91 90 0240
fax (33) 91 139 625

45

MONT-SANT-AIGNAN

Université de Rouen
Faculté de Droit, de Sciences Economiques
et de Gestion
Boulevard Siegried b.p. 158
76135 Mont-St-Aignan, cedex
France
tel. (33) 35 98 58 85 poste 355

MONTPELLIER

Université de Montpellier I
Bibliothèque Interuniversitaire
4, rue École Mage
34000 Montpellier
France
tel. (33) 64 84 7777
fax.(33) 67 60 63 97

NANCY

Université de Nancy
Centre Européen Universitaire,
Bibliotheque
15, place Carnot
54042 Nancy cedex
France
tel. (33) 83 36 52 84
fax.(33) 83 35 76 05

NANTES

Université de Nantes
Bibliothèque Universitaire
Domaine du Tertre -Chemin de la Sensice
du Tertre
44036 Nantes cedex 03
France
tel. (33) 40 14 12 30
fax.(33) 40 141 251

NICE

Université de Nice
Institute du Droit de la Paix
et du Développement
av Robert Schuman
06050 Nice cedex
France
tel. (33) 93 97 29 90
fax.(33) 93 44 85 70

ORLEANS

Université d'Orléans
Faculté de Droit, d'Economie et de Gestion
b p 6739
45067 Orléans cedex 02
France
tel. (33) 38 41 7026
fax.(33) 384 173 60

PARIS

Université de Paris X Nanterre I.PI.E.
2 rue de Rouen
92001 Nanterre cedex
France
tel. (33) 46 57 46 55

Université René Descartes   Paris V
Centre de la Porte de Vanves,
Bibliotheque
10 av Pierre Larousse
92241 Malakoff cedex
France
tel. (33) 46 57 46 55

Ecole Nationale d'Administration
13 rue de l'Université
75007 Paris
France
tel. (33-1) 49 26 43 12
fax.(33) 49 26 44 56

Université de Paris
Bibliothèque Cujas de Droit et Sciences
Économiques
2 rue Cujas
75005 Paris
France
tel. (33-1) 46 34 99 87
fax (33-1) 46 33 82 61

Université de Paris II Panthéon-Assa
Centre de Droit Européen
Boulevard Raspail,54
75006 Paris
France
tel. (33-1) 44 41 59 18
fax.(33-1) 46 34 08 52

**Université de Paris I Centre
Universitaire d'Etudes des
Communautés Européennes**
12, place du Panthéon
75231 Paris cedex 05
France
tel. (33-1) 46 34 97 55

**Centre de Documentation et de
Recherche Européennes**
Université de Paris sud (Paris XI) Faculté
de Droit Jean Monnet
54 bld Desgranges
92330 Sceaux cedex
France
tel. (33-1) 46 60 46 11 40911834
fax.(33) 466 09 262

**Université de Paris XII -Val de Marne
Faculté de Droit de Saint-Maur**
58, avenue Didier
94210 Varenne Saint Hilaire
France
tel. (33) 49 76 80 62
fax (33) 48 85 96 23

Université de Paris Nord (Paris XIII)
Faculté de Droit et Sciences. Politiques
93 ave. J.B. Clément
93430 Villetaneuse
France
tel. (33-1) 49 40 32 84

PAU

**Université de Pau et des pays de
l'Audour**
Faculté de Droit et des Sciences
Économiques
avenue du Doyen Poplawski
64000 Pau
France
tel. (33) 59 80 75 90

PERPIGNAN

**Centre de Documentation et de
Recherche Européennes**
Université de Perpignan
Faculté de Sciences Humaines et Sociales
b.p. 1062 Moulin a Vent, avenue de
Villeneuve
66025 Perpignan cedex
France
tel. (33) 68 66 20 90
fax.(33) 68 66 2019

POITIERS

Université de Poitiers
Centre d'Etudes Européennes
av. du Recteur Pineau 93
86022 Poitiers
France
tel. (33) 49 45 30 00
fax.(33) 494 165 72

REIMS

**Centre de Documentation et de
Recherches Européennes**
Université de Reims
UER Faculté de Droit et Sciences
Économiques
57 bis rue Pierre Taittinger
51096 Reims cedex
France
tel. (33) 26 05 36 00
fax.(33) 26 04 20 75

RENNES

**Centre de Documentation et
Recherches Européennes (C.E.D.R.E.)**
Université de Rennes I Faculté de Droit
9 rue Jean Macé
35042 Rennes cedex
France
tel. (33) 99 84 76 71
fax (33) 466 092 62

SAINT-DENIS

Université de la Réunion
Faculté de Droit et de Sciences
Economiques et Politiques
24, 26 Avenue de la Victoire,
97489 Saint-Denis
France
tel.(33) 21 74 75
fax (33) 41 25 05

STRASBOURG

Université Robert Schuman
Centre d'Etudes Internationales et
Européennes (CEIE)
11, rue du Marechal Juin b.p. 68
67046 Strasbourg
France
tel. (33) 88 143004
fax (33) 88 61 66 21

**Université Robert Schuman Institut
des Hautes Etudes Européennes**
8 rue des Écrivains
67081 Strasbourg cedex
France
tel. (33) 88 35 02 69 - 8835027
fax (33) 88 35 64 42

47

TOULON

Université de Toulon
Bibliothèque de la Faculté de Droit
b.p. 1206, 83070 Toulon cedex
France
tel. (33) 944 675 80
fax (33) 941 421 38

TOULOUSE

**Centre de Documentation et de
Recherche Européennes**
Université Sciences Sociales de Toulouse I
place Anatole France
31042 Toulouse cedex
France
tel. (33) 61 63 36 30 / 31
fax (33) 61 63 37 98

TOURS

**Centre de Documentation et de
Recherches Européennes**
Université François Rabelais de Tours
Faculté de Droit, d'Economie et des
Sciences Sociales
50, Avenue Portalis B.P. 0607,
37206 Tours cedex
France
tel. (33) 47 36 81 26
fax (33) 47 36 64 10

IRELAND

CORK

University College Cork Boole
Library
Cork
Ireland
tel. (353-21) 27 68 71 ext. 2428

DUBLIN

Trinity College Official Publications
Library
College Street
Dublin 2
Ireland
tel. (353-1) 702 23 42 / 77 29 41 ext. 1655
fax (353-1) 71 90 03

University College Dublin Main
Library
Belfield
Dublin 4
Ireland
tel. (353-1) 69 32 44 ext. 7508

GALWAY

University College James Hardiman
Library
Galway
Ireland
tel. (353-91) 244 11 ext. 549

LIMERICK

University of Limerick Library
Plassey Technological Park Limerick
Ireland
tel. (353-61) 33 36 44 ext. 2185
fax (353-61) 33 80 44

KILDARE

St Patrick's College Library
Maynooth Kildare
Ireland
tel. (353-1) 628 52 22
fax (353-1) 628 60 08

ITALIA

ACIREALE

**Scuola Superiore Publica
Amministrazione**
Biblioteca sede di Acireale
Via Collegio Pennisi
95024 Acireale
Italia
tel. 095 604 541
fax 095 601 909

ANCONA

Università degli Studi di Ancona
Biblioteca della Facoltà di Economia
Palazzo degli Anziani, Piazza Stracca 2
60121 Ancona
Italia
tel. (39-71) 220 39 61
fax (39-71) 220 39 95

48

BARI

Università degli Studi di Bari
Facoltà di Giurisprudenza, Istituto di
Diritto Internazionale e Scienze Politiche
70121 Bari
Italia
tel. (39-80) 31 72 91

BENEVENTO

Consorzio per gli Studi Universitari
Biblioteca Universitaria
Piazza Guerazzi
82100 Benevento
Italia
Tel 0824 54 441
Fax 0824 43 021

BOLOGNA

Università degli Studi di Bologna
Istituto Giuridico A.Cicu
via Zamboni 27/29
40126 Bologna
Italia
tel. (39-51) 25 96 51/0

CAGLIARI

Università degli Studi di Cagliari
Facoltà di Giurisprudenza
viale San Ignazio 17
09123 Cagliari
Italia
tel. (39-70) 65 62 21 / 65 96 49

CAMPOBASSO
Universitá degli Studi del Molise
Biblioteca Centrale
Viale Manzoni
86100 Campobasso
Italia
Tel 08 74 40 45 04 - 40 45 18
Fax 08 74 41 23 94

CATANIA

Università degli Studi di Catania
Dipartimento di Studi Politici
Via V. Emanuele, 49
95131 Catania
Italia
tel. (39-95) 532 886 - 532 645
fax 095 533 128

CASERTA

Scuola Superiore di Publica
Ammnistrazione
Biblioteca sede di Caserta
Via Nazionale Appia, 2/A
81100 Caserta
Italia
Tel 08 23 32 66 22
Fax 08 23 32 76 70

FERRARA

Centro di Documentazione e studi
sulle Comunità Europee
Università degli Studi di Ferrara   Istituto
di Economia e Finanza
44100 Ferrara
Italia
tel. (39-532) 481 84/258 93

FIRENZE

Archivi Storici delle C.E.
Villa Il Poggiolo Piazza Edison 11
50133 Firenze
Italia

Centro di Documentazione Europea
Dipartimento di Scienza Politica e
Sociologia Politica
Facoltá di Scienze Politiche "Cesare Alfieri"
Via S. Caterina d'Alessandria, 3,
50129 Firenze
Italia
tel. (39-55) 480 966

GENOVA

Università degli Studi di Genova
Facoltà di Economia e Commercio,
Istituto di Politica economica
1 Via Bertani 16125 Genova
Italia
tel. (39-10) 353 70 11 / 012

LECCE

Centro di Documentazione e studi sul-
le Comunità Europee
Università degli Studi di Lecce
Viale O. Quarta, 10
73100 Lecce
Italia
tel. (39-832) 33 16 80
fax (39-832) 30 49 41

49

MESSINA

Università degli Studi di Messina
Istituto di studi internazionali e comunitari,
Facoltà di Scienze Politiche
Via Nino Bixio, 9
98100 Messina
Italia
tel. (39-90) 293 10 38
fax (39-90) 292 44 48

MILANO

Centro Internazionale di Studi e Documentazione sulle Comunità Europee
Corso Magenta 61
20123 Milano
Italia
tel. (39-2) 48 00 90 72/74
fax.(39-2) 48 00 90 67

Università Commerciale Luigi Bocconi
Biblioteca, Sezione Economia e Commercio
Via R. Sarfatti 25
20136 Milano
Italia
tel. (39-2) 83 84 50 17
fax (39-2) 58 36 5016

Università degli Studi di Milano
Istituto di Diritto e Politica Internazionale
Via Conservatorio 7
20122 Milano
Italia
tel. (39-2) 760 74 24 09 / 78 36 46

MODENA

Centro di Documentazione e Ricerche sulle Comunitá Europee
Università degli Studi di Modena
Via Università 4
41100 Modena
Italia
tel (39-59) 41 75 61/68
fax(39-59) 23 04 43

NAPOLI

Società Italiana per l'organizzazione internazionale
Villa Pignatelli Riviera di Chiaia 200
80121 Napoli
Italia
tel. (39-81) 66 78 62

Università degli Studi di Napoli
Facoltá di Scienze Politiche, Istituto
Sociologico Giuridico
Via Guglielmo Sanfelice 47
80134 Napoli
Italia
tel. (39-81) 552 11 70

Università degli Studi di Napoli
Facoltá di Agraria, Dipartimento di
Economia e Politica Agraria
Via Università, 96
80055 Portici (Napoli)
Italia
tel. (39-81) 27 46 22/56 / 27 44 73

PADOVA

Università degli Studi di Padova
Facoltà di Giurisprudenza, Centro di Studi
Europei
Via VIII Febbraio
35100 Padova
Italia
tel. (39-49) 65 14 00

PALERMO

Università degli Studi di Palermo
Dipartimento di Diritto Pubblico
via maqueda 172
90134 Palermo
Italia
tel. (39-91) 58 26 59
fax (39-91) 611 03 61

PARMA

Università degli Studi di Parma
Instituto di Diritto e Organizzazioni
Internazionali
12 Via dell' Università
43100 Parma
Italia
tel. (39-521) 28 11 68/28 68 72
fax. (39) 521 286872

PAVIA

Università degli Studi di Pavia
Centro Studi sulle Comunità Europee
C.SO Strada Nuova 65
27100 Pavia
Italia
tel. (39-382) 233 00 / 38 62 39

50

PERUGIA

Università degli Studi di Perugia
Biblioteca Centrale
Piazza dell'Università, 1
06100 Perugia
Italia
tel. (39-75) 585 21 45

PESCARA

Universitá degli Studi "Gabrielle D'Annunzio"
Facoltá di Economia e Commercio, Istituto di Studi Giuridici
Viale Pindaro, 42
65127 Pescara
Italia
tel. (39-85) 69 48 43 / 38 01 12
fax (39-85) 69 24 80

PISA

Università degli Studi di Pisa
Dipartimento di Diritto Pubblico , Sezione di Diritto Internazionale
Via S. Giuseppe 22
56100 Pisa
Italia
tel. (39-50) 56 21 78
fax (39-50) 55 13 92

REGGIO CALABRIA

Istituto Superiore Europeo di Studi Politici (ISESP)
Via Torrione 101/f - Casella Postale 297
89100 Reggio Calabria
Italia
tel. (39-965) 33 14 79

ROMA

Centro Studi di Diritto Comunitario
Via Torino 117
00184 Roma
Italia
tel. (39-6) 474 45 94

Società Italiana per l'Organizzatione Internazionale (SIOI)
Biblioteca
Palazzetto di Venezia, Piazza San Marco 51
00186 Roma
Italia
tel. (39-6) 678 17 22

Università degli Studi "La Sapienza" di Roma
Facoltá di Economia e Commercio
Scuola di Specializzazione in Diritto ed Economia C.E.
Via del Castro Laurenziano, 9
00161 Roma
Italia

SAN DOMENICO FIESOLE

Istituto Universitario Europeo
Biblioteca
Via dei Roccettini
50016 San Domenico Fiesole
Italia
tel. (39-55) 509 21

SASSARI

Universitá degli Studi di Sassari
Biblioteca interfacoltà per le Scienze Giuridiche, Politiche ed Economiche
Antonio Pigliaru
Piazza Università 20
07100 Sassari
Italia
tel. (39-79) 21 9111
fax (39-79) 22 88 09

SIENA

Università degli Studi di Siena
Biblioteca Circolo Giuridico
Piazza San Francesco 7
53100 Siena
Italia
tel. (39-577) 29 87 42

TORINO

Università degli Studi di Torino
Istituto Universitario di Studi Europei
Via Sacchi 28 bis
10128 Torino
Italia
tel. (39-11) 562 54 58 / 54 41 93
fax (39-11) 53 02 35

TRIESTE

Università degli Studi di Trieste
Facoltá di Giurisprudenza, Istituto di Diritto Internazionale e Legislazione comparata Via Fabio Severo 158
34127 Trieste
Italia
tel. (39-40) 560 30 62

51

URBINO

Università degli Studi di Urbino
Centro Alti Studi Europei
Via Veterani, 1
 61029 Urbino (PS)
Italia
tel. (39-722) 32 00 051
fax (39-722) 26 66

VERONA

Università degli Studi di Verona
Istituto di Scienze Economiche
Via dell'Artigliere 19
37129 Verona
Italia
tel. (39-45) 809 82 44

LUXEMBOURG

LUXEMBOURG

Institut Universitaire International
Centre International d'Etudes et de
Recherches Européennes
162a, Av. de la Faïencerie
 1511 Luxembourg
Luxembourg
tel. (352) 47 18 11 / 46 66 44-1
fax (352) 47 16 77

NEDERLAND

AMSTERDAM

Universiteit van Amsterdam
Fac. der Rechtgeleerheid, Bibliotheek
Internationaal Recht
postbus 19123 Turfdraagsterpad 9
1000-6c Amsterdam
Nederland
tel. (31-20) 525 21 61
fax (31-20) 525 29 00

Vrije Universiteit Amsterdam
Bibliotheek Economie/Rechten
Vr. de Boelelaan 1105
1081 hv Amsterdam
Nederland
tel. (31-20) 548 43 15/46 13

DEN HAAG

T.M.C. Asser Instituut
22, Alexanderstraat , p.o. box 30461
2500 gl Den Haag
Nederland
tel. (31-70) 34 20-300/382
fax (31-70) 34 20-359

ENSCHEDE

Universiteit Twente
postbus 217 - Drienerbeeklaan 5
7500 Ae Enschede
Nederland
tel. (31-53) 89 22 42/20 64

GRONINGEN

Rijksuniversiteit Groningen
Faculteit Rechtsgeleerdheid, Bibliotheek
oude kijk in't jatstraat 26
9712 ek Groningen
Nederland
tel. (31-50) 63 56 64
fax. (31) 50 63 56 03

LEIDEN

Rijksuniversiteit Leiden
Hugo de Grootstraat 27 , postbus 9520
2300 ra Leiden
Nederland
tel. (31-71) 27 75 34
fax (31-71) 27 76 00

MAASTRICHT

**European Institute of Public
Administration**
Library Onze Lieve Vrouweplein 22 p.o.
box 1229
 6201 be Maastricht
Nederland
tel. (31-43) 29 62 74
fax (31-43) 29 62 96

**Raad der Europese Gemeenten
en Regio's**
Batterijstraat 36 a
6211 sj Maastricht
Nederland
tel. (31-43) 25 02 45

52

NIJMEGEN

Katholieke Universiteit
Fac. der Rechtsgeleerdheid, Instituut
Rechtsgeleerdheid
postbus 9049 Thomas van Aquinostraat 6
6500 kk Nijmegen
Nederland
tel. (31-80) 51 62 03 / 51 25 18

ROTTERDAM

Erasmus Universiteit Rotterdam
Universiteitsbibliotheek
Burgemeester Oudlaan 50
3062 pa Rotterdam
Nederland
tel. (31-10) 40811 11

TILBURG

Katholieke Universiteit Brabant
Bibliotheek informatie centrum, AFD.
Europese Gemeenschappen
hogeschoollaan 225
5037 gc Tilburg
Nederland
tel. (31-13) 66 22 13

UTRECHT

**Rijksuniversiteit Utrecht Juridische
Bibliotheek**
Ganzenmarkt 32
3512 ge Utrecht
Nederland
tel. (31-30) 53 62 50 / 53 84 09

WAGENINGEN

**Landbouwuniversiteit Wageningen
Bibliotheek**
p.o. box 9100
6700 ha Wageningen
Nederland
tel. (31-8370) 824 93/61

ÖSTERREICH

GRAZ

Karl-Franzens-Universität Graz
Forschungsinstitut für Europarecht
Merangasse 70/II
8010 Graz
Österreich
Tel (43-316) 38 38 71 / 380 36 25/26/27/30
Fax (43-316) 38 38 07

INNSBRUCK

**Leopold-Franzens-Universität
Innsbruck**
Institut für Völkerrecht und
Rechtsphilosophie
Innrain 52
6020 Innsbruck
Österreich
tel. (43-512) 227 24 26 35

KLAGENFURT

**Universität für
Bildungswissenschaften**
Universitätsbibliothek
Universitätsstr. 65-67
9020 Klagenfurt
Österreich
tel. (43-463) 270 02 95
fax (43-463) 270 02 96

KREMS

Donau-Universität Krems
Wissenschaftliche Landesakademie für
Niederösterreich
Dr Karl Dorrek-Str. 30
3500 Krems
Österreich
tel. (43-2732) 705 45
fax (43-2732) 414

LINZ

Johannes Kepler Universität Linz
Forschungsinstitut für Europarecht
Projektgruppe Eur.
4040 Linz Auhof
Österreich
tel. (43-70) 246 84 14
fax (43-70) 246 83 68

SALZBURG

Universität Salzburg
Forschungsinstitut für Europarecht
Churfürstgasse 1
5020 Salzburg
Österreich
tel. (43-662) 80 44 35 08
fax (43-662) 80 44 30 20

53

WIEN

Institut für Volkerrecht und Internationale Beziehungen
Universitätsstr. 2
1090 Wien
Österreich
tel. (43-222) 43 43 41-0

Wirtschafts Universität
Forschungsinstitut für Europafragen
Althanstr. 39-45
1090 Wien
Österreich
tel. (43-1) 31 336,4145
fax (43-1) 31 336,756

PORTUGAL

BRAGA

Universidade do Minho
Escola de Economia e Gestão
2¤ piso, sala 225 Estrada Nova de Gualtar
4700 Braga codex
Portugal
tel. (351-53) 67 63 94 / 60 42 28 (directo)
fax (351-53) 67 63 75

CASTELO BRANCO

Instituto Politecnico de Castelo Branco
Av. Pedro Alvares Cabral, 12
6000 Castelo Branco
Portugal
tel 22126/ 22128/23394
fax 331874

COIMBRA

Universidade de Coimbra
Centro Interdisciplinar de Estudos Jurídico-Económicos
Rua de Aveiro 11, 11
3000 Coimbra
Portugal
tel. (351-39) 259 54
fax (351-39) 339 29

COVILHA

Universidade da Beira Interior
Centro de Estudos de Desenvolvimento
Regional   Rua Marques d'Avila e Bolama
6200 Covillha
Portugal
tel. (351-75) 32 77 70 171
fax (351-75) 32 77 71

EVORA

Universidade de Evora
Gabinete de Informaçao e Apoio
Largo dos colegiais 1,
7001 Evora
Portugal
tel. (351) 255 72/3/4

FARO

Universidade do Algarve
Campus da Penha, Estrada da Penha
8000 Faro
Portugal
tel. (089) 80 01 00
fax.(089) 82 35 60

FUNCHALL

Universidade da Madeira
Lago de Municipio
9000 Funchall
Portugal
tel. (091) 230390/ 230209
fax (091) 230342

LISBOA

Universidade Catolica Portuguesa
Biblioteca Universitaria João Paulo II,
Centro de Documentaçao Europeia
caminho de Palma de Cima
1600 Lisboa
Portugal
tel. (351-1) 721 40 16
fax (351-1) 726 61 60

Universidade Nova de Lisboa
Faculdade de Economia
travessa Estevão Pinto- Campolide
1070 Lisboa
Portugal
tel. (351-1) 69 36 24
fax (351-1) 385 68 81

Universidade de Lisboa
Faculdade de Direito
Cidade Universitaria
1600 Lisboa
Portugal
tel. (351-1) 793 15 66
fax (351-1) 793 32 50

Universidade Lusíada
Centro de Documentaçao Europeia
Rua da Junqueira, 194
1300 Lisboa
Portugal
tel. (351-1) 363 99 44 362 29 50/1/2/3
fax (351-1) 363 83 07

Centro de Documentaçao Europeia
Universidade Tecnica
Instituto Superior de Economia e Gêstao
Rua Miguel Lupi 20
1200 Lisboa codex
Portugal
tel. (351-1) 60 70 99
fax (351-1) 397 26 84

OEIRAS

Instituto Nacional de Administração
Palácio dos Marqueses de Pombal
2780 Oeiras
Portugal
tel. (351-1) 441 32 31
fax (351-1) 443 27 50

PONTA DELGADA

Universidade dos Açores
Rua da Mãe de Deus, 58 apartado, 1422
9502 Ponta Delgada/ Açores codex
Portugal
tel. (351-96) 65 31 55 / 65 30 44 / 65 20 89
fax (351-96) 65 30 70

PORTO

Centro de Documentaçao e Estudos Europeus
Universidade do Porto
av. da Boavista, 1311   6
4100 Porto
Portugal
tel. (351-2) 60 64 303 / 60 97 086
fax (351-2) 60 64 303

SUOMI-FINLAND

HELSINKI

University of Helsinki
Institute of International Economic Law
p.o. box 4 (fabianinkatu 24)
00014 Helsinki
Suomi-Finland
tel. (358-0) 191 23 392
fax (358-0) 191 23 390

JOENSUU

Joensuu University
Library
p.o. box 107
80101 Joensuu 10
Suomi-Finland
tel. (358-73) 151 26 51 /72
fax. (358-73) 512691

JYVASKYLA

University of Jyvaskyla
Library
P.O.Box 35
40351 Jyvaskyla
Suomi-Finland

LAPPEENRANTA

Lappeenranta University
Technology Library
P.O.Box 20
53851 Lappeenranta
Suomi-Finland

OULU

University of Oulu
University Library
P.O. Box 450
Oulu 90571
Suomi-Finland
tel 358-81-5533530
fax 358-81-363135

ROVANIEMI

University of Lapland
Library
P.O. Box 122
Rovaniemi 96101
Suomi-Finland
tel 358 60 324 208

TAMPERE

University of Tempere
P.O.Box 607
33101 Tampere
Suomi-Finland

55

TURKU

Turku University
Institute for European Studies
p.o. box 110 - leminkäisenkatu 14 18c
20521 Turku
Suomi-Finland
tel. (358-21) 63 83556
fax (358-21) 63 83-268

VAASA

University of Vaasa
Library
P.O. box 331
65101 Vaasa
Suomi-Finland
tel. (358-61) 324 82 01
fax. (358-61) 324 82 00

SVERIGE

GOETEBORG

University of Goeteborg
Institute of Legal Science
Vasagatan 3
411 24 Goeteborg
Sverige
tel. (46-31) 773 15 23 / 63 15 23
fax (46-31) 11 93 78

LINKÖPING

Linköping University
University Library and Department of
Management and Economics
S 581 83 Linköping
Sverige

LUND

Lunds Universitet
Jurisdiska Fakulteten, Biblioteket for
Internationell Ratt
box 207 221 00 Lund
Sverige
tel. (46-46) 10 80 88

OREBRO

University College of Orebro
PO Box 923
S 701, 30 Orebro
Sverige
tel 46 19 301240
fax 46 19 331217

56

STOCKHOLM

**Stockholms Universitet, Juridiska
Fakulteten**
hus c9, eu-dok
106 91 Stockholm
Sverige
tel. (46-8) 16 27 58 / 16 28 34

SUNDVALL

**Mid-Sweden University in Sundsvall,
Mitthögskolan**
p.o. box 860
851 24 Sundsvall
Sverige
tel. (46-60) 18 86 00
fax (46-60) 12 66 40

UMEA

**Umea University, Social Sciences
Library**
box.1441
90184 Umea
Sverige
tel. (46-90) 16 53 91
fax (46-90) 16 66 77

UPPSALA

University of Uppsala, Law Library
p.o. box 512
751 20 Uppsala
Sverige
tel. (46-18) 18 20 05
fax (46-18) 15 27 14

VAXJO

Vaxjo University
Hogskolan in Vaxjo, Library
351 95 Vaxjo
Sverige
tel. (46-470) 686 18
fax (46-470) 832 17

UNITED KINGDOM

ABERDEEN

Aberdeen University
The Queen Mother Library
Meston Walk
AB9 2UE Aberdeen
Scotland
United Kingdom
tel. (44-224) 272 572
fax (44-224) 48 70 48

ASHFORD

Wye College
Library
TN25 5A WYE Ashford Kent
United Kingdom
tel. (44-233) 81 24 01 ext. 497

BATH

University of Bath
Library
Claverton Down   BA2 7 AY Bath
United Kingdom
tel. (44-225) 82 68 26 ext. 5594
fax (44-225) 82 62 29

BELFAST

The Queen's University of Belfast
Main Library
BTt7 1LS Belfast
United Kingdom
tel. (44-232) 24 51 33 ext. 3605
fax (44-232) 32 33 40

BIRMINGHAM

University of Central England in Birmingham
Perry Barr Library
B42 2SU Birmingham
United Kingdom

University of Birmingham
Main Library
PO Box 363   B15 2TT Birmingham
United Kingdom
tel. (44-21) 414 58 23

BRADFORD

University of Bradford
J.B. Priestley Library
Richmond Road BD7 1DP Bradford
United Kingdom
tel. (44-1274) 38 34 02 / 73 34 66 ext. 3402

BRIGHTON

University of Sussex
Library
BN19QL Falmer, Brighton
United Kingdom
tel. (44-273) 67 81 5

BRISTOL

The University of Bristol
Wills Memorial Library
Queen's Road BS8 1RJ Bristol
United Kingdom
tel. (44-272) 30 33 70

CAMBRIDGE

Cambridge University
Library
West Road CB3 9DR Cambridge
United Kingdom
tel. (44-223) 33 31 38
fax (44-223) 33 31 60

CARDIFF

University of Wales Arts & Social Studies Library
PO Box 430 CF1 3XT Cardiff
United Kingdom
tel. 0222874262

COLCHESTER

University of Essex
Library
PO Box 24 C04 3UA Colchester
United Kingdom
tel. (44-206) 873181
fax (44-206) 87 35 98

COVENTRY

Coventry University
Lanchester Library
Much Park street CV1 2HF Coventry
United Kingdom
tel. (44-203) 838295

The University of Warwick
Library
Gibbet Hill road CV4 7AL Coventry
United Kingdom
tel. (02-03) 52 30 33 / 52 35 23 ext. 2041

DUNDEE

The University of Dundee
Faculty of Law, Library
Perth Road dd1 4hn Dundee
United Kingdom
tel. (44-382)344 102

DURHAM

University of Durham
University Library
Stockton road DH1 3LY Durham
United Kingdom
tel. (44-91) 374 30 41/4

EDINBURGH

University of Edinburgh
The Europa Library
South Bridge EH8 9YL Edinburgh
United Kingdom
tel. (44-31) 650 20 41 / 667 10 11 ext. 4292
fax (44-31) 667 79 38

EXETER

Exeter University
Law Library
Amory Building - Rennes Drive EX4 4RJ
Exeter
United Kingdom
tel. (44-392) 262 072
fax (44-392) 26 31 08

GLASGOW

University of Glasgow
Library
Hillhead street G12 8QE Glasgow
United Kingdom
tel. (44-41) 339 88 55 ext. 67 40
fax (44-41) 357 50 43

GUILDFORD

University of Surrey
George Edwards Library
GU2 5XH Guildford, Surrey
United Kingdom
tel. (44-1483) 25 92 33
fax (44-1483) 25 95 00

HULL

The University of Hull
Brynmor Jones Library
Cottingham road HU6 7RX Hull
United Kingdom
tel. (44-482) 46 54 11

KEELE

University of Keele
Library
ST5 5BG Keele Staffordshire
United Kingdom
tel. (44-782) 584 162
fax (44-782) 61 38 47

KENT

The University of Kent at Canterbury
Library
CT2 7NU Canterbury,Kent
United Kingdom
tel. (44-227) 76 40 00 ext. 31 09

LANCASTER

University of Lancaster
University Library
Bailrigg LA1 4YH Lancaster
United Kingdom
tel. (44-524) 652 01
fax (44-524) 638 06

LEEDS

Leeds Metropolitan University
Library
Calverley street LS1 3HE Leeds
United Kingdom
tel. (44-113) 283 31 26
fax (44-113) 283 31 23

University of Leeds
The Law Library
20 Lyddon terrace, LS2 9JT Leeds
United Kingdom
tel. (44-532) 33 50 40 / 33 55 12

LEICESTER

University of Leicester
Library
PO Box 248 University road LE1 9QD
Leicester
United Kingdom
tel. (44-533) 52 20 44
fax (44-533) 52 20 66

LONDON

University of North London
Library
1 Prince of Wales road NW5 3LB   London
United Kingdom
tel. (44-71) 753 51 42 / 607 27 89 ext.
4110
fax (44-71) 753 50 78

London School of Economics
International Organisation Collection,
British Library of Political and Economic
Science
10 Portugal street WC2A2HD London
United Kingdom
tel. (44-71) 955 72 73
fax (44-71) 955 74 54

Queen Mary and Westfield College
Library
Mile End road E1 4NS London
United Kingdom
tel. (44-71) 775 33 21
fax (44-71) 975 55 00

The Royal Institute of International Affairs
Library
Chatham House 10 St James's Square
SW1Y 4LE London
United Kingdom
tel. (44-71) 957 57 21
fax (44-71) 957 57 10

LONDONDERRY

University of Ulster
Library
Cromore Road Coleraine BT52 1s CO
Londonderry
United Kingdom
tel. (44-265) 41 41 ext. 4257
fax (44-265) 555 13

LOUGHBOROUGH

University of Technology
Pilkington Library
LE113TU Loughborough Leicestershire
United Kingdom
tel. (44-509) 22 23 44

MANCHESTER

Manchester University
John Rylands University Library
Oxford road M13 9PP Manchester
United Kingdom
tel. (44-61) 275 37 51
fax (44-61) 275 37 64/51

NEWCASTLE UPON TYNE

The University of Northumbria at Newcastle
Library
Ellison Building - Ellison Place NE1 8ST
Newcastle upon Tyne
United Kingdom
tel. (44-91) 235 81 36
fax (44-91) 261 69 11

NORWICH

University of East Anglia
Library
University Plain NR4 7tTJ Norwich
United Kingdom
tel. (44-603) 561 61 ext. 2412
fax (44-603) 25 94 90

NOTTINGHAM

Nottingham University
 Library
NG7 2RD Nottingham
United Kingdom
tel. (44-602) 514 579

OXFORD

University of Oxford
The Bodleian Law Library
Manor road OX1 3UR Oxford
United Kingdom
tel. (44-865) 27 14 63
fax (44-865) 27 14 75

PORTSMOUTH

University of Portsmouth
Frewen Library
Cambridge road PO1 2T Portsmouth
United Kingdom
tel. (44-705)843 240

59

READING

University of Reading
Main Library
Whiteknights PO B ox 223 RG6 2AE
Reading
United Kingdom
tel. (44-734) 31 87 82
fax (44-734) 31 23 35

SALFORD

University of Salford
Clifford Whithworth University Library
M5 4WT Salford Lancashire
United Kingdom
tel. (44-61) 745 50 00, ext. 3662

SHEFFIELD

Sheffield Hallam University
Library
Pond street S1 1WB Sheffield
United Kingdom
tel. (44-742) 72 09 11

SOUTHAMPTON

Southampton University
Library
S09 5NH Southampton, Hants
United Kingdom
tel. (44-703) 55 90 00

WOLVERHAMPTON

University of Wolverhampton
The Robert Scott Library
St. Peter's Square WV1 1RH
Wolverhampton
United Kingdom
tel. (44-902) 31 30 05 ext. 2300

ALGÉRIE

**Institut National d'études
de stratégie globale**
Service de documentation
Rue les Vergers B.P. 137
BIRKHADEM - ALGER
ALGÉRIE
Tel. (213-2) 56 90 00

AUSTRALIA

La Trobe University
The Library
 3083 Bundoora ,
MELBOURNE-VICTORIA
AUSTRALIA
Tel. (61-3) 479 29 43
Fax (61-3) 471 09 93

University of Tasmania
Seraials Librarian
P.O. Box 252CN G P O
HOBART TASMANIA
AUSTRALIA
Tel. (61-02) 20 22 07
Fax (61-02) 20 76 42

University of Western Australia
Library, Periodicals Department
6009 NEDLANDS WA
AUSTRALIA
Tel. (61-9) 380 23 39
Fax (61-9) 380 11 77

University of Sidney
Serials Department
Fisher Library
2006 SYDNEY N.S.W.
AUSTRALIA
Tel. (61-2) 692 32 57
Fax (61-2) 692 45 93

BRASIL

**Escola de Administraçao de Empresa
de Sao Paulo**
Fundação Getulio Vargas, EAESEP / FGV
Av. 9 DE julho 2029
01313 SAO PAULO
BRASIL
Tel. (55-11) 284 23 11

BULGARIA

Bulgarian Academy of Sciences
Centre for European Studies
Ul. Dobromir Hriz 7
1124 SOFIA
BULGARIA
Tel. (359-2) 44 14 96
Fax (359-2) 88 44 48

CANADA

Dalhousie University
Killam Memorial Library
Government Documents Department
B3H 4H8 HALIFAX, NOVA SCOTIA
CANADA
Tel. (1-902) 424 36 34
Fax (1-902) 494 23 19

Queen's University
Documents Library, Mackintosh Corry Hall
K725C4 KINGSTON ONTARIO
CANADA
Tel. (1-613) 545 63 13

Université de Montreal
BLSH-Publications Officielles
Pav. Samuel-Broufman
C.P. 6128, SUCC. A
H3C 3J7 MONTRÉAL
CANADA
Tel. (1-514) 343 79 72

Mc Gill University
Government Documents Department
Mc Lennan Library
3459 Mc Tavish Street
H3A IYI MONTRÉAL QUEBEC
CANADA
Tel. (1-514) 398 47 37

Carleton University Library
Documents Division
1125 Colonel by Drive
K1S 5J7 OTTAWA, ONTARIO
CANADA
Tel. (1-613) 788 26 00 ext.27-48
Fax (1-613) 788 39 09

University of Saskatchewan
Government Publications Section
Saskatchewan
S7N OWO SASKATOON SK
CANADA
Tel. (1-306) 966 59 89
Fax (1-306) 966 60 40

Université Laval
Bibliothèque Pav Bonenfant
Division des Acquisitions
Cité Universitaire
G1K 7P4 STE FOY QUEBEC 10E
CANADA
Tel. (1-418) 656 21 31 ext. 6246

University of Toronto
John P. Robarts Library
M5S 1A5 TORONTO ONTARIO
CANADA
Tel. (1-416) 978 39 31

University of Manitoba
The Elisabeth Dafoe Library
Government Publications Section
R3T 2N2 WINNIPEG MANITOBA
CANADA
Tel. (1-204) 474 63 61/88 80
Fax (1-204) 275 25 97

CHILE

**Pontificia Universidad Católica
de Chile**
Instituto de Ciencia Política
AV. Bernardo O'Higgins, 340
SANTIAGO
CHILE
Tel. (56-2) 22 45 16 EXT 2581
Fax (56-2) 22 45 16 EXT 222 2590

CHINA

61

Chinese Academy of Social Sciences
Centre for EU Studies
Institute of Western Europea Studies
5 Jiaan Guo Nei Da Jie
BEIJING
CHINA

Foreign Affairs College
Programme of European Studies
24 Zhan Lan Road
BEIJING
CHINA
Tel. (86-1) 832 86 64
Fax (86-1) 832 86 64

Fudan University
Institute of World Economy
220 Handan Road
SHANGHAI
CHINA

Sichuan University
Economics Department
Chengdu
SICHUAN
CHINA

Nan-Kai University
Department of International Economics
Economics Buiding
94, Weijin Road
TIANJIN
CHINA

Institute of the Study of Economy of Western Europe
Department of Economics
Wuhan University
WUHAN HUBEI
CHINA

SOUTH KOREA

Pusan National University
Institute for European Studies
30 Changjon Dong-Kumsong-Gu
609 735 PUSAN
SOUTH KOREA
Tel. (82-51) 026 44
Fax (82-51) 290 49

Korea University
Central Library
1, 5-Ka -Anam-Dong Sungbuk-Ku
136-701 SEOUL
SOUTH KOREA
Tel. (82-2) 920 10 24
Fax (82-2) 922 58 20

Seoul National University
Institute of Economic Research
Sillim-Dong-Kwanak-Gu
SEOUL
SOUTH KOREA
Tel. (82-2) 880 54 32/3/4
Fax (82-2) 888 44 54

CROATIA

University of Zagreb
Institute of Development and International Relations (IRMO-EDOC)
Ljudevita Farkasa Vukotin
P.O. BOX 303
1000 ZAGREB
CROATIA
Tel. (38-41) 44 45 22
Fax (38-41) 44 40 59

ESTONIA

Tartu University Library
Information Department
Struve 1 EE
2400 TARTU
ESTONIA
Tel. (372-7) 43 24 67
Fax (372-7) 43 47 56

FYROM-MACÉDOINE

St Cyril and Methodius University
Faculty of Economics
Bul Kreste Misirkov
91000 SKOPJE
FYROM- MACÉDOINE
Tel. (38-91) 11 64 66
Fax (38-91) 11 60 54

HONGRIE

BUDAPEST University of Economics
Department of International Economics
Fovam Ter 8
1093 BUDAPEST
HONGRIE
Tel. (36-1) 117 66 52
Fax (36-1) 117 88 83

Institute of Law of Conflicts and International Economic Relations
Memzetkopi Maganjogi Tanszek
Egyetem Ter 1-3
1364 BUDAPEST
HONGRIE
Tel. (36-1) 266-59-99

Institute of Economics
hungarian Academy of Sciences, Library
Budaörsi UT 43-45
PO BOX 262
H-1502 BUDAPEST XI
HONGRIE
Tel. (36-1) 185 15 27
Fax (36-1) 185 11 20

Janus Pannonius University
Library
H- 7601 PECS
HONGRIE
Tel. (36-72)311433
Fax (36-72) 415148

University Joszef Attila of Szeged
Tisza Lajos Krt. 54
6720 SZEGED
HONGRIE
Tel. (36-62) 122 44
Fax (36-62) 109 46

INDIA

Indian Council of World Affairs
Library
Sapru House
Barakhamba Road
NEW DELHI 1
INDIA
Tel. (91-11) 331 72 46

ISRAEL

Bar-Ilan University
Faculty of Social Sciences
Center for European Community Studies
Mexico Building
52100 RAMAT GAN
ISRAEL
Tel. (972-3) 551 85 78

Tel-Aviv University
Brender Moss Library for Social Sciences &
Management
Ramat Aviv P.O.B. 39654
61396 TEL AVIV
ISRAEL
Tel. (972-3) 545-04-97
Fax (972-3) 640 95 27

JAPAN

Seinan Gakuin University
6-2-92 Nishijin-Sawaraku
FUKUOKA 814
JAPAN
Tel. (81-92) 823 34 10
Fax (81-92) 843 93 37

Fukuyama University
Faculty of Economics
985 Higashimura-Cho-Hirishima
729-02 FUKUYAMA-SHI
JAPAN
Tel. (81-849) 36 21 11
Fax (81-849) 3622 13

Kagawa University
Takamatsu -Shi-Saiwaicho
760 KAGAWA KEN
JAPAN
Tel. (81-878) 61 41 41
Fax. 81/ 878-34-68-58

Kanazawa University
Central Library
Kakuma-Machi
920-11 KANAZAWA   ISHIKAWA
JAPAN
Tel. (81-762) 64 52 12 EXT. 716
Fax (81-762) 64 52 16

Tohoku University
The Main Library
980 Kawauchi, Aoba-Ku
SENDAI
JAPAN
Tel. (81-22) 222 18 00
Fax (81-22) 222 15 37

Kobe University of Economics
The Institute of Economic Research
Gakuen -Nishimachi 8 Chome 2-1, Nishi-Ku
651-21 KOBE   SHI, HYOGO-KEN 673
JAPAN
Tel. (81-78) 794 61 64
Fax (81-78) 708 23 44

Doshisha University
Faculty of Law
Imadegawa-Dosi-Kamigyo-Ku
602 KYOTO
JAPAN
Tel. (81-75) 252 35 33
Fax (81-75) 251 30 60

Nagoya University
Library of School of Economics
Furoh-Chou, Chikusa-Ku
464-01 NAGOYA
JAPAN
Tel. (81-52) 781-51-11
Fax (81-52) 832-31-11

University of the Ryukyus
Library, Reference and Research
Subsection
1 Senbaru Nishihara-Cho
903-01 OKINAWA
JAPAN
Tel. (81-98) 895 22 21 EXT. 21-45
Fax (81-98) 895 26 51

63

Osaka City University
Institute for Economic Research, Library
3-3-138 Sugimoto-Sumiyoshu Ku
558 OSAKA
JAPAN
Tel. (81-6) 605 24 70

Kansai University Library
Suita P.O. Box 50, Suita-Shi
564 OSAKA-FU
JAPAN
Tel. (81-6) 388 11 21, EXT. 43-28
Fax (81-6) 330 14 64

Hokkaido University
Library
Kita-8-Nishi-5-Kitaku
SAPPORO
JAPAN
Tel. (81-11) 716 21 11
Fax (81-11) 747 28 55

Nihon University
College of International Relations
2-31-145 Bunkyo-Cho-Mishima-Shi
411 SHIZUOKA-KEN
JAPAN
Tel. (81-559) 86 55 00
Fax (81-559) 87 63 50

Hitotsubashi University
Eu Documentation Center
Library
2-1, Naka, Kunitachi 186
TOKYO
JAPAN
Tel. (81-3) (425) 72 11 01
Fax (81-3) (425) 73 03 16

Keio University
Library,
Mita-Minato-Ku
108 TOKYO
JAPAN
Tel. (81-3) 453 44 11 EXT. 2553
Fax (81-3) 453 02 54

Sophia University
Central Library
7/A, Kioicho-Chiyoda-Ku
TOKYO
JAPAN
Tel. (81-3) 238 35 07
Fax (81-3) 238 30 55

Waseda University
Institute for Research in Contemporary
Political & International Affairs
1-6-1 Nishiwasedda-Shinjuku-Ku
160 TOKYO
JAPAN
Tel. (81-3) 203 41 41 EXT. 71 33 24
Fax (81-3) 203 41 41

The University Of Tokyo
United Nations Depositary Lybrary
Hongo 7-Chome -Bunkyo-Ku
TOKYO 113
JAPAN
Tel. (81-3) 812 21 11 EXT. 26 45
Fax (81-3) 816 42 08

Chuo University
The Institute of Economics Research
742-1 Higashi Nakano-Hachioji-Shi
TOKYO 192 03
JAPAN
Tel. (81-3) 426 74 32 72
Fax (81-3) 426 74 33 01

LETTONIE

University of Latvia
Faculty of History and Philosophy
Department of Political Science
Brivibas Bould 32
1098 RIGA
LETTONIE
Tel. (371-13) 21 74 92
Fax (371-13) 22 50 39

MACAU

Universidade de Macau
P.O. BOX 3001, MACAU
MACAU
Tel. (853) 32 73 22
Fax (853) 32 06 94

MALTA

**European Documentation and
Research Centre**
University of Malta-Tal-Qroqq
Stà Paul's Street
VALLETTA
MALTA
Tel. (356) 33-39-04/8
Fax (356) 33 64 50

64

NORWAY

Agder College
4604 KRISTIANSAND S
NORWAY

University of Oslo
Karl Johans GT 47
0162 OSLO
NORWAY
Tel. (47) 22 85 93 52
Fax (47) 22 85 96 10

University of Bergen
Department of Research Management
N-5020 BERGEN
NORWAY

NEW ZEALAND

University of Auckland
Library; Official Publications and Statistics
Collection
Private Bag 92019
AUCKLAND 1
NEW ZEALAND
Tel. (64-9) 373 79 99 EXT. 89 95
Fax (64-9) 3660431

University of Canterbury
Serilas Department; The Librarian
Private Bag 4800
CHRISTCHURCH NZL
NEW ZEALAND
Tel. (64-3) 366 70 01
Fax (64-3) 364 20 55

POLOGNE

Centrun Dokunentacji Europejskiej
Europejska Akademia na Slasku
ul. Krasinskiego 8 b ,40 019 KATOWICE
POLOGNE
tel. (48-32) 155 57 60
fax (48-32) 156 17 62

**Akademia Ekonomicza, Wydzial
Ekonomii**
Katedra Studiow Europejskich
ul. Rakowicka 27, 31-510 KRAKOW
POLOGNE

European Documentation Centre
University of Lodz
ul. Piotrkowska 262/264 , 90-361 LODZ
POLOGNE
tel. (48-42) 33 14 34 / 32 03 82

Katholische Universität Lublin
Hauptbibliothek , ul. Chopina 27 , 20950
LUBLIN
POLOGNE
tel. (48-81) 212 20
fax (48-81) 218 80

**Centre for European Community
Studies and Documentation**
Akademia Ekonomiczna
Powstanicow Wielkopolskich 16 (p. 13) ,
61-967 POZNAN
POLOGNE
tel. (48-61) 69 92 61
fax (48-61) 66 89 24

**Uniwersytet Gdansky Instytut Teorii
Ekonomii**
Osrodek badan ewg
ul. Arnii Krajowej 119/121, 81 824 SOPOT
POLOGNE
tel. (48-58) 51 00 61/459

Fundacja Centrum Europejskie Natolin
Biblioteka College of Europe
Résidence Natolin - ul. Nowoursynowska
84, 02-766 WARZAWA
POLOGNE
tel. (48-2) 644 17 92
fax (48-2) 644 13 52

**Central School of Planning and
Statistics**
Centre for European Studies
ul. Niepodleglosci, 164 , 02-554 WARZAWA
POLOGNE
tel. (48-22) 49 12 51 ext. 366
fax (48-22) 49 26 29

Polski Instytut Spraw
Niedzynarodowych Biblioteka
Warecka 1a - p.o. box 1000 , WARZAWA
POLOGNE
tel. (48-22) 26 30 21 / 27 28 26
fax (48-22) 27 47 38

Warsaw University
European Studies Centre
ul. Ksawerow 13, 02-656 WARZAWA
POLOGNE
tel. (48-22) 31 32 01/58
fax (48-22) 31 28 46

65

Uniwersytet Wroclawski
Instytut nauk Ekonomicznych
ul. Uniwersytecka 22 / 26, 50 145 WRO-
CLAW
POLOGNE
tel. (48-71) 40 23 58
fax (48-71) 40 23 74

PUERTO RICO

University of Puerto Rico
Law Library
Box 23310
Rio Piedras
00931 PUERTO RICO
Tel. (1809) 764 97 77 EXT. 2357
Fax. (1809) 7642660

REPUBLIQUE TCHEQUE

Nasaryk University
Faculty of Law
Veveri 70
611 80 Brno
République Tchèque
tel. (42-5) 41 32 12 97 ext. 304
fax (42-5) 41 21 06 04

International School of Management
T.G. Nasaryk ; Nadrazni 226 -p.s. 25
744 01 Frenstat p.Radhosten
République Tchèque
tel. (42-41) 65 65 66 52
fax (42-42) 65 65 66 50

University of Economics
Faculty of National Economy
W. Churchill 4
130 67 Praha
République Tchèque
tel. (42-2) 29 54 41

Charles University
Taboritska 23
130 87 Praha 3
République Tchèque
tel. (42-2)2793515/ 27 65 416 ext. 1311,
1309
fax (42-2) 27 49 13

ROUMANIE

**National School of Political Studies
and Public Administration**
bd. Schitu Nagureanu, 1 - sector 5 / c.p. 1
792 Bucaresti
Roumanie
tel. (40-36) - 401-613-22-49
fax. (40-36) 401 312 25 35

Université de Bucarest
Faculté de Droit
Bdul n. Kogalniceanu, 64 - sector 5
Bucaresti
Roumanie
tel. (40-1) 15 59 47

RUSSIE

Institute of Europe
Academy of Sciences
Mokhovaja st. 8-3 b
103873 Moskva
Russie
tel. (7-095) 203 41 87
fax (7-095) 200 42 98

Université de Moscou
Centre de Recherches Spécifiques,
Enseignement Processus Integration
Leninskie gory
119899 Moskva
Russie
tel. (7-095) 93917 54
fax (7-095)9395338

SLOVAQUIE

Conenius University
Faculty of Law, Library
Afárikovo nán. 6
818 05 Bratislava
Slovaquie
tel. (42-7) 30 41 11
fax (42-7) 36 61 26

SLOVENIE

Univerza Ljubljana
Ekonomska Fakulteta
Kardeljeva pl. 17
61101 Ljubljana
Slovénie
tel. (386-61) 30 11 20 (direct) / 16 83-
333/328
fax (386-61) 30 11 10

The European House Maribor
Gospejna Ulica 10
6200 Maribor
Slovénie

SUISSE/ SCHWEIZ/ SVIZZERIA

Universität Basel
Institut für Rechtswissenschaft
Naiengasse 51
4056 Basel
Schweiz
tel. (41-61) 261 25 00 / 25 52 77
fax (41-61) 267 25 79

Universität Bern
Juristische Bibliothek
Hochschulstr. 4
3012 Bern
Schweiz
tel. (41-31) 65 82 72/67

Université de Fribourg
Institut des Sciences Économiques et
Sociales
Miséricorde
1700 Fribourg
Suisse
tel. (41-37) 21 93 33

**Institut Européen de l'Université de
Genève (IUEG)**
Uni-Bastions (aile Jura)
1211 Genève 4
Suisse
tel. (41-22) 705 72 72
fax (41-22) 705 78 52

**Centre d'Études Juridiques
Européennes**
102, bd Carl Vogt
1211 Genève 4
Suisse
tel. (41-22) 705 86 56
fax (41-22) 320 46 20

Fondation Jean Monnet pour l'Europe
Centre de Recherches Européennes
Ferme de Dorigny
1015 Lausanne
Suisse
tel. (41-21) 692 20 90
fax (41-21) 692 20 95

Université de Neuchâtel
Bibliothèque de Sciences Économiques et
Sociales
Pierre-a-Nazel 7
2000 Neuchâtel
Suisse
tel. (41-38) 25 72 05

Hochschule St. Gallen
Institut für Europarecht, Wirtschaftsrecht
und Rechtsvergleichung
Bodanstr. 4
9000 St Gallen
Schweiz
tel. (41-71) 30 24 40

Universität Zürich
Institut für Völkerrecht und Ausländisches
Verfassungsrecht
Hirschengraben 40
8001 Zürich
Schweiz
tel. (41-1) 257 20 51

TURQUIE

Ankara University
Egitin Bilinleri Fakultesi
kat: 3 - blok cebeci
Ankara
Turquie
tel. (90-4) 362 07 62

Ataturk University
Ziraat Fakultesi, European Community
Research Center
ve Uygulana Nerkezi Nudurlugu
Erzurun
Turquie

Anadolu Universitesi
Avrupa Ekonomik Toplulugu, Arastirna
Nerkezi
Yunus Enre Kanpusu
Eskisehir
Turquie
tel. (90-50583) 21 10

67

Narnara Universitesi
Avrupa Toplulugu Enstitusu
Kayisdagi cad./ goztepe
87040 Istanbul
Turquie
tel. (90-1) 338 41 96

Istanbul Universitesi
Hukuk Fakultesi
34452 Istanbul
Turquie
tel. (90-1) 528 04 23
fax (90-1) 174 63 03

Ege University
Ziraat Fakultesi, Tarin Ekonomisi Bolunu
Bornova
35100 Izmir
Turquie
tel. (90-51) 18 18 62

UKRANIA

Institute of Public Administration and Local Government
Cabinet of Ministers
20 Eugene Pottier street
252057 Kiev
Ukrania
tel. (44) 446 42 58
fax (44) 296 13 60

USA

George Mason University
Centre for European Community Studies
Arlington Campus, 4001 North Fairfax Dr.,
Suite 450
22203 ARLINGTON, VIRGINIA
USA
Tel. (1-703) 993 82 00
Fax (1-703) 993 82 15

University of Georgia
School of Law
Law Library
30602 ATHENES   GEORGIA
USA
Tel. (1-706) 542 19 22
Fax (1-706) 542 50 01

The American University
CERDEC / Center for Research and
Documentation on the European Union
W C L Library
20016 WASHINGTON, D.C.
USA

YOUGOSLAVIE

Institute of International Politics and Economics
Library
Nakedonska street 25 - p.o. box 750
11000 Beograd
Yougoslavie
tel. (38-11) 32 14 33-212
fax (38-11) 32 40 13

68

EUROPÄISCHE REFERENZZENTREN

➤ **Akronym**

ERZ

➤ **Trägerorganisation**

Die 1963 gegründeten ERZ sind den Hochschulen, an denen der Unterricht über Europa nur gering entwickelt ist, oder nicht-universitären Studienzentren angeschlossen.

➤ **Zielgruppe**

Das Hochschulmilieu (Professoren, Studenten, Forscher) und das universitätsexterne Publikum

➤ **Wirkungskreis**

79 Zentren in der Gemeinschaft
126 Zentren in den Drittländern

➤ **Ziele**

- Bereitstellung bestimmter grundlegender Dokumente über die Union und ihre Politik für die Öffentlichkeit
- Angabe von Referenzen für andere bestehende EG-Dokumente.

➤ **Ihnen zur Verfügung stehende Informationen**

Die ERZ erhalten grundlegende Dokumentationen und Nachschlagewerke über die europäischen Veröffentlichungen. Sie haben nicht automatisch Zugang zu den EG-Datenbanken.

➤ Europäische Kommission
Generaldirektion X
Referat X/A/4 - Informationsrelais und -netze
200 rue de la Loi
B - 1049 Brüssel
Tel.(32.2) 299 94 25/299 92 72

69

EUROPEAN REFERENCE CENTRES

➤ **Acronym**

E R C

➤ **Host structure**

The ERCs, set up in 1963, are assigned to the universities in which education on Europe is not very advanced, or to non-university study centres.

➤ **Target Public**

The university community (lecturers, students, researchers) and the non-university public

➤ **Community coverage**

79 centres in the Community;
126 centres in the non-EC countries

➤ **Objectives**

- make available to the public certain basic documents on the Union and its policies;
- provide references to other existing Community documents.

➤ **Information which they have available**

The ERCs receive the basic documentation and works of reference to European publications. They do not automatically have free access to Community databases.

➤ European Commission
Directorate-General X
Unit X/A/4 - Information relays and networks
200 rue de la Loi
B - 1049 Brussels
Tel.: (32.2) 299.94.25/299.92.72

CENTRES DE REFERENCE EUROPEENS

➤ **Acronyme**
C.R.E.

➤ **Structure hôte**

Les CRE, nés en 1963, sont attribués aux universités dans lesquelles l'enseignement sur l'Europe est peu développé, ou à des centres d'études non-universitaires.

➤ **Public cible**

Le milieu universitaire (professeurs, étudiants, chercheurs) et le public non-universitaire.

➤ **Rayonnement communautaire**

79 centres dans la Communauté;
126 centres dans les pays tiers

➤ **Objectifs**

- mettre à la disposition du public certains documents de base sur l'Union et ses politiques;
- fournir les références des autres documents communautaires existants.

➤ **Informations dont ils disposent**

Les CRE reçoivent la documentation de base et des ouvrages de référence sur les publications européennes. Ils n'ont pas automatiquement un accès gratuit aux bases de données communautaires.

➤ Commission européenne
Direction générale X
Unité X/A/4 - Relais et réseaux d'information
200 rue de la Loi
B - 1049 Bruxelles
Tél.: (32.2) 299.94.25/299.92.72

71

BELGIQUE-BELGIË

ANTWERPEN

Europees Studie en Informatiecentrum v.z.w.
Handelsbeurs
Twaalfmaandenstraat 1
2000 Antwerpen
Belgique-België
tel. (32-3) 231 22 66

ARLON

La Maison de l'Europe du Luxembourg (CIFEL)
Rue Zenobe Gramme
6700 Arlon
Belgique-België

MONS

Université de l'État
Bibliotheque
17 Place Warocque
7000 Mons
Belgique-België

Bibliothèque de la Fondation d'Utilité Publique Léon Losseau
Rue de Nimy 37
7000 Mons
Belgique-België
tel. (32-65) 32 84 09

SAINT-GHISLAIN

Centre International de Formation Européenne (C.I.F.E.)
Rue de Saint-Lo 67
7330 Saint-Ghislain
Belgique-België

DEUTSCHLAND

BONN

Interdisziplinares Institut für Europäische Fragen
U. internationale Entwicklung E.V.
Römerstr. 164
53117 Bonn
Deutschland
tel. 49-228 -550365
fax. 0228- 550376

DORTMUND

Universität Dortmund
Universitätsbibliothek
Vogelpothsweg 76,
44227 Dortmund
Deutschland
tel. (49-231) 75 54 04

EMDEN

Fachhochschule Ostfriesland
Hochschulbibliothek
Constantiaplatz 4
26723 Emden
Deutschland
tel. (49-4921) 80 72 23/69
fax. 49-21807201

ESSEN

Universität Essen
Universitätsbibliothek
Zeitschriftenstelle
45147 Essen
Deutschland
tel. (49-201) 183 36 95

FLENSBURG

Universität Flensburg
Bildungswissenschaftliche Hochschule
Bibliothek
Mürwiker str. 77
24943 Flensburg
Deutschland
tel. (49-461) 313 0 144-140
fax (49-461) 385 43

HAMBURG

Universität der Bundeswehr Hamburg
Bibliothek
Holstenhofweg 85
22043 Hamburg
Deutschland
tel. (49-40) 65 41 28 64
fax. 49/40-65-41-27-84

HEIDELBERG

Institut für Ausländisches und Internationales Privat und Wirtschaftrecht
Augustinergasse,9
69117 Heidelberg
Deutschland
tel. (49-6221) 54 22 00
fax (49-6221) 54 22 01

72

KARLSRUHE

Landesgewerbeamt Baden-Württemberg
Gewerbebücherei
Karl-Friedrich-Str. 17 - Postfach 41 69
76133 Karlsruhe
Deutschland
tel. (49-721) 135 40 54
fax (49-721) 135 40 20

KASSEL

Gesamthochschulbibliothek Kassel
Murhardsche Bibliothek der Stadt Kassel
Zeitschriftenstelle
Monchebergstr. 10
34127 Kassel
Deutschland
tel. (49-561) 804 21 66

KOBLENZ

Fachhochschule Rheinland-Pfalz, abt. Koblenz
European Centre for Community Education
(E.C.C.E.) e.v.
am finkenherd 4
56075 Koblenz
Deutschland
tel. (49-261) 566 17 / 40 86 17
fax (49-261) 569 53

MAINZ

Universität Mainz
Bibliothek
Postfach 40 20 - Saarstr. 21
55122 Mainz
Deutschland
tel. (49-6131) 39 26 44

NEUBIBERG

Universität der Bundeswehr München
Universitätsbibliothek
Werner-Heisenberg-weg 39/45
88579 Neubiberg
Deutschland
tel. (49-89) 60 04 33 19

OLDENBURG

Universität Oldenburg
Bibliothek
Ämmerländer heerstr.49-55 - Postfach 25 41
26129 Oldenburg
Deutschland
tel. (49-441) 79 82 260

OSNABRÜCK

Fachhochschule Osnabrück
Bibliothek
Albrechtstr. 30
49076 Osnabrück
Deutschland
tel. (49-541) 60 82 211

PFORZHEIM

Fachhochschule für Wirtschaft Pforzheim
Bibliothek
Tiefenbronner str. 65
75175 Pforzheim
Deutschland
tel. (49-7231) 60 31 125

STUTTGART

Württembergische Landesbibliothek
Konrad Adenauer str. 8 - Postfach 10 54 41
70195 Stuttgart
Deutschland
tel. (49-711) 212 43 83

SUHL

Umwelt-Center der Stadt Suhl
EU Umweltinformationszentru
bahnhofstraße 20
98527 Suhl
Deutschland
tel. (49-3681) 221 95
fax (49-3681) 220 57

WORMS

Fachhochschule Rheinland-Pfalz Abteilung Ludwigshafen/Worms Fachbereich bwv
Außenhandel/Außenwirtschaft
Erenburgerstr. 19
67549 Worms
Deutschland
tel. (49-6241)50 91 46,50 9147
fax. 49/6241-50 92 24

73

ELLAS

RHODES

**Chambre de Commerce et d'Industrie
du Dodecanese**
Section Communautés Européennes,
Relations Internationales
8 rue Grigoriou Lambraki - b.p. no. 5
851 00 Rhodes
Ellas
tel. (30-241) 222 81
fax (30-241) 222 83

ESPAÑA

GIJÓN

Universidad de Oviedo
Escuela Universitaria de Estudios
Empresariales
c/ Ramiro de Maeztu, 1
33201 Gijón (Asturias)
España
tel. (34-85) 34 14 22 ext. 30

MADRID

Escuela Diplomatica
Paseo Juan XXIII, 5
28040 Madrid
España

FRANCE

BASTIA

**Institut Régional d'Administration de
Bastia (IRA)**
Place des Martyrs
20200 Bastia
France

PARIS

Cour D'Appel de Paris
Centre Judiciaire
Documentation Européenne du Palais de
Justice Européen
34, Quai de Justice
75001 Paris
France
tel. (33-1) 43 29 12 55

BASE-TERRE

**Chambre de Commerce et d'Industrie
de Basse-Terre**
rue du dr. Cabre, 45 - b.p.19
F-97100 Base-Terre
France

CAYENNE
Chambre du Commerce et d'Industrie de
Cayenne
b.p. 49
F - 97203 Cayenne
France

FORT-DE-FRANCE

**Chambre de Commerce et d'Industrie
de la Martinique**
rue Victor Hugo, 53- b.p. 478
Fort-de France
France

POINTE-A-PITRE

**Chambre de Commerce et d'Industrie
de Pointe-a Pitre**
ex-Grand Hotel b.p. 64
f. 97152 Pointe-a-Pitre
France

SAINT DENIS

**Chambre de Commerce et d'Industrie
de la Reunion**
rue de Paris, 5 bis - b.p. 120
93463 Saint Denis
France
tel. 262/21 53 66

ITALIA

ARCAVACATA DI RENDE

Università degli Studi della Calabria
Biblioteca interdipartimentalle
87036 Arcavacata di Rende CS
Italia
tel. (39-984) 83 72 10

BERGAMO

Accademia della Guardia di Finanza
Ufficio Addestramento e Studi
via Statuto, 21
24100 Bergamo
Italia
tel. (39-35) 25 97 07
fax (39-35) 25 42 23

Istituto Universitario di Bergamo
Biblioteca
via Salvecchio 19
24100 Bergamo
Italia

BOLZANO

Presidenza Giunta Provinciale
Ufficio Affari Comunitari
Palazo Provinciale n. 1,
via Crispi,3
39100 Bolzano
Italia
tel. (39-471) 99 22 40
fax (39-471) 99 22 45

BRINDISI

Centro Informazioni e Studi sulle Comunità Europee
Corso Garibaldi 53
72100 Brindisi
Italia
tel. (39-831) 225 41

CAMPOBASSO

Associazione dei Comuni Molisani, ASCOM
via Roma 64
6100 Campobasso
Italia
tel. (39-874) 920 12

CASERTA

Scuola di Perfezionamento in Studi Storico-Politici
via Napoli Villa Vitrone
Caserta
Italia

CUNEO

Comune di Cuneo
Biblioteca Civica
via Cacciatori delle Alpi
12100 Cuneo
Italia
tel. (39-171) 69 31 69

FISCIANO SALERNO

Universitá degli Studi di Salerno
Facoltà di Economia e Comercio, Biblioteca
via don Melillo
I - 84100 Fisciano Salerno
Italia
tel. (39-9) 220164

MACERATA

Università degli Studi di Macerata
Istituto di Economia e Finanze
62100 Macerata
Italia
tel. (39-733) 483 51

MESSINA

Università degli Studi di Messina
Facoltá di Economia e Commercio,
Biblioteca
via Cesare Battisti
98100 Messina
Italia
tel. (39-90) 71 10 21

MILANO

Università Cattolica del Sacro Cuore
Biblioteca Centrale
Largo A. Gemelli 1
20123 Milano
Italia
tel. (39-2) 885 62 31

NUORO

Biblioteca "Sebastiano Satta"
Nuoro (Sardegna)
Italia
tel. (39-784) 23 00 45

PARMA

Collegio Europeo di Parma
Borgo Lalatta, 14
43100 Parma
Italia
tel. (39-521) 20 75 25

PERUGIA

Servizio Europa Umbria
Centro Direzionale Fontivegge
via Fontivegge, 51
06124 Perugia
Italia
tel. (39-75) 504 46 00
fax (39-75) 504 46 02

RAGUSA

Camera di Commercio, Industria, Artigianato e Agricoltura
via Natalelli
97100 Ragusa
Italia
tel. (39-932) 239 11

ROMA

Ufficio Studi delle Acli
Centro Studi e Informazione Europea
via Marcora 18-20
00153 Roma
Italia
tel. (39-6) 584 01

Comando Scuola Polizia Tributaria delle Guardia di Finanza
Biblioteca
piazza Armellini, 20
00162 Roma
Italia

Centro Italiano di Studi Europei C.I.S.E.
via del Corso,267
00187 Roma
Italia
tel. (39-6) 78 00 04

Scuola Superiore della Pubblica Amministrazione sede di Roma
Biblioteca
via dei Robilant 11
00194 Roma
Italia
tel. (39-6) 396 12 44/36 53

TRENTO

Libera Università degli Studi di Trento
Dipartimento di Economia
via Inama 1
38100 Trento
Italia
tel. (39-461) 88 22 01
fax (39-461) 88 22 22

Ufficio Studi della Regione Trentino Alto Adige
Palazzo della Regione, via Gazzoletti
38100 Trento
Italia
tel. (39-461) 370 22

NEDERLAND

DEN HAAG

Association for Netherlands Municipalities (VNG)
EU Informatiepunkt voor Gemeenten en Provincies
po box 30435
2500 GK Den Haag
Nederland
tel. (31-70) 373 83 91
fax (31-70) 346 02 60

PORTUGAL

LISBOA

Colegio Universitario Pio XI!
av. das Forcas Armadas
1599 Lisboa codex
Portugal
tel. (351-1) 76 71 46

SUOMI-FINLAND

HELSINKI

Suomen Kaupunkiliitto
Finlands Stadsfoerbund
Toinen Linja 14 Helsinki
Suomi-Finland
tel 358/07711
fax 358/07712291

UNITED KINGDOM

ABERYSTWYTH

University College of Wales Aberystwyth
Laura Place
SY23 3AX Aberystwyth Dyfed
United Kingdom
tel. (44-970) 62 23 64
fax (44-970) 62 23 64

CHALFONT ST. GILES

Buckinghamshire College
Library
Newland Park
Buckinghamshire HP8 4AD Chalfont St
Giles
United Kingdom
tel. (44-494) 87 44 41
fax (44-494) 60 30 82

CHELMSFORD

Anglia Polytechnic University
Library
Rivermead Campus, Bishop Lane
Chelmsford, Essex CM1 1SQ
United Kingdom
tel. (44-245) 49 31 31 ext. 200
fax (44-245) 49 08 35

CLEVELAND

Teesside Polytechnic
Library
Borough road Middlesbrough
TSI 3BA Cleveland
United Kingdom
tel. (44-642) 21 81 21, ext. 43 71

EDINBURGH

National Library of Scotland
George IV Bridge
EH1 1EW Edinburgh
United Kingdom
tel. (44-31) 226 45 31

EXMOUTH

Polytechnic South West
Library
Douglas avenue
EX8 2AT Exmouth, Devon
United Kingdom
tel. 44/395 255333
fax. 44/395 255331

HALIFAX

**Percival Whitley Centre European
Reference Centre**
College Library Information service
Francis street
HX1 3UZ Halifax
United Kingdom
tel. (44-4225) 35 82 21 ext 2117
fax (44-4225) 34 56 61

HATFIELD

Hertfordshire County Council
College Library & Information Service
p.o. box 110, AL109AD Hatfield
Hertfordshire
United Kingdom

INVERNESS

Highlands Regional Council
Regional Library Service
31 a Harbour road IV1 1UA Inverness
United Kingdom
tel. (44-) 23 41 21

IPSWICH

Suffolk County Library
Central Library
Northgate street
IP1 3DE Ipswich
United Kingdom
tel. (44-473) 25 24 77 ext. 34/37
fax (44-473) 23 07 58

LONDON

British Library Overseas
English section
Great Russell street
WC1b3DG London
United Kingdom
tel. (44-71) 636 15 44
fax (44-71) 323 70 39

Thames Valley University
Walpole House
18-22 bond St. - Ealing
W5 5AA London
United Kingdom
tel. (44-81) 231 22 48
fax (44-81) 231 26 31

Ealing College of Higher Education
Law Divison
St. Marys road Ealing
UK - W5 5RF London Northampton
United Kingdom

NORTHAMPTON

Nene College Library
Moulton park
NN2 7AL Northampton
United Kingdom
tel. (44-604) 71 55 0

77

PRESTON

Harris Library
Market square
PR1 2 TQ Preston
United Kingdom
tel. (44-772) 53 191

Lancashire Polytechnic
Library & Learning Resources service
st. Peter's Square
PR1 2TQ Preston, Lancashire
United Kingdom
tel. (44-772) 221 41

READING

University of Reading
European Education Centre, Bulmershe
Library
Woodlands avenue
RG6 1HY Reading
United Kingdom
tel. (44-734) 31 86 51
fax (44-734) 35 30 80

SHEFFIELD

University of Sheffield
Crookesmoor Library
SIO IEW Sheffield
United Kingdom
tel. (44-742) 76 85 55 ext. 67- 79
fax (44-742) 75 46 20

STIRLING

Stirling University
Library
FK4 4LA Stirling
United Kingdom
tel. (44-0786) 73171ext. 22-27
fax (44-0786) 46 68 66

SWANSEA

University College of Swanseathe
Library
Singleton park
SA2 8PP Swansea
United Kingdom

WREXHAM

The North Wales Institute of Higher Education
101 box lane
LL12 7RB Wrexham
United Kingdom
tel. (44-978) 357 073
fax (44-978) 356 426

AFRIQUE DU SUD

University of South Africa
Library, Serials Division
PO Box 392
0001 PRETORIA
AFRIQUE DU SUD

ARABIE SAOUDITE

King Sand University
Central Library, Government Publications
Department
P.O. Box 22480
11495, RIYADH
ARABIE SAOUDITE
Tel. (966-1) 467 61 14

Ministry of Planning
Library and Documentation Department,
Special publications Section
11 182 RIYADH
ARABIE SAOUDITE
Tel. (966-1) 401 04 17

The Cooperation Council of the Arab States of the Gulf
P O BOX 7153
RIYADH
ARABIE SAOUDITE

ARGENTINA

Biblioteca del Congreso de la Nación Argentina
C/ Adolfo Alsina 1861, 10 .
1090 BUENOS AIRES
ARGENTINA
Tel. (54-1) 40 76 57
Fax. 54/1 49 38 54

**Centro de Investigaciones Europeo-
Latinoamericanas (EURAL)**
Corrientes, 2554-3A "A"
1046 BUENOS AIRES
ARGENTINA
Tel. (54-1) 951 45 04 / 953 43 26
Fax (54-1) 953 15 39

Universidad del Salvador
Instituto de Investigación en Ciencias
Sociales (IDISCO)
Facultad de Ciencias Sociales
Teniente General Juan D. Perón 1818
1040 BUENOS AIRES
ARGENTINA
Tel. (54-1) 40 04 22

**Instituto para la Integración de
America Latina (INTAL)**
Casilla de Correo 39 - Sucursal 1
1401 BUENOS AIRES
ARGENTINA

Universidad de Buenos Aires
Facultad de Ciencias Económicas
Biblioteca
Av. Córdoba 2122
1120 BUENOS AIRES
ARGENTINA

Universidad Argentina de la Empresa
Biblioteca Central
Azcu Naga 1625
1128 BUENOS AIRES
ARGENTINA
Tel. (54-1)821 96 93

Universidad de Buenos Aires
Facultad de Derecho y Ciencias Sociales
Av. Presidente Figueroa Alcorta 2263
1425 BUENOS AIRES
ARGENTINA

Universidad Católica
Instituto de Ciencias de la Administración
CEPADE-CIPEAP-CIPAC
Trejo 323
5000 CÓRDOBA
ARGENTINA

Universidad Nacional de la Plata
Facultad de Ciencias Jurídicas y Sociales
Biblioteca "Joaquín V. González"
C/ 48 E/6 Y 7 P.B.
1900 LA PLATA
ARGENTINA

Universidad Nacional de Cuyo
Biblioteca Central
Casilla de Correo 420
5500 MENDOZA
ARGENTINA

Universidad Nacional del Litoral
Facultad de Ciencias Jurídicas y Sociales
Instituto de Derecho Internacional
Cándido Pujato 2751
3000 SANTA FE
ARGENTINA
Tel. 54/414-29 328-08

BOSTWANA

University of Botswana
University Library
Private Bag0022
GABORONE
BOSTWANA

BRASIL

**Centro de Desenvoluimento de
Administração Publica**
Mesuv de Ciencia e Technologia da Bahia
BAHIA
BRASIL

**Uniao de Ensino Superior do ParaNIAO
DE ENSINO SUPERIOR DO PARA**
Av. Alcindo Cacela, 287
CEP 66.030
BELEM   PARA
BRASIL
Tel. (55-91) 223 21 00
Fax (55-91) 225 39 09

Universidade Federal de Minas Gerais
Faculdade de Direitp
Av Alvares Cabral 211
30000 BELO HORIZONTE
BRASIL

Universidade de Brasilia
Biblioteca Cantral
Seção de Organismos Internacionais
Campus Universitario Asa Norte
C. POSTAL 15.2951
70910 BRASILIA D.F.
BRASIL

79

Universidade Federal do H.B. Schreiner
Biblioteca Central
Av Paulo Gama s/n
90001 PORTO ALEGRE
BRASIL
Tel. (55-512) 24 24 31

Fundação Gertulio Vargas
Biblioteca
Praia do Botafogo 190
22250 RIO DE JANEIRO RJ
BRASIL

Catholic University of Rio de Janeiro
Department of Economics
Rua Marques São Vincente 225
22453 RIO DE JANEIRO, RJ
BRASIL
Tel. (55-21) 529 99 22
Fax (55-21) 294 20 95

Universidade Federal da Bahia
Biblioteca Central
Campus Universitario do Canela, s/n¤
40.000 SALVADOR CEP BAHIA
BRASIL

Centro de Estatistica e Informacoes (CEI)
Secretaria do Planejamento, Ciencia y Technologia
Servicio de Documentação e Biblioteca(SDB)
Av. Luiz Viana Filho, s/n cab
41200 SALVADOR, BAHIA
BRASIL
Tel. (55-231) 99 85

Universidade Federal de Santa Maria
Centro de Ciencias Sociais e Humanas
Rua Floriano Peixoto, 1184, Sala 113
97015 SANTA MARIA
BRASIL
Tel. (55-221) 53 33 RAMAL 3

Universidade de São Paulo
Faculdade de Direito
Largo de São Francisco, N¤.95
ANDAR
01005 SÃO PAULO SP
BRASIL
Tel. (55-11) 239 30 77/274 / 239 07 01
Fax (55-11) 284 17 89

80

CANADA

Simon Fraser University
Wac Bennett Library, Serials Division
V5A 1S6 BURNABY B.C.
CANADA
Tel. (1-614) 291 36 77

University of Prince Edmard Island
Library, Government Publications
CHARLOTTETOWN P.E.I.
CANADA
Tel. (1-902) 566 04 52 / 892 41 21

York University
Library, Government Documents, room 113
Administration Building
4700 Keele Sreet
M3J 2R6 DOWNSVIEW ONT.
CANADA
Tel. (1-416) 736 51 39

University of Alberta
Library, Government Publications
T6G 2J8 EDMONTON ALBERTA
CANADA
Tel. (1-403) 492 37 76

University of New Brunswick
Harriet Irving Library
Documents Department
P O BOX 7500
E3B 5H5 FREDERICTON N B
CANADA
Tel. (1-506) 453 47 52
Fax (1-506) 453 45 96

Université de Moncton
Bibliothèque Champlain
E1A 3E9 MONCTON N.B.
CANADA
Tel. (1-506) 858 41 04

Université d'Ottawa
Bibliothèque Morisset, Documents Officiels
K1N 9A5 OTTAWA ONTARIO
CANADA
Tel. (1-613) 514 68 80

University of Regina
The Library
Government Publications Section
S4S OA2 REGINA, SASKATCHEWAN
CANADA
Tel. (1-306) 585 44 56
Fax (1-306) 585 4878

University of Saskatchewan
Library, Government Publications Section
SASKATCHEWAN
S7N OWO SASKATOON SK
CANADA
Tel. (1-306) 966 59 87
Fax (1-306) 966 60 40

University of Sherbrooke
Library, Government Publicaions
Bould. Université
University City
SHERBROOKE P.Q.
CANADA
Tel. (1-819) 821 75 59

Brock University
Library, Documents Department
ST. CATHARINES ONT. L25 3A1
CANADA
Tel. (1/416) 688 32 28

Memorial University of Newfoundland
Queen Elizabeth II Library, Government
Publications
A1B 3Y4 ST. JOHN'S
CANADA
Tel. (1-709) 737 74 25

Université Laurentienne
Dept. de Science Politique
P3E 2C6 SUDBURY ONT.
CANADA
Tel. (1-705) 675 11 51

University of British Columbia
Main Library, Government Publications
P.O. BOX 2194
V6B 3V9 VANCOUVER B.C.
CANADA
Tel. (1-604) 822 63 51
Fax (1-604) 822 91 22

WIlfried Laurier University
Library Periodicals
N2L 3C5 WATERLOO ONT.
CANADA
Tel. (1-519) 884 19 70
Fax (1-519) 886 93 51

University of Waterloo
Dana Porter Arts Library, Government
Publications Department
N2L 3G1 WATERLOO ONTARIO
CANADA
Tel. (1-519) 885 12 11

Acadia University
Department of Political Science
BOP 1XO WOLFVILLE NOVA SCOTI
CANADA
Tel. (1-902) 542 22 01

CHILE

Universidad de Tarapaca
General Velasquez, 1775
Casilla 7D
ARICA
CHILE
Tel. (56-58) 22 28 00
Fax.(56-32) 23 00 30

Biblioteca del Congreso
Hemeroteca de Organismos
Internacionales
Huérfanos, 1117, piso 2¤
SANTIAGO DE CHILE
CHILE
Tel. (56-2) 71 53 31

Universidad Católica de Valparaíso
Facultad de Derecho
Av Brasil 2950
VALPARAISO
CHILE
Tel. (56-58) 22 28 00
Fax. (56-58) 23 00 30

Universidad Austral de Chile
Biblioteca Central
Casilla 39-A
VALDIVIA
CHILE
Tel. (56-63) 22 12 90
Fax (56-63) 22 13 60

CHINE

Nationam Library of China
UN Materials Section
Dept of Western European Affairs
Ministry of Foreign Affairs
Jian Guo E. C.
BEIJING
CHINE
Tel. (86) 831 55 66

81

CYPRUS

Cyprus Chamber of Commerce and Industry
Chamber's Building
38, Grivas Dhigenis Ave
P.O. BOX 1455
NICOSIA
CYPRUS
Tel. (357-2) 44 95 00 / 46 23 12
Fax (357-2) 45 86 30 / 44 90 48

COLOMBIA

Universidad de los Andes
Facultad de Derecho
Apartado Aereo 4976
BOGOTÁ
COLOMBIA

Universidad de Gran Colombia
Departamento de Bibliotecas
Carrera 6, 13-92
co I.D.E.
BOGOTÁ
COLOMBIA
Tel. 2-411449

Universidad Javeriana
Facultad de Estudios Interdisciplinarios,
Centro de Documentación
Cra.7 #40-62/ Edif. 25/OF. 208
Apartado Aereo 56710
BOGOTÁ,
COLOMBIA
Tel. (57-1) 288 47 00

Universidad del Valle
Departamento de Bibliotecas
Apartado Aereo 25 360
CALI
COLOMBIA
Tel. (57-23) 39 85 17

COSTA RICA

Facultad Latinoamericana de Ciencias Sociales(FLASCO)
Apartado Postal 5429   1000
SAN JOSÉ
COSTA RICA

Instituto Centroamericano de Administración Pública (ICAP)
Apartado Postal 10.025
Edificio Schyfter, pisos 4,5,6
Avenida Central Y C/ 2
SAN JOSE
COSTA RICA
Tel. (506/53) 40 59
Fax. 506/25 2049

Universidad de Costa Rica
Facultad de Derecho
Ciudad de la Facultad de Derecho de Rodrigo Facio
SAN PEDRO DE MONTES DE OCA
COSTA RICA
Tel. (506) 53 61 52

CROATIE

University of Zagreb
ISIP International Permanent Exhibition of Publications
Trg Marsala Tita, 3
PO BOX 327
41001 ZAGREB
CROATIE
Tel. (38-41) 42 06 30
Fax (38-41) 42 79 03

CUBA

Universidad de la Habana
Dirección DE Información científica y técnica
San Lazaro YL
Colina Universitaria
Biblioteca Central " Rubén Martinez Villena"
CIUDAD LA HABANA 4
CUBA
Tel. (53) 755 73

EGYPTE

Helwan University
Department of Internationam Trade
Faculty of Commerce and Business Administration
43 SCHAREH ABU EL FEDA
ZAMALEK CAIRO
EGYPTE

82

EL SALVADOR

Universidad Centroamericana José Simeón Cañas
Biblioteca Central
Apartado (01) 168
SAN SALVADOR
EL SALVADOR
Tel. (503) 24 00 11

EQUATEUR

Universidad Central del Ecuador
Facultad de Jurisprudencia
Escuela de Ciencias Internacionales
C/ Clarvajal
QUITO
EQUATEUR

FIDJI

University of the South Pacific
Library
P.O. Box 1168
SUVA FIDJI
Tel. (679) 31 39 00
Fax (679) 30 08 30

GIBRALTAR

John Mackintosh Hall Library
Main Street
GIBRALTAR
Tel. (350) 780 00
Fax (350) 408 43

HONDURAS

Bibliotaca Nacional de Honduras
Avenida Salvador Mendieta, casa 411
TEGUCIGALPA
HONDURAS

HONGRIE

College of Commerce, Catering and Tourism
P.O.Box 21
1363 BUDAPEST
HONGRIE
Tel. (36-1) 32 71 50
Fax (36-1) 131 57 20

INDE

Jawaharlal Nehru University_
Central Library New Campus
New Mahrauli Road
110067 NEW DELHI
INDE

INDONESIE

Asean Secretariat
The Public Information Office
P.O. BOX 2072
70A Kebajoran Baru
701 Jalan Sisingamangalja
JAKARTA
INDONESIE
Tel. (62-21) 71 22 72

University of Indonesia
Faculty of Economics
Institute for Economic and Social Research
Jalan Salemba Raya 4
10430 JAKARTA
INDONESIE
Tel. (62-21) 33 31 77 / 33 02 25

Atma Jaya Research Centre
The Librarian
Jalan Jenderal Sudriman 51
P.O. Box 2639
10001 JAKARTA
INDONESIE
Tel. (62-21 570 3306 ext 230
Fax (62-21) 573 43 55

83

ISLAND

Haskolabokasafin
The University Library
101 REYKJAVIK
ISLAND

JAMAIQUE

University of the West Indies
Library, Gifts and Exchange
MONA KINGSTON 7
JAMAIQUE
Tel. (1-809) 927 21 23
Fax. (1- 809) 927 19 26

JAPON

Otaru University of Commerce
Faculty of Commerce
3-5-21 Midori
HOKKAIDO
JAPON
Tel. (81-134) 23 11 01

Nanzan University
The Centre for European Studies
18 Yamazato-Cho, Showa-Ku
NAYOGA 466
JAPON
Tel. (81-52) 832 31 11
Fax (81-52) 833 69 85

Saitama University
Library
255 Shimo Okubo Urawa-Shi
SAITAMA
JAPON
Tel. (81-48) 852 21 11
Fax (81-48) 855 03 90

KENYA

University of Nairobi
Diplomacy Trainig Programme
P.O. Box 30197
NAIROBI
KENYA

LIBAN

Université Saint-Joseph
Faculté de Sciences Economiques
B.P.293
BEYROUTH
LIBAN

Chambre de Commerce et d'Industrie de Beyrouth
Centre d'Etudes et de Doc. économique.
BP 11   1801 Samayeh
BEYROUTH
LIBAN

MALAWI

University of Malawi
Library
Chancellor College
P.O.B. 280
ZOMBA
MALAWI
Tel. (265) 52 22 22 EXT. 128/129

MALAYSIE

University of Malya
Central Library
Pantai Valley
59100 KUALA LUMPUR
MALAYSIE
Tel. (60-3) 756 00 22
Fax (60-3) 757 36 61

MALI

Centre Culturel Français
CITÉ (Centre d'Information technique et économique) EUREKA
B.P. 1547
BAMAKO
MALI
Tel. (223) 22 40 19

84

MAROC

Délégation de l'UE à Rabat
Service des Études et de la Documentation
du Ministère de l'Information
Rue Oqba
RABAT
MAROC

MÉXICO

**Universidad Nacional Autónoma de
México (UNAM)**
Facultad de Ciencias Políticas y Sociales
Biblioteca
Apartado Postal 70-266
MÉXICO 20 DF
MÉXICO
Tel. (52-5) 655 13 44 EXT. 7957

**Centro de Estudios economicos y
Sociales del tercer mundo**
Apart. Post. 85-03
Av. San Jeronimo N . 1387 San Jeronimo
Lidice
MX. 01000 D.F. MÉXICO
MÉXICO

El Colegio de México
Biblioteca Daniem Cosio Villegas, Series y
Documentos
Camino al Ajusco, 20
01000 MÉXICO DF
MÉXICO
Tel. (52-645 50 83
Fax (52-645 45 84

Universidad Autónoma del Nuevo León
Facultad de Economía
Loma Redonda, 1515 PTE
Col. Loma Larga
A.P. 288
64710 MONTERREY
MÉXICO
Tel. (52-83) 43 89 89

PAPOUASIE-NOUVELLE-GUINÉE

University of Papua New Guinea
Library, Periodical Department
P.O.B. 319 / NCD
PAPUA
PAPOUASIE-NOUVELLE-GUINÉE
Tel. (675) 24 52 80
Fax (675) 24 51 87

PARAGUAY

**Universidad Católica Nuestra Señora
de la Asunción**
Biblioteca Central Pablo VI
Casilla de Correos 1718
ASUNCIÓN
PARAGUAY

PERU

Universidad de Lima
Facultad de Derecho y Ciencias Políticas
Av Javier Prado Este, s/n
Monterrico
Apartado 852
LIMA
PERU
Tel. (51-14) 35 06 77 EXT. 2060

Pontificia Universidad Católica del Perú
CISEPA
Ciudad Universitaria
Apartado 1761
LIMA 21
PERU
Tel. (51-14) 62 25 40 EXT. 212

PHILIPPINES

University of the Philippines
School of Economics
Library
1101 QUEZON CITY
PHILIPPINES
Tel. (63-32) 98 20 44
Fax (63-32) 99 19 29

POLOGNE

**Centre de Référence auprés de
l'Institut de conjocture et des prix du
commerce exterieur**
Ul. Swietokrzyska, 12
00-916 WARSZAWA
POLOGNE
Tel. (48-2) 694 42 10/694 52 92
Fax (48-22) 26 55 62_

85

REPÚBLICA DOMINICANA

Universidad Central del Este
Biblioteca Central
Av Circunvalación, s/n.
SAN PEDRO DE MACORIS
REPÚBLICA DOMINICANA
Tel. (508) 529 35 62
Fax (508) 529 51 46

RÉPUBLIQUE DE CORÉE

The Institute of Foreign Affairs and
National Security (IFANS)
1376-2, Socho 2-Dong,
Socho-Ku
137-072 SEOUL
RÉPUBLIQUE DE CORÉE
Tel. (850) 571 10 20/330
Fax (850) 571 10 19

Yonsei University
College of law
120-749 SEOUL
RÉPUBLIQUE DE CORÉE

Kyung Hee University
Department of Political Science
131 SEOUL 131
RÉPUBLIQUE DE CORÉE

RUSSIE

All Russian Market Research Institute
Mr Valery Gorski
Pudovkin Str. 4
MOSKVA 119 285
RUSSIE
Tel. (795) 143 02 48
Fax (795) 143 0281

**Institut Mirovoji Economiki I
Meghdunarodnich**
Profsoyousnaia str.23
GSP 117 859
MOSKVA
RUSSIE

86

SIERRA LEONE

University of Sierra Leone
Library
Fourah Bay College
FREETOWN
SIERRA LEONE

SINGAPORE

National University of Singapore
Central Library, Serials Department (ISN
25393)
10 Kent Ridge Crescent
0511 SINGAPORE
Tel. (65) 772 20 35

SLOVAQUIE

Comenius University
Bajzikova Lubica
College of management_
Staré Grunty 55
841 04 BRATISLAVA
SLOVAQUIE
Tel. (42-7) 72 76 86
Fax (42-7) 72 39 70

Slovenska Technika Kniznica
Nam. Slobody C. 19
812 236 BRATISLAVA
SLOVAQUIE
Tel. (42-7) 361 428 / 323 527
Fax (42-7) 364 497

THAÏLANDE

Thammasat University
Faculty of Economics
Library
Prachand road
10200 BANGKOK 2
THAÏLANDE
Tel. (66-2) 224 13 80

TRINITÉ-ET-TOBAGO

University of the West Indies
Institute of International Relations
ST. AUGUSTINE
TRINITÉ-ET-TOBAGO

TUNISIE

Faculté de Droit et des Sciences Politiques et Économiques de Tunis
Campus Universitaire
TUNIS
TUNISIE

TURQUIE

Cukurova Universitesi
Library
Balcali; 0 1330 Adanaa
tel. (90-71) 14 17 24
ADANAA
TURQUIE

Union of Chambers of Commerce, Industry and Commodity Exchanges
Library
Ataturk Bulvari 149, Bakanliklar
ANKARA
TURQUIE
tel. (90-4) 117 77 00

URUGUAY

Biblioteca Nacional
División Técnica
18 de julio, 1790
MONTEVIDEO
URUGUAY

Universidad de Montevideo
Facultad de Ciencias Económicas y Adminidtración
Biblioteca
Casilla de Correo 5052
Sucursal AN1
MONTEVIDEO
URUGUAY

USA

Texas Christian University
Mary Couts Burnett Library, Documents Department
BOX 32904
76129 FORT WORTH, TEXAS
USA
Tel. (1-817) 921 76 69
Fax (1-817) 921 74 47

VENEZUELA

Universidad Central de Venezuela
Facultad de Derecho
Instituto de Derecho Público, Sección de Integreación
Apartado de Correos 61591 Chacao
CARACAS
VENEZUELA

Universidad de Los Andes
Servicios Bibliotecarios Generales
Edificio Administrativo, planta baja
5101 MÉRIDA
VENEZUELA
Tel. (58-74) 40 12 37
Fax (58-74) 40 25 07

ZAÏRE

Université Nationale du Zaïre
Bibliothèque Centrale
Campus de Kinshasa
BP 125
KINSHASA XI
ZAÏRE

Université Officielle du Zaïre
Faculté de Droit
Bibliothèque
B.P. 1825
LUBUMBASHI

ZIMBABWE

University of Zimbabwe
University Library
P.O. Box 45
Mount Pleasant
HARARE
ZIMBABWE

87

DEPOSITAR-BIBLIOTHEKEN

➤ **Akronym**

DEP

➤ **Trägerorganisation**

Die 1963 gegründeten DEP befinden sich in den großen
Staatsbibliotheken.
Im Prinzip gibt es nur eine DEP pro Land

➤ **Zielgruppe**

Alle Bürger

➤ **Wirkungskreis**

Es gibt 24 DEP in Europa, 73 weltweit.

➤ **Ziele**

- Bereitstellung der gesamten offiziellen Veröffentlichungen der
  Gemeinschaftsinstitutionen für die Öffentlichkeit.

➤ **Ihnen zur Verfügung stehende Informationen**

Die DEP erhalten eine Kopie aller offiziellen Veröffentlichungen der
Europäischen Union in einer der 9 Amtssprachen; sie haben nicht automatisch kostenlosen Zugang zu den Datenbanken der Kommission.

89

➤ Europäische Kommission
Generaldirektion
Referat X/A/4 - Informationsrelais und -netze
200 Rue de la Loi
B - 1049 Brüssel
Tel. (32.2) 299 94 25/299 92 72

EUROPEAN DEPOSITORY LIBRARIES

> **Acronym**

DEP

> **Host structure**

Set up in 1963, the DEP are situated in the large national libraries.
In principal, there is only one DEP per country.

> **Target public**

All citizens

> **Community coverage**

There are 24 DEP in Europe, 73 in the rest of the world.

> **Objectives**

- Make available to the general public all the official publications of the Community Institutions.

> **Information which they have available**

The DEP receive a copy of all the official publications of the European Union in one of the 9 Community languages; they do not automatically have free access to the Commission databases.

> European Commission
Directorate-General X
Unit X/A/4 - Information relays and networks
200 rue de la Loi
B - 1049 Brussels
Tel.: (32.2) 299.94.25/299.92.72

BIBLIOTHEQUES DEPOSITAIRES

➤ **Acronyme**

DEP

➤ **Structure hôte**

Nés en 1963, les DEP sont situés dans les grandes bibliothèques nationales.
En principe, il n'y a qu'un seul DEP par pays.

➤ **Public cible**

Tous les citoyens

➤ **Rayonnement communautaire**

Il existe 24 DEP en Europe, 73 dans le reste du monde.

➤ **Objectifs**

▪- Mettre à la disposition du public l'ensemble des publications officielles des Institutions communautaires.

➤ **Informations dont ils disposent**

Les DEP reçoivent une copie de toutes les publications officielles de l'Union européenne dans l'une des langues communautaires; ils n'ont pas automatiquement un accès gratuit aux bases de données de la Commission.

➤ Commission européenne
Direction générale
Unité X/A/4 - Relais et réseaux d'information
200 rue de la Loi
B - 1049 Bruxelles
Tél.: (32.2) 299.94.25/299.92.72

BELGIQUE-BELGIË

Bibliothèque Dépositaire
Bibliothèque Royale Albert Ier
Bld de l'Empereur 4
1000 Bruxelles
Belgique/België
Tel: 32/2-513-61-80

DANMARK

Depositary Library
Det Kongelige Bibliotek
Christians Brygge 8
1219 Koebenhavn
Danmark
Tel: 45/33-93-01-11

DEUTSCHLAND

Depositarbibliothek
Die Deutsche Bibliothek -
Bundesunmittelbare Anstalt d.öffentl.
Rechts Abt. Erwerbung
Deutscher Platz, 1
04103 Leipzig
Deutschland
Tel: 49/341-22-710
Fax: 49/341-22-71-444

Depositarbibliothek
Deutsche Bibliothek
Zeppelinallee 4-8
6035 Frankfurt
Deutschland
Tel: 49/69-75-66-201

Depositarbibliothek
Bayerische Staatsbibliothek
Ludwigstr. 16
80328 München
Deutschland
Tel: 49/89-28-63-83-11
Fax: 49/89-28-63-82-93

Depositarbibliothek
Staatsbibliothek Preussischer Kulturbesitz
Postdamer Str. 33
10772 Berlin
Deutschland
Tel: 49/30-26-62-471
Fax: 49/30-26-62-341

Depositarbibliothek
Deutscher Bundestag
Bibliothek - Bundeshaus Internationale
Organisationen
Gírresstr. 15
53113 Bonn
Deutschland
Tel: 49/228-16-29-43
Fax: 49/228-16-86-037

ELLAS

Depositary Library
Hellenic Centre for European Studies
Library (Ekem/Library)
G. Prassa 1 & Didotou
10680 Athenes
Ellas
Tel: 30/1-363-11-33 30/1-363-11-33

ESPAÑA

Biblioteca Depositaria
Biblioteca Nacional
Paseo de Recoletos, 20
28001 Madrid
España
Tel: 34/1-43-54-053

FRANCE

Bibliothèque Dépositaire
Bibliothèque Nationale de France
Agence bibliographique nationale
rue Vivienne, 2-4
75084 Paris-cedex 02
France
Tel: 33/1-47-03-85-46

IRELAND

Depositary Library
Oireachtas Library, Leinster House,
Kildare Street ,
Dublin
Ireland
Tel: 353/1-78-99-11
ext. 412 353/1-78-59-45

92

Depositary Library
The National Library of Ireland
Kildare Street
Dublin
Ireland
Tel: 353/1-61-88-11

ITALIA

Biblioteca Depositaria
Biblioteca Nazionale Vittorio Emanuele III
Palazzo Reale
80100Napoli
Italia

Biblioteca Depositaria
Biblioteca Nazionale Centrale
Piazza dei Cavalleggeri, 1/a
50122 Firenze
Italia

Biblioteca Depositaria
Consiglio Nazionale delle Ricerche
Biblioteca Centrale Direzione
Piazzale Aldo Moro, 7
00185 Roma
Italia
Tel: 39/6-49-931
Fax: 39/6-49-93-38-34

LUXEMBOURG

Bibliothèque Dépositaire
Bibliothèque Nationale de Luxembourg
Bld F.D. Roosevelt, 37
Luxembourg

ÖSTERREICH

Depositarbibliothek
Zentrale Verwaltungsbibliothek und
Dokumentation für Wirtschaft und Technik
Stubenring 1
1010 Wien
Österreich
Tel: 43/222-75-00 54-86

PORTUGAL

Biblioteca Depositaria
Biblioteca Nacional
Campo Grande, 83
1751 Lisboa codex
Portugal
Tel: 351/1-76-76-39

SUOMI-FINLAND

Depositary Library
Library of Parliament
Eduskunnan Kirjasto
Helsinki 00102
Suomi/Finland

SVERIGE

Depositary Library
Riksdagsbiblioteket
10012 Stockholm
Sverige
Tel: 46/8-786-40-00
Fax: 46/8-796-94-08

Kungh. Biblioteket
Sveriges Nationalbibliotek
The Royal Library of Sweden
P.O. Box 5039
S 10241 Stockholm
Sverige

UNITED KINGDOM

Depositary Library
Liverpool and District Scientif.,
Industriel and Research Library
Advisory Council (Ladsirlac)
William Brown Street
L3 8EW Liverpool
United Kingdom
Tel: 44/51-225-54-34
Fax: 44/51-207-13-42

Depositary Library
City of Westminster Libraries
Central Reference Library
St Mary's Street
London WC2 7HP
United Kingdom
Tel: 44/71-798-20-34

93

Depositary Library
The British Library Document Supply
Centre, EC Liaison Officer
Boston Spa
United Kingdom
Tel: 44/937-54-60-60

AFRIQUE DU SUD

Depositary Library
City Librarian
Market square
rsa -2001 Johannesburg
AFRIQUE DU SUD
Tel: 27/836-37-87 Fax: 27/836-66-07

Depositary Library
South African Library
p.o. box 496
rsa -8000 Cape Town
AFRIQUE DU SUD
Tel: 27/21-24-63-20

AUSTRALIA

Depositary Library
National Library of Australia
Preliminary processing (d 238/1)
au -2600 a c t Canberra
AUSTRALIA
Tel: 61/62- 61-12-66
Fax: 61/62-57-17-03

Depositary Library
State Library of New South Wales
Acquisitions librarian
Macquarie street
au -2000 Sydney
AUSTRALIA
Tel: 61/2-230-14-14 Fax: 61/2-233-20-03

Depositary Library
State Library of Victoria, serials section
Swanston street, 328
au -3000 Melbourne
AUSTRALIA
Tel: 61/3-669-98-88 Fax: 61/3-663-14-80

BULGARIA

Depositary Library
National Library Cyrill and Methodius
Boul. Tolbuhin 11 Sofia
BULGARIA

ESTONIE

Depositary Library
Eesti Rahvusraamatukogu,
National Library of Estonia
Kiriku Plats, 1
EE0106 Tallinn
ESTONIE
Tel: 7/142-44-20-94 7/142-44-20-94

LITHUANIA

Depositary Library
Lietuvos Nacionaline, National Library of
Lithuania
Martyno Mazvydo Biblioteka
Gedimino Pr. 51
232635 Vilnius
LITHUANIA

NORWAY

Depositary Library
Nobelinstituttets Bibliotek
Drammensveien 19
0255 Oslo
NORWAY
Tel: 47/2-44-20-63
Fax: 47/2-43-01-68

POLOGNE

Depositary Library
Council of Ministers EC Depository Library
Aleje Ujazdowskie, 1/3
00567 Warszawa
POLOGNE
Tel: 48/2-694-63-05
Fax: 48/2-229-48-88

ROUMANIE

Depositary Library
National Institute for Information and
Documentation
European Information Centre
George Enescu Street, 27-29 - P.O. Box
70074 Sector 1
Bucarest
ROUMANIE

TURKEY

Depositary Library
Iktisadi Kalkinma Vakfi
Rumeli Cad. no. 85 kat:7 Istanbul
TURKEY
Tel: 90/1-148-74-37 /146-94-37

CANADA

Depositary Library
National Library of Canada
Reference and Information Service
rm. 215 rue Wellington, 395
OttawaK1A ON4
CANADA
Tel: 1/613-99-67-464

CHINE

Depositary Library
National Library of China
Baishijiao road, 39
Prc - Beijing
CHINE
Tel: 86/1-831-55-66

INDE

Depositary Library
Parliament Library
Parliament House
New Delhi
IN -1110001 INDE

Depositary Library
Government of India National Library
Belvedere
IN -700027 Calcutta
INDE
Tel: 91/45-53-81-87

Depositary Library
Servants of India Society's, Library
IN-411004 Pune
INDE
Tel: 91/54287

ISRAEL

Depositary Library
the Jewish National and University Library,
European Communities Collection
p.o. box 503
isr -91000 Jerusalem
ISRAEL
Tel: 972/2-58-50-32

JAPON

Depositary Library
National Diet Library, Library cooperation
dept.
10-1, nagata-cho 1chome   chiyoda-ku
jp -100 Tokyo
JAPON
Tel: 81/3-581-23-31 Fax: 81/3-581-09-89

NOUVELLE ZELANDE

Depositary Library
Parliamentary Library
Parliament House
nz -1 Wellington
NOUVELLE ZELANDE
Tel: 64/4-471-96-12
Fax: 64/4-471-96-19

Depositary Library
Auckland city Library
Documents librarian
p.o. box 4138 nz -1 Auckland
NOUVELLE ZELANDE
Tel: 64/9-377-02-09
Fax: 64/9-307-77-41

USA

Depositary Library
Duke University Perkins Library
Public Documents and Maps Dept.
Box 90177
Durham N.C. 27708-0177
USA
Tel: 1/919- 684-23-80
Fax: 1/919-684-28-55

95

Depositary Library
University of Chicago Library
Serials Department Documents Processing
Xeast 57th Street, 2425
ChicagoUSA -IL 60637-1502
USA

Depositary Library
Emory University Law Library ,
Government Documents
Gambrell Hall
Atlanta USA-ga. 30322
USA
Tel: 1/404-727-67-96
Fax: 1/404-727-68-20

Depositary Library
University of Arkansas
documents dept ualr library
South University avenue, 2801
72204 Little Rock
USA
Tel: 1/501-569-88-11/ 569-88-06 Fax:
1/501-569-30-17

Depositary Library
University of California
Government Documents
dept. general library
Berkeley USA -ca 94720
USA

Depositary Library
University of California
public affairs service/int'l
University Research library
Hilgard avenue, 405
Los Angeles USA -ca. 90024
USA

Depositary Library
University of California, San Diego
University Library
Gilman Drive, 9500
La Jolla USA -ca 92093-0175
USA

Depositary Library
University of Arizona
University Library
Tucson USA -85721
USA

Depositary Library
University of Washington
Seattleusa -wa. 98195
USA

Depositary Library
State University of New York at Buffalo
Lockwood Memorial Library
Buffalo USA -n.y. 14260
USA

Depositary Library
University of Florida
Smathers libaries documents department
Library West
USA -fl. 32611 Gainesville
USA
Tel: 1/904-392-03-66
Fax: 1/904-392-72-51

Depositary Library
University of Hawaii Library
Government Documents Collection
Campus Road, 2425 USA -hi. 96822
Honolulu
USA

Depositary Library
University of Southern California
Doheny Memorial Library
University park - mc 0182
Los Angeles USA -ca. 90089
USA

Depositary Library
Yale University,
government documents center
Mansfield Street, 38 p.o. box 208294,
Yale Station
New Haven   USA -ct. 06520-8294
USA
Tel: 1/203-432-32-09
Fax: 1/203-432-32-14

Depositary Library
University of Colorado
Government Publication Library
Boulder, USA-CO. 80309-0184
USA

Depositary Library
Standford University
Hoover inst. central and western
european collections,
Stanford
USA -ca. 94305-1687
Tel: 1/415-725-35-95
Fax:1/415-723-16-87

Depositary Library
University of Illinois
College of Law   - Foreign Law School
104 law building East Pennsylvania ave.,
504 Champaign
USA-ill. 61820
Tel: 1/217-333-29-13
Fax: 1/217-244-85-00

Depositary Library
The University of New Mexico
Zimmerman Library gifts
and exchange section
Albuquerque, n.m. 87131 st. of New Mexico
USA

Depositary Library
Indiana University
Library documents department
USA -ind. 47405 Bloomington
Tel: 1/812-855-69-24
Fax: 1/812-855-34-60

Depositary Library
University of Notre-Dame
Memorial library document center
USA -ind. 46556 notre-dame

Depositary Library
University of Iowa
Libraries government publication dept.
USA -iowa 52242 iowa city

Depositary Library
Pennsylvania State University
Libraries documents section
USA -pa. 16802 university park

Depositary Library
University of Kentucky libraries
USA -ky 40506-0039 Lexington

Depositary Library
University of Kansas
Government documents and map Library
6001 malott hall
USA -Kansas 66045 Lawrence
Tel: 1/913-864-46-60

Depositary Library
University of Maine
Raymond h. Fogler Library
USA -maine 04473 Orono

Depositary Library
Haward University, Law School Library
Langdell Hall lw 431
USA -mas. 02138 Cambridge
Tel: 1/617-495-31-72
Fax: 1/617-495-44-49

Depositary Library
Michigan State University
Library documents
USA-mich. 48824 East Lansing

Depositary Library
University of Michigan , Law Library
USA -mich. 48104 Ann Arbor

Depositary Library
University of Minnesota
Government publications Library
409 wilson library ,
19th avenue south, 309
USA -min. 55455 Minneapolis
Tel: 1/612-624-02-41

Depositary Library
Washington University
Libraries serials unit
lindell & skinker bluds
USA -miss. 63130 St. Louis

Depositary Library
University of Nebraska
The University libraries acquisitions
department
USA -nebr. 68508 Lincoln

Depositary Library
University of New Orleans
Earl K. Long Library
lakefront
USA -la. 70148 New Orleans
Tel: 1/286-72-76
Fax: 1/286-72-77

Depositary Library
New York University , School of Law
Library
108 Vanderbilt Hall -
Washington Square South, 40
USA -n.y. 10012 New York

Depositary Library
University of Pennsylvania
Van Pelt-Dietrich Library center serial dept
Walnut street, 3420
USA -pa. 19104-6278 Philadelphia
Tel: 1/215-898-75-55
Fax: 1/215-898-05-59

Depositary Library
Princeton University Library
Documents division
One Washington road
USA -n.j. 08544 Princeton
Tel: 1/609-258-31-78

97

Depositary Library
Northwestern University
the University Library
Government publications department
USA -ill. 60208-2300 Evanston
Tel: 1/708-491-31-30
Fax: 1/708-491-56-85

Depositary Library
New york Public Library
Grand central station
p.o. box 2221
USA -n.y. 10017 New York

Depositary Library
Ohio State University
Neil avenue Mall, 1858
USA -ohio 43210 Colombus

Depositary Library
State University of New York at Albany
University Library
Western avenue, 1223
USA -n.y. 12203 Albany

Depositary Library
University of Oklahoma ,
The Library, room 440
West Brooks, 401
USA -okl. 73019 Norman
Tel: 1/405-325-26-11

Depositary Library
the Harold Pratt house council on foreign
relations, ins, Library
East 68th street, 58
USA -n.y. 10021 New York

Depositary Library
University of Pittsburgh
Government documents technical services
g-20k Hillman Library
USA -pa 15260 Pittsburgh

Depositary Library
University of Carolina
Thomas Cooper Library
USA -s.c. 29208 Columbia

Depositary Library
University of Texas at Austin
School of Law Library
East 26th street, 727
USA -texas 78705 Austin

Depositary Library
University of Utah
International documents librarian
documents division Marriott Library
USA -utah 84112 Salt Lake City
Tel: 1/801-581-83-94
Fax: 1/801-581-48-82

Depositary Library
University of Virginia
the Alderman Library
USA -vir.22903-2498 Charlottesville
Tel: 1/804-924-31-33
Fax: 1/804-924-43-37

Depositary Library
University of Wisconsin
Memorial library
State street, 728
USA -wi. 53706 Madison

Depositary Library
Library of Congress exchange and gift divi-
sion (igo - eudom)
First street s.e., 10
USA -d.c. 2054 Washington

Depositary Library
College of Law -
Library of international relations
8th floor of the Chicago-Kent
West Adams street, 565
USA -ill. 60661-d3691 Chicago
Tel: 1/312-906-56-22
Fax: 1/312-906-56-85

Depositary Library
University of Oregon
Knight Library USA -
ov 97403-1299 Eugene
Tel: 1/503-346-30-94

98

FORUM DES LÄNDLICHEN RAUMS

Die Foren des ländlichen Raums wurden im Anschluß an die 1988 veröffentlichte Mitteilung der Kommission über die "Zukunft des ländlichen Raums" gegründet.

> **Trägerorganisation**

Die Foren sind bestehenden regionalen Einrichtungen angegliedert, die in enger Synergie mit allen Komponenten der ländlichen Gesellschaft zusammenarbeiten (Landwirtschaftskammern, Agrar-Stiftungen, regionale Institute, Informationszentren, Kommunalbehörden...).

> **Zielgruppe**

Alle Akteure der Agrarwelt (Entwicklungsstellen, Berufsverbände, Gebietskörperschaften,Schulen, Vereinigungen, Bürger...).

> **Wirkungskreis**

Derzeit zählt das Netz 50 Foren auf dem gesamten Territorium der Gemeinschaft, doch diese Zahl ist nicht definitiv: das Netz soll langfristig alle europäischen Regionen erfassen.

> **Ziele**

Die Foren tragen die EG-Informationen in die ländlichen Gemeinschaften. Sie sind Treffpunkt und Diskussionsstätte, ein Ort, an dem Aktionen erstellt und innoviert werden können. Die Foren haben folgende Aufgaben:
- Unterrichtung der sozioökonomischen Akteure und der Öffentlichkeit über Gemeinschaftspolitik und -maßnahmen, die die Agrarwelt betreffen
- Anregung des Dialogs und der Zusammenarbeit von Akteuren der Agrarwelt
- Förderung von Erfahrungsaustausch zwischen den ländlichen Regionen Europas
- Errichtung einer Partnerschaft für Zugang zu den Gemeinschaftsprogrammen

> **Aktionen**

Die Foren:
- verwalten Dokumentationszentren
- erstellen Newsletter oder andere Veröffentlichungen, audiovisuelle Produkte, arbeiten mit den örtlichen und regionalen Medien zusammen...
- organisieren Seminare und Konferenzen sowie Ausbildungskurse
- fördern den Austausch zwischen verschiedenen lokalen Akteuren und den ländlichen Regionen der Gemeinschaft
- verbreiten Informationsmaterial der GD X und anderer Dienststellen der Kommission.

> Europäische Kommission
> Generaldirektion X
> Referat X/A/4
> 120 Rue de Trèves
> B - 1049 Brüssel
> Tel. 299 94 25 / 299 91 16

RURAL INFORMATION SOCIETY

The rural information Carrefours were created following the Commission Communication, "Future of the Rural World", published in 1988.

> **Host structure**

The Information Carrefours were established within existing regional organisations working in close harmony with all members of the rural society of the region (chambers of agriculture, rural foundations, regional institutes, information centres, community administrations,...).

> **Target public**

All the actors of the rural world (development organisations, professional organisations, local cooperatives, schools, associations, citizens,...).

> **Community coverage**

At present, the network has 50 carrefours spread over the whole of the Community territory, but this figure is not final: the network must, eventually, extend to all European regions.

> **Objectives**

The carrefours bring information on the Community to the heart of the rural communities. They are a place for meeting and discussion, a place where actions can be conceived and innovated. In particular, the Carrefours have as their tasks:
- inform the socio-economic actors and the public about the Union and its policies and community measures of interest to the rural world;
- stimulate dialogue and cooperation between the actors of the rural world;
- encourage an exchange of experiences between the European rural regions;
- urge the partnership to comply with Community programmes.

> **Actions**

The Carrefours:
- administer the documentation centres;
- create newsletters or other publications, audiovisual products, collaborate with the local and regional media...
- organise seminars and conferences , as well as training courses
- facilitate exchanges between the various local actors and between the rural regions of the Community
- disseminate information material produced by DG X and other Commission services.

> European Commission
Directorate-General X
Unit X/A/4 - Information relays and networks
200 rue de la Loi
B - 1049 Brussels
Tel.: 299.94.25 / 299.91.16

CARREFOURS D'INFORMATION ET D'ANIMATION RURALE

Les Carrefours ruraux ont été créés à la suite de la Communication de la Commission, publiée en 1988, sur l'"Avenir du Monde rural".

➤ **Structure hôte**

Les Carrefours sont établis auprès d'organismes existants au niveau régional travaillant en étroite synergie avec l'ensemble des composantes de la société rurale de la région (Chambres d'agriculture, Fondations rurales, Instituts régionaux, Centres d'information , Administrations communales,...).

➤ **Public cible**

Tous les acteurs du monde rural (organismes de développement,organisations professionnelles, collectivités locales, écoles, associations,citoyens,...).

➤ **Rayonnement communautaire**

Actuellement, le réseau compte plus de 50 carrefours répartis sur l'ensemble du territoire de la Communauté, mais ce chiffre n'est pas définitif: le réseau devrait, à terme, couvrir toutes les régions européennes.

➤ **Objectifs**

Les Carrefours portent l'information communautaire au sein des communautés rurales. Ils sont un lieu de rencontre et de discussion, un lieu où l'on peut concevoir des actions et innover. En particulier, les Carrefours ont pour tâche de:
* informer les acteurs socio-économiques et le public
  sur l'Union et sur les politiques et mesures communautaires
  intéressant le monde rural;
* stimuler le dialogue et la coopération entre les acteurs du monde rural;
* encourager les échanges d'expériences entre les régions
  rurales européennes;
* inciter au partenariat pour accéder aux programmes communautaires.

➤ **Activités**

Les Carrefours:
* gèrent des centres de documentation;
* créent des newsletters ou autres publications, des produits
  audiovisuels, collaborent avec les médias locaux et régionaux...
* organisent des séminaires et des conférences, ainsi que des cours de
  formation;
* facilitent les échanges entre les divers acteurs locaux et entre les
  régions rurales de la Communauté;
* diffusent le matériel d'information produit par la DG X et autres
  services de la Commission.

➤ Commission européenne
   Direction générale X
   Unité X/A/4 - Relais et réseaux d'information
   200 rue de la Loi
   B - 1049 Bruxelles
   Tél.: 299.94.25 / 299.91.16

BELGIQUE-BELGIË

Carrefour de Wallonie
Fondation rurale de Wallonie
rue des Déportés 140
B-6700 ARLON
Tel. 32/63/22.03.78
Fax 32/63/21.92.54

DANMARK

Jelling Carrefour
Brandbjerg Højskole
Brandbjergvej 12
DK-7300 JELLING
Tel. 45/75/87.25.52
Fax 45/75/87.26.75

Carrefour Bornholm
Fællesforvaltningen
Ullasvej 23
Postboks 160
DK-3700 Rønne
Tel. 45/56.95/60.00
Fax. 45/56.95/73.97

102

DEUTSCHLAND

Forum f. d. ländlichen Raum in Nordhessen
(Thoméestraße 3 - 34117 Kassel)
Postfach 101760
D-34117 Kassel
Tel. 49/561/7299-200
Fax 49/561/7299-359

Forum Westthüringen
Initiative zur Förderung des ländlichen
Raumes
Ev. Stift
D-99894 Reinhardsbrunn
Tel. 49/36 23 / 3608.530 / 3608.0
Fax 49/36 23 / 3608.600

Forum Franken
Ökologische Bildungsstätte Oberfranken
Unteres Schloß
D-96268 Mitwitz
Tel: 49/92 66/82 52
Fax: 49/92 66/64 42

ELLAS

Carrefour Aighio
D.E.Y.A. Aighio
Metropoleos & Meletopoulou 11
GR-25100 Aighio
Tel. 30/691/21526, 28066
Fax: 30/691/20663, 21089

Carrefour Ioanina
ACIC S.A.
Nikolaou Dosiou, 6
GR-45333 Ioannina
Tel. 30/651/709.61-4
Fax: 30/651/373.22

Carrefour Thessaloniki
American Farm School
Box 23
GR-55102 Thessaloniki
Tel. 30/31/475.693, 5, 6
Fax. 30/31/475.694

Development Agency of Karditsa (ANKA)
Artessianou Kolokotroni Street, 5
P.O. Box 178
GR-43100 Karditsa
Tel.
Fax

Organization for the Development
of Western Crete (O.A.DY.K.)
1866 Square Kriari Street
T.K. 73135 Chania - Crete
Tel. 30/821/983.93
Fax 30/821/933.50

ESPAÑA

Centro Europeo para la Información y Promoción del Medio Rural - CEIP
C/Gran Vía 56 entreplanta
E-26005 LOGROÑO
Tel. 34/41/20.88.33
Fax 34/41/20.95.52

Carrefour Galicia
Instituto de Desenvolvemento Comunitario
de Galicia
c/ San Pedro de Mezonzo, 48 bajo
E-15701 SANTIAGO DE COMPOSTELA
Tel. 34/81/59.91.00/15
Fax 34/81/59.08.75

**CAIRE - Centro Aragones
de información rural europea**
Plaza Mayor, 1
E-44556 MOLINOS (Teruel)
Tel. 34/78/84.94.31
Fax 34/78/84.94.03

Carrefour de Lérida
Patronat Català pro Europa
Anselm Clavé, 2 - 6
E - 25007 LERIDA
Tél. 34/73/23.02.60
Fax 34/73/23.92.84

**Centro Europea de Información rual
de Canarias**
C/ Arrieta S/N
Edificio de servicios multiples - 4 Planta
E-35004 LAS PALMAS DE GRAN CANARIA
Tél. 34/28/38.00.00
Fax 34/28/36.71.87

Carrefour des Baléares
Unió de Pagesos de Mallorca
C/. Manacor, 20, 2 , 2a
E-07006 PALMA (Illes Balears)
Tél. 34/71/46.41.42 / 46.76.57
Fax 34/71/46.40.61

Diputación Provincial de Ciudad Real
C/ Toledo, n¤ 17
E-13001 CIUDAD REAL
Tél. 34/26/25.25.75 / 25.25.87
Fax. 34/26/25.59.42

**Colectivo para el Desarrollo Rural de
Tierra de Campos**
C/ Los Huesos, n¤ 3
E-47800 Medina de Rioseco/VALLADOLID
Tél. 34/83/720.204
Fax 34/83/720.205

FRANCE

Carrefour Rural Européen
Poitou Charentes
B.P. 24
F-86550 Mignaloux-Beauvoir
Tel. 33/49/44.74.56
Fax 33/49/45.76.83

**Carrefour d'Information et
d'Animation sur l'Europe**
Horizon Europe
18, Rue Guy de Veyre
F-15000 Aurillac Cédex
Tél. 33/71/64.14.14
Fax 33/71/48.80.65

**Carrefour Européen d'Informations
Ville - Agriculture - Ruralité**
CIVAR Europe
37, avenue Jean Jaurès
F-62400 Béthune
Tél. 33/21/57.05.02
Fax 33/21/65.84.35

**Carrefour Rural Européen Pyrénées -
Languedoc-Roussillon**
Maison des Entreprises
Espace Alfred Sauvy
F-66500 Prades
Tél. 33/68/05.38.88
Fax 33/68/05.38.89

**Carrefour Rural Européen de Midi
Pyrénées - CARMIP**
110, avenue Marcel Unal
F-82017 Montauban Cédex
Tél. 33/63/63.60.00
Fax 33/63/66.57.87

Carrefour Rural Européen d'Auvergne
Chambre d'Agriculture d'Auvergne
12, avenue Marx-Dormoy / B.P. 455
F-63012 CLERMONT-FERRAND Cedex 1
Tél. 33/73/43.44.45
Fax: 33/73/93.56.73

Carrefour de la région Centre
Chambre d'Agriculture Région Centre
13, avenue des Droits de l'Homme /
B.P. 9019
F-45921 Orléans
Tél. 33/38/71.91.09
Fax: 33/38/71.91.12

IRELAND

**European Center for information and
the promotion of rural development**
University College Galway
IRL-GALWAY
Tel. 353/91/24411
Fax 353/91/24130
Telex 50023 UCG EI

Carrefour Waterford
Waterford Foods PLC and Waterford
Development Partnership Ltd.
Teagasc Centre
IRL-Lismore, Co. Waterford
Tel. 353/58/546.46
Fax 353/58/541.26

103

Carrefour South Rural Ireland
South Kerry Development Partnership Ltd
I.D.A. Industrial Estate
Valentia road
Cahersiveen
IR-County Kerry
Tél. 353/66/727.24
Fax 353/66/727/25

ITALIA

Carrefour Romagna
Centro di Formazione professionale in
Agricoltura
Via prov. le Bagnara, 17
I-48020 VILLA S. MARTINO DI LUGO (RA)
Tel. 39/545/32662
Fax 39/545/33004

**Carrefour europeo di informazione e
animazione rurale**
Associazione Regionale Pugliese
Tecnici e Ricercatori in Agricoltura
Piazza Mercantile, 22
I-70122 BARI
Tel. 39/80/523.32.99
Fax 39/80/523.30.63

Carrefour Siena
Fondazione OIKOS
Villa di Basciano
I-53010 Quercegrossa (Siena)
Tel. 39/577/327.327/8
Fax 39/577/327/329

Carrefour Maremma
Amministrazione Comunale
Corso Giosué Carducci 5
I-58100 Grosseto
Tel. 39/564/41.34.42 - 48.82.81 -
(numero verde): 167.01.97.99
Fax 39/564/21.500 (provisoire)

Carrefour Emilia
Centro Ricerche Produzioni Animali
Corso Garibalid, 42
I-42100 Reggio Emilia
Tel. 39/522/436.999
Fax 39/522/435.142

Carrefour "Sannio Beneventano"
Agridir
Via XXIV Maggio, 22
I-82100 Benevento
Tel. 39/824/31.09.66
Fax 39/824/31.66.07

Carrefour Parco del Ticino
Consorzio Parco Lombardo della Valle del
Ticino
Via. Isonzo 1
Fraz. Pontevecchio
I-20013 MAGENTA
Tel. 39/2/97.210.223/97.91.377
Fax 39/2/97.95.06.07

Carrefour Umbria
CESAR - Centro per lo Sviluppo Agricolo
e Rurale
Via Metastasio, 22
I-06081 Assisi
Tél. 39/75/81.62.44
Fax 39/75/81.67.97

Carrefour Veneto
Consulta per l'Agricoltura e le Foreste delle
Venezie
Corso del Popolo, 85/a
I-30172 Mestre
Tél. 39/41/96.22.38
Fax 39/41/96.18.03

Comunità Montana N. 9
Del Nuorese
Via Trieste n. 46
I-08100 NUORO (Sardegna)
Tél. 39/784/241.900
Fax 39/784/241.921

ÖSTERREICH

Carrefour Oberösterreich
Bildungszentrum St. Magdalena
Schatzweg 177
A-4040 Linz
Tél.: 43/732/25.30.41-0
Fax. 43/732/25.30.41-35

Carrefour Kärnten
Kammer für Land- und Forstwirtschaft
Museumstraße 5
A-9010 Klagenfurt
Tél. 43/463/58.50-264
Fax 43/463/58.50-251

PORTUGAL

Carrefour da Beira Litoral
Direcção Regional de Agricultura da Beira
Litoral
Av. Fernão de Magalhãos, 465
P-3000 COIMBRA
Tél. 351/39/241.45
Fax 351/39/336.79

Carrefour do Oeste
Direcção Regional de Agricultura do
Ribatejo e Oeste
Zona Agrária de Caldas da Rainha
Rua Leonel Sotto Mayor - Apt. 114
P-2500 Caldas da Rainha
Tél. 351/62/84.19.68
Fax. 351/62/84.19.69

Carrefour 'IN LOCO'
Intervenção - Formação - Estudos para o
desenvolvimento local
Rua da Marinha, 8 - 1 Dt
P-8000 Faro
Tél. 351/89/250.63
Fax. 351/89/271.75

**Centro de Actualização Propedêutica
e Formação Técnica de Entre Douro
e Minho**
Rua do Monte - Crasto
Vairão
P-4480 Vila do Conde
Tél. 351/52/66.23.99 / 66.19.99
Fax 351/52/66.17.80

Instituto Politécnico de Bragança
Quinta de Sta. Apolónia
Apartado 38
P- 5300 Bragança

SVERIGE

Carrefour South-East Scania
Sydöstra Skånes Samarbetskommitté
S-27180 Ystad
Tél. 46/411/77.197
Fax: 46/411/19.709

UNITED KINGDOM

**Scottish Agricultural College
Carrefour**
SAC - The National College for Food, Land
and Environmental Studies
Auchincruive
UK-Ayr, KA6 5HW
Tel. 44/1292/520.626
Fax 44/1292/521.119

Orbit Carrefour
Lancashire Orbit
Council Offices
UK-Garstang PR3 1EB
Tel. 44/1995/60.12.07
Fax 44/1995/60.12.08

**Highlands and Islands Rural
Carrefour**
Business Information Source Ltd
20 Bridge Street
UK-Inverness IV1 1QR
Tel. 44/1463/71.54.00
Fax: 44/1463/24.44.69

West Wales European Centre
Dyfed County Planning Department
40, Spilman Street
UK-CARMARTHEN SA31 1LQ (DYFED)
Tel. 44/1267/22.48.59/95
Fax 44/1267/23.42.79

ACRE - Carrefour
The Rural Communities Charity
Somerford Court
Somerford Road
Cirencester
UK-Glos GL7 1TW
Tel. 44/1285/65.34.77
Fax. 44/1285/65.45.37

Carrefour Ulster
Clogher Valley Rural Centre
47 Main Street
Clogher
Co. Tyrone
Northern Ireland BT 76 0AA
Tél. 44/16625/488.72
Fax 44/16625/482.03

105

LOKALE ZENTREN FÜR STÄDTISCHE INITIATIVEN

➢ **Akronym**

CIUL

➢ **Trägerorganisation**

Rathäuser, Institute für Städtebau, gemeinnützige Vereine...

➢ **Tätigkeitsbereich**

Unterrichtung und Sensiblisierung der sozioökonomischen Akteure und Bürger über die EG-Strategie für eine dauerhafte und umweltfreundliche Entwicklung der Städte.

➢ **Zielgruppe**

Sozioökonomische Akteure in den Städten, die Bürger.

➢ **Wirkungskreis**

8 schon gegründete Zentren, weitere sind in der Planung. Ein Netz auf Experimentierbasis.

➢ **Ziele**

Die CIUL sollen neue Mittel suchen und erproben, um:
- die verschiedenen Bevölkerungssparten über die EG-Politik und - Initiatven und ihre Anwendung auf verschiedene konstituierende Faktoren des Stadtbildes zu informieren
- Förderung und Unterstützung des Dialogs, konzertierte Planung und Zusammenarbeit der verschiedenen Bevölkerungssparten für eine Verbesserung des städtischen Milieus;
- Förderung des Informationsaustausches zwischen den Städten über angetroffene Probleme und ihre Erfahrungen mit Abhilfemaßnahmen.

Die CIUL zeigen ebenfalls wie Information und Kommunikation in Arbeitsinstrumente für eine dauerhafte und umweltfreundliche Entwicklung der Städte eingesetzt werden können.

➢ **Ihnen zur Verfügung stehende Informationen**

- Dokumentationen über die Maßnahmen und Aktionen der Gemeinschaft wird den Zentren zur Verfügung gestellt
- bevorrechtigter Zugang zu den Datenbanken der Kommission.

➢ **Betreuung des Netzes und Kommunikationstechnik**

Sitzungen in Brüssel mit den Verantwortlichen der Zentren.

➢ Europäische Kommission
Generaldirektion X
Referat X/A/4
200 Rue de la Loi
B - 1049 Brüssel
Tel. (+32-2) 299 94 25

LOCAL URBAN INITIATIVE CENTRES

> **Acronym**

LUIC

> **Host structure**

Town halls, urban institutes, non-profit making organisations...

> **Field of activity**

Inform and heighten awareness of socio-economic actors and city dwellers on the Community strategy of sustainable development in cities.

> **Target public**

Socio-economic actors in cities and city dwellers.

> **Community coverage**

8 centres already set up, others projected. This is an experimental network.

> **Objectives**

The LUIC must look for and experiment with new ways of:
- informing the different sectors of the population on Community policies and initiatives and of their application to various component factors of urban reality;
- encourage and assist dialogue, joint planning and cooperation between the different categories of city dwellers with a view to improving the urban environment;
- facilitate information exchange between cities on the problems which they face and on their experiences in finding solutions.

The LUIC show how information and communication can be transformed into a tool to serve sustainable development in cities.

> **Information which they have available**

- Documentation relative to Community policies and actions provided to the centres;
- privileged access to Commission databases.

> **Network animation and methods of communication**

Meetings in Brussels with those in charge of the centres.

> European Commission
Directorate-General X
Unit X/A/4 - Information relays & networks
200 rue de la Loi
B - 1049 Brussels
Tel.: (+32.2) 299.94.25

CENTRES D'INITIATIVES URBAINES LOCALES

> **Acronyme**

CIUL

> **Structure hôte**

Mairies, instituts d'urbanisme, asbl,...

> **Domaine d'activité**

Information et sensibilisation des acteurs socio-économiques et des citadins sur la stratégie communautaire du développement soutenable des villes.

> **Public cible**

Acteurs socio-économiques dans les villes, les citadins.

> **Rayonnement communautaire**

8 centres déjà créés, d'autres sont en projet. C'est un réseau expérimental.

> **Objectifs**

Les CIUL doivent rechercher et expérimenter de nouveaux moyens pour:
- informer les différents secteurs de la population des politiques et initiatives communautaires et de leur application aux divers facteurs constitutifs de la réalité urbaine;
- encourager et aider le dialogue, la planification concertée et la coopération entre les différentes catégories de citadins en vue d'améliorer l'environnement urbain;
- faciliter l'échange d'information entre les villes sur les problèmes qu'elles rencontrent et sur leurs expériences quant aux moyens d'y remédier.

Les CIUL démontrent ainsi comment information et communication peuvent être transformées en outil de travail au service du développement soutenable des villes.

> **Informations dont ils disposent**

- Documentation relative aux politiques et actions de la Communauté fournie aux centres;
- accès privilégié aux bases de données de la Commission.

> **Animation du réseau et techniques de communication**

Réunions à Bruxelles avec les responsables des centres.

> Commission européenne
Direction générale X
Unité X/A/4 - Relais et réseaux d'information
200 rue de la Loi
B - 1049 Bruxelles
Tél.: (+32-2) 299.94.25

BELGIQUE-BELGIË

Espace- Environnement
Rue de Montignies, 29
6000 Charleroi
Tél.: +32/71/300300
Fax: +32/71/300254

DANMARK

Aalborg kommune
Box 462
9100 AALBORG
Tel: 45/99 31 31 31
Fax: 45/99 31 31 32

DEUTSCHLAND

EG-Umweltinformationszentrum
Ökologische Bildungsstätte
Bahnhofstrasse, 20
0-6000 SUHL
Tél.: +49/3681/22195
Fax: +49/3681/22057

Öko-Zentrum NRW
Sachsenweg, 8
59073 HAMM
Tel 49/2381/30 22 00
Fax 49/2381/30 22 030

FRANCE

Atelier Urbain
Franche -Comté
Porte Rivotte
25000 BESANCON
Tél.: +33/81/83 28 91

ITALIA

Comune di Terni
Centro iniziative urbane locali
Arch. Sig TARQUINI
Via G. Garibaldi, 128
05100 TERNI (Umbria)
Tél.: +39/744/549960
Fax: +39/744/549965

Forum per la Laguna di Venezia
Via Circonvallazione, 23
30170 MESTRE (Venezia)
Tel: +39/41/77 01 67
Fax: +39/41/27 014 68

NEDERLAND

The European Centre for the Urban
Environment
De Heer Tjeerd DEELSTRA
Nickersteeg, 5
2611 EK DELFT
Tél.: +31/15/623279
Fax: +31/15/624873

110

EURO-JUS

> **Trägerorganisation**

Die Kommissionsvertretungen in den Mitgliedstaaten

> **Tätigkeitsbereich**

Praktische Informationen über die EG-Gesetzgebung, die insbesondere den Alltag der Bürger betrifft (Freizügigkeit von Waren, Personen, Dienstleistungen und Kapital; Anerkennung der Diplome; Umwelt; Verbraucher; sozialer Schutz; Aufenthaltsrecht ...).

> **Zielgruppe**

Alle Bürger

> **Wirkungskreis**

Ein Rechtsexperte in jedem Mitgliedstaat

> **Aktivitäten**

Die Rechtsexperten antworten auf telefonische, schriftliche Anfragen oder vereinbaren einen Gesprächstermin. Die Antwort erfolgt unverzüglich, falls es sich um eine allgemeine Frage handelt; erfordert das Thema einige Recherchen, wird der Bürger so schnell wie möglich informiert.

> **Betreuung des Netzes und Kommunikationstechnik**

- Erstellung und Verteilung von Broschüren über spezifische Themen, Veröffentlichung von Newslettern und Teilnahme an Kolloquien, Fernseh- oder Hörfunksendungen für die Rechtsexperten
- Koordinierungssitzung in Brüssel
- Veröffentlichung eines jährlichen Tätigkeitsberichts.

> Europäische Kommission
> Generaldirektion X
> Referat X/A/5
> 200 Rue de la Loi
> B - 1049 Brüssel
> Tel. (+32-2) 295.43.23

EURO-JUS

➣ **Host structure**

Representative offices of the Commission in the Member States.

➣ **Field of activity**

Practical information on Community legislation of particular interest to citizens' daily lives (free circulation of property, people, services and capital; recognition of qualifications; environment; consumers; social protection; rights of residence;...).

➣ **Target public**

All citizens.

➣ **Community coverage**

An expert lawyer in each Member State.

➣ **Actions**

The expert lawyers answer questions which are put to them by telephone, in writing or in person. The reply is immediate if the question is common; if the subject requires research, the citizen is re-contacted as soon as possible.

➣ **Network animation and methods of communication**

- Production and distribution of manuals on specific subjects, publication of newsletters and participation in symposiums, television programmes or radio broadcasts by the expert lawyers;
- coordination meeting in Brussels;
- publication of an annual activity report.

➣ European Commission
Directorate-General X
Unit X/A/5
200 rue de la Loi
B - 1049 Brussels
Tel.: (+32.2) 295.43.23

EURO-JUS

> **Structure hôte**

Les Représentations de la Commission dans les Etats membres.

> **Domaine d'activité**

Information pratique sur la législation communautaire intéressant particulièrement la vie quotidienne des citoyens (libre circulation des biens, des personnes, des services et des capitaux; reconnaissance des diplômes; environnement; consommateurs; protection sociale; droit de séjour;...).

> **Public cible**

Tous les citoyens

> **Rayonnement communautaire**

Un expert juriste dans chaque État membre

> **Actions**

Les experts juristes répondent aux questions qui leur sont posées par téléphone, par écrit ou sur rendez-vous. La réponse est immédiate si la question est courante; si le sujet demande une recherche, le citoyen est recontacté au plus tôt.

> **Animation du réseau et techniques de communication** 113

- Création et distribution de fascicules sur des sujets spécifiques, publication de newsletters et participation à des colloques, des émissions télévisées ou radiodiffusées pour les experts juristes;
- réunion de coordination à Bruxelles;
- publication d'un rapport d'activité annuel.

> Commission européenne
> Direction générale X
> Unité X/A/5
> 200 rue de la Loi
> B - 1049 Bruxelles
> Tél.: (+32-2) 295.43.23

EURO-BIBLIOTHEKEN

➢ **Trägerorganisation**

Öffentliche Bibiliotheken.

➢ **Zielgruppe**

Breites Publikum.

➢ **Wirkungskreis**

39 Euro-Bibliotheken auf dem gesamten spanischen Territorium,
80 auf dem britischen Territorium,
15 in Dänemark.

➢ **Ziele**

Dezentralisierung der Gemeinschaftsdokumentation, Zugänglichkeit
für die Bürger, auf lokaler Ebene Informationen über die EU-Politik.

➢ **Aktionen**

Die Euro-Bibliotheken stellen ihrem Publikum Nachschlagewerke bereit
sowie zu verteilende Gemeinschaftsdokumentationen.
Einige Euro-Bibliotheken veranstalten Ausstellungen oder
Wettbewerbe in bezug auf die EU oder erstellen Mitteilungsblätter.
Einige können auf spezifische Fragen antworten oder ggf. auf andere
Informationsquellen vor Ort aufmerksam machen.

115

➢ **Betreuung des Netzes und Kommunikationstechnik**

Jede Euro-Bibliothek:
- erhält folgende Dokumente kostenlos: Verträge, Amtsblatt, KOM-
  Dokumente,Verzeichnis der EU-Gesetzgebung, Allgemeiner
  Tätigkeitsbericht, grundlegende Statistiken, SCAD-Bulletin,
  Broschüren, Falthefte und Videos;
- wird zu besonderen Schulungen und zu jährlich stattfindenden
  Sitzungen mit anderen Außenstellen eingeladen.

➢ **Verantwortliche Stellen**

Die Vertretungen der Europäischen Kommission in Madrid, London
und Kopenhagen (siehe weiter unten das Kapitel "Vertretungen
in den Mitgliedstaaten")

EUROLIBRARIES

> **Host structure**

Public Libraries.

> **Target public**

General Public.

> **Community coverage**

39 Eurolibraries throughout the Spanish territory,
80 on British territory,
15 in Denmark.

> **Objectives**

Decentralize Community documentation, make information on EU
policies accessible to the public on the local level.

> **Actions**

Eurolibraries are equipped with reference material for the use of its
public as well as Community documentation for distribution.
Some Eurolibraries organize exhibits or contests relative to the EU,
or publish bulletins. Some are able to answer specific questions or,
if necessary, can direct visitors to other local information sources.

> **Network animation and methods of communication**

Each library:
• receives the following documents free of charge: Treaties, OJEC,
  COM documents, Directory of Community Legislation, General
  Activities Report, Basic Statistics, SCAD Bulletin, brochures,
  pamphlets and videos;
• is invited to specific training sessions and to annual meetings with
  the other relays.

> **Responsible Office**

The European Commission Representation Offices in Madrid,
London and Copenhagen (see chapter on Representation Offices
in the Member States).

EUROBIBLIOTHEQUES

➤ **Structure hôte**

Les bibiliothèques publiques.

➤ **Public cible**

Grand Public.

➤ **Rayonnement communautaire**

39 Eurobibliothèques sur l'ensemble du territoire espagnol,
80 sur le territoire britannique,
15 au Danemark.

➤ **Objectifs**

Décentraliser la documentation communautaire, rendre accessibles aux
citoyens, au niveau local, les informations sur les politiques de l'UE.

➤ **Actions**

Les Eurobibliothèques ont à la disposition de leur public des
documents de référence, ainsi que de la documentation
communautaire à distribuer.
Certaines Eurobibliothèques organisent des expositions ou
des concours en relation avec l'UE, ou créent des bulletins.
Certaines peuvent répondre à des questions spécifiques ou, si
nécessaire, aiguiller les visiteurs vers d'autres sources
d'informations locales.

➤ **Animation du réseau et techniques de communication**

Chaque Eurobibliothèque:
* reçoit gratuitement les documents suivants: Traités, JOCE,
  documents COM, Répertoire de la législation communautaire,
  Rapport général d'activités, Statistiques de base, Bulletin SCAD,
  brochures, dépliants et vidéos;
* est invitée à des sessions de formation spécifique et à des réunions
  annuelles avec les autres relais.

➤ **Bureaux responsable**

Les Représentations de la Commission Européenne à Madrid, Londres
et Copenhague (voir plus loin le chapitre consacré aux Représentations
dans les Etats membres)

DANMARK

Euro Library
Bornholms Centralbibliotek
Pingels Alle 1
3700 Ronne
Danmark
Tlf. 56 95 07 04
Fax. 56 95 45 93

Euro Library
Frederiksberg Bibliotek
Solbjergvej 21
2000 Frederiksberg
Danmark
Tlf. 38 34 48 77
Fax. 38 33 36 77

Euro Library
Helsingor Kommunes Biblioteker
Marienlyst Alle 4
3000 Helsingor
Danmark
Tlf. 49 21 73 00
Fax. 49 21 00 14

Euro Library
Kobenhavns Kommunes Bibioteker
Krystalgade 15
1172 Kobenhavn K
Danmark
Tlf. 33 93 60 60
Fax. 33 12 60 80

Euro Library
Odense Centralbibliotek
Orbaekvej 95
5220 Odense SO
Danmark
Tlf. 66 13 13 72
Fax. 66 15 49 37

Euro Library
Slagelse Centralbibliotek
Stenstuegade 3
4200 Slagelse
Danmark
Tlf. 53 52 12 45 - 4620
Fax. 58 50 12 88 - 4519

Euro Library
Biblioteket for Vejle By og Amt
Vestre Engvej 55
7100 Vejle
Danmark
Tlf. 75 82 32 00
Fax. 75 82 32 13

Euro Library
Det Nordjvdske Landsbibliotek
Nytorv 26, Postboks 839
9100 Alborg
Danmark

Tlf. 99 31 43 30
Fax. 99 31 43 33

Euro Library
Centralbiblioteket for Ribe Amt
Norregade 19, Postboks 69
6701 Esbjerg
Danmark
Tlf. 75 12 13 77
Fax. 75 45 35 09

Euro Library
Gentofte Kommunebibliotek
Ahlmanns Alle 6
2900 Hellerup
Danmark
Tlf. 31 62 75 00
Fax. 31 62 33 32 -304

Euro Library
Herning Centralbibliotek
Braendegardevej
7400 Herning
Danmark
Tlf. 97 12 18 11
Fax. 97 12 54 80

Euro Library
Nykobing F Centralbibliotek
Rosenvaenger 17, Postboks 171
4800 Nykobing F
Danmark
Tlf. 54 85 05 00 Fax. 54 82 27 49

Euro Library
Roskilde Bibliotek
Dronning Margrethes Vej 14, Postboks 229
4000 Roskilde
Danmark
Tlf. 42 35 63 00
Fax. 46 32 01 70

Euro Library
Det Sonderjydske Landsbibliotek
Haderslevvej 3, Postboks 1037
6200 Abenra
Danmark
Tlf. 74 62 25 62
Fax. 74 62 14 80

Euro Library
Viborg Centralbibiotek
Vesterbrogade 15, Postboks 1224
8800 Viborg
Danmark
Tlf. 86 62 44 88 Fax. 86 62 80 96

Euro Library
Arhus Kommunes Biblioteker
Molleparken
8000 Arhus C
Danmark
Tlf. 86 13

ESPAÑA

Eurobiblioteca
Biblioteca Pública de Albacete
San José de Calasanz, 14
E-02002 Albacete
España
Tel.: +34/967/23.80.53

Eurobiblioteca
Biblioteca Pública del Estado Fco
Villaespesa
Hermanos Machado s/n
E-04004 Almeria
España
Tel.: +34/950/23.03.75
Fax: +34/950/26.49.60

Eurobiblioteca
Biblioteca Pública del Estado
c/Tostado, 4
E-05001 Avila
España
Tel.: +34/920/21.21.32
Fax: +34/920/25.27.02

Eurobiblioteca
Biblioteca de la Universidad de Barcelona
Gran Vía de las Cortes Catalanas, 585
E-08007 Barcelona
España
Tel.: +34/93/318.42.66 ext. 2205

Eurobiblioteca
Biblioteca de la Diputación Foral de
Vizcaya
Astarloa, 10
E-48008 Bilbao
España
Tel.: +34/94/420.77.02
Fax: +34/94/415.51.84

Eurobiblioteca
Biblioteca Pública del Estado
Plaza de San Juan, s/n
E-09004 Burgos
España
Tel.: +34/947/20.23.12
Fax +34/947/27.74.10

Eurobiblioteca
Biblioteca Pública de Cáceres
Calle de Alfonso IX, 6
E-10004 Cáceres
España
Tel.: +34/927/24.33.00

Eurobiblioteca
Biblioteca Pública del Estado
Av.da Ramón de Carranza, 16
E-11006 Cádiz
España
Tel.: +34/956/22.24.39
Fax: +34/956/22.16.33

Eurobiblioteca
Biblioteca Pública de Castellón
Carrer Rafalafena, 29
E-12003 Castellón
España
Tel.: +34/964/22.43.09
 Fax et Tel.: +34/964/23.65.57

Eurobiblioteca
Biblioteca Pública de Ciudad Real
c/ Del Prado, 10
E-13002 Ciudad Real
España
Tel: +34/926/22.33.10

Eurobiblioteca
Biblioteca Pública del Estado
San Carlos 10 - 12, 1er piso
E-15001 La Coruña
España
Tel.: +34/981/20.96.83

Eurobiblioteca
Biblioteca Pública de Cuenca
Glorieta González Palencia, 2
E-16002 Cuenca
España
Tel: +34/22.23.11 - 22.28.15

Eurobiblioteca
Biblioteca Pública de Girona
Plaza del Hospital, 6
E-17001 Girona
España
Tel.: +34/972/20.22.52 - 20.27.97
Fax: +34/972/22.76.95

119

Eurobiblioteca
Biblioteca Pública Provincial
Plaza de los Caidos, 11
E-19001 Guadalajara
España
Tel.: +34/949/21.17.87

Eurobiblioteca
Biblioteca Pública de Huelva
Avda. de los Pirineos, 2
E-22004 Huesca
España
Tel. +34/974/22.87.61
Fax: +34/974/22.87.61

Eurobiblioteca
Biblioteca Pública Provincial
c/ Santo Reino, 1
E-23008 Jaén
España
Tel.: +34/953/22.39.50-54

Eurobiblioteca
Biblioteca Pública del Estado
c/Santa Nonia, 5
E-24003 León
España
Tel.: +34/987/20.67.10 Fax:
+34/987/20.30.25

Eurobiblioteca
Biblioteca Pública de Lérida
Plaza de San Antonio María Claret, 5
E-25002 Lérida
España
Tel.: +34/973/26.75.51

Eurobiblioteca
Biblioteca Pública del Estado
c/ de la Merced, 1
E-26001 Logroño
España
Tel.: +34/941/29.12.20
Fax: +34/941/29.12.35

Eurobiblioteca
Biblioteca Pública Provincial
Avda. Ramón Ferreirp, s/n
E-27071 Lugo
España
Tel.: +34/982/22.85.25

Eurobiblioteca
Biblioteca Popular Salamanca
Azcona, 42
E-28028 Madrid
España
Tel.: +34/91/726.37.01 - 361.28.22

Eurobiblioteca
Edificio de Gobernación
Av. de la Aurora, 57
E-29006 Málaga
España
Tel.: +34/952/35.40.12 ext. 34

Eurobiblioteca
Biblioteca Pública del Estado
Concejo, 11
E-32003 Orense
España
Tel.: +34/988/21.07.00 Fax:
+34/988/21.85.50

Eurobiblioteca
Biblioteca Pública de Palencia
Eduardo Dato, 4
E-34005 Palencia
España
Tel.: +34/979/75.11.00 Fax:
+34/979/75.11.21

Eurobiblioteca
Biblioteca Pública del Estado
Plaza de la Constitución, 3
E-35003 Las Palmas de Gran Canaria
España
Te.: +34/928/36.10.77 Fax:
+34/928/38.17.18

Eurobiblioteca
Biblioteca General de Navarra
Plaza de San Francisco, s/n
E-31001 Pamplona
España
Tel.: +34/948/10.77.97

Eurobiblioteca
Biblioteca Pública
Alfonso XIII, 3
E-36002 Pontevedra
España
Tel.: +34/986/85.08.38 Fax:
+34/986/86.21.27

Eurobiblioteca
Biblioteca Pública de Salamanca
Casa de las Conchas   Compañía, 2
E-37002 Salamanca
España
Tel.: +34/923/26.93.17 - 26.93.72
Fax: +34/923/26.97.58

Eurobiblioteca
Biblioteca Pública del Estado
c/ Gravina, 4
E-39007 Santander
España
Tel.: +34/942/37.44.14

Eurobiblioteca
Biblioteca Pública del Estado
Juan Bravo, 11
E-40001 Segovia
España
Tel.: +34/921/43.07.80 - 44.05.17
Fax: +34/921/44.28.02

Eurobiblioteca
Biblioteca Pública
c/Nicolás Rabal, 25
E-42002 Soria
España
Tel.: +34/975/22.18.00

Eurobiblioteca
Biblioteca Pública de Tarragona
c/Fortuny, 30
E-43001 Tarragona
España
Tel.: +34/977/24.03.31 - 24.05.44
Fax: +34/977/24.53.12

Eurobiblioteca
Biblioteca Pública
Plaza de Pérez Prado, 3
E-44001 Teruel
España
Tel.: +34/978/60.13.59

Eurobiblioteca
Biblioteca Pública del Estado
Paseo del Miradero, 4
E-45001 Toledo
España
Tel.: +34/925/22.12.24

Eurobiblioteca
Biblioteca Pública de Valencia
Hospital, 13
E-46001 Valencia
España
Tel.: +34/96/351.09.39-99.96
Fax: +34/96/351.66.61

Eurobiblioteca
Biblioteca Pública Provincial de Vitoria
Paseo de la Florida, 9
E-01071 Vitoria-Gasteiz (Alava)
España
Tel.: +34/945/13.44.05
Fax: +34/945/13.93.04

Eurobiblioteca
Biblioteca Pública del Estado
Plaza de Claudio Moyano, s/n
E-49001 Zamora
España
Tel.: +34/980/53.15.51
Fax: +34/980/51.60.32

Eurobiblioteca
Biblioteca Pública de Zaragoza
Dr. Cerrada, 22
E-50005 Zaragoza
España
Tel.: +34/976/23.33.23 - 21.73.24
Fax: +34/976/21.12.67

UNITED KINGDOM

Euro Library
Reference Services Officer
Central Library
Victoria Square
Middlesborough - Cleveland TS1 2AY
United Kingdom
Tel: 01642 248 155

Euro Library
Information Services Manager
Arts, Libraries and Museums Department
Durham County Council - County Hall
 Durham DH1 5TY
United Kingdom
Tel: 0191 383 4231

Euro Library
Director of Libraries & Arts , Central
Library
Prince Consort Rd
Gateshead - Tyne & Wear, NE8 4LN
United Kingdom
Tel: 0191 477 3478

Euro Libary
Business and Sciences Librarian, Central
Library
Princess Square
Newcastle upon Tyne NE99 1DX - Tyne and
Wear
United Kingdom
Tel: 0191 261 0691

121

Euro Library
County Amenities Officer, Amenities
Division
Central Library
The Willows
Morpeth Northumberland NE61 1TA
United Kingdom
Tel: 01670 512 385

Euro Library
Central Area Librarian, Central Library
Le Mans Crescent
Bolton - Lancashire BL1 1SE
United Kingdom
Tel: 01204 522 311

Euro Library
Reference and Information Services
Librarian ,Central Library
Manchester Road
Bury - Greater Manchester BL9 ODG
United Kingdom
Tel: 0161 705 5871

Euro Library
Principal Librarian ,Central library
Civi Way - Ellesmere Park
South Wirral - Cheshire L65 OBG
United Kingdom
Tel: 0151 356 7606

Euro Library
Senior Librarian ,Workington Library
Vulcans Lane
Workington - Cumbria CA14 2ND
United Kingdom
Tel: 01900 603 744

Euro Library
Information Services Manager ,Huyton
Library
Derby Road
Huyton - Knowsley - Merseyside
Merseyside L36 9UJ
United Kingdom
Tel: 0151 443 3738

Euro Library
Principal Librarian , Reader Services -
County Library HQ
143 Corporation St
Preston - Lancashire PR1 2UQ
United Kingdom
Tel: 01772 264 007

Euro Library
Business and Information Library
William Brown Street
Liverpool - Merseyside L3 8EW
United Kingdom
Tel: 0151 225 5430

Euro Library
European Information Officer - European
Information Unit
Manchester Central Library
St Peter's Square
Manchester M2 5PD Greater Manachester
United Kingdom
Tel: 0161 234 1992

Euro Library
St Helen's Metropolitan Borough Council
,Town Hall
Corporation St
 St Helens, Merseyside, WA10 1HP
United Kingdom
Tel: 01744 382 121

Euro Library
Head of information Services ,Stockport
Central Library
Welliongton Road South
 Stockport SK1 3RS Greater Manchester
United Kingdom
Tel: 0161 342 2031

Euro Library
Reference & Information Librarian
,Tameside Reference Library
Mulberry Street
Ashton-under-Lyne Tameside OL6 6EY
Greater Manchester
United Kingdom
Tel: 0161 342 2031

Euro Library
Reference Librarian
Altrincham Library
20 Stamford New Road
Altrincham Trafford Cheshire
United Kingdom
Tel: 0161 875 0956

Euro Library
Information Unit
Leisure Services Department
Hodson Street
Wigan Greater Manchester WN3 4EN
United Kingdom
Tel: 01942 828 153

Euro Library
Information Services Librarian
Birkenhead Central Library
Borough Road
Birkenhead Wirral Merseyside L41 2XB
United Kingdom
Tel: 0151 652 6106

Euro Library
European Information Officer, Central
Library
Shambles Street
Barnsley South Yorkshire S70 2JF
United Kingdom
Tel: 01226 773 935

Euro Library
Principal Librarian , Central Library
Princes Way
Bradford West Yorkshire BD1 1NN
United Kingdom
Tel: 01274 753 653

Euro Library
Senior Librarian Reference Library
,Doncaster Central Library
Waterdale Doncaster
South Yorkshire DN1 3JE
United Kingdom
Tel: 01302 734 320

Euro Library
Assistant Chief Officer, Central Library
Albion Street
Hull Humberside HU1 3TF
United Kingdom
Tel: 01482 883 043

Euro Library
Principal Librarian ,The Library
Museum Street
York, North Yorkshire YO1 2DS
United Kingdom
Tel: 01904 626 429

Euro Library
Prinicipal Librarian , Central Library
Walker Place
Rotherham South Yorkshire SG5 1JH
United Kingdom
Tel: 01709 823 614

Euro Library
Central Library
Surrey Street
Sheffield South Yorkshire S1 1X2
United Kingdom
Tel: 0114 273 4751

Euro Library
Derbyshire Library Service, County
Education Department
County Offices
Matlock Derbyshire DE4 3AG
United Kingdom
Tel: 01629 580 000

Euro Library
Reference, Information and Local Studies
Bishop Street
Leicester Leicestershire LE1 6AA
United Kingdom
Tel: 0116 255 6699

Euro Library
Reference Librarian , Lincoln Central
Library
Greyfriars Building
Brodadgate Lincoln Lincolnshire LN1
United Kingdom
Tel: 01522 549 160

Euro Library
Subject Specialist Librarian, Central Library
Abington Street
Northampton Northamptonshire NN1 2BA
United Kingdom
Tel: 01604 202 62

Euro Library
Central Librarian,
County Library
Angel Row
Nottingham Nottinghamshire NG1 6HP
United Kingdom
Tel: 0115 941 2121

Euro Library
Central Library
Chamberlain Square
Birmingham West Midlands B3 3HQ
United Kingdom
Tel: 0121 235 4545

Euro Library
Reference Librarian , Dudley Libarary
St James Road
Dudley West Midlands DY1 1HR
United Kingdom
Tel: 01384 453 554

Euro Library
Droitwich Library
Victoria Square
Droitwich, Worcester, Hereford &
Worcester WR5 2NP
United Kingdom
Tel: 01905 797 399

123

Euro Library
Library Services Column House
7 London Road
Shrewsbury Shropshire SY2 6NW
United Kingdom
Tel: 01743 253 666

Euro Library
Staffordshire Libraries HQ
Friars Terrace
Stafford, Staffordshire ST17 4AY
United Kingdom
Tel: 01785 278 351

Euro Library
Information Services Walsall Central Library
Lichfield Street
Walsall, West Midlands
United Kingdom
Tel: 01922 653 110

Euro Library
Area Manager South West, SW Operations
Unit Dunstable Library
Vernon Place
Dunstable, Bedfordshire LU5 4HA
United Kingdom
Tel: 01582 301 61

Euro Library
Libraries and Heritage HQ Babbage House,
Shire Hall
Cambridge, Cambridgeshire CB3 OAP
United Kingdom
Tel: 01223 317 061

Euro Library
Head of Information Services, Chelmsford
Library
P O Box 882 - Market Road
Chelmsford, Essex CM1 1LH
United Kingdom
Tel: 01245 492 758

Euro Library
Central Resources Librarian,
Hertfordshire Libraries New Barnfield
Travellers' Lane
Hatfield, Hertfordshire AL10 8XG
United Kingdom
Tel: 01707 281 511

Euro Library
Reference Librarian
Northgate Street
Ipswich, Suffolk IP1 3DE
United Kingdom
Tel: 01473 232 041

Euro Library
Acting Head of Reference and Information
Services , Bristol Central Library
College Green
Bristol, Avon BS1 5TL
United Kingdom
Tel: 0117 927 6121

Euro Library
County Reference Library
Union Place
Truro, Cornwall TR1 1EP
United Kingdom
Tel: 01872 727 02

Euro Library
County Librarian's Dept, Library
Headquarters, Barley House
Isleworth Rd
Exeter, Devon EX4 1RQ
United Kingdom
Tel: 01392 384 300

Euro Library
County Librarian & Arts Officer, Dorset
County Library HQ
Colliton Park
Dorcester, Dorset DT1 1XJ
United Kingdom
Tel: 01305 224 456

Euro Library
County Library, Quayside Wing
Shire Hall
Gloucester, Gloucestershire GL1 2HY
United Kingdom
Tel: 01452 425 020

Euro Library
Information & Specialist Services Manager,
Library Administration Centre
Mount Street
Bridgwater, Somerset TA6 3ES
United Kingdom
Tel: 01278 451 201

Euro Library
Information Services Manager
Bythesea Road
Trowbridge, Wiltshire BA14 8BS
United Kingdom
Tel: 01225 713 727

Euro Library
Information Manager, Berkshire County
Council
Shire Hall, Shinfield Park
Reading, Berkshire RG2 9XD
United Kingdom
Tel: 01934 233 270

124

Euro Library
County Reference Library County Hall
Walton Street
Aylesbury, Buckinghamshire HP20 1UU
United Kingdom
Tel: 01296 382 570

Euro Library
Hove Central Library
182 - 186 Church Road
Hove, East Sussex BN3 2EG
United Kingdom
Tel: 012703 770 473

Euro Library
Central Library
Civic Centre
Southampton, Hampshire SO14 7LW
United Kingdom
Tel: 01703 832 459

Euro Library
Lord Louis Library
Orchard Street
Newport, Isle of Wight PO30 1LL
United Kingdom
Tel: 01983 527 655

Euro Library
Springfield Maidstone
Kent ME14 2LH
United Kingdom
Tel: 01622 671 411

Euro Library
Department of Leisure and Arts
Holton
Oxfordshire OX33 1QQ
United Kingdom
Tel: 01865 810 210

Euro Library
Woking Library
Gloucester Walk
Woking, Surrey GU21 1HL
United Kingdom
Tel: 01483 770 591

Euro Library
South Division Office Worthing Library
Richmond Road
Worthing, West Sussex BN11 1HD
United Kingdom
Tel : 0903 212 414

Euro Library
Central Library
Barking
Essex IG11 7NB
United Kingdom
Tel: 0181 517 8666

Euro Library
Central Library
Townley Road
Bexley, Kent DA16 7HJ
United Kingdom
Tel: 0181 301 5151

Euro Library
Brent Town Hall Library
Forty Lane
Wembley, Brent, Middlesex HA9 9HX
United Kingdom
Tel: 0181 908 7196 n

Euro Library
Central Reference Library
High Street
Bromley , Kent BR1 1EX
United Kingdom
Tel: 0181 460 9955

Euro Library
City Business Library
1 Brewers' Hill Garden
Corporation of London,
London EC2V 5BX
United Kingdom
Tel: 0171 332 1881

Euro Library
Central Library
Katharine Street
Croydon, Surrey CR9 1ET
United Kingdom
Tel: 0181 760 5400

Euro Library
Central Library
103 Ealing Broadway Centre
Ealing W5 5JY
United Kingdom
Tel: 0181 579 2424

Euro Library
Business Information Officer
Edmonton Green Library
36 - 44 South Mall
Edmonton Green, Enfield, Middlesex N9
OTN
United Kingdom
Tel: 0181 967 9484

Euro Library
Principal Reference and Information
Librarian, Woolwich Reference Library
Calderdale Street
Greenwich, London SE18 6QZ
United Kingdom
Tel: 0181 854 8888

Euro Library
Shoreditch Town Hall
380 Old Street
Hackney, London EC1V 9LT
United Kingdom
Tel 0181 985 8262

Euro Library
Reference Services Civic Centre
Station Road
Harrow, Middlesex HA1 2UU
United Kingdom
Tel: 0181 424 1055

Euro Library
Central Reference Library
St Edward's Way
Romford, Havering , Essex RM1 3AR
United Kingdom
Tel: 01708 772 393

Euro Library
Central Reference Library
Phillimore Walk
Kensington and Chelsea, London W8 7RX
United Kingdom
Tel: 0171 361 3036

Euro Library
Surbiton Library
Ewell Road
Surbiton, Kingston upon Thames, Surrey
KT6 6AG
United Kingdom
Tel: 0181 399 2331

Euro Library
London Borough of Lambeth Tate Library
(Brixton)
Brixton Oval
Lambeth, London SW2 1JQ
United Kingdom
Tel: 0171 926 9325

Euro Library
London Borough of Lewisham
199 - 201 Lewisham High St
Lewisham, London SE13 6LG
United Kingdom
Tel: 0181 297 9430

Euro Library
Head of Information & Community
Services, Merton Civic Centre
London Road Morden, Merton
Surrey SM4 5DX
United Kingdom
Tel: 0181 545 4089

Euro Library Old Town Hall
Whittaker Avenue, Richmond upon Thames
Surrey TW9 1TP
United Kingdom
Tel: 0181 940 5529

Euro Library
Principal Reference & Information Library
55-157 Walworth Rd
Southwark, London SE17 1RS
United Kingdom
Tel: 0171 708 0516

Euro Library
Sutton Central Library
St Nicholas Way
Sutton, Surrey SM1 1EA
United Kingdom
Tel: 0181 770 4700

Euro Library
Battersea Reference Library
Altenburg Gardens
Wandsworth, London SW11 1JQ
United Kingdom
Tel: 0181 871 7467

Euro Library
Westminster Central Reference Library
(DEP)
35 St Martin's Street
Westminster, London WC2 7HP
United Kingdom
Tel: 0171 798 2034

Euro Library
Belfast Public Libraries Central Library
Royal Avenue
Belfast BT1 1EA
United Kingdom
Tel: 01232 243 233

Euro Library
North Eastern Education and Library Board
Area Library
25 - 31 Demesne Avenue
Ballymena BT43 7BG
United Kingdom
Tel: 01266 415 31

126

Euro Library
South Eastern Education and Library Board
Library HQ
Ballynahinch, Co. Down BT24 8DH
United Kingdom
Tel: 01238 562 639

Euro Library
Southern Education & Library Board Library
HQ
1 Markethill Road
Armagh BT60 1NR
United Kingdom
Tel: 01762 335 247

Euro Library
Western Education and Library Board
Library HQ
1 Spillars Place
Omagh Co. Tyrone BT78 1HL
United Kingdom
Tel: 01662 244 821

Euro Library
Central Library
Aberdeen, Grampian AB9 1GU
United Kingdom
Tel: 01224 634 622

Euro Library
Argyll and Bute District Library
Hunter Street
Kirn, Dunoon, Argyll, Strathclyde PA23 8JR
United Kingdom
Tel: 01369 3214

Euro Library
Bearsden and Milngavie Libraries
166 Drymen Road
Bearsden, Strathclyde G61 3RJ
United Kingdom
Tel: 0141 943 0121

Euro Library
Borders Regional Library
St. Mary's Hill
Selkirk, Borders TD7 5EW
United Kingdom
Tel: 01750 208 42

Euro Library
Reference Librarian, District Library HQ
26 - 28 Drysdale Street
Alloa
Clackmannan, Central FK10 1JL
United Kingdom
Tel: 01259 722 262

Euro Library
Central Library
Hope Street
Lanark, Clydesdale, Strathclyde Ml11 7LZ
United Kingdom
Tel: 01555 661 331

Euro Library
Cumbernauld and Kilsyth District Library
8 Allander Walk
Cumbernauld, Strathclyde G67 1EE
United Kingdom
Tel: 01236 725 664

Euro Library
District Library HQ
Council Offices
Lugar Cumnock & Doon , Strathclyde
KA18 3JQ
United Kingdom
Tel: 01290 422 111

Euro Library
District Library HQ
39 - 41 Princes Street
Ardrossan, Cunninghame, Strathclyde
KA22 8BT
United Kingdom
Tel: 01294 469 137

Euro Library
District Libraries HQ Levenford House
Helensee Road
Dumbarton, Strathclyde G82 4AH
United Kingdom
Tel: 01389 651 00

Euro Library
Dumfries & Galloway Libraries Ewart
Library
Catherine Street
Dumfries, Dumfries and Galloway DG1 1JB
United Kingdom
Tel: 01387 253 820

Euro Library
Central Library
The Wellgate
Dundee , Tayside DD1 1D8
United Kingdom
Tel: 01382 231 41

Euro Library
Central Library
Abbot Street
Dunfermline , Fife KY12 7NL
United Kingdom
Tel: 01383 723 661

127

Euro Library
Central Library
Olympia Centre
East Kilbride, Strathclyde G74 1PG
United Kingdom
Tel: 013552 200 46

Euro Library
District Librarian, District Library HQ
Lodge Street
Haddington, East Lothian, Lothian EH41 3DX
United Kingdom
Tel: 0162 082 4161

Euro Library
Eastwood Park
Rouken Glen Road
Eastwood, Strathclyde G46 6UG
United Kingdom
Tel: 0141 638 6511

Euro Library
Central Library
George IV Bridge
Edinburgh , Lothian EH1 1EG
United Kingdom
Tel: 0131 225 5584

Euro Library
Falkirk Library
Hope Street
Falkirik , Central FK1 5AU
United Kingdom
Tel: 01324 624 911

Euro Library
The Mitchell Library
North Street
Glasgow, Strathclyde G3 7DN
United Kingdom
Tel: 0141 305 2850

Euro Library
District Libraries HQ
8 Cadzow Street
Hamilton, Strathclyde Ml3 6HQ
United Kingdom
Tel: 01698 282 323

Euro Library
Central Services
31A Harbour Road
Inverness, Highland IV1 1UA
United Kingdom
Tel: 01463 235 713

Euro Library
Central Library
Clyde Square
Greenock, Inverclyde,
Strathclyde PA15 1NA
United Kingdom
Tel: 01475 726 211

Euro Library
District Library HQ
East Fergus Place
Kirkcaldy , Fife KY1 1XT
United Kingdom
Tel: 0592 268 386

Euro Library
Library HQ
2 Clerk Street
Loanhead, Midlothian ,
Lothian EH20 9DR
United Kingdom
Tel: 0131 440 2210

Euro Library
Coatbridge Library
Academy Street
Coatbridge, Monklands,
Strathclyde ML5 3AW
United Kingdom
Tel: 01236 424 150

Euro Library
District HQ
High Street
Elgin, Moray, Grampian IV30 1BX
United Kingdom
Tel: 01343 543 451

Euro Library
Cultural Services Division
P.O. Box 14 Civic Centre
Motherwell , Strahclyde ML1 1TW
United Kingdom
Tel: 01698 266 166

Euro Library
County Buildings
St Catherine Street
Cupar, North East Fife, Fife KY15 4TA
United Kingdom
Tel: 01334 653 722

Euro Library
AK Bell Library
York Place
Perth, Tayside PH2 8EP
United Kingdom
Tel: 01738 444 949

Euro Library
Central Library
Paisley, Renfrewshire,
Strathclyde PA1 2BB
United Kingdom
Tel: 0141 887 3672

Euro Library
Lower Hillhead
Lerwick , Shetland ZE1 0EL
United Kingdom
Tel: 01595 3868

Euro Library
Stirling District Libraries
Borrowmeadow Road
Stirling , Central FK7 7TN
United Kingdom
Tel: 01786 432 381

Euro Library
William Patrick Library
2 West High Street
Kirkintilloch, Strathkelvin,
Strathclyde G66 1AD
United Kingdom
Tel: 0141 775 1613

Euro Library
Western Isles Libraries
Keith Street
Stornoway, Isle of Lewis,
Western Isles PA87 2QG
United Kingdom
Tel: 01851 703 064

Euro Library
District Library HQ
Wellpark Marjoribanks Street
Bathgate, West Lothian ,
Lothian EH48 1AN
United Kingdom
Tel: 0506 528 66

Euro Library
Gwynedd County Council
County Offices
Caernarfon, Gwynedd LL55 1SH
United Kingdom
Tel: 01554 773 538

Euro Library
Borough Librarian
Vaughan Street
Llanelli, Dyfed SA15 3AS
United Kingdom
Tel: 01554 773 538

Euro Library
County Librarian
Mid Glamorgan County Library,
Coed Parc, Park Street
Brigend, Mid Glamorgan CF31 4BA
United Kingdom
Tel: 01656 767 451

Euro Library
Borough Librarian, Central Library
John Frost Square
Newport, Gwent NP9 1PA
United Kingdom
Tel: 01633 265 539

Euro Library
Information Librarian , Cardiff Central
Library
St Davids Link Frederick Street
Cardiff, South Glamorgan CF1 4DT
United Kingdom
Tel: 0222 382 116

Euro Library
West Glamorgan County Council
County Hall
Swansea SA1 3SN West Glamorgan
United Kingdom
Tel: 0192 471 759

129

EURO-INFO-ZENTREN

> **Akronym**

E I C

> **Tätigkeitsbereich**

Unterrichtung der Unternehmen, insbesondere der KMU (kleine und mittlere Unternehmen) und der Handwerksbetriebe über die Gemeinschaftsaktionen zugunsten ihrer Integration und ihrer Entwicklung in der Europäischen Union durch Inanspruchnahme des Mehrwerts eines dezentralisierten europäischen Netzes.

> **Zielgruppe**

Unternehmen, vor allem KMU und Handwerksbetriebe.

> **Wirkungskreis**

Das Netz setzt sich aus 235 EIC verteilt auf 15 Mitgliedstaaten, sowie Norwegen und Island, zusammen. Das Netz umfaßt ebenfalls 16 Korrespondenzzentren(EICC), die in Drittländern geöffnet sind, hauptsächlich in Mittel- und Osteuropa sowie im Mittelmeerbecken.

> **Aktionen**

- Verbreitung von gezielten Informationen bei Unternehmen und Bereitstellung eines Gutachtens, das alle Gemeinschaftsbereiche erfaßt
- Unterstützung und Beratung für KMU zur Förderung der Internationalisierung ihrer Aktivitäten durch ihre Teilnahme an Gemeinschaftsprogrammen und ihr Zugang zu öffentlichen Aufträgen;
- Organisation von Partnerschaften zwischen KMU über "Interprise"- und "Euro-Partnerschafts"-Veranstaltungen sowie andere Kooperationsmissionen;
- Informationsaustausch der EIC über die nationale Gesetzgebung und die Handelspraktiken in anderen Mitgliedstaaten.

> **Betreuung des Netzes und Kommunikationstechnik**

Jedes EIC:
- erhält vom Amt für amtliche Veröffentlichungen der Europäischen Gemeinschaft und von anderen Generaldirektionen der Kommission eine kostenlose Dokumentation;
- kann bevorzugte Zugangs- und Abfragebedingungen für die Datenbanken in Anspruch nehmen (Eurobase-Server, ECHO, Datastar ...);
- wird regelmäßig zum Besuch von Ausbildungskursen eingeladen (EG-Bereiche, spezialisierte Workshops, Consulting);
- ist am Netzwerkeffekt beteiligt und kann die entwickelten Spezialisationen in Anspruch nehmen;
- hat Zugang zu den Mehrwertdiensten eines Netzes (VANS): E-Mail, Dateitransfer, Abfrage von Datenbanken.

> Europäische Kommission
> Generaldirektion XXIII
> Referat XXIII/B/1
> Jean-Pierre HABER
> 200 Rue de la Loi
> B - 1049 Brüssel
> Tel. (+32-2) 287 15 11 / 296 13 50
> Fax (+32-2) 230 05 20 / 295 55 40

EURO INFO CENTRES

> **Acronym**

EIC

> **Field of activity**

Informing companies, particularly SME (small and medium-sized enterprises) and the craft industry, about Community activities favouring their integration and development in the European Union through the added value of a decentralized European network.

> **Target public**

Companies, especially SME and the craft industry.

> **Community coverage**

Network composed of 235 EIC spread over the 15 Member States, Norway and Iceland. The network also includes 16 Correspondence Centres (EICC) opened in non-EC countries, mainly in Central and Eastern Europe and the Mediterranean Basin region.

> **Actions**

- Disseminating specific information to companies, making expertise available on all Community issues and looking out anticipatively for information on the European programmes;
- Assistance and consulting for SME in order to favour the internationalism of their activities through the participation of SME in Community programmes and their access to public markets;
- Establishment of partnerships among SME, especially through Interprise and Europartenariat events as well as other cooperation missions;
- Information exchanges among EIC on issues related to national legislation and commercial practices of the other Member States.

> **Network animation and methods of communication**

Each EIC:
- receives free documentation from OOPEC, other Directorates-General of the Commission and other European institutions;
- benefits from preferential conditions for access to and consultation of databanks (Eurobases, ECHO, Datastar servers...);
- is invited regularly to training sessions (Community matters, specialised workshops, consulting);
- contributes to the value of the networks and benefits from the specializations developed among them;
- has access to the services of a value-added network (VANS): electronic mail, transfer of data files, consultation of databanks.

> European Commission
Directorate-General XXIII
Unit XXIII/B/1
Jean-Pierre HABER
200 rue de la Loi
B - 1049 Brussels
Tel.: (+32.2) 287.15.11 / 296.13.50
Fax: (+32-2) 230.05.20 / 295.55.40

EURO INFO CENTRES

➢ **Acronyme**

E.I.C.

➢ **Domaine d'activité**

Informer les entreprises et plus particulièrement les PME (petites et moyennes entreprises) et l'artisanat sur les actions communautaires favorisant leur intégration et leur développement dans l'Union européenne en bénéficiant de la valeur ajoutée d'un réseau européen décentralisé.

➢ **Public cible**

Les entreprises, surtout PME et artisanat.

➢ **Rayonnement communautaire**

Réseau composé de 235 EIC répartis sur les 15 Etats membres, la Norvège et l'Islande. Le réseau comporte également 16 Euro Info Centres de Correspondance (EICC) ouverts dans les pays tiers, principalement d'Europe centrale et orientale et du Bassin méditérranéen.

➢ **Actions**

- Diffusion auprès des entreprises d'une information ciblée et mise à disposition d'une expertise couvrant l'ensemble des matières communautaires et veille informative anticipative sur les programmes européens;
- Assistance-conseil aux PME pour favoriser l'internationalisation de leurs activités par leur participation aux programmes communautaires et leur accès aux marchés publics;
- Organisation de partenariats entre PME par le biais notamment de manifestations Interprise et Europartenariat et autres missions de coopérations;
- Echange d'informations entre EIC sur la législation nationale et les pratiques commerciales des autres Etats membres.

➢ **Animation du réseau et techniques de communication**

Chaque EIC:
- reçoit de l'OPOCE, d'autres Directions générales de la Commission et d'autres institutions européennes une documentation gratuite;
- bénéficie de conditions préférentielles d'accès et de consultation des banques de données (serveurs Eurobases, ECHO, DataStar...);
- est invité régulièrement à suivre des sessions de formation (matières communautaires, ateliers spécialisés, consultance...);
- participe à l'effet réseau et bénéficie des spécialisations développées entre eux;
- a accès aux services d'un réseau à valeur ajoutée (VANS): messagerie, transfert de fichiers, consultation de banques de données.

➢ Commission européenne
Direction générale XXIII
Unité XXIII/B/1
Jean-Pierre HABER
200 rue de la Loi
B - 1049 Bruxelles
Tél.: (+32-2) 287.15.11 / 296.13.50
Fax: (+32-2) 230.05.20 / 295.55.40

BELGIQUE-BELGIË

Euro Info Centre
Bureau Economique de la Province de
Namur (B.E.P.N.)
Avenue Sergent Vrithoff, 2
B-5000 Namur
Belgique/België
Tel: 32 81 73 52 09
Fax: 32 81 74 29 45
P FR 6 11021 527

Euro Info Centre
Kamer van Koophandel en Nijverheid van
Antwerpen
Markgravestraat, 12
B-2000 Antwerpen
Belgique/België
Tel: 32 3 232 22 19
Fax: 32 3 233 64 42
P EN 4 11017 511

Euro Info Centre
C.D.P. - Idelux
Avenue Nothomb, 8
B-6700 Arlon
Belgique/België
Tel: 32 63 21 99 48
Fax: 32 63 22 65 84
E FR 244 526

Euro Info Centre
Chambre de Commerce et
d'Industrie de Bruxelles/Fabrimétal
Avenue Louise, 500
B-1050 Bruxelles
Belgique/België
Tel: 32 2 648 58 73
Fax: 32 2 640 93 28
E FR 16 11012 522

Euro Info Centrum
Ministerie van de Vlaamse Gemeenschap
Administratie Economie Markiesstraat, 1-
5e Ver.
B-1000 Brussel
Belgique/België
Tel: 32 2 507 37 30
Fax: 32 2 502 47 02
E FR 51

Euro Info Centre
Euroguichet Hainaut-Est
Avenue Général Michel, 1E
B-6000 Charleroi
Belgique/België
Tel: 32 71 33 14 60
Fax: 32 71 30 54 48
E FR 523

134

Euro Info Centre
Gewestelijke Ontwikkelingsmaatschappij
voor Oost-Vlaanderen
Floraliapaleis, bus 6
B-9000 Gent
Belgique/België
Tel: 32 9 221 55 11
Fax: 32 9 221 55 00
E EN 518

Euro Info Centre
Kamer voor Handel en Nijverheid van
Limburg
Gouverneur Roppesingel, 51
B-3500 Hasselt
Belgique/België
Tel: 32 11 28 44 00
Fax: 32 11 28 44 06
E EN 5151

Euro Info Centre
NCMV Internationaal
Lange Steenstraat, 10
B-8500 Kortrijk
Belgique/België
Tel: 32 56 22 41 23
Fax: 32 56 22 96 94
E FR 228 11035 519

Euro Info Centre
Institut Provincial des
Classes Moyennes Le Vertbois
Rue du Vertbois, 13 A
B-4000 Liège
Belgique/België
Tel: 32 41 20 11 11
Fax: 32 41 20 11 20
E FR 398 11018 524

Euro Info Centre
Euro Info Centre Hainaut
Site du Grand Hornu
Rue Sainte Louise, 82
B-7301 Hornu (Mons)
Belgique/België
Tel: 32 65 77 79 70
Fax: 32 65 77 90 91
E FR 211 11023 523

Euro Info Centre
Euro Info Centre Zaventem
Kamer voor Handel en
Nijverheid Halle-Vilvoorde
Brucargo Gebouw, 706 - Lokaal 7614
B-1931 Zaventem
Belgique/België
Tel: 32 2 751 90 56
Fax: 32 2 751 78 11
E FR 512

Euro Info Centre
Stellenvermittlungsamt
Arbeitsbeschassung - Forem
(Antenne de BE-010 Liège)
Borngasse, 3 & 5
B-4700 Eupen
Belgique/België
Tel: 32 87 74 21 80
Fax: 32 87 55 70 85
A FR   524

Euro Info Centre
Chambre de Commerce et d'Industrie du
Tournaisis
(Antenne de BE011-Mons)
Rue Beyaert, 75
B-7500 Tournai
Belgique/België
Tel: 32 69 22 11 21
Fax: 32 69 21 27 84
A FR   523

Euro Info Centre
ARIES Association
Réseau d'Information de l'Economie Sociale
c/o CECOP Avenue Guillaume Tell, 59
B-1060 Bruxelles
Belgique/België
Tel: 32 2 537 57 40
Fax: 32 2 537 09 17
E EN

DANMARK

Euro Info Center
Haslegaardsvænget 18-20
DK-8210 Århus
Danmark
Tel: 45 86 15 25 77
Fax: 45 86 15 43 22
P EN   9036

Euro Info Center Fyn
Lucernemarken, 1 P.O. BOX 504
DK-5260 Odense
Danmark
Tel: 45 66 14 60 30
Fax: 45 66 14 60 34
P EN   9031

Euro Info Center
Sonderjyllands Erhversråd
Bjerggade 4 L
DK-6200 Aabenraa
Danmark
Tel: 45 74 62 23 84
Fax: 45 74 62 67 60
E EN   81018   9032

Euro Info Center
Herning Erhvervsråd
Uldjydevej 5
DK-7400 Herning
Danmark
Tel: 45 97 12 92 00
Fax: 45 97 12 92 44
E EN   433   81019   9035

Euro Info Center
Danish Technological Institute (DTI)
Gregersensvej Postbox 141
DK-2630 Kobenhavn-Tåstrup
Danmark
Tel: 45 43 71 17 55
Fax: 45 43 71 63 60
E EN   274 81004 9012

Euro Info Center
Det Danske Handelskammer Borsen
DK-1217 Kobenhavn
Danmark
Tel: 45 33 95 05 00
Fax: 45 33 32 52 16
E EN   9012

Euro Info Center
Håndværksrådet - Viborg A/S
Lille Sankt Hansgade 20
DK-8800 Viborg
Danmark
Tel: 45 86 62 77 11
Fax: 45 86 61 49 21
E EN   9037

Euro Info Center
Storstroms Erhvervscenter
Marienbergvej 80
DK-4760 Vordingborg
Danmark
Tel: 45 55 34 05 55
Fax: 45 55 34 03 55
E EN   81007 9022

DEUTSCHLAND

**Euro Info Centre/EG-Beratungsstelle
für Unternehmen**
Zenit GmbH
Dohne 54 - Postfach 10 22 64
D-45468 Mülheim an der Ruhr
Deutschland
Tel: 49 208 300 04 21
Fax: 49 208 300 04 29
P EN 15

135

Euro Info Centre/EG-Beratungsstelle
Rationalisierungs-Kuratorium der
Deutschen Wirschaft (RKW)
Heilwigstrasse 33
D-20249 Hamburg
Deutschland
Tel: 49 40 460 20 87
Fax: 49 40 482 032
P EN 41058 12

Euro Info Centre
EG-Beratungsstelle für Unternehmen
Deutscher Industrie-und Handelstag-DIHT
Adenauerallee 148 - Postfach 1446
D-53004 Bonn
Deutschland
Tel: 49 228 10 46 21/22
Fax: 49 228 10 41 58
P EN 416 41021 15

Euro Info Centre
EG-Beratungsstelle
Wirtschaftsförderung Brandenburg GmbH
Am Lehnitzsee
D-14476 Neufahrland-Potsdam
Deutschland
Tel: 49 33 1 9675-0
Fax: 49 33 1 9675-222
E EN 41137

Euro Info Centre
Industrie-und Handelskammer Regensburg
EG-Beratungsstelle
Martin-Luther-Straße 12 - Postfach 11 03 55
D-93016 Regensburg
Deutschland
Tel: 49 941 56940
Fax: 49 941 5694279
P EN 333 19

Euro Info Centre
EG-Beratungsstelle für Unternehmer beim
Deutschen Handwerkskammertag (DHKT)
Johanniterstraße 1 - Postfach 12 02 70
D-53044 Bonn
Deutschland
Tel: 49 228 545 299/211
Fax: 49 228 545 205
P EN 15

Euro Info Centre
EG-Beratungsstelle für Unternehmer
Handwerkskammer Stuttgart
Heilbronner Straße, 43 - Postfach 10 21 55
D-70017 Stuttgart
Deutschland
Tel: 49 711 1657 280
Fax: 49 711 1657 222
P EN 46 41057 18

Euro Info Centre/EG-Beratungsstelle
Industrie- und Handelskammer zu Aachen
Theaterstraße 6-10 - Postfach 6 50
D-52007 Aachen
Deutschland
Tel: 49 241 438 223
Fax: 49 241 438 259
E EN 15

Euro Info Centre / ERIC Berlin
BAO Berlin - Marketing Service GmbH
Hardenbergstraße 16-18
D-10623 Berlin
Deutschland
Tel: 49 30 315 10 240
Fax: 49 30 315 10 316
E EN 41060 1B

Euro Info Centre Deutsches
Informationszentrum für Technische
Regeln (DITR) im DIN e.V.
Burggrafenstraße 6
D-10787 Berlin
Deutschland
Tel: 49 30 2601 2605/2836
Fax: 49 30 2628 125
E EN 1B

Euro Info Centre
Genossenschaftliche EG-Beratungs- und
Informationsgesellschaft (GEBI) mbH
Rheinweg 67
D-53129 Bonn
Deutschland
Tel: 49 228 23 75 44
Fax: 49 228 23 75 48
E EN 456 41066 15

Euro Info Centre
EG-Beratungsstelle für Unternehmen beim
Deutschen Sparkassen- und Giroverband
Simrockstraße, 4
D-53113 Bonn
Deutschland
Tel: 49 228 204 319/323
Fax: 49 228 204 725
E EN 41059 15

Euro Info Centre
AXON Technologie Consult GmbH
Hanseatenhof 8
D-28195 Bremen
Deutschland
Tel: 49 421 17 55 55
Fax: 49 421 17 16 86
E EN 41142 14

136

Euro Info Centre

NATI - Niedersächsische Agentur für
Technologietransfer und Innovation GmbH
Vahrenwalder Straße 7
D-30165 Hannover
Deutschland
Tel: 49 511 9357 121/2
Fax: 49 511 9357 439
E EN   13

Euro Info Centre

EG-Beratungsstelle
Investitionsbank Schleswig-Holstein
Fleethörn 29-31 Postfach 1128
D-24103 Kiel
Deutschland
Tel: 49 431 900 3497/99
Fax: 49 431 900 3207
E EN   41067 11

Euro Info Centre

Bundesstelle für Außenhandels-
Information (BfAI)
Agrippastraße 87/93 Postfach 10 05 22
D-50445 Köln
Deutschland
Tel: 49 221 20 57 273/274 Fax: 49 221
20 57 212/262
E EN   15

Euro Info Centre

Europäisches Beratungs-Zentrum
der Deutschen Wirtschaft
Gustav-Heinemann-Ufer 84-88
D-50968 Köln
Deutschland
Tel: 49 221 370 86 21
Fax: 49 221 370 88 40
E EN 45   15

Euro Info Centre

Industrie- und Handelskammer
Südlicher Oberrhein
Lotzbeckstraße 31 Postfach 1547
D-77905 Lahr
Deutschland
Tel: 49 78 21 270 30
Fax: 49 78 21 270 322
E EN   41065 18

Euro Info Centre

EG-Beratungsstelle
Landesgewerbeanstalt Bayern (LGA)
Marientorgraben, 8
D-90403 Nürnberg
Deutschland
Tel: 49 911 2017 588
Fax: 49 911 2017 580
E EN   41040

Euro Info Centre

Zentrale fur Produktivität und Technologie
Saar e.V
Franz-Josef-Röder-Straße, 9
D-66104 Saarbrücken
Deutschland
Tel: 49 681 95 20 450/1/2
Fax: 49 681 58 46 125
E EN   41043 1A

Euro Info Centre Trier

c/o Technologie-Zentrum Trier
Gottbillstraße 34a
D-54294 Trier
Deutschland
Tel: 49 651 19 92/8100945
Fax: 49 651 81 00 919
E EN   41123 17

Euro Info Centre

EG-Beratungsstelle
Wirtschaftsförderung Hessen
Investitionsbank AG - HLT
Abraham-Lincoln-Straße 38-42
Postfach 3107
D-65021 Wiesbaden
Deutschland
Tel: 49 611 774202/774-0
Fax: 49 611 774265
E EN   41061 16

Euro Info Centre

Kreis Steinfurt Amt für Wirtschaft und
Verkehr , (Satellite of NL455-Enschede)
Tecklenburger Straße 10
D-48565 Steinfurt
Deutschland
Tel: 49 25 51 69 20 18
Fax: 49 25 51 69 24 00
A EN   15

Euro Info Centre

Industrie- und Handelskammer Dresden
Niedersedlitzer Straße, 63
D-01257 Dresden
Deutschland
Tel: 49 351 2802 185/186
Fax: 49 351 2802 280
E EN

Euro Info Centre

Omnibera Wirtschaftsberatungsgesellschaft
mbH (Satellite)
Coburger Straße 1c
D-53113 Bonn
Deutschland
Tel: 49 228 23 80 78
Fax: 49 228 23 39 22
A EN   15

137

Euro Info Centre
EG-Beratungsstelle für Unternehmen der
Landesbank Hessen-Thüringen
Bahnhofstraße, 4a Postfach 167
D-99004 Erfurt
Deutschland
Tel: 49 361 56 24 798
Fax: 49 361 66 57 233
E EN   41143 1

Euro Info Centre
EG-Beratungsstelle für Unternehmen in der
Industrie und Handelskammer zu Leipzig
Goerdelerring 5
D-04091 Leipzig
Deutschland
Tel: 49 341 1267323
Fax: 49 341 1267421
E EN 510 41138

Euro Info Centre
EG-Beratungsstelle
Industrie- und Handelskammer Rostock
Ernst-Barlach-Straße 7 Postfach 10 52 40
D-18010 Rostock
Deutschland
Tel: 49 381 466 98 26/27
Fax: 49 381 459 11 56
E EN   41139

Euro Info Centre
Handswerkskammer Magdeburg
Bahnhofstraße 49 a Postfach 15 68
D-39005 Magdeburg
Deutschland
Tel: 49 391 561 91 61
Fax: 49 391 561 91 62
E EN   41140

Euro Info Centre
EG-Beratungsstelle für Unternehmen
Industrie- und Handelskammer München
Max-Joseph-Straße 2
D-80323 München
Deutschland
Tel: 49 89 511 62 09
Fax: 49 89 511 64 65
E EN   11

Euro Info Centre
Industrie- und Handelskammer
Frankfurt/Oder Logenstrasse 8 (im
Oderturm)
Postfach 343
D-15203 Frankfurt/Oder
Deutschland
Tel: 49 335 23863
Fax: 49 335 322271
E EN

138

ELLAS

Euro Info Centre (EIC)
Athens Chamber of Commerce and
Industry
Akadimias Street, 7
GR-10671 Athens
Ellas
Tel: 30 1 362 73 37
Fax: 30 1 360 78 97
P EN 101   A3

Euro Info Centre
(EOMMEX) Hellenic Organization of Small
and Medium Sized Industries and
Handicrafts
Xenias Street, 16
GR-11528 Athens
Ellas
Tel: 30 1 779 42 29
Fax: 30 1 777 86 94
P EN 97 51012 A3

Euro Info Centre
Association of Industries of Northern
Greece
Morihovou Square, 1
GR-54625 Thessaloniki
Ellas
Tel: 30 31 539817/539682
Fax: 30 31 541491
P   EN 103 51002 A12

Euro Info Centre
(EOMMEX) Hellenic Organization of Small
and Medium Sized Industries and
Handicrafts
Leoforos Dimokratias 150
GR-68100 Alexandroupolis
Ellas
Tel: 30 551 33 565
Fax: 30 551 33 566
E EN   A11

Euro Info Centre
Panhellenic Exporters Association
Kratinou, 11
GR-10552 Athens
Ellas
Tel: 30 1 522 89 25
Fax: 30 1 524 25 68
E EN   51006 A3

Euro Info Centre
Chamber of Commerce and Industry of
Iraklion
Koronaeou Street, 9
GR-71202 Iraklion, Crete
Ellas
Tel: 30 81 285829/342134
Fax: 30 81 225730
E EN   A43

Euro Info Centre
Chamber of Kavala
Omonias Street, 50
GR-65302 Kavala
Ellas
Tel: 30 51 83 39 64
Fax: 30 51 83 59 46
E EN 644   51014 A11

Euro Info Centre
(EOMMEX) Hellenic Organization of Small
and Medium Sized Industries and
Handicrafts
Marinou Antipa & Kouma Street
GR-41222 Larissa
Ellas
Tel: 30 41 22 60 77
Fax: 30 41 25 30 19
E EN   51110 A14

Euro Info Centre
(EOMMEX) Hellenic Organization of Small
and Medium Sized Industries and
Handicrafts
Iktinou, 2 Platia Kyprion Agoniston
GR-81100 Mytilini
Ellas
Tel: 30 251 24 906
Fax: 30 251 41 501
E EN   A41

Euro Info Centre
(EOMMEX) Hellenic Organization of Small
and Medium Sized Industries and
Handicrafts
Aratou Street, 21
GR-26221 Patras
Ellas
Tel: 30 61 22 02 48
Fax: 30 61 22 34 96
E EN   51108 A23

Euro Info Centre
Chambre de Commerce et
d'Industrie du Pirée
Rue Loudovicou, 1 Place Roosevelt
GR-18531 Pirée
Ellas
Tel: 30 1 41 70 529
Fax: 30 1 41 74 601
E EN 627 51109 A3

Euro Info Centre
Association of Industries in Thessaly and in
Central Greece
El. Venizelou Rd., 4
GR-38221 Volos
Ellas
Tel: 30 421 28111/29407
Fax: 30 421 26394
E EN 643 51013 A14

Euro Info Centre
Chamber of Ioannina
X.Trikoupi & O.Poutetsi Str.14
GR-45332 Ioannina
Ellas
Tel: 30 651 76 589
Fax: 30 651 25 179
E EN   A21

139

ESPAÑA

Euro Info Centre
Centro Europeo de Información
Empresarial-CIDEM/FTN (Eurofinestreta)
Av. Diagonal, 403 1r
E-08008 Barcelona
España
Tel: 343 4151114
Fax: 343 2186747
P FR   B51

Euro Info Centre
Cámara Oficial de Comercio Industria y
Navegación de Bilbao
Alameda de Recalde, 50
E-48008 Bilbao
España
Tel: 34 4 410 45 03
Fax: 34 4 443 41 45
P FR 63 61007 B21

Euro Info Centre
Confederación de Empresarios de
Andalucía
Isla de la Cartuja, s/n
E-41010 Sevilla
España
Tel: 34 5 446 00 01
Fax: 34 5 446 16 44
P FR   61044 B61

Euro Info Centre
Confederación Española de Organisaciones
Empresariales
Diego de León, 50
E-28006 Madrid
España
Tel: 34 1 563 96 41
Fax: 34 1 564 01 35
P FR 60   B3

Euro Info Centre
Centro Europeo de Información
Empresarial ICEX-IMPI
Paseo de la Castellana, 141-2a Planta
E-28046 Madrid
España
Tel: 34 1 571 46 40/54 04
Fax: 34 1 571 59 12
P FR 379 61060 B3

Euro Info Centre
Confederación Regional de Empresarios de
Castilla la Mancha
Calle Rosario, 29
E-02001 Albacete
España
Tel: 34 67 21 73 00
Fax: 34 67 24 02 02
E FR   B42

Euro Info Centre
Euroventanilla Grupo Banco Popular
Español
Rambla de Méndez Núñez, 12
E-03002 Alicante
España
Tel: 34 6 521 62 91
Fax: 34 6 520 19 54
E FR   B52

Euro Info Centre
Banco Exterior de España (BEX)
Manila, 56 - 58
E-08034 Barcelona
España
Tel: 34 3 204 13 66
Fax: 34 3 205 73 35
E FR   61070 B51

Euro Info Centre
Cámara Oficial de Comercio Industria y
Navegación
Avenida Diagonal, 452-454
E-08006 Barcelona
España
Tel: 34 3 416 93 89
Fax: 34 3 416 07 35
E FR   61029 B51

Euro Info Centre
Ayuntamiento de Cáceres, Edificio la
Chicuela
c/ Sánchez Herrero, 2
E-10004 Cáceres
España
Tel: 34 27 21 71 83
Fax: 34 27 21 00 66
E FR   B43

Euro Info Centre
Asociación de la Industria Navarra
P.O. Box 439
E-31191 Cordovilla - Pamplona
España
Tel: 34 48 101 101
Fax: 34 48 101 100
E EN   547 61006 B22

Euro Info Centre
Gobierno de Canarias
Consejería de Economía y Hacienda
C/Nicolás Estévanez, 33
E-35007 Las Palmas de Gran Canaria
España
Tel: 34 28 271142
Fax: 34 28 275144/227812
E EN   B7

Euro Info Centre
Federación de Empresarios de la Rioja
Calle Hermanos Moroy, 8 - 4¤
E-26001 Logroño
España
Tel: 34 41 25 70 22
Fax: 34 41 26 25 37
E FR   B23

Euro Info Centre
Cámara de Comercio e Industria de Madrid
Plaza de la Independencia, 1
E-28001 Madrid
España
Tel: 34 1 538 36 10
Fax: 34 1 538 36 43
E FR   61015 B3

Euro Info Centre
Centro Europeo de Información
Empresarial - Euroventanilla IMADE
c/ Miguel Angel, 23
E-28010 Madrid
España
Tel: 34 1 3198048
Fax: 34 1 3103269
E FR   B3

Euro Info Centre
Proyecto Europa - Banesto Centro Europeo
de Información
Plaza de la Constitución, 9
E-29008 Málaga
España
Tel: 34 5 222 09 59/79
Fax: 34 5 222 09 36
E FR 66 61022 B61

Euro Info Centre/Euroventanilla
Instituto de Fomento de la Región de
Murcia
Plaza San Agustín, 5
E-30005 Murcia
España
Tel: 34 68 36 28 00
Fax: 34 68 29 32 45
E FR 537 61067 B62

Euro Info Centre
Instituto de Fomento Regional del
Principado de Asturias
Parque Tecnológico de Asturias
E-33420 Llanera
España
Tel: 34 85 26 00 68
Fax: 34 85 26 44 55
E FR 554 61122 B12

Euro Info Centre
Centro Baleares Europa
Calle Patronato Obrero, 30
E-07006 Palma de Mallorca
España
Tel: 34 71 46 10 02
Fax: 34 71 46 30 70
E FR   B53

Euro Info Centre
Euroventanilla del País Vasco
C/Tomas Gros, 3 bajo
E-20001 Donostia San Sebastián
España
Tel: 34 43 27 22 88
Fax: 34 43 27 16 57
E FR   61071 B21

Euro Info Centre
Confederación de Empresarios de Galicia
Rúa del Villar, 54
E-15705 Santiago de Compostela
España
Tel: 34 81 56 06 95
Fax: 34 81 56 57 88
E EN   61069 B11

Euro Info Centre
Cámara de Comercio e Industria de Toledo
Plaza San Vicente, 3
E-45001 Toledo
España
Tel: 34 25 21 44 50
Fax: 34 25 21 39 00
E EN 61 61065 B42

Euro Info Centre
Cámara Oficial de Comercio, Industria y
Navegación de Valencia
c/ Poeta Querol, 15
E-46002 Valencia
España
Tel: 34 6 351 13 01
Fax: 34 6 351 63 49
E FR 59 61039 B52

Euro Info Centre Sodical
C/Claudio Moyano, 4 - 1¤
E-47001 Valladolid
España
Tel: 34 83 35 40 33
Fax: 34 83 35 47 38
E FR   B41

Euro Info Centre
Confederación Regional de Empresarios
de Aragón
Plaza Roma F-1, 1a planta
E-50010 Zaragoza
España
Tel: 34 76 32 00 00
Fax: 34 76 32 29 56
E FR   61063 B24

Euro Info Centre
Federación Asturiana de Empresarios
F.A.D.E. (Antenne de ES218-Llanera)
c/ Dr. Alfredo Martinez, 6 - 2a planta
E-33005 Oviedo
España
Tel: 34 85 23 21 05
Fax: 34 85 24 41 76
A FR   B12

141

FRANCE

Euro Info Centre (EIC)
Chambre de Commerce et d'Industrie de
Lyon
16, Rue de la République
F-69289 Lyon CEDEX 02
France
Tel: 33 72 40 57 46
Fax: 33 78 37 94 00
P   FR   80 31045 271

Euro Info Centre (EIC)
Comité d'Expansion Aquitaine
2, Place de la Bourse
F-33076 Bordeaux CEDEX
France
Tel: 33 56 01 50 10/09 Fax: 33 56 01 50
05
P   FR   473 31059 261

Euro Info Centre (EIC)
Euro Info Centre Région de Lorraine
World Trade Centre - Tour B
2, Rue Augustin Fresnel
F-57070 Metz
France
Tel: 33 87 20 40 90
Fax: 33 87 74 03 15
P   FR   90   241

Euro Info Centre (EIC)
Euro Info Centre Pays de la Loire
Chambres de Commerce et d'Industrie de
Nantes et de Saint Nazaire
Centre des Salorges-BP 718
16, Quai Renaud
F-44027 Nantes CEDEX 04
France
Tel: 33 40 44 60 60
Fax: 33 40 44 60 90
P   FR 87 31035 251

Euro Info Centre (EIC)
Maison du Commerce International de
Strasbourg (MCIS)
4, Quai Kléber
F-67080 Strasbourg CEDEX
France
Tel: 33 88764224
Fax: 33 88764200
P   FR 84   242

Euro Info Centre (EIC)
Chambre Régionale de Commerce et
d'Industrie de Picardie
36, Rue des Otages
F-80037 Amiens CEDEX 01
France
Tel: 33 22 82 80 93
Fax: 33 22 91 29 04
E   FR 300 31065 222

Euro Info Centre (EIC)
Chambre Régionale de Commerce et
d'Industrie de Franche-Comté
Valparc Zac de Valentin
F-25043 Besançon
France
Tel: 33 81 80 41 11
Fax: 33 81 80 70 94
E   FR 553   243

Euro Info Centre (EIC)
Euro Info Centre Toulouse-Blagnac
Chambre Régionale de Commerce et
d'Industrie Midi-Pyrénées
5, Rue Dieudonné Costes -BP 32
F-31701 Toulouse-Blagnac
France
Tel: 33 62 74 20 00
Fax: 33 62 74 20 20
E   FR 233 31067 262

Euro Info Centre (EIC)
Euro Info Centre de Basse-Normandie CRCI
Basse-Normandie
21, Place de la République
F-14052 Caen CEDEX
France
Tel: 33 31 38 31 67
Fax: 33 31 85 76 41
E   FR   225

Euro Info Centre (EIC)
Chambre de Commerce et d'Industrie de
Guyane Française
Place de l'Esplanade - BP 49
F-97321 Cayenne CEDEX
Guyane Française
Tel: 594 299601/299600 Fax: 594
299634/299645
E   FR 461   293

Euro Info Centre (EIC)
CCI de Châlons-sur-Marne Point Europe
Champagne Ardenne
2, Rue de Chastillon - BP 533
F-51010 Châlons-sur-Marne
France
Tel: 33 26 21 11 33
Fax: 33 26 64 16 84
E   FR   31061 221

142

Euro Info Centre Ile de France
Chambre Régionale de Commerce et
d'Industrie Ile-de-France
9 A, rue de la Porte de Buc
F-78021 Versailles
France
Tel: 33 1 39 20 58 54
Fax: 33 1 39 53 78 34
E FR   31020

Euro Info Centre (EIC)
Euro Info Centre Auvergne
Chambre de Commerce et d'Industrie de
Clermont-Ferrand/Issoire
148, Boulevard Lavoisier
F-63037 Clermont-Ferrand
France
Tel: 33 73 43 43 32
Fax: 33 73 43 43 25
E FR 464   272

Euro Info Centre (EIC)
Chambre Régionale de Commerce et
d'Industrie de Bourgogne
68, Rue Chevreul - BP 209
F-21006 Dijon
France
Tel: 33 80 63 52 63
Fax: 33 80 63 52 53
E FR 294 31066 226

Euro Info Centre (EIC)
Chambre de Commerce et d'Industrie de la
Martinique
50, Rue Ernest Deproge BP 478
F-97241 Fort de France CEDEX
La Martinique
Tel: 596 55 28 00 Fax: 596 60 66 68
E FR 424 31075 292

Euro Info Centre (EIC)
Euro Info Centre Nord-Pas de Calais
185, Boulevard de la Liberté BP 2027
F-59013 Lille CEDEX
France
Tel: 33 20 40 02 77
Fax: 33 20 40 04 33
E FR 86 31029 23

Euro Info Centre (EIC)
Chambre Régionale de Commerce et
d'Industrie de Limousin/Poitou/Charentes
Boulevard des Arcades
F-87038 Limoges
France
Tel: 33 55 04 40 25
Fax: 33 55 04 40 40
E FR 386 31076 263

Euro Info Centre (EIC)
Société du Centre Méditerranéen de
Commerce International, (SOMECIN)
2, Rue Henri-Barbusse
F-13241 Marseille CEDEX 01
France
Tel: 33 91 39 33 77
Fax: 33 91 39 33 60
E FR 279   282

Euro Info Centre (EIC)
Comité Liaison Chambres Economiques
Languedoc Roussillon - Région
254, Rue Michel Teule ZAC d'Alco - BP
6076
F-34030 Montpellier CEDEX 1
France
Tel: 33 67 61 81 51
Fax: 33 67 61 81 10
E FR 536   281

Euro Info Centre (EIC)
Chambre Régionale de Commerce et
d'Industrie (Centre)
35, Avenue de Paris
F-45000 Orléans
France
Tel: 33 38 54 58 58
Fax: 33 38 54 09 09
E FR   31070 224

Euro Info Centre (EIC)
Centre Français du Commerce Extérieur
10, Avenue d'Iéna
F-75783 Paris
France
Tel: 33 1 40 73 30 00
Fax: 33 1 40 73 30 48
E FR 260 31018 21

Euro Info Centre (EIC)
Ministère de l'Industrie, des P&T et du
Commerce Extérieur
20, Rue de Ségur
F-75353 Paris 07 SP
France
Tel: 33 1 43 19 28 16
Fax: 33 1 43 19 27 06
E FR   21

Euro Info Centre (EIC)
Euro Info Centre Réseau Point Europe - Ile
de France
Chambre de Commerce et d'Industrie Paris
2, Rue de Viarmes
F-75040 Paris CEDEX 01
France
Tel: 33 1 45 08 35 90
Fax: 33 1 45 08 36 80
E FR 310 31014 21

143

Euro Info Centre (EIC)
Association Poitou-Charentes-Europe
47, Rue du Marché - BP 229
F-86006 Poitiers
France
Tel: 33 49 60 98 00
Fax: 33 49 41 65 72
E FR 368   253

Euro Info Centre (EIC)
Chambre Régionale de Commerce et
d'Industrie de Bretagne
1, Rue du Général Guillaudot
F-35044 Rennes
France
Tel: 33 99 25 41 57
Fax: 33 99 63 35 28
E FR   252

Euro Info Centre (EIC)
Chambre Régionale de Commerce et
d'Industrie de Haute Normandie
9, Rue Robert Schuman - BP 124
F-76002 Rouen CEDEX
France
Tel: 33 35 88 44 42
Fax: 33 35 88 06 52
E FR   223

144

Euro Info Centre (EIC)
Chambre de Commerce et d'Industrie de la
Réunion
5 bis, Rue de Paris - BP 120 F-97463 Saint
Denis CEDEX
Ile de la Réunion
Tel: 262 28 46 00
Fax: 262 28 83 23
E FR   31069 294

Euro Info Centre (EIC)
Chambre de Commerce et d'Industrie
d'Annecy et de Haute-Savoie, (Antenne de
FR251-Lyon)
2, Rue du Lac - BP 2072
F-74011 Annecy CEDEX
France
Tel: 33 50 33 72 05
Fax: 33 50 33 72 39
A FR   271

Euro Info Centre (EIC)
Chambre de Commerce et d'Industrie
d'Avignon et de Vaucluse, (Antenne de
FR268-Marseille)
46, Cours Jean Jaurès - BP 158
F-84008 Avignon
France
Tel: 33 90 82 40 00
Fax: 33 90 85 56 78
A FR   282

Euro Info Centre (EIC)
GREX/Centre de Commerce International
Chambre de Commerce et d'Industrie
(Antenne de FR251-Lyon)
5, Place Robert Schuman
F-38025 Grenoble CEDEX 1
France
Tel: 33 76 28 28 43
Fax: 33 76 28 28 35
A FR   558   31057 271

Euro Info Centre (EIC)
C.C.I. Nice Côte d'Azur, (Antenne de
FR268-Marseille)
20, Boulevard Carabacel BP 259
F-06005 Nice CEDEX 1
France
Tel: 33 93 13 73 05/74 90
Fax: 33 93 13 74 74
A FR   282

Euro Info Centre (EIC)
Chambre de Commerce et d'Industrie de
Pointe-à-Pitre
Complexe WTC de Pointe-à-Pitre/Jarry
F-97122 Baie-Mahaut
La Guadeloupe FWI
Tel: 590 250616
Fax: 590 250606
E FR   291

IRELAND

Euro Info Centre
Irish Trade Board / An Bord Trachtala
Merrion Hall, P.O. Box 2198 Strand Road,
Sandymount
IRL Dublin 4
Ireland
Tel: 353 1 269 50 11
Fax: 353 1 269 58 20
P EN 142 22004 8001

Euro Info Centre
Shannon Free Airport Development
Company
The Granary
Michael Street, IRL Limerick
Ireland
Tel: 353 61 410 777
Fax: 353 61 315 634
P EN   143 22009 8008

Euro Info Centre
67, South Mall
IRL Cork
Ireland
Tel: 353 21 50 90 44
Fax: 353 21 27 13 47
E EN 626   8002

Euro Info Centre
Galway Chamber of Commerce and
Industry
Commerce House, Merchants Road
IRL Galway
Ireland
Tel: 353 91 62 624
Fax: 353 91 61 963
E EN   8008

Euro Info Centre
16, Quay Street
IRL Sligo
Ireland
Tel: 353 71 61 274
Fax: 353 71 60 912
E EN   8009

Euro Info Centre
European Business Information Centre
CTT Office Industrial Estate, Cork Road
IRL Waterford
Ireland
Tel: 353 51 72 639
Fax: 353 51 79 220
E EN   8003

ITALIA

Euro Info Centre
Eurosportello
Azienda Speciale della Camera di
Commercio Industria, Artigianato e
Agricoltura di Milano
Via delle Orsole, 4
I-20123 Milano
Italia
Tel: 39 2 8515 5692/5693
Fax: 39 2 8515 5687
P EN 146 71015 32

Euro Info Centre
Camera di Commercio Industria
Artigianato e Agricoltura di Napoli
Corso Meridionale, 58
I-80143 Napoli
Italia
Tel: 39 81 5536106/284217
Fax: 39 81 287 675
P FR 152 71047 37

Euro Info Centre
Eurosportello per l'Impresa Rete
Artigianato
Via Giovanni Bruni, 17
I-25121 Brescia
Italia
Tel: 39 30 377 47 70/75
Fax: 39 30 377 48 12
P FR 145   32

Euro Info Centre/Eurosportello
Confindustria - Direzione PMI
Viale dell' Astronomia, 30
I-00144 Roma
Italia
Tel: 39 6 5903525
Fax: 39 6 5903291/5910629
P FR   36

Euro Info Centre
Eurosportello Associazione degli Industriali
della Provincia di Bologna
Via San Domenico, 4
I-40124 Bologna
Italia
Tel: 39 51 52 96 11
Fax: 39 51 52 96 13
P EN 71066 34

Euro Info Centre
Eurosportello Camera di Commercio
Industria Artig.e Agricoltura di Ascoli
Piceno
Via L. Mercantini, 23/25
I-63100 Ascoli Piceno
Italia
Tel: 39 736 27 92 55/33
Fax: 39 736 27 92 37
E FR 276 71131 353

Euro Info Centre
Istituto Finanziario Regionale Pugliese
(Finpuglia)
Via Lenin, 2
I-70125 Bari
Italia
Tel: 39 80 5016735/890
Fax: 39 80 5016809
E   EN   71070 391

Euro Info Centre
Eurosportello Camera di Commercio
Industria, Artigianato e Agricoltura
Viale Diaz, 221 c/o Centro Servizi
I-09126 Cagliari
Italia
Tel: 39 70 306877/308977
Fax: 39 70 340328
E EN   3B

145

Euro Info Centre
Eurosportello Camera di Commercio
Industria, Artigianato e Agricoltura
Salita Cappuccini, 2
I-95124 Catania
Italia
Tel: 39 95 71 50 176
Fax: 39 95 71 50 265
E FR   71125 3A

Euro Info Centre
Eurosportello Azienda Speziale Agenzia di
Sviluppo della Camera di Commercio
Corso Marrucino, 168
I-66100 Chieti
Italia
Tel: 39 871 33 12 72
Fax: 39 871 33 12 18
E FR   71133 381

Euro Info Centre
Eurosportello Promofirenze, Artigianato e
Agricoltura di Firenze
Via Faenza, 111
I-50123 Firenze
Italia
Tel: 39 55 28 01 32/03 29
Fax: 39 55 28 33 04
E FR   71130 351

Euro Info Centre
Consorzio Eurosportello Confesercenti
Piazza Piervettori, 8/10
I-50143 Firenze
Italia
Tel: 39 55 27 05 247/218
Fax: 39 55 22 40 96
E FR   245 71129 351

Euro Info Centre
Eurosportello Camera di Commercio di
Genova
Torre World Trade Center ,
Via de Marini, 1
I-16149 Genova
Italia
Tel: 39 10 20 94 252
Fax: 39 10 20 94 297
E FR   313

Euro Info Centre
Camera di Commercio Industria
,Artigianato ed Agricoltura Isernia
Corso Risorgimento, 302
I-86170 Isernia
Italia
Tel: 39 865 41 29 23
Fax: 39 865 23 50 24
E FR   71128 382

Euro Info Centre
Associazione Industriale Lombarda
Via Pantano, 9
I-20122 Milano
Italia
Tel: 392 58370382/411/459
Fax: 392 58370416
E FR 261 71241 32

Euro Info Centre Centro Estero Umbria
Camera di Commercio di Perugia
Via Cacciatori delle Alpi, 40
I-06100 Perugia
Italia
Tel: 39 75 5748206
Fax: 39 75 5728088
E FR   352

Euro Info Centre
Eurosportello Associazione 'Compagnia
delle Opere'
Via Rossi, 2
I-61100 Pesaro
Italia
Tel: 39 721 410088
Fax: 39 721 414174
E EN 402 71119 353

Euro Info Centre
Eurosportello Azienda Speciale 'Sportello
di Informazione e Documentazione per le
Imprese'
Viale L.C. Farini, 14
I-48100 Ravenna
Italia
Tel: 39 544 481311/481418
Fax: 39 544 218731
E FR 585 71124 34

Euro Info Centre
Confederazione Generale dell'Agricoltura
taliana
Corso Vittorio Emanuele, 101
I-00186 Roma
Italia
Tel: 39 6 685 23 78
Fax: 39 6 686 17 26
E EN   36

Euro Info Centre
Confederazione Generale Italiana del
Commercio e del Turismo
Piazza G.Gioacchino Belli, 2
I-00153 Roma
Italia
Tel: 39 6 5898973/5897613
Fax: 39 6 5814984
E FR 334 71067 36

146

Euro Info Centre
Istituto per la Promozione Industriale
Viale M. Pilsudski, 124
I-00197 Roma
Italia
Tel: 39 6 80972210/3/6/9
Fax: 39 6 80972212
E EN   71127 36

Euro Info Centre
Istituto Nazionale per
il Commercio Estero (ICE)
Viale del Lavoro, 8
I-37135 Verona
Italia
Tel: 39 45 8201155
Fax: 39 45 8203233
E FR   36

Euro Info Centre
Eurosportello Unioncamere -
Mondimpresa - Cerved
Piazza Sallustio, 21
I-00187 Roma
Italia
Tel: 39 6 47041/4704206
Fax: 39 6 4704343
E FR   71003 36

Euro Info Centre
Camera di Commercio Industria,
Artigianato e Agricoltura di Torino
Via San Francesco da Paola, 24
I-10123 Torino
Italia
Tel: 39 11 571 63 70
Fax: 39 11 571 65 17
E FR   311

**Euro Info Centre Federazione delle
Associazioni**
Industriali del Piemonte (Federpiemonte)
Corso Stati Uniti, 38
I-10128 Torino
Italia
Tel: 39 11 54 92 46
Fax: 39 11 51 75 204
E FR 209 71068 311

Euro Info Centre
CEFCE - Division CCIAA Servizi srl
Viale Ungheria, 15
I-33100 Udine
Italia
Tel: 39 432 248826
Fax: 39 432 503919
E EN 486   333

**Euro Info Centre/Eurosportello
Veneto**
Centro Estero delle Camere
di Commercio del Veneto
Via G. Pepe, 104
I-30172 Venezia Mestre
Italia
Tel: 39 41 98 82 00
Fax: 39 41 98 95 48
E FR 251 71123 332

Euro Info Centre
Associazione Industriali
della Provincia di Vicenza
Piazza Castello, 3
I-36100 Vicenza
Italia
Tel: 39 444 232580
Fax: 39 444 232686
E FR   339 71072 332

LUXEMBOURG

Euro Info Centre
Chambre de Commerce du Grand-Duché
de Luxembourg FEDIL
Rue Alcide de Gasperi, 7 - BP. 1503
L-2981, Luxembourg
Tel: 352 43 58 53
Fax: 352 43 83 26
P FR 157 13001 6

Euro Info Centre
Chambre des Métiers
du Grand-Duché de Luxembourg
Circuit de la Foire Internationale, 2 -
B.P.1604
L-1016 Luxembourg
Tel: 352 42 67 67 1
Fax: 352 42 67 87
E FR   13002 6

NEDERLAND

Euro Info Centre
Kamer van Koophandel en Fabrieken
voor Amsterdam de Ruyterkade 5
P.O. Box 2852
NL-1000 CW Amsterdam
Nederland
Tel: 31 20 5236 706
Fax: 31 20 5236 732
P EN 432 12210

147

Euro Info Centre
EG-Adviescentrum Zuid-Nederland
Kamer van Koophandel / INDUMA / BOM
P.O. Box 70060 Pettelaarpark, 10
NL-5201 DZ s-Hertogenbosch
Nederland
Tel: 31 73 87 44 20
Fax: 31 73 12 32 10
P EN 108 12008 451

Euro Info Centre Nederland
EVD & Bureau EG-Liaison
Bezuidenhoutseweg, 151
den Haag NL-2594
Nederland
Tel: 31 70 379 88 11
Fax: 31 70 379 78 78
E EN 4

Euro Info Centre Oost Nederland
Hengelosestraat, 585 P.O. Box 5508
NL-7500 GM Enschede
Nederland
Tel: 31 53 849 890
Fax: 31 53 849 897
E EN 12120 423

Euro Info Centre Noord-Nederland
Damsport, 1 - P.O. Box 424
NL-9700 AK Groningen
Nederland
Tel: 31 50 21 44 70
Fax: 31 50 21 44 00
E EN 411

Euro Info Centre
Europees Advies-en Informatiecentrum
Oost-Nederland
Kerkenbos 10-02 - Postbus 38326
NL-6503 AH Nijmegen
Nederland
Tel: 31 80 78 00 75
Fax: 31 80 77 70 29
E EN 12018 424

Euro Info Centre
Midden-Nederland
St. Jacobsstraat, 16 - P.O. Box 48
NL-3500 AA
Utrecht
Nederland
Tel: 31 30 36 32 81
Fax: 31 30 36 85 41
E EN 471

148

ÖSTERREICH

Euro Info Centre
Wirtschaftkammer Österreich
Wiedner Hauptstrasse, 63 Postfach 150
A-1045 Wien
Österreich
Tel: 43 1 501054191
Fax: 43 1 50206297
X EN 1 90382

Euro Info Centre
Industriellenvereinigung
Schwarzenberplatz 4 - Postfach 61
A-1030 Wien
Österreich
Tel: 43 1 711352405
Fax: 43 1 711352914
X EN

Wiener Wirtschaftsförderungsfonds
Friedrich Schmidt Platz, 3
A-1082 Wien
Österreich
Tel: 43 1 400086775
Fax: 43 1 40007070
X EN

Euro Info Centre
Wirtschaftskammer Salzburg
Julius- Raab-Platz 1
A-5020 Salzburg
Österreich
Tel: 43 662 8888 400
Fax: 43 662 8888 582
X EN

Euro Info Centre
Wirtschaftskammer Oberösterreich
Hessenplatz 3-Postfach 253
A-4010 Linz
Österreich
Tel: 43 732 7800279
Fax: 43 732 7800520
X EN

Euro Info Centre
Wirtschaftskammer Steiermark
Körblergasse 111-113-Postfach 1038
A-8021 Graz
Österreich
Tel: 43 316 601600
Fax: 43 316 601535
X EN

Euro Info Centre
Wirtschaftskammer Tirol
Meinhardstraße 12-14
A-6021 Innsbrück
Österreich
Tel: 43 512 531 0293
Fax: 43 512 531 0275
X EN

PORTUGAL

Euro Info Centre
Eurogabinete/Exponor
Associaçao Industrial Portuense
Leça da Palmeira
P-4450 Matosinhos (Porto)
Portugal
Tel: 351 2 9961 529
Fax: 351 2 9957 017
P FR 174 62001 C11

Euro Info Centre
Eurogabinete Banco de Fomento e Exterior
Av. Casal Ribeiro, 59
P-1000 Lisboa
Portugal
Tel: 351 1 356 01 44
Fax: 351 1 343 17 28
P FR 272 62002 C13

Euro Info Centre
Eurogabinete Associaçao Industrial do
Distrito de Aveiro
Av. Dr. Lourenço Peixinho, 146 - 5¤ A
P-3800 Aveiro
Portugal
Tel: 351 34 20 095/2
Fax: 351 34 24 093
E FR 62016 C12

Euro Info Centre
Eurogabinete Comissao
de Coordenacao da Regiao Centro
Rua Luis de Camoes, 150
P-3000 Coimbra
Portugal
Tel: 351 39 701475/701562
Fax: 351 39 405688
E FR C12

Euro Info Centre
Eurogabinete PME Instituto de Apoio as
Pequenas e Medias Empresas e ao
Investimento
Rua de Valasco, 19
P-7000 Evora
Portugal
Tel: 351 66 218 75/6
Fax: 351 66 297 81
E FR C14

Euro Info Centre
Eurogabinete Commissao de Coordenaçao
da Regiao do Algarve
Praça da Liberdade, 2
P-8000 Faro
Portugal
Tel: 351 89 80 27 09
Fax: 351 89 80 66 87
E FR 62107 C15

Euro Info Centre
Eurogabinete Associaçao Comercial e
Industrial do Funchal/C.C.I. da Madeira
Avenida Arriaga, 41
P-9000 Funchal (Madeira)
Portugal
Tel: 351 91 23 01 37/8/9
Fax: 351 91 22 20 05
E FR 62204 C3

Euro Info Centre
Eurogabinete Associaçao Industrial
Portuguesa Date - Apoio Tecnico as
Empresas
Praça das Industrias
P-1399 Lisboa
Portugal
Tel: 351 1 363 94 58
Fax: 351 1 364 67 86
E FR 309 62018 C13

Euro Info Centre
Eurogabinete Caixa Geral de Depositos
Apartado 1795
P-1017 Lisboa Cedex
Portugal
Tel: 351 1 790 50 47
Fax: 351 1 790 50 97
E FR 62017 C13

149

Euro Info Centre
Eurogabinete da Camara do Comercio
e Industria dos Açores
Rua Ernesto do Canto, 13
P-9500 Ponta Delgada (Açores)
Portugal
Tel: 351 96 27073/23235
Fax: 351 96 27073/24268
E FR   C2

**Associacao Comercial e Industrial de
Coimbra   (A.C.I.C.)**
(Satellite of PT504-Coimbra)
Parque de Feiras e Exposiçoes Alto da
Relvinha
P-3020 Coimbra
Portugal
Tel: 351 39 492402
Fax: 351 39 492064
A EN   C12

Euro Info Centre
Camara do Comercio de Angra do
Heroismo, (Antenne de PT510-Ponta
Delgada)
Rua da Palha, 32/34
P-9700 Angra do Heroismo
Portugal
Tel: 351 95 234 70
Fax: 351 95 271 31
A FR   C2

SUOMI-FINLAND

Euro Info Centre
The Finnish Foreign Trade Association
Arkadiankatu, 2 - P.O. Box 908
SF-00101 Helsinki
Suomi-Finland
Tel: 358 0 1992
Fax: 358 0 6940028
X EN   373 90321

Euro Info Centre
MTI, Regional Business
Service Office in Oulu
Asemakatu, 37
SF-90100 Oulu
Suomi-Finland
Tel 358 81 374 699
Fax 358 81 379 946

Euro Info Centre
Lahti Chamber of Commerce and South
Karelia Chamber of Commerce
Niemenkatu, 73 Neopoli
SF-15210 Lahti
Suomi-Finland
Tel 358 18 811 4211
Fax 358 18 751 1524

Euro Info Center
Ostrobothnia Chamber of Commerce,
Vaasa Office
Raastuvankatu, 20
SF-65100 Vaasa
Suomi-Finland
Tel 358 61 317 2279
Fax 358 61 312 6656

Euro Info Center
Kuopio Chamber of Commerce
Kasarmikatu, 2
SF-70110 Kuopio
Suomi-Finland
Tel 358 71 282 0291
Fax 358 71 282 3304

Euro Info Center
MTI Regional Business Service in Turku
Puolalankatu, 1
SF-20100 Turku
Suomi-Finland
Tel 358 921 2510 051
Fax 358 921 2310 667

Euro Info Center
Technology Development Centre, TEKES
Malminkatu, 34, P.O. Box 69
SF-00101 Helsinki
Suomi-Finland
Tel 358 0 693 691
Fax 358 0 694 9196

SVERIGE

Euro Info Centre
Nutek - Swedish National Board for
Industrial and Technical Development
Liljeholmsvägen, 32
S-117 86 Stockholm
Sverige
Tel: 46 8 681 91 00/94 65
Fax: 46 8 744 40 45
X EN   90301

EICC-SYD Ltd
IDEON Science Park
P A Hanssons väg 41
Malmö
Sverige
Tel 46 40 32 10 32
Fax 46 40 32 10 33

Euro Info Center
Europa Institutet i Västeras
Stora Gatan, 38
S-722 12 Västeras
Sverige
Tel 46 021 10 65 35
Fax 46 021 10 65 39

Euro Info Center
The Federation of Private Enterprises
Ölandsgatan, 6, P.O. Box 1958
S-791 19 Falun
Sverige
Tel 46 23 580 60
Fax 46 23 580 65

Euro Info Center
Östsvenska EuropaKontoret
Nya Radstugugatan, 3
S-602 24 Norrköping
Sverige
Tel 46 11 12 11 19
Fax 46 11 13 77 19

Euro Info Center
ALMI Företagspartner Kronoberg AB
P.O. Box 1501
S-35115 Växjö
Sverige
Tel 46 470 230 40
Fax 46 480 279 37

Euro Info Center
Trade & Industryy Development Agency
Göteborg, TID
Norra Hamngatan, 14
S-411 14 Göteborg
Sverige
Tel 46 31 61 24 07
Fax 46 31 61 24 01

Euro Info Center
ALMI Företagspartner Stockholm AB
Stockholm Mark och Lokaliseringbolag AB
Swedish Trade Council
P.O. Box 23 135
S-104 35 Stockholm
Sverige
Tel 46 8 15 14 00
Fax 46 8 33 01 04

Euro Info Center
Jönköping County Administration
EuropaCenter Jönköpings County
Elmiavägen
S-554 54 Jönköping
Sverige
Tel 46 36 12 70 01
Fax 46 36 12 95 79

UNITED KINGDOM

Euro Info Centre Limited
Host: Scottish Enterprise, Atrium Court
21, Bothwell Street
G2 6NL Glasgow
United Kingdom
Tel: 44 141 221 09 99
Fax: 44 141 221 65 39
P EN 134   7A

Euro Info Centre
Birmingham Chamber of Industry and
Commerce
75, Harborne Road P.O. Box 360
B15 3DH Birmingham
United Kingdom
Tel: 44 121 454 61 71
Fax: 44 121 455 86 70
P EN   77

Euro Info Centre
Northern Development Company
Great North House
Sandyford Road
NE1 8ND Newcastle Upon Tyne
United Kingdom
Tel: 44 191 261 0026/5131
Fax: 44 191 222 1779
P EN 664   71

**Euro Info Centre Local Enterprise
Development Unit**
(L.E.D.U.) Ledu House Upper Galwally
BT8 4TB Belfast
United Kingdom
Tel: 44 1232 49 10 31
Fax: 44 1232 69 14 32
E EN   7B

Euro Info Centre
Sussex Chamber of Commerce and
Industry
169, Church Road
BN3 2AS Hove
United Kingdom
Tel: 44 1273 326 282
Fax: 44 1273 207 965
E EN   278 21207 75

151

Euro Info Centre
Bristol Chamber of Commerce and Industry
16, Clifton Park
BS8 3BY Bristol
United Kingdom
Tel: 44 117 973 73 73
Fax: 44 117 974 53 65
E EN 116 76

Euro Info Centre Southwest
Exeter Enterprises
Reed Hall University of Exeter
EX4 4QR Exeter
United Kingdom
Tel: 44 1392 21 40 85
Fax: 44 1392 26 43 75
E EN 290 76

Euro Info Centre
European Business Services
Business Information Source
20, Bridge Street
IV1 1QR Inverness
United Kingdom
Tel: 44 1463 715400
Fax: 44 1463 715600
E EN 21067 7A

Euro Info Centre
Humberside European Business nformation
Centre (HEBIC)
(Satellite of UK571-Bradford)
University of Hull Brynmor Jones Library
HU6 7RX Hull
United Kingdom
Tel: 44 1482 46 59 40/35
Fax: 44 1482 46 64 88
A EN 72

Euro Info Centre
Leicester European Information Centre
The Business Centre
10, York Road
LE1 5TS Leicester
United Kingdom
Tel: 44 116 255 99 44
Fax: 44 116 255 34 70
E EN 73

Euro Info Centre North West
Liverpool Central Libraries
William Brown Street
L3 8EW Liverpool
United Kingdom
Tel: 44 151 298 19 28
Fax: 44 151 207 13 42
E EN 21127 78

Euro Info Centre
Kent European Information Centre
Springfield
ME14 2LL Maidstone Kent
United Kingdom
Tel: 44 1622 69 41 09
Fax: 44 1622 69 14 18
E EN 442 75

Euro Info Centre
Manchester Euro Info Centre
Business Link Manchester Churchgate
House
56 Oxford Street
M60 7BL Manchester
United Kingdom
Tel: 44 161 237 4190/4020
Fax: 44 161 236 9945
E EN 78

Euro Info Centre
Norfolk and Waveney Chamber of
Commerce and Industry
112, Barrack Street
NR3 1UB Norwich
United Kingdom
Tel: 44 1603 62 59 77
Fax: 44 1603 63 30 32
E EN 129 21063 74

Euro Info Centre
Nottingham Chamber of Commerce
and Industry
309, Haydn Road
NG5 1DG Nottingham
United Kingdom
Tel: 44 115 962 46 24
Fax: 44 115 985 66 12
E EN 114 21010 73

Euro Info Centre
Wales Euro Info Centre
UWCC Guest Building
P.O. Box 430
CF1 3XT Cardiff
United Kingdom
Tel: 44 1222 22 95 25
Fax: 44 1222 22 97 40
E EN 349 79

Euro Info Centre
Thames Valley, Commerce House
2 - 6 Bath Road
SL1 3SB Slough
United Kingdom
Tel: 44 1753 577 877
Fax: 44 1753 524 644
E EN 75

152

Euro Info Centre
Shropshire and Staffordshire
Euro Info CentreTrevithick House
Stafford Park 4
TF3 3BA Telford
United Kingdom
Tel: 44 1952 208 213/228
Fax: 44 1952 208 208
E EN   77

Euro Info Centre
Southern Area
Civic Centre
SO14 7LW Southampton
United Kingdom
Tel: 44 1703 832866
Fax: 44 1703 231714
E EN   21064   75

Euro Info Centre
West Yorkshire European Business,
Information Centre (WYEBIC)
4 Manchester Road Mercury House - 2nd
Floor
BD5 0QL Bradford
United Kingdom
Tel: 44 1274 754262
Fax: 44 1274 393226
E EN   21126   72

Euro Info Centre
Staffordshire European Business Centre
Business Innovation Centre (Satellite of
UK569-Telford)
Staffordshire Technology Park Beaconside
ST18 0AR Stafford
United Kingdom
Tel: 44 1785 222300/59528
Fax: 44 1785 53207
A EN   21033 77

Euro Info Centre
London Chamber of Commerce and
Industry
33, Queen Street
EC4R 1AP London
United Kingdom
Tel: 44 171 489 19 92
Fax: 44 171 489 03 91
E EN 132   75

BULGARIA

Euro Info Centre
Union for Private Economic Enterprise
54, Dr G.M. Dimitrov Blvd Business Centre
- 4th Floor
BG-1125 Sofia
Bulgaria
Tel: 359 2 73 84 48
Fax: 359 2 73 04 35
C EN

CHYPRE

Euro Info Centre
Cyprus Correspondence Centre
to the Euro Info Centre Network
Cyprus Chamber of Commerce and
Industry
P.O. BOX 1455 - 38, Grivas Dhigenis
Avenue
Nicosia
Chypre
Tel: 357 2 44 95 00
Fax: 357 2 36 10 44
C EN 26 96002

ICELAND

Euro Info Centre
Trade Council of Iceland
Hallveigarstig, 1- POB 1000
IS-128 Reykjavik
Iceland
Tel: 354 5517272
Fax: 354 5517222
X EN

JORDAN

Euro Info Centre
Jordan Export Development and
Commercial Centers Corporation (JEDCO)
Shmeisani i Akrama Al-Karashi
P.O.BOX 7704
JO-11118 Amman
Jordan
Tel: 962 6 603507
Fax: 962 6 684568
C EN

153

LITHUANIA

Euro Info Centre
Vilniaus Narutis/Lithuanian
Association of CCI
Pilies Street, 24
LT-2600 Vilnius
Lithuania
Tel: 3702 223613/220373
Fax: 3702 220580
C EN

MALTA

Euro Info Centre
Malta Export Trade Corporation (METCO)
P.O.BOX 08
MT SGN 01 San Gwann
Malta
Tel: 356 497 560
Fax: 356 496 687
C EN

MAROC

Euro Info Centre
Euro Info Maroc
Centre Européen pour l'Information des
Entreprises au Maroc
71b, Av. Forces Armées Royales
Casablanca
Maroc
Tel: 212 2 44 74 10/11/12
Fax: 212 2 44 72 62
C FR

NORWAY

Euro Info Centre
EC Information Office for Business and
Industry
Drammensveien, 40
N-0243 Oslo
Norway
Tel: 47 22 92 65 70
Fax: 47 22 43 16 40
X EN

Euro Info Center
VINN-North Norwegian Institute of
Technology and Innovati
Teknologiveien, 10, P.O. Box 253
N-8501 Narvik
Norway
Tel 47 76 92 22 22
Fax 47 76 94 72 60

Euro Info Center
Vestlandforsking
P.O. Box 163
N-5890 Sogndal
Norway
Tel 47 57 67 61 50
Fax 47 57 67 61 90

Euro Info Center
Agder Research Foundation
Tordenskjolsgate, 65
P.O. Box 2074, Posebyen
N-4602 Kristiansand
Norway
Tel 47 38 02 50 55
Fax 47 38 02 50 90

Euro Info Center
Sor-Trondelag Naeringsservice
Sluppenvn 12E
P.O. Box 6018
N-7003 Trondheim
Norway
Tel 47 73 96 22 30
Fax 47 73 96 22 18

POLOGNE

Euro Info Centre
the Cooperation Fund
Ul. Zurawia 6/12
PL-00-503 Warszawa
Pologne
Tel: 48 2 625 13 19
Fax: 48 2 625 12 90
C EN

RÉPUBLIQUE TCHÈQUE

Euro Info Center
Korespondencni Stredisko
NIS - National Information Center
Havelkova 22
CZ-130 00 Praha 3
République Tchèque
Tel: 42 2 24 23 11 14
Fax: 42 2 24 23 11 14
C EN 428

154

SLOVAQUIE

Euro Info Centrum
National Agency for Development of SMEs
Nevadzova, 5
SK-821 01 Bratislava
Slovaquie
Tel: 42 7 237563/231873
Fax: 42 75222434
C EN

SLOVÉNIE

Euro Info Centre
Small Business Development Centre
Kotnikova 5/ii
SLO-61000 Ljubljana
Slovénie
Tel: 386 61 1713230
Fax: 386 61 1324210
C EN

SUISSE

Euro Info Centre
OSEC - Euro Center Schweiz
Euro Centre Suisse- Euro Centro Svizzera
Stampfenbachstrasse, 85
CH-8035 Zurich
Suisse
Tel: 41 1 365 54 54
Fax: 41 1 365 54 11
C EN   90361

TUNISIE

Euro Info Centre
Correspondance de Tunisie
Agence de Promotion de l'Industrie (API)
63, rue de Syrie
Tunis-Belvedère T-1002
Tunisie
Tel: 216 1 782 144
Fax: 216 1 782 482
C FR

TURQUIE

Euro Info Center
(SMIDO) Small and Medium Industry
Development Organization
M.K.E.K. Binasi, Kat: 9
Tandogan-Ankara
Turquie
Tel: 90 312 212 23 82
Fax: 90 312 223 87 69
C EN 477 90521

155

ARIES

> **Genaue Bezeichnung**

Interaktives Informations- und Kommunikationsnetz für
Sozialwirtschaft in Europa.

> **Zielgruppe**

Akteure der Sozialwirtschaft:
Genossenschaften, Krankenkassen, Verbände, europäische Stiftungen.

> **Zieles**

- Anregung des Informationsaustausches von Akteuren der
  Sozialwirtschaft;
- Antwort auf besondere Informationsbedürfnisse.

> **Betreuung des Netzes und Kommunikationstechnik**

Rund fünfzehn besondere Anzeigetafel zu diversen Themen, die
Akteure der Sozialwirtschaft betreffen können, werden von Spezialisten
für europäische Informationen aufgefüllt, die auf dem GeoNet-Netz
tätig sind.

> **Angebotene Informationen**   157

Alle Gemeinschaftsinformationen bezüglich der Sozialwirtschaft, der
"Humanressourcen"-Programme, die zweite Reform der Strukturfonds,
die EG-Ausschreibungen, die die Akeure in diesem Sektor interessieren
könnten usw.

> **Adresse**

ARIES
59 Rue Guillaume Tell
B-1060 Brüssel
Tel. +32/2/537 52 81
Fax +32/2/537 09 17

ARIES

> **Full title**

Network of interactive information and communication on the social economy in Europe.

> **Target public**

Social economic actors:
cooperatives, mutual insurance systems, associations, European foundations.

> **Objectives**

- to stimulate information exchanges among the social economic actors;
- to respond to their specific information needs.

> **Network animation and methods of communication**

Some fifteen specific bulletin boards on various topics of interest to social economic actors are kept up-to-date by specialists in European information operating on the GeoNet network.

> **Information which they have available**

All information regarding, for example, social economics, the "Human Resources" programmes, the second reform of the structural funds, EC calls for tender of interest to actors in the sector, etc.

> **Address**

ARIES
59 Rue Guillaume Tell
B - 1060 Brussels
Tel.: (32.2) 537.52.81
Fax.: (32.2) 537.09.17

ARIES

> **Intitulé exact**

Réseau d'Information et de Communication interactif
de l'économie sociale en Europe.

> **Public cible**

Acteurs de l'économie sociale:
coopératives, mutualités, associations, fondations européennes.

> **Objectifs**

- Susciter des échanges d'information entre les acteurs
  de l'économie sociale;
- répondre à leurs besoins d'informations spécifiques.

> **Animation du réseau et techniques de communication**

Une quinzaine de tableaux d'affichage spécifiques sur des thèmes
divers, qui peuvent intéresser les acteurs de l'économie sociale, sont
alimentés par des spécialistes de l'information européenne opérant sur
le réseau GeoNet.

> **Informations offertes**

159

Toutes informations communautaires concernant, par exemple,
l'économie sociale, les programmes "Ressources humaines", la
deuxième réforme des fonds structurels, les appels d'offres CE
pouvant intéresser les acteurs de ce secteur, etc.

> **Adresse**

ARIES
59 Rue Guillaume Tell
B-1060 Bruxelles
Tél.: +32/2/537.52.81
Fax: +32/2/537.09.17

COLINE

➤ **Genaue Bezeichnung**

Consumer Line

➤ **Tätigkeitsbereich**

Antwort auf Fragen des Verbraucherschutzes, damit die Verbraucher ihre Rechte in ihrem eigenen Land sowie in einem anderen Land der Gemeinschaft geltend machen können.

➤ **Zielgruppe**

Alle Verbraucher und sonstigen Akteure des Wirtschaftslebens (Verbraucherschutzverbände, Juristen ...).

➤ **Wirkungskreis**

Transeuropäisches Netz mit derzeit fünf Zentren; die Erweiterung auf zehn Zentren wird derzeit geprüft.

➤ **Aktionen**

- Datenbanken, die das gesamte Verbraucherschutzrecht sowie die nationalen Vorschriften und EG-Richtlinien enthalten. Sie wird fortlaufend aktualisiert und berücksichtigt auch die Rechtsprechung.
- Gestaltung der gemeinsamen Initiativen, wobei jedem Zentrum die freie Wahl bezüglich der wirksamsten Verbreitungsweisen auf lokaler Ebene überlassen wird.

161

➤ **Betreuung des Netzes und Kommunikationstechnik**

Kommunikationsnetz verschiedener Zentren.
Praktische Info-Hefte sind sofort je nach gestellter Frage erhältlich.

➤ Europäische Kommission
S.P.C.
SPC/2 J 70 07/18
Mercedes DE SOLA
200 Rue de la Loi
B - 1049 Brüssel
Tel. (32.2) 295 62 72 / 295 77 74

COLINE

> **Full title**

Consumer Line

> **Field of activity**

Answer questions raised in the field of consumer rights, so that
consumers can defend their rights in their own country as well as in
other countries of the Community.

> **Target public**

All consumers and the other actors in economic life (consumer
organisations, lawyers...).

> **Community coverage**

Trans-European network currently comprised of five centres;
a possible enlargement to ten centres is being considered.

> **Actions**

- Databases covering the whole subject of consumer rights, including
  national regulations as well as Community Directives. Updating is
  continuous and also takes account of judicial precedent.
- Conceptualisation of common initiatives leaving to each centre
  the choice as to the most efficient methods of dissemination
  at the local level.

> **Network animation and methods of communication**

Communication network between the different centres.
Practical index cards available immediately specific to
the question raised.

> European Commission
  S.P.C.
  SPC/2 J 70 07/18
  Mercedes DE SOLA
  200 Rue de la Loi
  B - 1049 Brussels
  Tel.: (32.2) 295.62.72 / 295.77.74

COLINE

➤ **Intitulé exact**

Consumer Line

➤ **Domaine d'activité**

Réponse aux questions posées dans le domaine du droit de la consommation, afin que les consommateurs puissent faire valoir leurs droits dans leur propre pays comme dans un autre pays de la Communauté.

➤ **Public cible**

Tous les consommateurs et les autres acteurs de la vie économique (organisations de consommateurs, juristes...).

➤ **Rayonnement communautaire**

Réseau transeuropéen composé actuellement de cinq centres; l'extension à dix centres est à l'étude.

➤ **Actions**

- Bases de données reprenant l'ensemble du droit de la consommation, comprenant aussi bien les règles nationales que les directives communautaires.
  La mise à jour est continue et tient compte aussi de la jurisprudence.
- Conceptualisation des initiatives communes en laissant à chaque centre le choix des modes de diffusion les plus efficaces au plan local.

➤ **Animation du réseau et techniques de communication**

Réseau de communication entre les différents centres.
Fiches pratiques disponibles immédiatement en fonction
de la question posée.

➤ Commission européenne
S.P.C.
SPC/2 J 70 07/18
Mercedes DE SOLA
200 Rue de la Loi
B - 1049 Bruxelles
tél: (32.2) 295.62.72 / 295.77.74

163

Verbraucherzentrale Nordrhëin-Westfalen
Mintropstraße 27
D-4000 DÜSSELDORF
Tel.: +49/211/38.09.139
M. Klaus Schmidbauer

Institut Catalá del Consum
Gran Vía Carles III, 105, lletera I
E-08028 BARCELONA
Tel.: +34/3/330.98.12
Mme Isabel Segura

Centre Régional da la Consommation
du Nord Pays de Calais
47 bis rue Barthélémy Delespaul
F-59000 LILLE
Fax : +33/20/54.44.44
Mme Martine Demeyere

Union Luxembourgeoise
des Consommateurs
55 rue des Bruyères
L-1274 HOWALD
LUXEMBOURG
Tel.: +352/49.60.22
M. Elmer Krings

164

Instituto do Consumidor
Praça Duque de Saldanha 31, 3¤
P-1000 LISBOA
Tel.: +351/1/54.43.83
Mme Cristina Portugal

GRENZÜBERGREIFENDE INFORMATIONS- UND BERATUNGSZENTREN FÜR VERBRAUCHER

➤ **Akronym**

CTIC

➤ **Genaue Bezeichnung**

Siehe unten; umgangssprachlich: "Euro-Verbraucherdesks".

➤ **Tätigkeitsbereich**

Alle Fragen bezüglich grenzübergreifender Verbrauchstransaktionen:
Marktanalyse auf beiden Seiten der Grenze, Beratung und
Unterstützung in bezug auf die private Einfuhr von Produkten für den
persönlichen Verbrauch und im Streitfall, Beziehungen zu staatlichen,
nationalen und regionalen Behörden usw.

➤ **Zielgruppe**

Der Verbraucher im allgemeinen, in der Region oder auf der Durchreise,
Ausgangspunkt für die Arbeit der CTIC ist der "Mikro-Binnenmarkt" der
Grenzregionen.

➤ **Wirkungskreis**

Ein Netz mit zehn Zentren, vier davon verfügen über Außenstellen (acht
insgesamt), aufgrund lokaler/regionaler Initiative gegründet;
die Ausweitung des Netzes auf die neuen Mitgliedstaaten wird derzeit
geprüft.

➤ **Aktionen**

Alle Arten der Information, Beratung und Unterstützung: persönlicher
und telefonischer Gesprächsdienst, Untersuchungen,
Veröffentlichungen, Beziehung zu den Medien usw.

➤ **Betreuung des Netzes und Kommunikationstechnik**

Selbstverwaltung: Die schon bestehenden Verbraucherschutzverbände
in den Grenzregionen haben die CTIC gegründet; folglich stellen sie
kein Netz dar, das von der Kommission verwaltet wird.
Die GD XXIV spielt in zweifacher Hinsicht eine Rolle: für die
Koordination und Förderung der Aktivitäten, z. B. durch die
Veranstaltung einer jährlichen Sitzung mit allen CTIC durch die
Bereitstellung von Seiten in ihrem Mitteilungsblatt "Info-C"
für einen regelmäßigen Informationsaustausch.

➤ Europäische Kommission
Generaldirektion XXIV
XXIV/5
Kenneth I. ROBERTS
200, Rue de la Loi
B-1049 Brüssel
Tel. (32.2) 295 56 57/295 86 33
Fax: (32.2) 296 32 79

TRANS-BORDER INFORMATION AND CONSULTING CENTRES FOR CONSUMERS

> **Acronym**

CTIC

> **Full title**

See above. Commonly referred to as consumer "euroguichets."

> **Field of Activity**

All questions relating to cross-border consumer transactions: analyses of markets on both sides of the border, consulting and assistance for private import of products for personal consumption and, in the event of a litigation, in relations with national and regional public authorities, etc.

> **Target public**

Consumers in general, in the region or travelling through it, the starting point for the work of CTICs being the "mini internal market" character of cross-border regions.

> **Community coverage**

Network composed of ten centres, four of which have agencies (eight in all) established on the initiative of local/regional actors; enlargement of the network, particularly to include the new Member States, is being examined.

> **Actions**

All kinds of information, consulting and assistance: physical and phone assistance, publications, media relations, etc.

> **Network animation and methods of communication**

Self-animated: Consumer organizations already present in the cross-border regions created the TICCs. Consequently, this is not a Commission-lead network. DG XXIV plays a double role in coordinating and stimulating the development of activities, for example, by organizing an annual meeting of all TICCs and by opening the pages of its "Info-C" bulletin for the regular exchange of information.

> European Commission
Directorate-General XXIV
XXIV/5
Kenneth I. ROBERTS
200, rue de la Loi
B - 1049 Brussels
Tel.: (32.2) 295.56.57 / 295.86.33
Fax.: (32.2) 296.32.79

CENTRES TRANSFRONTALIERS D'INFORMATION ET DE CONSEIL DES CONSOMMATEURS

➤ **Acronyme**

CTIC

➤ **Intitulé exact**

Voir ci-dessus; en langage courant : "Euroguichets consommateurs".

➤ **Domaine d'activité**

Toutes questions relatives aux transactions transfrontalières de consommation :
analyse des marchés des deux côtés de la frontière, conseil et assistance en relation avec l'importation privée de produits pour consommation personnelle et en cas de litiges, relations avec les autorités publiques, nationales et régionales, etc.

➤ **Public cible**

Consommateurs en général, dans la région ou de passage, le point de départ du travail des CTIC étant le caractère de "marché unique en minuscule" des régions frontalières.

➤ **Rayonnement communautaire**

Réseau composé de dix centres, dont quatre disposent d'antennes (huit au total), établis sur initiative locale/régionale; l'extension du réseau, notamment vers les nouveaux pays membres, est à l'étude.

➤ **Actions**

Toute sorte d'information, de conseils et d'assistance : permanences physiques et téléphoniques, enquêtes, publications, relations avec les médias, etc.

➤ **Animation du réseau et techniques de communication**

➤ Auto-animation : Les organisations de consommateurs déjà présentes dans les régions transfrontalières ont créé les CTIC; par conséquent, ceux-ci ne représentent pas un réseau dirigé par la Commission.
La DG XXIV joue un double rôle de coordination et de stimulation du développement des activités, par ex. en organisant une réunion annuelle avec tous les CTIC et en leur ouvrant les pages de son bulletin "Info-C" pour un échange d'informations régulier.

➤ Commission européenne
Direction générale XXIV
XXIV/5
Kenneth I. ROBERTS
200, rue de la Loi
B-1049 Bruxelles
Tél.:(32.2) 295.56.57/295.86.33
Fax: (32.2) 296.32.79

AACHEN (D/B/NL)

Eurokon Verbraucherberatung
Bendelstrasse 37
D - 520620 AACHEN
Tel: 49-241-40.45.26

> Antenne St-Vith (B)
> Mühlenbachstrasse 12
> B - 4780 ST- VITH
> Tel: 32-80-22.97.00

> Antenne Eupen (B)
> Neustrasse 44
> B - 4700 EUPEN
> Tel: 32-87-55.55.40

> Antenne Heerlen-Hoensbroek (NL)
> Hoofdstraat 11
> NL - 6431 LA HOENSBROEK
> Tel: 31-45-22.61.61

FLENSBURG (D/DK)

**EUROCON, Euro-
Verbraucher/Forbruger-Information**
Rathausstrasse 20
D - 24937 FLENSBURG
Tel: 49-461-28705

KEHL (D/F)

**Euro-Info
Consommateurs/Verbraucher**
Kinzigstrasse 5
D - 77694 KEHL
Tel: 49-7851-48.28.62

GRONAU (D/NL)

EUREGIO
Grenzüberschreitende
Verbraucherberatung
Enschederstrasse 362
D - 48599 GRONAU
Tel: 49-2562-70.20

BARCELONA (E)

**Agencia Europea de Información
sobre el Consumo**
Gran Via Carles III, 105 lletra 1
E - 08028 BARCELONA
Tel: 34-3-33.09.812

> Antenne Montpellier (F)
> R. Marceau, 18 BP 2123
> F - 34000 MONTPELLIER

BILBAO (E)

**Agencia Europea de Información al
Consumidor**
Calle Simón Bolivar 27 - 1¤, Dpto. 12
E - 48000 BILBAO
Tel: 34-45-18.99.97

LILLE (F)

**Agence Européenne d'Information sur
la Consommation**
79, rue Gantois
F - 59000 LILLE
Tel: 33-20.21.92.50

> Antenne Mons (B)
> Grand-Place 22 - Jardin du Mayer
> B - 7000 MONS
> Tél: 32-65-84.07.38

> Antenne Kortrijk (B)
> Wijngaardstraat 48
> B - 8500 KORTRIJK
> Tél: 32-56-23.37.03

TORINO (I)

**Agenzia Europea d'Informazione dei
Consumatori**
Via XX Settembre 74
I - 10121 TORINO
Tel: 39-11-4.436.23.19

LUXEMBOURG (L)

Euroguichet Consommateur
rue des Bruyères 55
L - 1274 HOWALD
Tel: 352-49.60.22

GUIMARÃES (P)

**Agência Europeia de Informação sobre
Consumo**
R. Capitão Alfredo Guimarães 1
P - 4800 GUIMARÃES
Tel: 351-53-51.37.00

> Antenne Pontevedra (E)
> Jofre de Tenorio 1
> (Pza. de C. de Arenal, Edf. Fontoira)
> E - 36002 PONTEVEDRA
> Tel: 34-86-86.22.33

> Antenne Santiago de Compostela (E)
> Avda. de A. Coruña, 6 baixo
> E - 15706 SANTIAGO DE COMPOSTELA
> Tel: 34-81-54.55.64

TEAM EUROPE

➤ **Tätigkeitsbereich**

Unterrichtung der breiten Öffentlichkeit über die Verwirklichung des Binnenmarktes und seine Auswirkungen sowie alle Aspekte der Gemeinschaftspolitik.

➤ **Zielgruppe**

Breite Öffentlichkeit

➤ **Wirkungskreis**

- Eine Koordinationsstelle in Brüssel
- Ein Koordinator in jeder Vertretung der Kommission in den Mitgliedstaaten
- Netz mit 760 Referenten in 19 Ländern Europas.

➤ **Aktionen**

Über 2.500 Konferenzen werden jährlich von 760 Referenten für ein Publikum von rund 250.000 Personen abgehalten.

➤ **Betreuung des Netzes und Kommunikationstechnik**

Versendung von Pressemitteilungen, Reden und anderen maßgeblichen Dokumenten über die Vollendung des Binnenmarkts an die Mitglieder des Netzes; auf Anfrage Informationsdienst für die Vortragsredner; Erstellung von Ausbildungsprogrammen für die Mitglieder des Netzes; Zugang zu den Datenbanken CELEX, SCAD, RAPID und INFO 92.

169

➤ Europäische Kommission
Generaldirektion X
Referat X/C/5
William MARTIN
200 Rue de la Loi
B - 1049 Brüssel
Tel. (+32-2) 299 94 02

TEAM EUROPE

> **Field of activity**

Information for the general public on the achievement of the internal market and its consequences, and on all aspects of Community policy

> **Target public**

General public

> **Community coverage**

- a coordination agency in Brussels;
- a coordinator in each office of the Commission in the Member States;
- a network of 760 speakers spread over 19 European countries.

> **Actions**

More than 2,500 lectures are given annually by the 760 speakers to an audience of around 250,000 people.

> **Network animation and methods of communication**

Dispatch of press releases, speeches and other documents to network members relating to the completion of the internal market;
an information service at the request of speakers;
putting into place training programmes for network members;
access to CELEX, SCAD, RAPID and INFO 92 databases.

> European Commission
Directorate-General X
Unit X/C/5
200, rue de la Loi
B - 1049 Brussels
Tel.: (+32.2) 299.94.02

TEAM EUROPE

> **Domaine d'activité**

Information du grand public sur la réalisation du marché intérieur et ses conséquences, et sur tous les aspects de la politique communautaire.

> **Public cible**

Grand public

> **Rayonnement communautaire**

- Une agence de coordination à Bruxelles;
- un coordinateur dans chaque représentation de la Commission dans les États membres;
- réseau de 760 conférenciers répartis dans 19 pays d'Europe.

> **Actions**

Plus de 2.500 conférences sont données par les 760 conférenciers pour un auditoire d'environ 250.000 personnes par an.

> **Animation du réseau et techniques de communication**

Envoi aux membres du réseau des communiqués de presse, discours et autres documents de référence sur l'achèvement du marché intérieur;
service d'information à la demande pour les conférenciers;
mise en place de programmes de formation pour les membres du réseau;
accès aux bases de données CELEX, SCAD, RAPID et INFO 92.

171

> Commission européenne
Direction générale X
Unité X/C/ 5
200 rue de la Loi
B - 1049 Bruxelles
Tél.: (+32-2) 299.94.02

2

Allgemeine und berufliche Bildung, Jugend

Eurydice
Naric
Aktion Jean Monnet
Socrates
Leonardo
Jugend für Europa
Tempus
Impact

Education, Training, Youth

Eurydice
Naric
Jean Monnet Project
Socrates
Leonardo
Youth for Europe
Tempus
Impactt

Education, Formation, Jeunesse

Eurydice
Naric
Action Jean Monnet
Socrates
Leonardo
Jeunesse pou l'Europe
Tempus
Impact

EURYDICE

➤ **Genaue Bezeichnung**

Informationsnetz für das Bildungswesen in der Europäischen
Gemeinschaft

➤ **Tätigkeitsbereich**

Informationsaustausch über die Bildungssysteme und -politik in der
Gemeinschaft;
Unterstützung der EG-Kooperation im Bildungsbereich.

➤ **Zielgruppe**

Entscheidungsträger der Bildungspolitik

➤ **Wirkungskreis**

Europäische EURYDICE-Stelle in Brüssel;
Nationale Stelle(n) in jedem Mitgliedstaat.

➤ **Aktionen**

Frage- und Antwortsystem zugunsten der Bildungsbehörden;
Erstellung von Vergleichsanalysen, Berichten und Zusammenfassungen;
Verbreitung von im Netz erhältlichen Produkten an ein breiteres
Publikum.

175

➤ **Betreuung des Netzes und Kommunikationstechnik**

Datenbank über Bildungssysteme;
Veröffentlichungen von in den Bildungssystemen der Mitgliedstaaten
allgemeingültigen Themen;
Terminologiehilfen: Thesaurus und Glossare.

➤ Europäische Kommission
Task Force "Humanressourcen"
TF RHEJ
Domenico LENARDUZZI
200 Rue de la Loi
B -1049 Brüssel

EURYDICE

➤ **Full title**

Education Information Network in the European Community

➤ **Field of activity**

Information exchange on educational systems and policies in the
Community;
Support to Community cooperation in the educational field.

➤ **Target public**

Those responsible for educational policies

➤ **Community coverage**

EURYDICE European Unit in Brussels;
National Unit(s) in each Member State.

➤ **Actions**

Question and answer system for educational authorities;
preparation of comparative analyses, reports and summaries;
dissemination to a wider public of products available in the network.

➤ **Network animation and methods of communication**

Databank on educational systems;
Publications on common themes of educational systems in the Member
States;
Terminological resources: thesaurus and glossaries.

➤ European Commission
Directorate-General XXII
Domenico LENARDUZZI
200 rue de la Loi
B -1049 Brussels

EURYDICE

> **Intitulé exact**

Réseau d'information sur l'éducation dans la Communauté européenne

> **Domaine d'activité**

Échange d'informations sur les systèmes et les politiques de l'éducation dans la Communauté;
support à la coopération communautaire dans le domaine de l'éducation.

> **Public cible**

Responsables des politiques de l'éducation.

> **Rayonnement communautaire**

Unité européenne EURYDICE à Bruxelles;
Unité(s) nationale(s) dans chaque État membre.

> **Actions**

Système de questions et réponses en faveur des autorités de l'éducation;
élaboration d'analyses comparatives, de rapports et de synthèses;
diffusion des produits disponibles dans le réseau à un public plus large.

> **Animation du réseau et techniques de communication**

Banque de données sur les systèmes éducatifs;
Publications sur des thèmes communs aux systèmes éducatifs des États membres;
Outils terminologiques: Thesaurus et glossaires.

> Commission européenne
Direction Générale XXII
Domenico LENARDUZZI
200 rue de la Loi
B -1049 Bruxelles

AGENCE DE COORDINATION

Unité Européenne Eurydice
15, rue d'Arlon
B - 1040 BRUXELLES
Fax: +32/2/2306562

UNITES NATIONALES DANS LES ÉTATS MEMBRES

BELGIQUE-BELGIË

Unité Belge d'Eurydice
(Communauté française)
Ministère de l'Education, de la Recherche et
de la Formation - Secrétariat Général
Bd. Pachéco, 19 Boîte 0, 7ème étage
Cité Administrative de l'Etat
B - 1010 BRUXELLES
Fax: +32/2/2105538

Belgische Eurydice - Eenheid
(Vlaamse Gemeenschap)
Ministerie van Vlaamse Gemeenschap
Departement Onderwijs
Centrum voor Informatie en Documentatie
Koningsstraat 71
B- 1000 BRUSSEL
Fax: +32/2/2197773

DANMARK

Euridyce Informationskontor i
Danmark
Undervisningsministeriet
Frederiksholms Kanal 25 D
DK - 1220 KOBENHAVN K
Fax: +45/33/925567

DEUTSCHLAND

Eurydice- Informationstelle beim
Bundesministerium
für Bildung und Wissenschaft
Heinemannstrasse 2
D - 53170 BONN
Fax: +49/228/572096

Eurydice- Informationstelle im
Sekretariat der Ständigen Konferenz
der Kulturminister der Länder
Nassestrasse 8
D - 53113 BONN
Fax: +49/228/501301

ELLAS

Ministère de l'Education Nationale et
des Cultes
Direction CEE - Section C "Eurydice"
15 , rue Mitropoléos
GR - 10185 ATHENES
Fax: +30/1/3248264

ESPAÑA

Unidad de Eurydice
Centro Nacional de Investigacion y
Documentacion Educative
C/ San Augustin 5
E - 28014 MADRID
Fax: +34/1/5437390

FRANCE

Unité Eurydice
Ministère de l'Education Nationale -
Direction des Affaires Générales,
Internationales et de Coopération
Sous-Direction des Affaires Multilatérales
Bureau de l'Evaluation, de l'Information et
des Comparaisons Internationales
110, rue de Grenelle
F - 75357 PARIS
Fax: +33/1/45445787

IRELAND

Eurydice Unit - EC Section
Department of Education
6th floor
Apollo House
Tara Street
IRL - DUBLIN 2
Fax: +353/1/6791315

ITALIA

Ministero della Pubblica Istruzione
Biblioteca di Documentazione pedagogica
Palazzo Gerini
Via Buonarroti, 10
I - 50122 FIRENZE
Fax: +39/55/242884

LUXEMBOURG

Unité Eurydice
Centre de Psycologie et d'Orientation
Scolaire
280, route de Longwy
L - 1940 LUXEMBOURG
Fax: +352/454544

NEDERLAND

Dienst van Eurydice
Bibliotheek en Documentatie
Ministerie van Onderwijs en
Wetenschappen
Postbus 25000
NL - 2700 LZ ZOETERMEER
Fax: +31/79/531953

PORTUGAL

Unidade de Eurydice
Ministerio da Educaçao
Departamento de Programaçao e Gestào
Financeira
(DEPGEF)
Praça de Alvalade, 12
P - 1700 LISBOA
Fax: +351/1/8472482

UNITED KINGDOM

Eurydice Unit London
National Foundation for Educational
Research
The Mere
Upton Park
UK - SLOUGH, BERKSHIRE, SL1 2DQ
Fax: +44/753/691632

Eurydice Unit Scotland
Scottish Office Education Department
Room 803
43, Jeffrey Street
UK - EDINBURGH EH1 1DG
Fax: +44/31/2445387

179

NARIC

> **Genaue Bezeichnung**

National Academic Recognition Information Center

> **Tätigkeitsbereich**

Gemeinschaftsnetz der nationalen Informationszentren für die akademische Anerkennung von Diplomen.

> **Zielgruppe**

Hochschuleinrichtungen; Studenten, Eltern, Lehrpersonal und potentielle Arbeitgeber

> **Wirkungskreis**

Nationales Zentrum in jedem Mitgliedstaat;
Koordinierung des Gemeinschaftsnetzes der nationalen Informationszentren für die akademische Anerkennung der Diplome.

> **Aktionen**

Informationsverbreitung und individuelle Beratung bezüglich der akademischen Anerkennung von Diplomen und der absolvierten Studienzeiten in einem anderen Mitgliedstaat sowie in den EFTA-Ländern.

> **Betreuung des Netzes und Kommunikationstechnik**

Alle zwei Jahre Sitzungen mit den Direktoren der nationalen Zentren; Veröffentlichungen: Sammlung der bilateralen oder multilateralen Abkommen für gegenseitige Anerkennung von Diplomen zwischen den Mitgliedstaaten.
NARIC-Broschüre.

> Europäische Kommission
Generaldirektion XXII
Direktion A
200 Rue de la Loi
B - 1049 Brüssel

181

NARIC

➤ **Full title**

National Academic Recognition Information Centre.

➤ **Field of activity**

Community network of national information centres on the academic recognition of qualifications.

➤ **Target public**

Institutes of higher education;
students, parents, teachers and potential employers.

➤ **Community coverage**

A national centre in each Member State;
Coordination of the Community network at the level of national information centres on the academic recognition of qualifications.

➤ **Actions**

Dissemination of information and individual advice relative to the academic recognition of qualifications and of periods of study undertaken in another Member State as also in the EFTA countries.

➤ **Network animation and methods of communication**

Biennial meetings with the directors of the national centres;
Publications: collection of agreements of bilateral or multilateral recognition between Member States;
NARIC Brochure.

➤ European Commission
Directorate-General XXII
Directorate A
200 rue de la Loi
B - 1049 Brussels

NARIC

> **Intitulé exact**

National Academic Recognition Information Center

> **Domaine d'activité**

Réseau communautaire des centres nationaux d'information sur la reconnaissance académique des diplômes.

> **Public cible**

Instituts d'enseignement supérieur;
étudiants, parents, enseignants et employeurs potentiels

> **Rayonnement communautaire**

Centre national dans chaque État membre;
Coordination du réseau communautaire au niveau des centres nationaux d'information sur la reconnaissance académique des diplômes.

> **Actions**

Diffusion d'information et de conseils individuels relatifs à la reconnaissance académique des diplômes et des périodes d'études entreprises dans un autre État membre,
ainsi que dans les pays de l'AELE.

> **Animation du réseau et techniques de communication**

réunions bisannuelles avec les directeurs des centres nationaux;
Publications: recueil des accords d'équivalence bilatéraux ou multilatéraux entre les États membres
Brochure NARIC.

> **Commission européenne**
Direction Générale XXII
Direction A
200 rue de la Loi
B - 1049 Bruxelles

BELGIQUE-BELGIË

Academic recognition NARIC /
Professional recognition /
Contact point for the directive 89/48:

Chantal Kaufmann (fr)
Equivalence de l'Enseignement Supérieur
Ministère de l'Education et de la Recherche
Scientifique de la Communauté française
Quartier des Arcades / 6ème étage
Rue Royale 204
B-1000 BRUXELLES
Tél.: +32/2/210.55.77
Fax: +32/2/210.55.17

Daniël de Schrijver (nl)
Dienst Gelijkwaardigheid
Ministerie van Onderwijs
Bestuur van het Hoger Onderwijs
en Wetenschappelijk Onderzoek
Koningstraat 136
B-1000 BRUXELLES
Tél.: +32/2/211.42.65
Fax: +32/2/211.42.50

DANMARK

Academic recognition NARIC:
Jette Kirstein
Rektorkollegiet Secretariat
c/o Undervisningsministeriet
Frederiksholms Kanal 26
DK-1220 KØBENHAVN K
Tél.: +45/33/92.54.06
Fax: +45/33/92.50.75

Professional recognition /
Contact point for the directive 89/48:

Niels Anker Ring
Erhvervs og Selskabsstyrelsen
Kampmannsgade 1
DK-1780 KØBENHAVN
Tel.: +45/33/12.42.80
Fax: +45/33/92.50.75

DEUTSCHLAND

Academic recognition NARIC /
Professional recognition /
Contact point for the directive 89/48:

Dr. Günter Reuhl
Zentralstelle für Ausländisches
Bildungswesen im
Sekretariat der KMK
Nassesstrasse 8
D-53113 BONN
Tél.: +49/228/50.10
Fax: +49/228/50.14.86

ELLAS

Academic recognition NARIC /
Professional recognition /
Contact point for the directive 89/48:

Theodoros Lianos
DI.K.A.T.S.A.
leoforos Sygrou 112
GR-11741 ATHINA
Tel.: +30/1/922.25.26
Fax: +30/1/921.80.52

Theodosios Papatheodosiou
ITE - Institute of Technological Education
Leoforos Sygrou 56
GR-11742 ATHINA
Tél.: +30/1/922.10.00
Fax: +30/1/922.77.16

ESPAÑA

Academic recognition NARIC /
Professional recognition /
Contact point for the directive 89/48:

Miguel Angel Martín, Mariano Labarta
Ministerio de Educación y Ciencia
Subdirección General de Títulos
Paseo del Prado 28 - 4a planta
E-28014 MADRID
Tél.: +34/1/420.16.93
Fax:+34/1/420.33.25
            420.35.35

FRANCE

**Academic recognition NARIC /
Professional recognition /
Contact point for the directive 89/48:**

Solange De Serre
Direction des Affaires Générales,
Internationales et de la Coopération
Ministère de l'Education Nationale
Bureau DAGIC B3
Rue de Grenelle 110
F-75007 PARIS
Tél.: +33/1/40.65.65.90
Fax: +33/1/45.44.57.87

Isabelle Delacroix
Département des Affaires Européennes,
Internatioanles et Francophones
Ministère de l'Enseignement Supérieur et
de la Recherche
rue Dutot 61-65
F-75015 PARIS
Tel.: +33/1/40.65.65.89
Fax: +33/1/40.65.67.54

IRELAND

**Academic recognition NARIC /
Professional recognition /
Contact point for the directive 89/48:**

Brendan O'Dea
Higher Education Authority
Fitzwilliam Square 21
IRL-DUBLIN 2
Tél.: +353/1/661.27.48
Fax: +353/1/661.04.92

ITALIA

Academic recognition NARIC:

Carlo Finocchietti
CIMEA
Fondazione Rui
Viale XXI Aprile 36
I-00162 ROMA
Tel.: +39/6/86.32.12.81
Fax: +39/6/86.32.28.45

**Professional recognition /
Contact point for the directive 89/48:**

Armanda Bianchi Conti
Presidenza Consiglio Ministri
Ministero Coordinamento Politiche
Comunitarie
Via Giardino Theodoli 66
I-00189 ROMA
Tel.: +39/6/699.83.73
Fax: +39/6/679.53.51

LUXEMBOURG

**Academic recognition NARIC /
Professional recognition /
Contact point for the directive 89/48:**

Ernest Weis
Ministère de l'Education Nationale
Centre d'Information sur la Reconnaissance
Académique des Diplômes et des Périodes
d'Etudes
29 rue Aldringen
L-2926 LUXEMBOURG
Tél.: +352/478.51.27
Fax: +352/478.51.30

NEDERLAND

Academic recognition NARIC:

Kees Kouwenaar
NUFFIC
Postbus 29777
Kortenaerkade 11
NL-2502 LT DEN HAAG
Tél.: +31/70/426.02.71
Fax: +31/70/426.03.95

**Professional recognition /
Contact point for the directive 89/48:**

D. Haaksman
IRAS-Informatie Centrum Richtlijn
Algemeen Stesel
Postbus 29777
NL-2502 RT DEN HAAG
Tel.: +31/70/426.03.90
Fax: +31/70/426.03.95

185

ÖSTERREICH

Academic recognition NARIC:

Heinz Kasparovsky
Bundesministerium für Wissenschaft,
Forschung und Kunst
Rosengasse 4
A-1014 WIEN
Tel.: +43/1/531.205.920
Fax: +43/1/531.206.205

**Professional recognition /
Contact point for the directive 89/48:**

Christoph Demand
Bundesministerium für Wissenschaft,
Forschung und Kunst
Rosengasse 4
A-1014 WiEN
Tel.: +43/1/531.205.922
Fax: +43/1/531.206.205

PORTUGAL

Academic recognition NARIC:

Maria Dos Anjos Cohen Caseiro
Núcleo Padagógico
Ministério da Educação
Depatamento do Ensino Superior
Av. Duque d'Avila, 137-4° esq.
P-1000 LISBOA
Tél.: +351/1/57.52.92
Fax: +351/1/54.78.73

**Professional recognition /
Contact point for the directive 89/48:**

Manuela Paiva
Núcleo Pedagógico
Ministério da Educação
Depatamento do Ensino Superior
Av. Duque d'Avila, 137-4° esq.
P-1000 LISBOA
Tel.: +351/1/54.72.70
Fax: +351/1/57.96.17

SUOMI-FINLAND

Academic recognition NARIC / Professional
recognition / Contact point for the
directive 89/48:

Anita Lehikoinen
Ministry of Education
Dept. for Higher Education and Research
P.O. Box 293
SF-00171 HELSINKI
Tel.: +358/0/13.41.74.24
Fax: +358/0/65.67.65

SVERIGE

**Academic recognition NARIC /
Professional recognition /
Contact point for the directive 89/48:**

Marianne Hildebrand
National Agency for Higher Education
Box 7851
S-10399 STOCKHOLM
Tel.: +46/8/453.51.41
        453.50.00
Fax: +46/8/453.51.40

UNITED KINGDOM

Academic recognition NARIC:

Patricia Hibbell
The British Council
Medlock Street
UK-MANCHESTER M15 4AA
Tél.: +44/61/957.70.63
Fax: +44/61/957.75.61

**Professional recognition /
Contact point for the directive 89/48:**

Nicolette Divecha
Department of Trade & Industry
Ashdown House
123 Victoria Street
UK-LONDON SW1E 6RB
Tel.: +44/71/215.46.48
        215.56.10
Fax: +44/71/22.52.26

EFTA LÄNDER:
EFTA COUNTRIES:
PAYS DE L'AELE:

SUISSE

Academic recognition NARIC /
Professional recognition /
Contact point for the directive 89/48:

Marianne Trempe
Central Office of the Swiss Universities
Seidenweg 68
CH-3012 BERN
Tel.: +41/31/302.23.34
Fax: +41/31/302.68.11

ISLANDE

Academic recognition NARIC:

Thordur Kristinsson
Office of Academic Affairs
University of Iceland
Sudurgata
IS-101 REYKJAVIK
Tel.: +354/1/69.43.60
Fax: +354/1/69.43.17

Professional recognition /
Contact point for the directive 89/48:

Hördur Larusson
Ministry of Culture and Education
Sölunolsgata 4
IS-150 REYKJAVIK

NORVEGE

Academic recognition NARIC:

Kaja Schiötz
NAIC-National Academic Information
Centre
The University of Oslo
Dept. of International Relations
Postboks 1081 Blindern
N-0317 OSLO
Tel.: +47/22/85.88.60
Fax: +47/22/85.88.69

Professional recognition /
Contact point for the directive 89/48:

Fritjof Lund
Kirke,-undervisnings- og
forskningsdepartementet
PB 8119, Dep
N-0032 OSLO

187

AKTION JEAN MONNET

➤ **Genaue Bezeichnung**

Hochschulunterricht über europäische Integration

➤ **Tätigkeitsbereich**

Hilfsprogramm für die Einrichtung von ständigen Unterrichtsstrukturen im Bereich der europäischen Integration in den Bereichen EG-Recht, europäische Wirtschaft, europäische Politikwirtschaft und Geschichte des europäischen Aufbaus.

➤ **Zielgruppe**

Universitäten und Hochschuleinrichtungen; Akademiker.

➤ **Gemeinschaftlicher Wirkungskreis**

• In der Europäischen Union
252 Lehrstühle Jean Monnet: Ganztagslehrstellen für europäische Integration;
471 ständige Kurse von mindestens 60 Stunden für europäische Integration;
329 europäische Module: Kurzausbildungen von mindestens 30 Stunden für europäische Integration;
70 Forschungshilfen und 19 ergänzende Initiativen in Verbindung mit den Lehrstühlen Jean Monnet.

• Außerhalb der Europäischen Union
16 Lehrstühle Jean Monnet in Polen und Ungarn, 1 Lehrstuhl Jean Monnet in Montreal (Kanada) und 1 Lehrstuhl Jean Monnet in Harvard (USA);
67 ständige Kurse und europäische Module in Polen und Ungarn;
39 Forschungsprojekte, 53 materielle Unterstützungen und 12 Doktorats-Stipendien in Polen und Ungarn.

➤ **Betreuung des Netzes und Kommunikationstechnik**

Veranstaltung von nationalen und transnationalen Sitzungen pro Fachbereich;
Hilfe bei der Einrichtung von Netzen, gemeinsamen Veröffentlichungen, Konferenzen über Themen der Integration in die Gemeinschaft.
Organisation von Reflexionsgruppen und Themenforschungsgruppen.

➤ Europäische Kommission
Generaldirektion X
Referat X/C/6
Jacqueline LASTENOUSE BURY
200 Rue de la Loi
B - 1049 Brüssel
Tel. (+32-2) 299 94 53
Fax: (+32-2) 296.31.06

189

JEAN MONNET PROJECT

> **Full title**

European Integration in University Studies

> **Field of activity**

Assistance programme for the establishment of courses on European integration in the fields of Community law, European economy, European politics and the history of European construction.

> **Target public**

Universities and establishments of higher education; the academic community.

> **Community coverage**

- 252 Jean Monnet Chairs corresponding to-full time teaching positions devoted to European integration;
  471 Permanent Courses of minimum 60 hrs. on European integration;
  329 European Modules of minimum 30 hrs. corresponding to short study courses;
  70 Research Assistance projects and 19 Complementary Initiatives tied to Jean Monnet Chairs.

- Outside of European Union:
  16 Jean Monnet Chairs in Poland and Hungary, 1 Jean Monnet Chair at Montreal (Canada) and 1 Jean Monnet Chair at Harvard (USA);
  67 Permanent Courses and European Modules in Poland and Hungary;
  39 research projects, 53 material assistance projects and
  12 doctorate scholarschips in Poland and Hungary.

> **Network animation and methods of communication**

Organisation of national and transnational meetings by discipline; assistance to setting up networks, joint publications, organisation of reflection and thematic-research groups and conferences on topics of Community integration.

> European Commission
Directorate-General X
Unit X/C/6
Jacqueline LASTENOUSE BURY
200 rue de la Loi
B - 1049 Brussels
Tel.: (+32.2) 299.94.53
Fax: (+32.-2) 296.31.06

ACTION JEAN MONNET

➤ **Intitulé exact**

Enseignement sur l'intégration européenne dans l'université

➤ **Domaine d'activité**

Programme d'aide à la mise en place d'enseignements sur l'intégration européenne en Droit communautaire, en Economie européenne, en Etudes Politiques européennes et en Histoire de la construction européenne.

➤ **Public cible**

Universités et Etablissements d'enseignement supérieur;
Milieux académiques.

➤ **Rayonnement communautaire**

- Dans l'Union européenne:
  252 *Chaires Jean Monnet* correspondant à des postes d'enseignement consacrés à temps complet à l'intégration européenne;
  471 *Cours permanents* sur l'intégration européenne d'un minimum de 60H;
  329 *Modules européens* correspondant à des formations courtes, de minimum 30H, sur l'intégration européenne;
  70 *Aides à la recherche* et 19 *Initiatives complémentaires* liées à des Chaires Jean Monnet.

- En dehors de l'Union européenne:
  16 Chaires Jean Monnet en Pologne et Hongrie, 1 Chaire Jean Monnet à Montreal (Canada) et 1 Chaire Jean Monnet à Harvard (USA);
  67 Cours permanents et Modules européens en Pologne et Hongrie;
  39 projets de recherche, 53 aides matérielles et 12 bourses de doctorat en Pologne et Hongrie.

➤ **Animation du réseau et techniques de communication**

Organisation de réunions nationales et transnationales par discipline, aide à la mise en place de réseaux, publications en commun, organisation de groupes de réflexion et de recherche thématiques, conférences sur des thèmes de l'intégration européenne.

➤ Commission européenne
Direction générale X
Unité X/C/6
Jacqueline LASTENOUSE-BURY
200 rue de la Loi
B - 1049 Bruxelles
Tél.: (+32-2) 299.94.53

SOCRATES

> **Genaue Bezeichnung**

Aktionsprogramm der Gemeinschaft im Bildungsbereich.

> **Tätigkeitsbereich**

SOCRATES schließt an die von ERASMUS (Mobilität der Studenten) und LINGUA (Förderung der Kenntnis von Fremdsprachen in der Union) durchgeführten Aktionen an und ist innovativ mit der Planung von Aktionen in allen Bildungsstufen tätig.

> **Zielgruppe**

Studenten aller Bildungsniveaus, Dozenten, Schuleinrichtungen, Hochschulen.

> **Wirkungskreis**

Fachreferat in Brüssel;
Nationale Agenturen für die Vergabe von Stipendien bzw. Erteilung von Auskünften in jedem Mitgliedstaat (ist noch zu benennen).

> **Aktionen**

Das Programm ist in drei Kapitel aufgeteilt.
- Kapitel I:Hochschulbildung (Erasmus).
Dieses Kapitel soll die europäische Dimension in den Hochschulstudien fördern, insbesondere durch die Zusammenarbeit der Hochschulen zu Themen von allemeinem Interesse, Förderung der Mobilität von Studenten und Dozenten, Bildung von Hochschul-Pools.
- Kapitel II: Vorschul-, Primär- und Sekundarbildung (Comenius).
Dieses Kapitel soll die Partnerschaften zwischen den Schuleinrichtungen fördern (um miteinander pädagogische Aktivitäten mit einem gemeinsamen Ziel durchzuführen);
Förderung des Informationsaustausches der Einrichtungen, die an solchen Partnerschaften beteiligt sind; Verbesserung oder Realisierung neuer pädagogischer Produkte;
Förderung der Einschulung von Kindern von Zuwanderern und Zigeunern; Aktualisierung und Verbesserung der Kompetenzen des Lehrkörpers.
- Kapitel III: transversale Maßnahmen in allen Bildungsstufen.
Dieses Kapitel sieht die Verbesserung der sprachlichen Kenntnisse vor, insbesondere durch das Angebot von Auslandspraktika für zukünftige Sprachlehrer;
es räumt eine offene Bildungsaktion auf Distanz ein, sowie Erwachsenenbildung und die Entwicklung von Informationen und den Erfahrungsaustausch in all seinen Formen, insbesonder durch die Verstärkung des Netzes"Eurydice". Multilaterale Studienbesuche für Bildungsspezialisten (Arion) werden ebenfalls weiter ausgebaut.

> **Generaldirektion**

Europäische Kommission
Generaldirektion XXII
Direktion A
200 Rue de la Loi
B - 1049 Brüssel

SOCRATES

> **Full title**

Community action programme in the field of education.

> **Field of activity**

SOCRATES continues the activities already carried out by ERASMUS
(student mobility) and LINGUA (promoting the knowledge of foreign
languages in the Union) and is planning new, innovative activities
aimed at all levels of education.

> **Target public**

Students of all levels, teachers, schools and universities.

> **Community coverage**

A technical assistance office in Brussels;
national agencies for granting scholarships and/or providing
information in each Member State (to be announced).

> **Actions**

The programme is divided into three parts.
- Part I: higher education (Erasmus).
  This part promotes a European dimension in higher studies, notably
  through inter-university cooperation on themes of common interest,
  through encouraging the mobility of students and teachers and through
  the creation of university centres.
- Part II: preschool, primary and secondary education (Comenius).
  This part aims at encouraging partnerships among schools (in view of
  carrying out joint teaching activities with common objectives);
  facilitating information exchanges among the schools involved in such
  partnerships; improving or creating new teaching material; promoting
  schooling for children of migrant workers or Gypsies;
  updating and improving the skills of educators.
- Part III: flexible measures applicable at all levels of education.
  This part focuses on improving language skills, in particular, by
  offering temporary "assistant" positions and student jobs abroad to
  future language teachers. It promotes open- and distance education as
  well as adult education, and seeks to develop information and the
  exchange of know-how in all manners, particularly by strengthening the
  "Eurydice" network. Multilateral study visits for education specialists
  (Arion) will also be reinforced.

> **Head Office**
European Commission
Directorate-General XXII
Directorate A
200 rue de la Loi
B - 1049 Brussels

SOCRATES

> **Intitulé exact**
Programme d'action communautaire dans le domaine de l'éducation.

> **Domaine d'activité**

SOCRATES poursuit les actions déjà menées par ERASMUS (mobilité des étudiants) et LINGUA (promotion de la connaissance des langues étrangères dans l'Union) et innove aussi en prévoyant des actions à tous les niveaux d'enseignement.

> **Public cible**
Etudiants de tous les niveaux, enseignants, établissement scolaires, Universités.

> **Rayonnement communautaire**

Un bureau d'assistance technique à Bruxelles;
agences nationales d'attribution des bourses et/ou d'information dans chaque pays membre (encore à nommer).

> **Actions**
Le programme est divisé en trois chapitres.
- Chapitre I: enseignement supérieur (Erasmus).
Ce chapitre propose la promotion de la dimension européenne dans les études supérieures, notamment par la coopération interuniversitaire sur des thèmes d'intérêt commun, l'encouragement de la mobilité des étudiants et des enseignants, la création de pôles universitaires.
- Chapitre II: enseignement préscolaire, primaire et secondaire (Comenius).
Ce chapitre veut encourager les partenariats entre les établissements scolaires (en vue de mener conjointement des activités pédagogiques ayant un objectif commun);
faciliter les échanges d'information entre les établissements engagés dans de tels partenariats; améliorer ou réaliser de nouveaux produits pédagogiques; promouvoir la scolarisation des enfants de travailleurs migrants et de tziganes;
actualiser et améliorer les compétences du personnel éducatif.
- Chapitre III: mesures transversales applicables à tous les niveaux d'éducation.
Ce chapitre prévoit l'amélioration des compétences linguistiques, notamment par l'offre de périodes d'assistanat et de stages d'immersion à l'étranger pour les futurs professeurs de langues ; il consent une action à l'éducation ouverte et à distance, ainsi qu'à l'éducation des adultes et cherche à développer l'information et l'échange d'expérience sous toutes ses formes, notamment par le renforcement du réseau "Eurydice". Les visites multilatérales d'études pour spécialistes de l'éducation (Arion) seront également renforcées.

> **Direction générale**
Commission Européenne
Direction générale XXII
Direction A
200 rue de la Loi
B - 1049 Bruxelles

LEONARDO

> **Genaue Bezeichnung**

Aktionsprogramm für eine europäische Berufsbildungspolitik.

> **Tätigkeitsbereich**

LEONARDO (das die vormaligen Programme COMETT, FORCE, PETRA, EUROTECNET und zum Teil LINGUA integriert) soll die Initiativen der Mitgliedstaaten im Berufsbildungsbereich unterstützen und ergänzen, wobei der Schwerpunkt auf die Zusammenarbeit der Ausbildungsbereiche und die Kontinuität der Ausbildung während des ganzen Lebens gelegt wird.

> **Zielgruppe**

Junge Lehrlinge und Studenten, junge Arbeitnehmer, Ausbilder, Tutoren oder Bildungsverantwortliche, öffentliche Entscheidungsträger, Sozialpartner.

> **Wirkungskreis**

Fachreferat in Brüssel;
nationale Agentur in jedem Mitgliedstaat (ist noch zu benennen).

> **Aktionen**

- Gestaltung, Entwicklung und Erprobung transnationaler Pilotprojekte, z. B. für die Einrichtung von gemeinsamen Ausbildungseinheiten, die Anpassung der Lehrpläne und der Methoden, Ausbildung von Ausbildern, frühzeitige Erkennung von Bedürfnissen, Verbesserung der sprachlichen Fähigkeiten;
- Durchführung von Programmen für die Vermittlung und den Austausch von Ausbildern, Studenten und Praktikanten, damit sie einen Teil ihrer Ausbildung in einem anderen Mitgliedstaat verfolgen können;
- Ausbau der Kenntnisse im Berufsbildungsbereich durch Untersuchungen und Analysen, die auf Gemeinschaftsebene durchgeführt werden.

> **Generaldirektion**
Europäische Kommission
Generaldirektion XXII
Direktion B
200 Rue de la Loi
B-1049 Brüssel

LEONARDO

> **Full title**

Action programme for a European policy on vocational training.

> **Field of activities**

LEONARDO (which combines the former COMETT, FORCE, PETRA,EUROTECNET and, in part, LINGUA programmes) aims at supporting and complementing Member State initiatives in the field of vocational training, focusing on cooperation among the different types of training and life-long training.

> **Target public**

Young apprentices and students, young workers, instructors, tutors or training coordinators, public authorities, employers' and employees organizations.

> **Community coverage**

A technical assistance office in Brussels;
national agencies in each Member State (to be announced).

> **Actions**

- Creation, perfection and experimentation of transnational pilot projects for, e.g. setting up joint training modules, adapting content and methods, instructor training, anticipating needs, improving language skills;
- Managing placement and exchange programmes for instructors, students and student workers, allowing them to receive part of their training in another Member State;
- Developing knowledge in the field of vocational training through surveys and analyses made on a Community level.

> **Directorate-General**

European Commission
Directorate-General XXII
Directorate B
200 rue de la Loi
B - 1049 Brussels

LEONARDO

> **Intitulé exact**

Programme d'action pour une politique européenne de formation professionnelle.

> **Domaine d'activité**

LEONARDO (qui intègre les anciens programmes COMETT, FORCE, PETRA, EUROTECNET et, pour partie, LINGUA) vise à appuyer et compléter les initiatives des Etats membres dans le domaine de la formation professionnelle, en mettant l'accent sur la coopération entre les domaines de formation et la continuité de la formation tout au long de la vie.

> **Public cible**

Jeunes apprentis et étudiants, jeunes travailleurs, formateurs, tuteurs ou responsables de formation, décideurs publics, partenaires sociaux.

> **Rayonnement communautaire**

Un bureau d'assistance technique à Bruxelles;
agences nationales dans chaque pays membre (encore à nommer).

> **Actions**

* Conception, mise au point et expérimentation de projets pilotes transnationaux pour, par exemple, mettre en place des modules de formation communs,
  adapter les contenu et les méthodes, former les formateurs, anticiper les besoins, améliorer les compétences linguistiques;
* Réalisation de programmes de placements et d'échanges de formateurs, étudiants et stagiaires afin de leur permettre de suivre une partie de leur formation dans un autre Etat membre;
* Développement des connaisances dans le domaine de la formation professionnelle par des enquêtes et analyses réalisées sur un plan communautaire.

> **Direction générale**
Commission européenne
Direction générale XXII
Direction B
200 rue de la Loi
B-1049 Bruxelles

JUGEND FÜR EUROPA III

➤ **Genaue Bezeichnung**

Aktionsprogramm zur Förderung des Austausches und der Mobilität von Jugendlichen in der Gemeinschaft.

➤ **Tätigkeitsbereich**

Verbesserung, Ausbau und Diversifizierung des Jugendaustausches in der Gemeinschaft außerhalb von Bildungssystemen und Berufsausbildung.

➤ **Zielgruppe**

➤ Jugendliche im Alter von 15 bis 25 Jahren mit Wohnsitz in den Mitgliedstaaten

➤ **Wirkungskreis**
Fachreferat in Brüssel:
Nationale Agentur in jedem Mitgliedstaat (dezentral verwaltetes Programm).

➤ **Aktionen**

Direkte finanzielle Unterstützung und Beratung für die Durchführung von Jugendaustauschprojekten;
Studienaufenthalte und Ausbildungsunterstützung für Betreuer und Entscheidungsträger der Einrichtungen für Jugendaustausch.

201

➤ **Betreuung des Netzes und Kommunikationstechnik**

Veröffentlichungen: Broschüren für die breite Öffentlichkeit, Informationshefte für nationale Agenturen und andere Stellen (alle zwei Monate in Französisch und Englisch):
von den nationalen Agenturen erstellte Dokumentation;
Sitzungen:
1. beratender Ausschuß "Jugend für Europa";
2. Arbeitssitzungen mit den nationalen Agenturen;
3. Fachseminare.

➤ Europäische Kommission
Task Force "Humanressourcen"
TF RHEJ /1
200 Rue de la Loi
B - 1049 Brüssel
Tel. 295 99 81/ 295 41 58

YOUTH FOR EUROPE III

> **Full title**

Action programme for the promotion of youth exchanges in the Community.

> **Field of activity**

Improvement, development and diversification of the youth exchanges in the Community apart from educational systems and professional training.

> **Target public**

Young people from 15 to 25 years old resident in the Member States

> **Community coverage**

Technical assistance unit in Brussels:
National agency in each Member State (programme managed in a decentralised manner).

> **Actions**

Direct financial support and advice for carrying out projects for youth exchanges;
Study visits and assistance in training for animators and those in charge of organisations for youth exchanges.

> **Network animation and methods of communication**

Publications: brochures for the general public, information bulletin intended for national agencies and other intermediaries (bimonthly, in French and English):
Documentation produced by the national agencies;
Meetings:
1. Consultative Committee "Youth for Europe";
2. Working meetings with the national agencies;
3. Thematic seminars.

> European Commission
Directorate-General XXII
Directorate C
200 rue de la Loi
B - 1049 Brussels
Tel.: 295.99.81/ 295.41.58

JEUNESSE POUR L'EUROPE III

➤ **Intitulé exact**

Programme d'action visant à promouvoir les échanges et la mobilité des jeunes dans la Communauté.

➤ **Domaine d'activité**

Amélioration, développement et diversification des échanges de jeunes dans la communauté en dehors des systèmes d'éducation et de formation professionnelle.

➤ **Public cible**

Jeunes de 15 à 25 ans résidant dans les États membres.

➤ **Rayonnement communautaire**

Unité d'assistance technique à Bruxelles:
Agence nationale dans chaque État membre (programme géré de manière décentralisée).

➤ **Actions**

Soutien financier direct et conseils pour la réalisation de projets d'échanges de jeunes;
visites d'études et d'assistance en formation pour animateurs et responsables d'organismes d'échanges de jeunes.

➤ **Animation du réseau et techniques de communication**

Publications: brochures grand public, bulletin d'information à l'attention des Agences nationales et autres intermédiaires (bimestriel, en français et anglais):
Documentation élaborée par les agences nationales;
Réunions:
1. Comité consultatif "Jeunesse pour l'Europe";
2. Réunions de travail avec les agences nationales;
3. Séminaires thématiques.

Commission européenne
Direction générale XXII
Direction C
200 rue de la Loi
B - 1049 Bruxelles
Tél.: 295.99.81/ 295.41.58

UNITE D'ASSISTANCE TECHNIQUE

**Bureau d'échanges de jeunes
dans la CE**
Place du Luxembourg 2-3
B - 1040 BRUXELLES
Tél.: +32/2/511.15.10
Fax: +32/2/511.19.60

**AGENCES NATIONALES DANS LES
ETATS MEMBRES:**

BELGIQUE-BELGIË

Communauté française de Belgique
Mylène Laurant
Agence pour la Promotion des Activités
Internationales de Jeunesse
13-17 Boulevard Adolphe Max
B - 1000 BRUXELLES
Tél.: +32/2/219.09.06
Fax: +32/2/218.81.08

Vlamse Gemeenschap
Koen Lambert
Jint v.Z.W.
Grétrystraat 26
B- 1000 BRUSSEL
Tél.: +32/2/218.64.55
Fax: +32/2/219.46.55

Deutschsprachige Gemeinschaft
Wilfried Heyen
Agentuur "Jungend für Europa"
Neustrasse 93
B - 4700 EUPEN
Tél.: +32/87/55.48.72
Fax: +32/87/55.66.06

DANMARK

Lars Hoegm Hansen
ICU
Dronningensgade 75
DK - 1420 KØBENHAVN
Tél.: +45/33/14.20.60
Fax: +45/33/14.36.40

DEUTSCHLAND

Hartwig Lürick
Maria Deisel
Deutsches Büro "Jungend für Europa"
Hockkreuzallee, 20
D - 5300 BONN
Tél.: +49/228/95060
Fax: +49/228/9506222

ELLAS

Vassiliki Vallianou
Theodora Giannakaki
Hellenic National Agency for the EC
Programme "YFE"
(General Secretariat for Youth National
Foundation)
417, Archanon str.
GR - 11143 ATHINAI
Tél.: +30/1/253.13.49
Fax: +30/1/258.14.20

ESPAÑA

Francisco Garcia Pliego Campillo
Insituto de la Juvendud
C/ Marques de Riscal, 16
E - 28010 MADRID
Tél.: +34/1/3477865
Fax: +34/1/3199338

FRANCE

Mr. Serge Mauvilain
Institut National de la Jeunesse
Val Flory
Rue Paul Leplat
F - 78160 MARLY-LE-ROI
Tél.: +33/1/39580257
Fax: +33/1/39165779

IRELAND

James Mullin
Mary Bigley
Youth Exchange Bureau
Avoce house
189 -193 Parnell Street
IRL - DUBLIN 1
Tél.: +353/1/731049
Fax: +353/1/731316

ITALIA

Mr. Giorgio Radicati
Agenzia Nazionale "Gioventù per l'Europa"
Piazzale della Farnesina, 1
I - 01000 ROMA
Tél.: +39/6/3236218
Fax: +39/6/3233552

LUXEMBOURG

Nico Meisch
Myriam Putzeys
Julia Recktenvald
Centre d'Information et d'Echange de
Jeunes
Boulevard de la Pétrusse, 76
L - 2320 LUXEMBOURG
Tél.: +352/405552
Fax: +352/405556

NEDERLAND

Thea Meinema
Ben Sllijkhuis
EXIS
Postbus 15344
NL - 1001 MH AMSTERDAM
Tél.: +31/20/6261276
Fax: +31/20/6228590

ÖSTERREICH

Mr. Helmut Fennes
Interkulturelles Zentrum
Kettenbrückengasse 23
A-1050 WIEN
Tel.: +43/1/58.67.54.40
Fax: +43/1/58.67.54.49

PORTUGAL

Odette Bernardes
Alzira Sousa
Instituto da Juventude
Av. de la Libertade, 194
P - 1100 LISBOA
Tél.: +351/1/3191961
Fax: +351/1/3151959

SUOMI-FINLAND

Dr. Lauri Lantto
Ulla Naskali
Centre for International Mobility-CIMO
P.O. Box 343
SF-00530 HELSINKI
Tel.: +358/0/77.47.70.33
Fax: +358/0/77.47.70.64

SVERIGE

Bengt Persson
Stiftelsen för Internationellt
Ungdomsutbyte (SIU)
Kungsgatan 48
S-11135 STOCKHOLM
Tel.: +46/8/20.19.80
Fax: +46/8/20.35.30

UNITED KINGDOM

Gordon Blakely
Hilary Jarman
Youth Exchange Centre
Seymour Mews House
UK - LONDON W1H 9PE
Tél.: +44/71/4875961
Fax: +44/71/2244506

ISLANDE

Erlendur Kristjansson
Margrét Sverrisdottir
Hitt Husid
Brautarholt 20
IS-105 REYKJAVIK
Tel.: +354/1/62.43.20
Fax: +354/1/62.43.41

NORVEGE

Kjersti Thoen
Torgeir Knutsen
Atlantis Youth Exchange
Rolf Hofmos gate 18
N-0655 OSLO
Tel.: +47/22/67.00.43
Fax: +47/22/68.68.08

205

TEMPUS

➤ **Genaue Bezeichnung**

Transeuropäisches Kooperationsprogramm für die
Hochschulausbildung

➤ **Tätigkeitsbereich**

Ausbau des Hochschulwesens in den mittel- und osteuropäischen
Ländern sowie den Republiken der ehemaligen Sowjetunion durch
Zusammenarbeit mit den Universitäten der EG und der G-24;
Förderung der Kooperation zwischen Universitäten und Unternehmen.

➤ **Zielgruppe**

Lehrpersonal im Hochschulbereich, Studenten, Unternehmer.
Für das akademische Jahr 1993/1994 handelt es sich um folgende
Länder:
Albanien, Bulgarien, Estland, Ungarn, Lettland, Litauen, Polen,
Rumänien, Slowakei, Slowenien, Tschechien, Weißrußland, Rußland und
Ukraine.

➤ **Wirkungskreis**

Ein Koordinierungsbüro in Brüssel;
nationale Kontaktstellen in allen Mitgliedstaaten.

➤ **Aktionen**

Unterstützung der gemeinsamen europäischen Projekte von
Universitäten und gegebenenfalls von Unternehmen;
im Rahmen dieser gemeinsamen Projekte Beihilfen für die Mobilität des
Lehrpersonals und der Studenten;
Beihilfen für Zusatzaktivitäten.

➤ **Betreuung des Netzes und Kommunikationstechnik**

Durch das Koordinierungsbüro TEMPUS in Brüssel in Zusammenarbeit
mit den nationalen TEMPUS-Büros in den Empfängerländern.

➤ Europäische Kommission
Generaldirektion XXII
Direktion C
200 Rue de la Loi
B - 1049 Brüssel
Tel. (+32-2) 295 46 46 / 295 99 19 / 295 75 07

TEMPUS Office
Avenue des Arts 19H
B - 1040 Brussels
Tel.: (+32.2) 212.04.11/12 - Fax: (+32.2) 212.04.00

TEMPUS

➢ **Full title**

Trans-European Cooperation Scheme for Higher Education

➢ **Field of activity**

Development of higher education in the countries of central and eastern European and the Republics of the former Soviet Union through cooperation with universities of the EC and of the G-24; stimulation of the development of cooperation between universities and companies.

➢ **Target public**

Higher education teachers, students, industry.
For the academic year 1993/1994, the countries concerned are: Albania, Bulgaria, Estonia, Hungary, Latvia, Lithuania, Poland, Roumania, Slovakia, Slovenia, the Czech Republic, Byelorussia, Russia and the Ukraine.

➢ **Community coverage**

A coordination office in Brussels; national contact points in all the Member States.

➢ **Actions**

Support to joint European projects between universities and, if need be, companies; assistance, in the framework of joint projects, to the mobility of teachers and students; assistance for complementary activities.

➢ **Network animation and methods of communication**

By the TEMPUS coordination office in Brussels in cooperation with the national TEMPUS offices in the beneficiary countries.

➢ European Commission
Directorate-General XXII
Directorate C
200 rue de la Loi
B - 1049 Brussels
Tel.: (+32.2) 295.46.46 / 295.99.19 / 295.75.07

TEMPUS Office
Avenue des Arts 19H
B - 1040 Brussels
Tel.: (+32.2) 212.04.11/12 - Fax: (+32.2) 212.04.00

TEMPUS

> **Intitulé exact**

Programme transeuropéen de coopération pour l'enseignement supérieur

> **Domaine d'activité**

Développement de l'enseignement supérieur des pays d'Europe centrale et orientale et des Républiques de l'ex-Union soviétique par la coopération avec les universités de la CE et du G-24; stimulation du développement de la coopération universités/entreprises.

> **Public cible**

Professeurs de l'enseignement supérieur, étudiants, industriels. Pour l'année académique 1993/1994, les pays concernés sont: l'Albanie, la Bulgarie, l'Estonie, la Hongrie, la Lettonie, la Lituanie, la Pologne,la Roumanie, la Slovaquie, la Slovénie, la Tchéquie, la Biélorussie, la Russie et l'Ukraine.

> **Rayonnement communautaire**

Un bureau de coordination à Bruxelles; des points de contact nationaux dans tous les États membres.

> **Actions**

Soutien à des projets européens communs entre universités et, le cas échéant, entreprises; aides, dans le cadre de ces projets communs, à la mobilité des enseignants et des étudiants; aides à des activités complémentaires.

> **Animation du réseau et techniques de communication**

Par le bureau de coordination TEMPUS à Bruxelles en collaboration avec les bureaux TEMPUS nationaux dans les pays bénéficiaires.

> Commission européenne
Direction générale XXII
Direction C
200 rue de la Loi
B - 1049 Bruxelles
Tél.: (+32-2) 295.46.46 / 295.99.19 / 295.75.07

TEMPUS Office
Avenue des Arts 19H
B - 1040 Brussels
Tel.: (+32.2) 212.04.11/12 - Fax: (+32.2) 212.04.00

IMPACT

➢ **Genaue Bezeichnung**

National Awareness Partners (NAP)

➢ **Tätigkeitsbereich**

Förderung von elektronischen Informationsdiensten in Europa.

➢ **Zielgruppe**

Potentielle Benutzer der Informationsdienste, hauptsächlich in
Universitäten, Bibliotheken sowie kleineren und mittleren
Unternehmen.

➢ **Wirkungskreis**

Zielgruppen in allen Ländern des Europäischen Wirtschaftsraums.

➢ **Aktionen**

Veranstaltung von Seminaren, Mailings, Teilnahme an Ausstellungen.

➢ **Betreuung des Netzes und Kommunikationstechnik**

Zentraler Träger für Erstausbildung, regelmäßig stattfindende
Sitzungen, elektronischer Postdienst.

211

➢ Europäische Kommission
Generaldirektion XIII
Referat XIII/E/2
A. SZAUER
Rue Alcide de Gasperi
L-2920 Luxemburg
Tel. (+352) 4301.3526 - Fax: (+352) 4301.2847

IMPACT

> **Full title**

National Awareness Partners (NAP's)

> **Field of activity**

Promotion of electronic information services in Europe.

> **Target public**

Potential users of information services, mainly in the universities, libraries and small and medium-sized enterprises.

> **Community coverage**

Target groups in all countries of the European Economic Area.

> **Actions**

Organisation of seminars, mailings, participation in exhibitions.

> **Network animation and methods of communication**

Central support for initial training, regular meetings, electronic mail service.

> European Commission
Directorate-General XIII
Unit XIII/E/2
A. SZAUER
Rue Alcide de Gasperi
L-2920 Luxembourg
Tel.: (+352) 4301.33526 - Fax: (+352) 4301.32847

IMPACT

> **Intitulé exact**

National Awareness Partners (NAP)

> **Domaine d'activité**

Promotion des services d'information électronique en Europe.

> **Public cible**

Utilisateurs potentiels des services d'information, essentiellement dans les universités, les bibliothèques et les petites et moyennes entreprises.

> **Rayonnement communautaire**

Groupes cibles dans tous les Pays de l'Espace Economique Européen.

> **Actions**

Organisation de séminaires, mailings, participation à des expositions.

> **Animation du réseau et techniques de communication**

Support central pour la formation initiale, réunions régulières, service de courrier électronique.

213

> Commission européenne
Direction générale XIII
Unité XIII/E/2
A. SZAUER
Rue Alcide de Gasperi
L-2920 Luxembourg
Tél.: (+352) 4301.33526 - Fax: (+352) 4301.32847

BELGIQUE-BELGIË

CNDST (Centre National de Documentation Scientifique et Technique)
NCWTD (Nationaal Centrum voor Wetenschappelijke en Technische Documentatie)
Boulevard de l'Empereur,4/Kaizerslaan, 4
B-1000 BRUSSELS
Contact: Mr. Paul Heyvaert
Tel.: +32/2/519.56.59
Fax: +32/2/519.56.45

DANMARK

INFOSCAN
Sigurdsgade 41
DK-2200 COPENHAGEN N
Contact: Mr Alex Gorski
Tel.: +45/31.81.66.66
Fax: +45/35.82.16.55

DEUTSCHLAND

TVA / Technologie-Vermittlungs-Agentur Berlin e.V.
Informationsdienste
Kleiststrasse 23-26
D-10787 BERLIN
Contact: Mr. Stephan Kurby
Tel.: +49/30/21.29.54.69
Fax: +49/30/31.30.807

IW / Institut der Deutschen Wirtschaft
Gustav-Heinemann-Ufer 84-88
D-50968 KÖLN
Contact: Mr. Bernd Risch
Tel.: +49/221/37.65.522
Fax: +49/221/37.65.556

DGD c/o Infratest Burke AG/Information and Documentation Division
Landsberger Strasse 338
D - 80687 MUNICH
Contact: Dr. Sabine Graumann
Tel.: +49/89/560.02.21
Fax: +49/89/580.19.96

ELLAS

NDC / National Documentation Centre
48 Vas Constantinou Avenue
GR-11635 ATHENS
Contact: Mr. Filippos Tsimpoglou
Tel.: +30/1/72.42.172
Fax: +30/1/72.46.824
ESPAÑA

CINDOC/Consejo Superior de Investigaciones Ciéntificas
Centro de Información y Documentación científica (C.I.N.D.O.C.)
c/Joaquín Costa, 22
E - 28002 MADRID
Contact: Mr. José Ramón Pérez / Mr. Isidro Aguilló
Tel.: +34/1/563.54.82-208
Fax: +34/1/564.26.44

ASEDIE / Asiciación Española de Distribuidores de
Información Electrónica
c/Londres 17   2 Dcha
E-28028 MADRID
Contact: Mr. Jaime Tascón
Tel.: +34/1/726.10.39
Fax: +34/1/726.10.70

FRANCE

AF 2i / Association Française des Intermédiaires en Information
43 rue La Bruyère
F-75009 PARIS
Contact: Mr. François Libmann / Mme Madeleine Wolff-Terroine
Tel.: +33/1/42.85.17.14
Fax: +33/1/42.85.41.65

ADBS / Association Française des Professionnels de l'Information et de la Documentation
10 rue Carnot
F-64000 Pau
Contact: Ms. Michèle Battisti
Tel.: +33/59.02.54.16
Fax: +33/59.02.07.15

214

CCIP / Chambre de Commerce et d'Industrie de Paris
27 avenue de Friedland
F-75008 PARIS
Contact: Mr. George Fischer / Mrs. Evelyne Houdard-Duval
Tel.: +33/1/42.89.72.27
Fax: +33/1/42.89.72.10

IRELAND

FORBAIRT / Technology Services
Glasnevin
IRL-DUBLIN 9
Contact: Dr. Barry Harrington
Tel.: +353/1/837.01.01
        837.23.03
Fax: +353/1/837.90.82

BTIS/Univesitry of Limerick Business Technical Information Service
Plassey Technological Park
IRL - LIMERICK
Contact: Ms Martina Flynn
Tel: +353/61/33.36.44
Fax: +353/61/33.80.44

ITALIA

ENEA/Dipartimento Innovazione
Senore INN-DIFF
VIA Don G. Flammelli 2
I-40129 BOLOGNA
Contact: Mr. Massimo Gazzotti/Mr. Ermes Ridolfi
Tel.: +39/51/609.81.97
Fax: +39/51/609.80.84

AIB / Associazione Italiana Biblioteche
c/o Istituto Nazionale di Economia Agraria
Via Barberini 36
I-00187 ROMA
Contact: Mrs. Maria Luisa Ricciardi
Tel.: +39/6/487.07.93
Fax: +39/6/47.41.984

PITAGORA S.p.A.
Banche dati e servizi telematici economico-finanziari
Località S. Stefano
I-87036 RENDE (Cosenza)
Contact: Mr. Salvatore Mesina/Mrs Liliane Le Piane
Tel.: +39/984/8361
Fax: +39/984/83.62.00

LUXEMBOURG

EIC / Chambre des Métiers du G.D. de Luxembourg
2, Circuit de la Foire Internationale
L-1347 LUXEMBOURG
Contact: Mme Marie-Andrée Colbach-Haas
Tel.: +352/426.767-1
Fax: +352/426.787

NEDERLAND

NBBI /Project Bureau for Information Management
Burg. van Karnebeeklaan 19
NL-2585 GM DEN HAAG
Contact: Mr F.J. Andriessen/Ms Annemiek Wiercx
Tel.: +31/70/360.78.33
Fax: +31/70/361.50.11

ÖSTERREICH

215

TECHINFORM/WKÖ/Wirtschaftskammer Österreich
Aussenwirtschaft
Wiedner Hauptstrasse 63
Postfach 150
A-1045 WIEN
Contact: Mr. Egon Kratochvil / Dr. Johann Kafka
Tel.: +43/1/501.05.4523-4566
Fax: +43/1/502.06.277-212

ÖGDI/Österreichische Gesellschaft für Dokumentation und Information
Heinestrasse 38
A - 1020 WIEN
Contact: Dr Gerhard Buclin
Tel: (+43) 1 21.30.03.10
Fax: (+43) 1 216.32.72

PORTUGAL

INETI / Instituto Nacional de Engenharia e Tecnologia Industrial
Azinhaga dos Lameiros à Estrada do Paço do Lumiar
Edificio A
P-1699 LISBOA Cedex
Contact: Ms. Ana Maria Ramalho Correia
Tel.: +351/1/716.51.41 ext. 2980
Fax: +351/1/716.47.32

SUOMI-FINLAND

VTT / Technical Research Centre of Finland Information Service
Vuorimiehentie 5, Espoo
P.O. Box 2000
FIN-02044 VTT, Suomi-Finland
Contact: Mrs. Elisabet Mickos
Tel.: +358/0/456.44.09
Fax: +358/0/456.43.74

SVERIGE

IDC / KTHB/ Information and Documentation Center
Royal Institute of Technology Library
S-10044 STOCKHOLM
Contact: Mrs. Marie Wallin
Tel.: +46/8/790.89.50
Fax: +46/8/790.89.54

Statskontoret
Norra Riddarholmshamnen 1
Box 2280
S-10317 STOCKHOLM
Contact: Mr. Söran Lindh
Tel.: +46/8/454.47.04
Fax: +46/8/454.46.93

UNITED KINGDOM

ASLIB / The Association for Information Management
Information House/20-24 Old Street
UK-LONDON EC1V 9AP
Contact: Ms. Julia Dickmann
Tel.: +44/71/253.44.88
Fax: +44/71/430.05.14

SET / University of Dundee
Dept. of Medical Physics
Ninewells Hospital and Medical School
UK-DUNDEE DD1 9SY
Contact: Dr. Ian Chapman
Tel.: +44/1382/63.26.04
        1382/66.01.11 ext. 364
Fax: +44/1382/64.01.77

ICELAND

SIFT / Icelandic Forum of IT & T Users
Viöskiptavakinn, 7
Kringlan 7
IS-103 REYKJAVIK
Contact: Dr. Jon Thorhallsson / Mrs. Harpa Halldórsdóttir
Tel.: +354/1/88.66.66
Fax: +354/1/68.65.64

NORWAY

Statskonsult / IT. Division
Advisory Department
Falbesgt 5 Box 8115 Dep
N-0032 OSLO
Contact: Mr. Rolf Borgerud
Tel.: +47/22.45.10.00
Fax: +47/22.60.21.11

INFOSØK / The Technical University Library of Norway
Høgskoleringen 1
N- 7034 TRONDHEIM
Contact: Ms. Aud Lamvik
Tel.: +47/73.59.51.07
            51.20
Fax: +47/73.59.51.03

216

Beschäftigung

Misep
Sysdem
Eures
E.C. bic
Ergo 2
Leda

Employment

Misep
Sysdem
Eures
EC BIC
Ergo 2
Leda

Emploi

Misep
Sysdem
Eures
EC BIC
Ergo 2
Leda

MISEP

> **Genaue Bezeichnung**

System für gegenseitige Unterrichtung über beschäftigungspolitische Maßnahmen.

> **Tätigkeitsbereich**

Informationsnetz bezüglich der Beschäftigungspolitik in den Mitgliedstaaten.

> **Zielgruppe**

Nationale Regierungen der Mitgliedstaaten und insbesondere mit Beschäftigungspolitik befaßte Personen, Verbände oder Direktionen.

> **Wirkungskreis**

Ein Fachsekretariat in Berlin (Deutschland);
Nationales Korrespondenznetz.

> **Aktionen**

Sammlung von Informationen über die Beschäftigungspolitik in den Mitgliedstaaten;
Funktion als Anlaufstelle für multilaterale Fragen und Antworten;
Veranstaltung von Seminaren.

> **Betreuung des Netzes und Kommunikationstechniken**

Quartalsheft "Maßnahmen" (EN/FR/DE);
Quartalsheft "Ostdeutschland" (EN/FR/DE)
Berichte mit Grundlageninformationen: Vergleiche der von den Mitgliedstaaten durchgeführten Aktionen und der Beschäftigungspolitik;
Bewertung der Ergebnisse bezüglich der Beschäftigungspolitik der Mitgliedstaaten.

> Europäische Kommission
Generaldirektion V
Referat V/A/2 - ARCH 1 - 7/13
Sergio PICCOLO
200 Rue de la Loi
B - 1049 Brüssel
Tel. (+32-2) 295 71 09 / 295 39 40

MISEP

> **Full title**

Mutual Information System on Employment Policies

> **Field of activity**

Information network concerning employment policies in the Member States.

> **Target public**

National governments of Member States and more particularly the persons, associations or management involved with employment policies.

> **Community coverage**

A technical secretariat in Berlin (Germany);
network of national correspondents.

> **Actions**

Collection of information relative to national employment policies in the Member States;
"Clearing House" function for multilateral questions and answers;
Organisation of seminars.

> **Network animation and methods of communication**

Quarterly Policy Bulletin (EN/FR/GE);
Quarterly East German Bulletin (EN/FR/GE)
Basic Information Reports: comparable information on the actions and policies taken by Member States on the labour market;
Evaluation of results concerning the employment policies of Member States.

> European Commission
Directorate-General V
Unit V/A/2 - ARCH 1 - 7/13
Sergio PICCOLO
200 rue de la Loi
B - 1049 Brussels
Tel.: (+32.2) 295.71.09 / 295.39.40

MISEP

> **Intitulé exact**

Système Mutuel d'Information sur les Politiques de l'Emploi

> **Domaine d'activité**

Réseau d'information concernant les politiques de l'Emploi dans les États membres.

> **Public cible**

Gouvernements nationaux des États membres et plus particulièrement les personnes, associations ou directions liées aux politiques de l'emploi.

> **Rayonnement communautaire**

Un secrétariat technique à Berlin (Allemagne);
réseau de correspondants nationaux.

> **Actions**

Collecte d'informations relatives aux politiques nationales de l'emploi dans les États membres;
Fonction de "Clearing House" pour les questions et les réponses multilatérales;
Organisation de séminaires.

221

> **Animation du réseau et techniques de communication**

Bulletin trimestriel Politiques (EN/FR/DE);
Bulletin trimestriel Allemagne de l'Est (EN/FR/DE);
Rapports d'Information de Base: une information comparable sur les actions et les politiques du marché du travail menées par les États membres;
Evaluation des résultats concernant les politiques de l'emploi des États membres.

> Commission européenne
Direction générale V
Unité V/A/2 - ARCH 1 - 7/13
Sergio PICCOLO
200 rue de la Loi
B - 1049 Bruxelles
Tél.: (+32-2) 295.71.09 / 295.39.40

BELGIQUE-BELGIË

Mr. Joseph REMY
Ministère de l'Emploi et du Travail
Administration de l'Emploi
Direction de l'Etude des problèmes du
travail
Rue Belliard, 51
B-1040 BRUXELLES
Tél.: +32/2/233.46.67
Fax: +32/2/233.47.38

DANMARK

Mrs Karen THRYSOE
Ministry of Labour
International Relation Division
Laksgade 19
DK-1063 COPENHAGEN K
Tél.: +45/33/92.99.50
Fax: +45/33/12.13.78

DEUTSCHLAND

Dr. Jochen JAHN
**Bundesministerium für Arbeit und
Sozialordnung**
Postfach 140280
D-53107 BONN
Tél.: +49/228/527.26.76
Fax: +49/228/527.11.21

Mr. Detlef HEIN
Bundesanstalt für Arbeit
Regensburgerdstrasse 104
D-90327 NÜRNBERG
Tél.: +49/911/179.22.86
Fax: +49/911/179.33.41

ELLAS

Ms. Ekaterini KRITIKOU
Ministry of Labour
Employment Division
40, Pireos Street
GR-10182 ATHENS
Tél.: +30/1/52.95.400
Fax: +30/1/52.42.942

ESPAÑA

Ms. Delmira Paz SEARA SOTO
Dorec. General de Empleo
**Ministerio de Trabajo
y Seguridad Social**
Calle Pio Baroja 6
E-28009 MADRID
Tél.: +34/1/409.09.41 ext. 51.29
Fax: +34/1/574.96.02

FRANCE

Mme Claudine ELHAÏK
ANPE
Direction Générale
Division Relations Internationales
LE GALILEE
4, Rue de Galilée
F-93198 NOISY-Le-Grand-Cédex
Tél.: +33/1/49.31.77.11 – 49.31.77.14
Fax: +33/1/43.03.13.47

Mr. Henri ROUX
Délégation à l'Emploi
Division Synthèses
168, Rue de Grenelle
F-75007 PARIS
Tél: +33/1/47.05.73.06
Fax: 33/1/47.05.68.82

IRELAND

Mr. Vincent LANDERS
Planning Unit
Department of Enterprise and Employment
Kildare Street
IRL-DUBLIN 2
Tél.: +353/1/661.44.44
Fax: +353/1/676.26.54

ITALIA

Ms. Mariarosaria DAMIANI
Direzione Generale per l'Impiego
Ministero del Lavoro
Via Flavia, 6
I-00100 ROMA
Tél.: +39/6/468.32.446
Fax: +39/6/478.87.174
Télex: 621.108 mipscm i

LUXEMBOURG

Mr. Jean HOFFMANN
Administration de l'Emploi
38/a, Rue Philippe II
B.P. 23
L-2010 LUXEMBOURG
Tél.: +352/478.53.00
Fax: +352/46.45.19

NEDERLAND

Mr. Ronald VAN BEKKUM
**Afdeling Internationale
Arbeidsmarktvraagstukken (IAV)**
P.O. Box 415
NL-2280 AK RIJSWIJK
Tel.: +31/70/313.09.11 (switchboard)
           313.06.12 (Mr. van Bekkum)
           313.07.44 (Ms. Dora van Meurs)
Fax: +31/70/313.06.30

ÖSTERREICH

Dr. Johannes SCHWEIGHOFER
**Bundesministerium
für Arbeit und Soziales**
Abteilung III 1
Stubenring 1
A - 1010 WIEN
Tel: +43/1/711.00.20.56
Fax: +43/1/715.82.55

PORTUGAL

Mr.Victor VIEGAS
**Ministério do Emprego
e da Segurança Social**
Avenida da republica, 62
P-1000 LISBOA
Tél.:+351/1/796.93.61 ext. 44
Fax: +351/1/797.52.69

SUOMI-FINLAND

Ms Tuuli RAIVIO
Ministry of Labour
Unit of International Affairs
Etelaesplanadi 4
Tel: +358/0/18.56.80.27
Fax: +358/0/18.56.80.13

SVERIGE

Mr. Mats WADMAN
Ministry of Labour
S - 10333 STOCKHOLM
Tel: +46/8/763.13.54
Fax: +46/8/20.73.69

UNITED KINGDOM

Mr.Graham ARCHER
Dept. of Employment
R 235 Caxton House
Tothill Street
UK-LONDON SW 1H 9NF
Tél.:+44/71/273.47.02
Fax: +44/71/273.48.14

Mr John FRANKHAM
Business Strategy Unit
Employment Service, Room 2/1
Rockingham House
123 West Street
GB-Sheffield, Yorkshire S14ER
Tél.: +44/742/59.64.00
Fax: +44/742/59.64.96

223

MISEP SECRETARIAT

I.A.S. – Institute for Applied Socio-Economics
Institut de recherche appliquée en socio-économie
Gesellschaft für Angewandte Sozial- und Wirtschaftwissenschaften mbH
Novelisstr. 10
D - 10115 BERLIN
Tél.:   +49/30/282.10.47
            Ms Angelika Zierer-Kuhnle
            +49/30/282.63.78
            Mr Peter Auer
Fax: +49/30/85.80.52

Mr Tony HUBERT & Ms Heinke HUBERT
European Association of National Productivity Cantres
60, rue de la Concorde
B-1050 BRUSSELS
Tél.: +32/2/511.71.00
Fax: +32/2/511.02.97

Wissenschaftszentrum Berlin für Sozialforschung (WZB)
Reichpietschufer 50
D-10785 BERLIN
Tél.:   +49/30/25.49.10
            +49/30/25.49.11.29
            Mr. Günther SCHMIDT
            (project director for evaluation)
            +49/30/25.49.11.28
            Mr Klaus SCHÖMANN
            +49/30/25.49.11.26
            secretariat: Ms Karin Reinsch
            +49/30/254.91.124
            Ms Birgit MEDING
            (Newsletter "East Germany")
Fax: +49/30/25.49.16.84
Télex 2627-308897=wz

SYSDEM

➤ **Genaue Bezeichnung**

Europäisches Dokumentationssystem für Beschäftigte

➤ **Tätigkeitsbereich**

Forschung, Analyse, Zusammenfassung und Verbreitung von
verfügbaren Informationen über die Beschäftigungsentwicklung in der
Gemeinschaft.

➤ **Zielgruppe**

Gemeinschaftsinstitutionen, Behörden der Mitgliedstaaten,
Universitäten, Forschungszentren und Sozialpartner

➤ **Wirkungskreis**

Informationsdienst in Brüssel;
Dienst für Analysen in Birmingham;
Korrespondenznetz in jedem Mitgliedstaat.

➤ **Aktionen**

Das Korrespondenznetz liefert Daten über Arbeitsmarkt- und
Beschäftigungslage in den Mitgliedstaaten und bereitet Quartals- und
Jahresberichte vor;
die Dienstelle "Analysen" faßt die eingeholten Auskünfte zusammen
und gewährleistet die Veröffentlichung von Berichten und
Mitteilungsblättern;
die Dienstelle "Information" verwaltet ein Dokumentationszentrum
(Informationen und Datenbanken).

➤ **Betreuung des Netzes und Kommunikationstechnik**

Veröffentlichungen: regelmäßig erscheinende Mitteilungsblätter
(vierteljährlich, jährlich);
Veranstaltung von Konferenzen;
Datenbank.

➤ Europäische Kommission
  Generaldirektion V
  Referat V/A/1
  Panayotis SIGONIS
  200 Rue de la Loi
  B - 1049 Brüssel
  Tel. (+32-2) 295 67 46 / 295 51 38

225

SYSDEM

➢ **Full title**

European System of Documentation on Employment.

➢ **Field of activity**

Research, analysis, synthesis and dissemination of information available on trends in employment in the Community.

➢ **Target public**

Community Institutions, the public authorities of Member States,universities, research centres and the two sides of industry.

➢ **Community coverage**

Information service in Brussels;
Analytical service in Birmingham;
Network of Correspondents in each Member State.

➢ **Actions**

The network of correspondents provides data on the labour market and employment in the Member States and prepares quarterly and annual reports;
the Analytical service summarises the information obtained and arranges for the publication of reports and bulletins;
the Information service administers a documentation centre (Information and Databases).

➢ **Network animation and methods of communication**

Publications: periodic bulletins (quarterly, annually);
Organisation of conferences;
Database.

➢ European Commission
Directorate-General V
Unit V/A/1
Panayotis SIGONIS
200 rue de la Loi
B - 1049 Brussels
Tel.: (+32.2) 295.67.46 / 295.51.38

SYSDEM

➤ **Intitulé exact**

Système Européen de Documentation sur l'Emploi

➤ **Domaine d'activité**

Recherche, analyse, synthèse et diffusion d'informations disponibles sur l'évolution de l'emploi dans la Communauté.

➤ **Public cible**

Institutions communautaires, Autorités publiques des États membres, universités, centres de recherche et partenaires sociaux

➤ **Rayonnement communautaire**

Service d'information à Bruxelles;
Service d'analyses à Birmingham;
Réseau de Correspondants dans chaque État membre.

➤ **Actions**

Le réseau de correspondants fournit des données sur le domaine du marché du travail et de l'emploi dans les États membres et prépare des rapports trimestriels et annuels;
le service Analyses fait la synthèse des renseignements obtenus et assure la publication de rapports et de bulletins;
le service Information gère un centre de documentation (Informations et Banques de données).

➤ **Animation du réseau et techniques de communication**

Publications: bulletins périodiques (trimestriels, annuels);
Organisation de conférences;
Banque de données.

➤ Commission européenne
Direction générale V
Unité V/A/1
Panayotis SIGONIS
200 rue de la Loi
B - 1049 Bruxelles
Tél.: (+32-2) 295.67.46 / 295.51.38

SERVICE D'INFORMATION

ECOTEC Research and Consulting Ltd
Av. de Tervueren, 13b
B- 1040 BRUXELLES
Tél.: +32/2/7327818
Fax: +32/2/7327111

SERVICE D'ANALYSE

ECOTEC Research and Consulting Ltd
Priestley House
28-34 Albert Street
BIRMINGHAM, B4 7UD UK
Tél.: +44/21/6161010
Fax: +44/21/6161099

CORRESPONDANTS NATIONAUX

BELGIQUE-BELGIË

Prof. François PICHAULT / Jean Noël BROUIR
LENTIC - Université de Liège
Faculté d'Economie, de Gestion et de Sciences Sociales
Boulevard du Rectorat 7
Bâtiment B31 - Boîte 48
B - 4000 LIEGE
Tél.:+32/41/663070
Fax: +32/41/662947

DANMARK

Dr. Saren VILLADSEN
Institute of Economics and planning
University of Roskilde
Post Office Box 260
DK - 4000 ROSKILDE
Tél.: +45/46.75.77.11
Fax: +45/46.75.66.18

DEUTSCHLAND

Mr Kurt VOGLER-LUDWIG
IFO Institute for Economic Research
Poschingerstr. 5
D-81631 MÜNCHEN
Tel: 49/89.922.40
Fax: 49/89.985.369

ELLAS

Prof. Theo PAPATHEODOSSIOU
Institute of technological Education
Leoforos Syngrou 56
GR - 11742 ATHENS
Tél.: +30/1/8941419 - 8941260
Fax: +30/1/3225259 - 3235609

ESPAÑA

Prof. Luis TOHARIA/ Gloria MORENO
Universidad de Alcalà de Henares
Plaza de la Victoria 3
E - 28802 ALCALÁ DE HENARES
Tél.:+34/1/8854272
Fax: +34/1/8854206

FRANCE

Mme Brigitte SIVAN
BIPE Conseil
Axe Seine 21
F - 92442 ISSY-LES-MOULINEAUX CEDEX
Tel: 33/1/46.62.33.00
Fax: 33/1/46.62.62.20

IRELAND

Prof. Jerry SEXTON
Research professor
Economic and Social Research Institute
4, Burlington Road
IRL - DUBLIN 4
Tél.: +353/1/6760115-9
Fax: +353/1/6686231

ITALIA

Dr. Manuela SAMEK
Istituto per la Ricerca Sociale
Via XX Settembre 24
I- 20123 MILANO
Tél.: +39/2/4815653
Fax: +36/2/48008495

NEDERLAND

Prof. Jacques SIEGERS
Economic institute / CIAV
Utrecht University
romme Nieuwergracht 22
NL - 3512 HH UTRECHT
Tél.: +31/30/537100
Fax: +31/30/537131

ÖSTERREICH

Mr. Fernand LECHNER
L&R Sozialforschung
Proschkogasse 1/12
A-1060 VIENNA
Tel: (43) 1 581 81 71 0
Fax: (43) 1 581 81 71 9

PORTUGAL

Prof. Maria Joao RODRIGUES
DINAMIA
Avenida das Forças Armadas
P-1600 LISBOA
Tel: 35/11/793.86.38
Fax:35/11/794.00.42

SUOMI-FINLAND

Ms Tuire SANTAMÄKI-VUORI
Research Director
Labour Institute for Economic Research
Hämeentie 8A
SF-00530 HELSINKI
Tel: (358) 0 737.733
Fax: (358) 0 7013.807

SVERIGE

Ms Anna Thoursie
Swedish Institute of Social Research
S-106 91 STOCKHOLM
Tel: +46/8/16.20.00
     +46/8/16.24.97 (direct)
Fax: +46/8/15.46.70

UNITED KINGDOM

Mr Kenneth Walsh
T.E.R.N.
7, Station Road
Stoffessdon
NR Kidderminster
UK-WORCS. DY14 8TT
Tél.: +44/1746/718530
Fax: +44/1746/718728

229

EURES

> **Genaue Bezeichnung**

European Employment Services

> **Tätigkeitsbereich**

Mobilität der Arbeitnehmer in Europa.

> **Zielgruppe**

Unternehmen, Arbeitnehmer.

> **Wirkungskreis**

450 Euroberater in den Ländern der Europäischen Union.

> **Ziele**

Förderung der Mobilität von Arbeitnehmern auf europäischer Ebene durch die Verbreitung von Stellenangeboten und -gesuchen.

> **Aktionen**

Information, Beratung und Hilfe bei der Vermittlung und Einstellung über Euroberater, die größenteils der Zuständigkeit der nationalen Arbeitsverwaltungen unterliegen.
Ihre Aufgabe sieht wie folgt aus:
- Sensibilisierung der Arbeitnehmer und Arbeitgeber für die Möglichkeiten eines erweiterten Arbeitsmarkts;
- Unterstützung für erfolgreiche Mobilität oder Einstellung von Personal in anderen Mitgliedstaaten.

> **Ihnen zur Verfügung stehende Informationen**

Die Euroberater sind an eine elektronische Datenbank angeschlossen, die folgendes enthält:
- europaweite Stellenangebote;
- allgemeine Informationen über die Lebens- und Arbeitsbedingungen in den Ländern der Union, angefangen vom Wohnungswesen über Vertragsrecht bis hin zur Besteuerung.

> Europäische Kommission
Generaldirektion V
Referat V/D/4
Vassiliki KOLOTOUROU
200 Rue de la Loi
B - 1049 Brüssel
Tel. (+32-2) 295 50 90

EURES

> **Full title**

European Employment Services

> **Field of activity**

Worker mobility in Europe.

> **Target public**

Companies and workers.

> **Community coverage**
450 Eurocounsellors spread over the countries of the European Union.

> **Objectives**

Facilitate the mobility of workers on the European scale by the dissemination of job offers and applications.

> **Actions**

Information, advice and help in placement and recruitment through the intermediary of Eurocounsellors, who, for the most part, report to national employment agencies.
Their role consists of:
- making workers and their employers aware of the opportunities offered by an enlarged employment market;
- assist in achieving successful mobility or recruitment of personnel from other Member States.

> **Information which they have available**

The Eurocounsellors are linked to a computer database which includes:
- job offers within Europe;
- general information on living and working conditions in the countries of the Union in fields extending from housing through contract law to taxation.

> European Commission
Directorate-General V
Unit V/D/4
Vassiliki KOLOTOUROU
200 rue de la Loi
B - 1049 Brussels
Tel.: (+32.2) 295.50.90

EURES

➤ **Intitulé exact**

European Employment Services

➤ **Domaine d'activité**

Mobilité des travailleurs en Europe.

➤ **Public cible**

Entreprises, travailleurs.

➤ **Rayonnement communautaire**

450 euroconseillers répartis dans les Pays de l'Union européenne.

➤ **Objectifs**

Faciliter la mobilité des travailleurs à l'échelle européenne par la diffusion d'offres et de demandes d'emploi.

➤ **Actions**

Information, conseil et aide au placement et au recrutement par l'intermédiaire d'euroconseillers relevant pour la plupart des agences nationales pour l'emploi.
Leur rôle consiste à:
- sensibiliser les travailleurs et les employeurs aux opportunités offertes par un marché de l'emploi élargi;
- aider à réaliser avec succès la mobilité ou le recrutement de personnel dans d'autres Pays membres.

➤ **Informations dont ils disposent**

Les euroconseillers sont raccordés à une base de données informatisée qui comporte:
- des offres d'emploi à dimension européenne;
- des informations générales sur les conditions de vie et de travail dans les Pays de l'Union dans des domaines allant du logement à l'imposition fiscale, en passant par le droit des contrats.

➤ Commission européenne
Direction générale V
Unité V/D/4
Vassiliki KOLOTOUROU
200 rue de la Loi
B - 1049 Bruxelles
Tél.: (+32-2) 295.50.90

E.C. BIC

➤ **Genaue Bezeichnung**

European Community Business Innovation Centre

➤ **Tätigkeitsbereich**

Ziel ist die Förderung der optimalen Nutzung der lokalen, natürlichen und finanziellen Ressourcen sowie des Humankapitals und des Know-hows für die Schaffung und Entwicklung von Industrietätigkeiten sowohl auf regionaler als auch lokaler Ebene.

➤ **Zielgruppe**

Unternehmensgründer;
bestehende KMU (es handelt sich um Unternehmen und Industriedienstleistungen).

➤ **Wirkungskreis**

Eine Koordinierungsstelle in Brüssel - EBN;
60 Europäische Unternehmens- und Innovationszentren in der ganzen Gemeinschaft (Ziel: 100).

➤ **Aktionen**

Anregung des Unternehmertums;
Bewertung, Auswahl und Orientierung der potentiellen Unternehmer;
Ermittlung von KMU, die für die Lancierung von neuen Aktivitäten geeignet sind;
Entwicklung von Verwaltungskompetenzen;
Angebot von Dienstleistungen für die Vorbereitung von Geschäftsplänen: Bewertungsdienste;
Finanzdienste; Empfangsdienste.

➤ **Betreuung des Netzes und Kommunikationstechnik**

Zwischen E.C. BIC und/oder unter Schirmherrschaft von EBN:
• beruflicher Austausch (Gutachten, Verwaltungsinstrumente);
• Kooperationsprojekte;
• Entwicklung von Kommunikationsinstrumenten (Mitteilungsblätter, Zeitschriften, audiovisuelles Material);
• Kommunikationskampagnen.

➤ Europäische Kommission
Generaldirektion XVI
Referat XVI/3 - CSTM 8/123
Francesco PETTINI
200 Rue de la Loi
B - 1049 Brüssel
Tel. (+32-2) 295 45 67 / 296 14 43

235

EC BIC

➤ **Full title**

European Community Business Innovation Centre

➤ **Field of activity**

The aim is to promote optimal utilisation of local-, human-, natural-, financial resources and know-how, to help in the development of industrial activities at regional as well as at local level.

➤ **Target public**

Business promoters;
Existing SME (companies and services to industry).

➤ **Community coverage**

A coordination agency in Brussels - EBN;
60 European Business Innovation Centres spread over the whole of the Community
(objective: 100).

➤ **Actions**

Stimulation of the company spirit;
evaluation, selection and orientation of potential entrepreneurs;
detection of SME likely to launch new activities;
development of management skills; offer of services for the preparation of business plans: advisory services;
financial services; reception services.

➤ **Network animation and methods of communication**

Between EC BIC and/or under the aegis of EBN:
• professional exchanges (appraisals, management tools);
• cooperation projects;
• development of communication tools (bulletins, newsletter, audiovisual material);
• communication campaigns.

➤ European Commission
Directorate-General XVI
Unit XVI/3 - CSTM 8/123
Francesco PETTINI
200 rue de la Loi
B - 1049 Brussels
Tel.: (+32.2) 295.45.67 / 296.14.43

E.C. BIC

➤ **Intitulé exact**
European Community Business Innovation Centre

➤ **Domaine d'activité**

Le but est de favoriser l'utilisation optimale des ressources locales, humaines, naturelles, de savoir-faire et financières, afin d'aider la création et le développement d'activités industrielles aussi bien au niveau régional que local.

➤ **Public cible**

Créateurs d'entreprises;
PME existantes (il s'agit d'entreprises et de services à l'industrie).

➤ **Rayonnement communautaire**

Une agence de coordination à Bruxelles - EBN;
60 Centres Européens d'Entreprise et d'innovation répartis sur l'ensemble de la Communauté
(objectif: 100).

➤ **Actions**

Animation d'esprit d'entreprise;
évaluation, sélection et orientation des entrepreneurs potentiels;
détection des PME susceptibles de lancer des activités nouvelles;
développement des compétences de gestion;
offre de services pour la préparation de plans d'entreprises:
services conseil, services financiers, services d'accueil.

➤ **Animation du réseau et techniques de communication**

Entre E.C. BIC et/ou sous l'égide d'EBN:
• échanges professionnels (expertises, outils de gestion);
• projets de coopération;
• développement d'outils de communication (bulletins, journal, matériel audiovisuel);
• campagnes de communication.

➤ Commission européenne
Direction générale XVI
Unité XVI/3 - CSTM 8/123
Francesco PETTINI
200 rue de la Loi
B - 1049 Bruxelles
Tél.: (+32-2) 295.45.67 / 296.14.43

AGENCE DE COORDINATION

**European Business
and Innovation Centre**
89/93 Rue Froissart
B-1040 BRUXELLES
Tél.: +32/2/231.07.47

BELGIQUE-BELGIË

Charleroi

**CENTRE D'ENTREPRISE ET
D'INNOVATION "3E"**
1E, Bld. Général Michel
B-6000 CHARLEROI
Mr. Philippe Chèvremont
Tél.: +32/71/32.04.74
Fax: +32/71/31.67.35
Télex 51847

Liège

**S.O.C.R.A.N./ Société pour la création
d'activités nouvelles**
Parc Scientifique de Sart-Tilman
Av. Pré-Aily
B-4031 ANGLEUR
Mr. Robert Frédéric
Tél.: +32/41/67.83.30
Fax: +32/41/67.83.00
Télex 42501 SOCRAN

Nivelles

Centre de Technologie et de
Gestion des Affaires (CTG)
Rue de l'Industrie, 20
B-1400 NIVELLES
M. Jean-Claude ETTINGER
Tel.: +32/67/88.36.11
Fax: +32/67/88.38.88

Turnhout

INNOTEK
Kleinhoefstraat 5
B-2440 GEEL
Mr. Luc Peeters
Tél.: +32/14/57.00.57
Fax: +32/14/58.13.25
Télex 33087

238

DEUTSCHLAND

Brandenburg

Business and Innovation Centre
Frankfurt (Oder) Gmbh
Im Technologiepark 1
D-15236 FRANKFURT (ODER)
Mr. Uwe Hoppe
Tél.: +49/335/55.71.100
Fax: +49/335/55.71.110

Sachsen

BIC-Zwickau GmbH
Lessingstr. 4
D-08058 ZWICKAU
Mr. Peter Michel
Tél.: +49/375/54.10
Fax: +49/375/54.13.00

Sachsen/Anhalt

BIC Stendal
Lüdertzer Str., 101-102
D-39576 STENDAL
Mr. Christian Krause
Tel.: +49/39.31/21.68.40
Fax: +49/39.31/21.68.84

Thüringen

BIC NORDTHÜRINGEN GmbbH
Landratsamt Sondershausen
Postfach 15
D-99701 SONDERSHAUSEN
Mr. Helmut Nüchter
Tel.: +49/36.32/41.300
Fax: +49/36.32/41.135

ELLAS

Grèce Occidentale

Patrs BIC
Chamber of Achaia Building
58, Michalakopoulo Street
POB. 1385
GR-26110 PATRAS
Mr. G. Kontogeorgakis
Mr. Evangelos Floratos
Tél.: +30/61/27.78.30
Fax: +30/61/27.65.19

Crète

**Chania Business
and Technology Centre**
Chamber of Chania
4, El. Venizelou Street
GR-73132 CHANIA
Mr. Theokritos Zervakis
Tél.: +30/821/22.329
             29.343
Fax: +30/821/26.362

Thessalia

E.C. BIC Larissa
44, Papakiriazi Street
GR-41222 LARISSA
Mr. Dimitrios Stylopoulos
Tel.: +30/41/53.49.17
Fax: +30/44/25.75.22

Centre Makedonia

Serres E.C.
Business & Innovation Centre
12, D. Solomou
GR-62122 SERRES
Mr. Karanasios
Mr Yiannis Kafetzopoulos
Tel.: +30/321/56.030
Fax: +30/321/56.031

ESPAÑA

Aragón

CEEI - Aragón, S.A.
María de Luna, 11 (Pol. Actur)
E-50015 ZARAGOZA
Mr. Javier Sánchez
Tél.: +34/76/73.35.00
Fax: +34/76/73.37.19

Asturias

**CEEI Asturias Centro Europeo de
Empresa e Innovación de Asturias**
Parque Tecnológico de Asturias
E-33420 LLANERA
Mr. José Luis Suárez
Tel.: +34/8/52.60.068
Fax: +34/8/52.64.455

Cataluña

**Centre de Empresas
de Noves Tecnologies S.A.**
Parc Tecnológic del Vallés
E-08290 CERDANYOLA
Tél.: +34/3/58.20.200
Fax: +34/3/58.01.354

Cantabria

SODERCAN
Avda Isabel II, 24
E-39002 SANTANDER
Mr. Ricardo Laporte
Tel.: +34/42/31.15.53
Fax: +34/42/31.16.53

País Vasco

BEAZ
Centro de Empresas e Innovación de
Bizkaia
Alda, Recalde, 18-6A
E-48009 BILBAO
Mr. Javier Maqueda Lafuente
Tel.: +34/4/423.92.27-8
Fax: +34/4/423.10.13

Castilla y León

**CEICALSA / Centro de Empresas e
Innovación de Castilla y León**
Parque Tecnológico de Boecillo
E-47151 BOECILLO (Valladolid)
Mr. Ramón Bocos Muñoz
Tél.: +34/83/55.22.11
Fax: +34/83/55.23.69

Extremadura

**CEI - Centro de Empresas e
Innovación de Extremadura**
C/ Doctor Marañón 2
E-10002 CÁCERES
Mr. Manuel Del Hoyo Macias
Tél.: +34/27/21.59.50
Fax: +34/27/21.59.89

Galicia

BIC-GALICIA
Avda Alcalde Portanet, 37
(Edificio Zona Franca, 2˚)
E-36211 VIGO
Mr. Santiago G.-Babé Ozores
Tel.: +34/86/20.98.49
Fax: +34/86/20.78.82

239

Madrid

BIC HENARES

Plaza de la Victoria 1
Alcalá de Henares
E-28807 MADRID
Mr. Ignacio Gamboa Maier
Tél.: +34/1/882.41.69
         882.77.07
Fax: +34/1/882.41.43

Navarra

CEIN , S.A.

Polígono Elorz s/n
E-31110 NOAIN (Navarra)
Mme Celia Oiz Gil
Tél.: +34/48/10.60.00-1
Fax: +34/48/10.60.10

Andalucía

BIC-EURONOVA, S.A.

Parque Tecnológico de Andalucía
Apartado de Correos, 81
E-29590 CAMPANILLAS (Málaga)
Mr. Alavro Simón De Blas
Tel.: +34/5/26.19.125
Fax: +34/5/26.19.128

EUROCEI - Centro Europeo de

Empresas e Innovación S.A.
Apartado de Correos, 76
Coria S/N
San Juan de Aznalfaracche
E-41920 SEVILLA
Mr. Enrique Piriz Salgado
Tél.: +34/5/417.05.17
Fax: +34/5/417.11.17

Comunidad Valenciana

CEEI VALENCIA

Parque Tecnológico
Calle 3, sector oeste, s/n
E-46980 PATERNA (Valencia)
Mr. Jesús Casanova Payá
Tel.: 34/96/199.42.00
Fax: +34/96/199.42.20

CEEI ALCOY

Pl. Emilio Sala, 1
E-03800 ALCOY (Alicante)
Mr. Jorge Seguí Roma
Tel.: +34/96/554.16.66
Fax: +34/96/554.40.85

CEEI ELCHE

Ronda Vall D'Uxó, 125
E-03205 ELCHE (Alicante)
Mr. Joaquín Alzár Cano
Tel.: +34/96/666.10.17
         666.11.25
Fax: +34/96/666.10.40

Murcia

CEEIC

Polígono Industrial Cabezo
Baeza
c/Berlín, Parcela 3-F
E-30395 CARTAGENA (Murcia)
Mr. Ramón Gómez
Tel. +34/68/52.10.17
Fax: +34/68/50.08.39

FRANCE

Aveyron

CEI 12

38, Bld. de l'Ayrolle
BP 408
F-12100 MILLAU Cédex
Mr. Gérard Revel
Tél.: +33/65/61.25.89
Fax: +33/65/60.41.88

Bouches-du-Rhône

Association du CEEI Multipolaire des Bouche-du-Rhône

Domaine du Petit Arbois
BP 88
F-13762 AIX-LES-MILLES Cédex
Mr. Luc Sollier-Bresset
Tel.: +33/42/24.59.59
Fax: +33/42/24.59.60

Haute Garonne

CEEI THEOGONE

Route de Mondavezan
F-31220 MARTRES-TOLOSANE
Mr. Daniel Blondé
Tél.: +33/61/28.56.56
         98.85.00
Fax: +33/61/28.56.00

240

Charente-Maritime

CEEI CAPE 17
Rue du Bois D'Huré
F-17140 LAGORD
Mme Marie-Thérèse Lucot
Tél.: +33/46.00.00.50
Fax: +33/46.00.00.51
Telex: 793 084

Lorraine

CEEI SYNERGIE
29, Place de Chambre
F-57000 METZ
Mr. Hubert Trost
Tél.: +33/87/76.36.36
Fax: +33/87/76.23.03

PROMOTECH NANCY
6, Allée Pelletier Doisy
F-54603 VILLERS-LES-NANCY Cédex
Mr. Jacky Chef
Tel.: +33/83/50.44.44
Fax: +33/83/44.04.82
Telex: 961742F (code 137)

Herault

CEEI CAP-ALPHA
Avenue de l'Europe-Clapiers
F-34940 MONTPELLIER Cédex
Mr. Jean-Claude Monnier
Tél.: +33/67/59.30.00
Fax: +33/67/59.30.10

Vienne

CEEI POITIERS
15, rue Carnot-B.P.175
F-86004 POITIERS
Mme Maïté Sasulla
Tél.: +33/49/88.66.90-1
Fax: +33/49/88.70.65

Loire

CEEI St-Etienne
Maison de la Productique
74, rue des Acieries
F-42000 SAINT-ETIENNE
M.Bassereau
Tél.: +33/77/43.19.59
Fax: +33/77/79.25.50

Ille-et-Villaine

CEEI CREAT'IV
Espace Performance
Boîte F
F-35769 SAINT-GRÉGOIRE Cédex
Mr. Jean-Luc Hannequin
Tel.: +33/99/23.79.00
Fax: +33/99/23.78.11

Var

CEEI TOULON
Place G. Pompidou
Quartier Mayol
F-83000 TOULON
Mr. Jean-Noël Loiseau
Tél.: +33/94.03.89.01
Fax:+33/94.03.89.14

IRELAND

South West

SOUTHWEST BUSINESS & TECHNOLOGY CENTRE
IDA Enterprise Centre
North mall
IRL-CORK CITY
(vacant)
Tél.: +353/21/39.77.11
Fax: +353/21/39.53.93
Télex 76159

Dublin

Dublin Business Innovation Centre
The Tower
IDA Enterprise Centre
Pearse Street
IRL-DUBLIN 2
Mr. Desmond Fahey
Tél.: +353/1/671.31.11
Fax: +353/1/671.33.30

West

Galway Business Innovation Centre
Hardiman House
5, Eyre Square
IRL-GALWAY
Mr. Joe Greaney
Tél.: +353/91/679.74
Fax: +353/91/679.80
Télex 50137

241

Mid West

Limerick Innovation Centre
The Innovation Centre
Enterprise House
Plassey Technological Park
CASTLETROY
IRL-County Limerick
Ms. Alice Morgan
Tél.:+353/61/33.81.77
Fax: +353/61/33.80.65
Télex 70182 INO EI

ITALIA

Marche

EURO BIC PICENO APRUTINO
Centro d'Impresa e Innovazione della
Comunità Europea
Ascoli Piceno
Zona industriale Marino
I-63100 ASCOLI PICENO
Mr. Umberto Fanuzzi
Tél.: +39/736/34.21.60
            34.25.70
Fax: +39/736/34.21.70

BIC MARCHE Srl
Via Cimabue 21
I-60019 SENIGALLIA
Prof. Tullio Piersantelli
Tel.: +39/71/66.08.537
Fax: +39/71/66.09.581

EUROBIC Marche
Business and Innovation Centre
c/o Innova
I-TOLENTINO
Mr. Marcolini
Tel.: +39/733/49.28.02
Fax: +39/733/49.21.88

Puglia

BIC PUGLIA S.p.A.
Centro Europeo di Impresa e Innovazione
Via A. Gioia, 131
I-70054 GIOVINAZZO (Bari)
Dott. Cosimo Del Vecchio
Tél.: +39/80/894.34.99
Fax: +39/80/894.37.95

CISI
Contrada Carmine
Quartiere Paolo VI
I-74100 TARANTO
Dott. Francesco Ruggieri
Tel.: +39/99/47.30.444
Fax: +39/99/42.12.40

Abruzzo

EUROBIC ABRUZZO
Via dei Frentani 191
I-66100 CHIETI
Dott. Antonio Sutti
Tél.: +39/871/33.17.92
Fax: +39/871/33.17.95

Lazio

BIC LAZIO
Via La Botte, 22
I-03100 FROSINONE
Dott. Paolo Palomba
Tél.: +39/775/27.05.72 (Frosinone)
            +39/6/807.98.53 (Roma)
                807.94.35 (Roma)
                858.71.59 (Roma)
Fax: +39/6/807.88.39

Liguria

BIC LIGURIA
Via Greto di Cornigliano, 6
I-16152 GENOVA
Dott. Filippo Gabani
Tél.: +39/10/65.631
Fax: +39/10/65.18.752

Toscana

CSP/BIC LIVORNO-PIOMBINO
Scali degli Olandesi, 43
I-57125 LIVORNO
Dott. Giorgio Starnini
Tél.: +39/586/88.05.68
Fax: +39/586/88.74.13

EBTS-EUROBIC
Toscana Sud
Via San Gimignano 69-71
I-53036 POGGIBONSI (Siena)
Dott. Franco Bartoli
Tel.: +39/577/93.82.27
Fax: +39/577/98.32.19

242

Sicilia

BIC
Sicilia Occidentale
Via Maggiore Toselli, 87/b
I-90143 PALERMO
Ing. Giorgio Chimenti
Tél.: +39/91/625.06.27
Fax: +39/91/625.06.20

INNOVA CEII
Viale Libertà is.521
I-98100 MESSINA
Mr. Nunzio Venuti
Tel.: +39/90/34.35.65
Fax: +39/90/51.533

Piemonte

BIC PIEMONTE
Via Curtatone 5
I-10131 TORINO
Dott. Giovanni Bertone
Tél.: +39/11/660.26.66
Fax: +39/11/660.33.33

Campania

BIC Caserta
Business and Innovation Centre
Via Redentore 10
I-81100 CASERTA
Dr. Pasquale Rivello
Tél.: +39/823/32.69.88
Fax: +39/823/32.62.27

Sardegna

BIC SARDEGNA S.p.A.
Centro Europeo Impresa e Innovazione
Via S. Margherita, 8
I-09124 CAGLIARI
Dott. Giuseppe Matolo
Tél.: +39/70/66.35.34
Fax: +39/70/65.92.73

Friuli-Venezia-Giulia

BIC Trieste
Via Flavia 23/1
I-34148 TRIESTE
Dott. Francesco Zacchigna
Tel.: +39/40/899.22.70
Fax: +39/40/899.22.57

Basilicata

**Centro Europeo d'Impresa
e Innovazione-SYSTEMA**
Via Pretoria 77
I-85100 POTENZA
Dott. Raffaele Ricciuti
Tel.: +39/971/35.836
Fax: +39/971/41.02.66

Emilia-Romagna

BIC-EMILIA-ROMAGNA
Business and Innovation Centre
c/o SOPRIP
Via Verdi
I-PARMA
Mr. Edoardo Terenziani
Tel.: +39/521/28.25.92
Fax: +39/521/23.54.07

NEDERLAND

Oost-Nederland

Business Innovation Centre
Twente b.v.
Instituten weg 4
Postbus 545
NL-7500 AM ENSCHEDE
Mr. R. Lawerman
Tél.: +31/53/88.53.33
Fax: +31/53/33.74.15

Zuid-Nederland

Europees Bedrijven
Centrum Heerlen B.V.
Valkenburgerweg, 19
P.O. Box 576
NL-6400 AN HEERLEN
Mr. J. Bogman
Tél.: +31/45/71.66.31
Fax: +31/45/71.83.81

BIC HELMOND
PRINS Hendriklaan, 21a
P.Bus 211
NL-5700 HELMOND
Mr. J.J. Steeman
Tél.: +31/4920/34.35
Fax: +31/4920/23.895

243

PORTUGAL

Lisboa e Vale do Tejo

CPIN - Centro Promotor de Inovaçao e Negócios
Av. Almirante Reis, 178
P-1000 LISBOA
Mr. José Carlos Amaral
Tél.: +351/1/848.80.08
          847.68.84
Fax: +351/1/847.58.93

CEISET Centro de Empresas e Inovação de Setúbal
Av. Luisa Todi, 375
P-2900 Setúbal
Mr. Vasco A. Lemos Vieira
Tel.: +351/65/535.242-107
Fax; +351/65/535.356-159
Telex: 202.24

Norte

NET-Novas Empresas
e Tecnologias, S.A.
Rua doa Salazares, 842
P-4100 PORTO
Mr. Jorge Monteiro
Tél.: +351/2/617.05.79
          617.98.51
Fax: +351/2/617.76.62
Télex 20224

Alentejo

CIEA-Centro de Inovação
Empresarial do Alentejo
Parque Industrial e Tecnológico de Evora
Rua da Barbarala, 1 Ap. 479
P-7005 EVORA CODEX
Mr. Luis Sotto Mayor
Tel.: +351/66/74.42.72-73
Fax: +351/66/74.42.74

Centro
CIEBI-Centro de Inovação
Empresarial de Beira Interior
c/o Centro de Estudos de
Desenvolvimento Regional
Edifício de Universidade de Beira Interior
Rua Marques d'Avila e Bolama
P-6200 COVILHÃ
Mr. João Carvalho
Tel.: +351/75/32.77.70
Fax: +351/75/32.77.71

BIC Viseu-Centro de Innovação
Empresarial de Viseu
c/o Associação
Industrial Da Região
de Viseu
Rua Cândido dos Reis, 22
P-3500 VISEU
Mr. Alfredo Alexandre
Tel.: +351/32/42.41.55
Fax: +351/32/42.11.50

UNITED KINGDOM

England

BARNSLEY BIC LIMITED
Innovation Way
BARNSLEY
UK-South Yorkshire S75 IJL
Mr. Tim Milburn (Acting CED)
Tél.: +44/226/24.95.90
Fax: +44/226/24.96.25

GREATER MANCHESTER CENTRE
C.C.E. Business Centre
Windmill Lane
Denton, Tameside
UK- GREATER MANCHESTER M34 30S
Mr. Philip Ellison
Tel.: +44/61/337.86.48-49-50
Fax: +44/61/337.86.51

LANCASHIRE BUSINESS AND INNOVATION CENTRE
Suites 302-304
Daisyfield Business Centre
Appleby Street-Blackburn
UK-LANCASHIRE BB1 3BL

Wales

SEWBIC-South East Wales
Business and Innovation Centre
Cardiff Business Technology Centre
Senghennydd Road
Cathays Park
UK-CARDIFF CF4 ZAY
Mr. Douglas Hampson
Tél.: +44/222/37.23.11
Fax: +44/222/37.34.36

244

Northern Ireland

INNOVATION CENTRE NORIBIC
Springrowth House
Balliniska Road
Springtown Industrial Estate
UK-DERRY BT48 ONA
Mr. William Duffy
Tél.: +44/504/26.42.42
Fax: +44//504/26.90.25

Scotland

STRATHCLYDE INNOVATION
Unit A1, Blg 1
Templeton Business Centre
62, Templeton Street
UK-GLASGOW G40 IDA
Mr. Douglas Martyn
Tél.: +44/41/55.45.995
Fax: +44/41/55.66.320

ERGO 2

➤ **Genaue Bezeichnung**

Aktionsprogramm der Gemeinschaft zugunsten der
Langzeitarbeitslosen

➤ **Tätigkeitsbereich**

Bekämpfung der Langzeitarbeitslosigkeit

➤ **Zielgruppe**

Öffentliche oder private Einrichtungen zur Bekämpfung der
Langzeitarbeitslosigkeit (nationale Verwaltungsstellen, Verbände,
Gebietskörperschaften, Ausbildungszentren),
Interessenvertretungen der Arbeitslosen.

➤ **Wirkungskreis**

Zwei für die Programmverwaltung zuständige Einrichtungen.

➤ **Aktionen**

Ermittlung, Bewertung und Verbreitung von auf nationaler, regionaler
oder lokaler Ebene besonders wirksamer bzw. problemgerechter
Aktionen oder Praktiken in den Mitgliedstaaten zur Bereicherung der
nationalen und gemeinschaftlichen Instrumente für die Bekämpfung
der Langzeitarbeitslosigkeit (siehe Broschüre).

247

➤ **Betreuung des Netzes und Kommunikationstechnik**

Zeitschrift ERGONEWS (vierteljährlich Fr/En/De/Es/It, 17.000
Exemplare).

Die jüngsten Entwicklungen der Beschäftigungspolitik und
insbesondere die Schlußfolgerungen des Europäischen Rats von
Dezember 1994 in Essen veranlaßten die Kommission, dem Rat eine
Umstrukturierung, einhergehend mit einer Verstärkung ihrer
Aktivitäten im Beschäftigungsbereich, vorzuschlagen. Dieser Prozeß,
der zur Einrichtung eines neuen Aktions- und Kooperationsrahmens
zur Förderung einer engeren Zusammenarbeit zwischen der
Kommission und den Mitgliedstaaten in der Beschäftigungspolitik
führt, wird auch **die Beendung des Programms Leda/Ergo zum
Ende des Jahres 1995** zur Folge haben.

➤ Europäische Kommission
Generaldirektion V
Referat V/A/1
200 Rue de la Loi
B - 1049 Brüssel
Tel. (+32-2) 295 51 84

ERGO 2

> **Full title**

European Community Action Programme for the long-term unemployed

> **Field of activity**

Combatting unemployment

> **Target public**

Public or private bodies who combat unemployment (National administrations, associations, local communities, training centres), bodies representing the unemployed.

> **Community coverage**

Two private bodies responsible for the management of the programme.

> **Actions**

Identification, evaluation and dissemination, in the Member States,of actions or practices at national, regional or local level which are particularly effective or applicable, so enabling the enrichment of national or Community tools to combat unemployment (see booklet).

> **Network animation and methods of communication**

ERGONEWS Journal (quarterly Fr/En/De/Es, 17,000 copies).

Recent developments in employment policy and, particularly, the Conclusions of the European Council of Essen in December, 1994, led the Commission to propose to the Council a reorganization process accompanied with the strengthening of its activities in the field of employment. Such a process, which will lead to the establishment of a new framework for action and cooperation favouring closer collaboration between the Commission and Member States as regards employment policy, will also, consequently, result in the **termination of the Leda/Ergo programme by the end of 1995.**

> European Commission
Directorate-General V
Unit V/A/1
200 rue de la Loi
B - 1049 Brussels
Tel.: (+32.2) 295.51.84

ERGO 2

➢ **Intitulé exact**

Programme d'action communautaire en faveur des chômeurs de longue durée

➢ **Domaine d'activité**

Lutte contre le chômage de longue durée.

➢ **Public cible**

Organismes publics ou privés de lutte contre le chômage de longue durée (Administrations nationales, associations, collectivités locales, centres de formation), organismes représentant les chômeurs.

➢ **Rayonnement communautaire**

Deux organismes privés responsables de la gestion du programme.

➢ **Actions**

Identification, évaluation et diffusion dans les États membres des actions ou des pratiques menées au niveau national, régional ou local particulièrement efficaces ou adaptées et permettant d'enrichir les outils nationaux ou communautaires de lutte contre le chômage de longue durée (voir plaquette).

249

➢ **Animation du réseau et techniques de communication**

Journal ERGONEWS (trimestriel Fr/En/De/Es/It, 17.000 exemplaires).

Les évolutions récentes en matière de politique de l'emploi et particulièrement les Conclusions du Conseil européen d'Essen en décembre 1994 ont conduit la Commission à proposer au Conseil une réorganisation assortie d'un renforcement de ses activités dans le domaine de l'emploi. Ce processus qui conduira à la mise en place d'un nouveau cadre d'action et de coopération favorisant une collaboration plus étroite entre la Commission et les Etats membres en matière de politique de l'emploi aura également pour conséquence la **clôture du programme Leda/Ergo à la fin de 1995.**

➢ Commission européenne
Direction générale V
Unité V/A/1
200 rue de la Loi
B - 1049 Bruxelles
Tél.: (+32-2) 295.51.84

**RESPONSABLE DU DOMAINE
"COMMUNICATION ET ANIMATION
DU RESEAU"**

Groupe Ten
93, rue de la Jonquière
F-75017 Paris
Tél.:   +33/1/40.25.39.00
Fax: +33/1/40.25.39.01

**RESPONSABLE DU DOMAINE
"EVALUATION ET RECHERCHE"**

P.A Cambridge Economic Consultants
62-64 Hills Road
UK-CAMBRIDGE CB2 1LA
Tél.:   +44/12.23/31.16.49
Fax: +44/12.23/62.913

BUREAU D'INFORMATION ERGO1

Marie Cristine ASHBY
Rue Van Campenhout 37
B-1040 Bruxelles
Tel.: +32/2/736.79.22
           353.19.22
Fax: +32/2/736.11.47

250

LEDA

➤ **Genaue Bezeichnung**
Local Employment Development Action
Aktionsprogramm zur örtlichen Beschäftigungsförderung

➤ **Tätigkeitsbereich**
Aktionsprogramm für die Untersuchung von Strategien für
Beschäftigungsförderung in den von Arbeitslosigkeit betroffenen
Gebieten. LEDA ermittelt positive Ideen und Erfahrungen und
gewährleistet die Verbreitung in der gesamten Gemeinschaft.

➤ **Zielgruppe**
Alle Regionen oder Körperschaften der Gemeinschaft mit
Beschäftigungsproblemen auf dem Arbeitsmarkt.

➤ **Wirkungskreis**
Studienbüro für die Umsetzung des LEDA-Programms in Brüssel und
London;
Netz von lokalen Entwicklungsagenturen in 42 Gebieten der
Gemeinschaft, die schwer von Arbeitslosigkeit getroffen sind;
Sachverständigengruppe für regionale Entwicklung.

➤ **Aktionen**
Umsetzung von Pilotprojekten;
Erstellung von Methoden und Techniken für Entscheidungsträger und
lokale Akteure zur Erarbeitung von Strategien für verbesserte
Arbeitsmarktgestaltung und Förderung der örtlichen Entwicklung.

251

➤ **Betreuung des Netzes und Kommunikationstechnik**
Informationsverbreitung und Förderung des Austausches von
Fachkenntnissen:
• Veröffentlichungen:
Grundlagendokumente für politische Entscheidungsträger;
Fachberichte für die lokalen Akteure;
Erstellung von Informationsmitteilungen.
• Sitzungen:
Austauschbesuche zwischen Pilotprojekten;
Veranstaltung von Workshops, Seminaren und Konferenzen.

Die jüngsten Entwicklungen der Beschäftigungspolitik und
insbesondere die Schlußfolgerungen des Europäischen Rats vom
Dezember 1994 in Essen veranlaßten die Kommission, dem Rat eine
Umstrukturierung, einhergehend mit einer Verstärkung ihrer
Aktivitäten im Beschäftigungsbereich, vorzuschlagen. Dieser Prozeß,
der zur Einrichtung eines neuen Aktions- und Kooperationsrahmens
zur Förderung einer engeren Zusammenarbeit zwischen der
Kommission und den Mitgliedstaaten in der Beschäftigungspolitik
führt, wird auch **die Beendung des Programms Leda/Ergo zum
Ende des Jahres 1995** zur Folge haben.

➤ Europäische Kommission
Generaldirektion V
Referat V/A/1
Gerda Mira LOEWEN
200 Rue de la Loi
B - 1049 Brüssel
Tel. (+32-2) 295 64 39

LEDA

➤ **Full title**
Local Employment Development Action.

➤ **Field of activity**
Action programme for the study of strategies used for job promotion in areas affected by unemployment.
LEDA identifies the ideas and positive experiences and ensures their dissemination throughout the Community.

➤ **Target public**
All the regions and localities of the Community characterised by problems on the employment market.

➤ **Community coverage**
Consultancy group responsible for the implementation of the LEDA programme in Brussels and London;
Network of local development agents in 42 zones of the Community severely affected by unemployment;
group of regional development experts.

➤ **Actions**
Implementation of pilot projects;
devise, for the benefit of decision makers and local actors, methods and techniques to develop strategies likely to improve planning in the local employment market and to promote local development.

➤ **Network animation and methods of communication**
Dissemination of information and promotion of information exchange:
- Publications:
Background documents for the benefit of the political decision makers;
Technical reports for the local actors;
Preparation of information notes.
- Meetings:
Exchange visits between the pilot projects;
Organisation of workshops, seminars and conferences.

Recent developments in employment policy and, particularly, the Conclusions of the European Council of Essen in December, 1994, led the Commission to propose to the Council a reorganization process accompanied with the strengthening of its activities in the field of employment. Such a process, which will lead to the establishment of a new framework for action and cooperation favouring closer collaboration between the Commission and Member States as regards employment policy, will also, consequently, result in the **termination of the Leda/Ergo programme by the end of 1995.**

➤ European Commission
Directorate-General V
Unit V/A/1
Gerda Mira LOEWEN
200 rue de la Loi
B - 1049 Brussels
Tel.: (+32.2) 295.64.39

252

LEDA

> **Intitulé exact**
Local Employment Development Action
Programme d'Action pour le Développement Local de l'Emploi

> **Domaine d'activité**
Programme d'action pour l'étude des stratégies utilisées en vue de la promotion de l'emploi dans les zones touchées par le chômage. LEDA identifie les idées et expériences positives et en assure la diffusion dans l'ensemble de la Communauté.

> **Public cible**
L'ensemble des régions ou localités de la Communauté caractérisées par les problèmes sur le marché de l'emploi.

> **Rayonnement communautaire**
Bureaux d'études chargés de la mise en oeuvre du programme LEDA à Bruxelles et Londres;
Réseau d'agents de développement local dans 42 zones de la Communauté durement touchées par le chômage;
Réserve d'experts en développement régional.

> **Actions**
Mise en oeuvre de projets pilotes;
élaboration à l'intention des décideurs et des acteurs locaux de méthodes et techniques pour élaborer des stratégies susceptibles d'améliorer la planification du marché local de l'emploi et de promouvoir le développement local.

253

> **Animation du réseau et techniques de communication**
Diffusion d'information et promotion de l'échange des connaissances techniques:
• Publications:
Documents de fond à l'attention des décideurs politiques;
Rapports techniques pour les acteurs locaux;
Rédaction de notes d'information.
• Réunions:
Échanges de visites entre les projets pilotes;
Organisation d'ateliers de travail, séminaires et conférences.

Les évolutions récentes en matière de politique de l'emploi et particulièrement les Conclusions du Conseil européen d'Essen en décembre 1994 ont conduit la Commission à proposer au Conseil une réorganisation assortie d'un renforcement de ses activités dans le domaine de l'emploi. Ce processus qui conduira à la mise en place d'un nouveau cadre d'action et de coopération favorisant une collaboration plus étroite entre la Commission et les Etats membres en matière de politique de l'emploi aura également pour conséquence la **clôture du programme Leda/Ergo à la fin de 1995.**

> Commission européenne
Direction générale V
Unité V/A/1
Gerda Mira LOEWEN
200 rue de la Loi
B - 1049 Bruxelles
Tél.: (+32-2) 295.64.39

ORGANISME CHARGE DE LA MISE EN OEUVRE DU PROGRAMME

L.R.P.D.-Local and Regional Development Planning
10 Grosvenor Gardens
UK-LONDON SW1W 0DH
Tel.: +44/71/411.43.00
Fax: +44/71/411.43.01

ou

L.R.D.P.
Rue Franklin 106
B-1040 BRUXELLES
Tél: +32/2/732.42.50
Fax: +32/2/732.49.73

RELAIS DANS LES ZONES LEDA

BELGIQUE-BELGIË

M. Mathieu Arits
Guidance Centre
Evence Coppéelaan 91
3600 GENK
Tel.: +32/89/36.44.45
Fax: +32/89/36.43.03

Mrs. Francine Quanten
Coordinator
Community Development Programme Municipality of Genk
Dieplaan 2
B-3600 GENK
Tel.: +32/89/35.39.11
Fax: +32/89/35.64.55

Luc Toussaint
Echevinat des Affaires Economiques et du Commerce de Liège
Place des Carmes 8
B-4000 LIÈGE
Tel.: +32/41/23.19.60
Fax: +32/41/22.44.45

Mr Robert Frédéric
Directeur général
SOCRAN
Av. Pré Aily
B-4031 ANGLEUR
Tel.: +32/41/67.83.11
Fax: +32/41/67.83.00

Marie Corman
FOREM
Place Xavier Neujean 37
B - 4000 LIÈGE
Tel: +32/41/22.43.22
Fax: +32/41/23.47.34

Mme Roxane Picard, M. Marc Myle
Comité Subrégional de l'Emploi et de la Formation du Hainaut Occidental-CSEF
Rue du Moulin de Marvis 9
B-7500 TOURNAI
Tel.: +32/69/22.21.78
Fax: +32/69/22.19.68

M. Eric Hellendorff
FOREM
Stets
B-7500 TOURNAI
Te.: +32/69/88.28.11
Fax: +32/69/21.00.57

DANMARK

Mr. Anders Munksgaard
Youth School
Godthaabsgade 8
DK-9400 NØRRESUNDBY
Tel.: +45/98/9931.41.92
Fax: +45/98/98.17.27.02

Lis Rom Andersen
Ungdomskontoret
Badehusvej 9
DK-9000 AALBORG
Tel.: +45/99/31.25.50
Fax: +45/99/13.11.45

Kristian Primdal/Hans B. Petersen
Storstøm Amt Labour Market Office
Marienbergvej 80
DK-4760 VORDINGBORG
Tel.: +45/55/34.01.55
Fax: +45/55/34.03.55

254

DEUTSCHLAND

Peter Prill
Behörde für Arbeit, Gesundheit und Soziales
Abteilung Arbeitsmarkt Politik
Hamburger Straße 118
D-22083 HAMBURG
Tel.: +49/40/291.88.29.15
Fax: +49/40/291.88.33.69

Frank Glücklich
SBB
Wendenstr. 493
D-20537 HAMBURG
Tel.: +49/40/21.11.20
Fax: +49/40/21.11.22.00

Andreas SchaederHaus
Oberkreisdirektor
Dieter Schröer
Director
Amt für Wirtschaftsförderung
und Fremdenverkehr
Elke Ukena
Eberhardt Lüpkes
Landkreis Leer
Friesenstrasse 46
D-26787 LEER
Tel.: +49/491/83.202
Fax: +49/491/83.388

Dr. Manfred Pühl
Stadtdirektor
Stadt Leer
Rathaustrasse 1
Postfach 2060
D-26789 LEER
Tel.: +49/491/82.385
Fax: +49/491/82.399

Burkhard Drescher
Oberstadtdirektor
Stadt Oberhause
Rathaus Schwartzstrasse 72
D-46042 OBERHAUSEN
Tel.: +49/208/825.22.83
Fax: +49/208/281.59

Annette Stilleke-Holobar
Stadt Oberhausen
Amt für Statistik und Wahlen
Schwartzstr. 71
D-46042 OBERHAUSEN
Tel.: +49/208/825.25.81

Jochen Kamps
Geschäftsf¨hrer
ZAQ Oberhausen e.v.
D-46042 OBERHAUSEN I
Tel. +49/208/690.00.14
Fax: +49/208/690.00.31

Herr Hollmann
Geschäftsführer Entwicklungsgesellschaft
Oberhausen (EGO)
Schwartzstrasse 53
D-46042 OBERHAUSEN I
Tel.: +49/208/85.40.12

Harald Elke
Stadt Oberhausen
Regionalsekretariat
Roncallistr. 26
D-46042 OBERHAUSEN
Tel.: +49/208/825.29.28
Fax: +49/208/85.18.30

Dr. Kilimann
Oberbürgermeister
Senat der Hansestadt Rostock
Neuer Markt,
D-18055 ROSTOCK
Tel.: +49/381/381.38.10
Fax: +49/381/381.19.03

Harr Werner
Senator für Wirtschaft
Senat der Hansestadt Rostock
Neuer Markt, 1
D-18055 ROSTOCK
Tel.: +49/381/381.16.07
Fax: +49/381/237.63

Thomas Hergert
EG Beauftragter
Neuer Markt, 1
D-18055 ROSTOCK
Tel.: +49/381/381.13.89
Fax: +49/381/381.17.73

Trägergesellschaft Schiffbau
Carl-Hopp Str. 17
D-18069 ROSTOCK
Tel.: +49/381/381.19.03
Fax: +49/381/237.63

Dr. Peter Röhlinger
Oberbürgermeister
Am Anger 15
D-07703 JENA
Tel.: +49/36.41/20.00
Fax: +49/36.41/228.43

255

Christoph Schwind
Dezernat für Wirtschaft
Am Anger, 15
D-07703 JENA
Tel.: +49/36.41/57.21.30
Fax: +49/36.41/228.43

Prof. Dr. Werner Melle
LEDA Konkord
Burg Weg 11
D-07749 JENA
Tel.: +49/36.41/270.41
Fax: +49/36.41/246.47

ELLAS

Dimitrios Konstantopoulos
President,
**TEDKA (Association of Local
Authorities of Arcadia)**
Helen Hioti (LEDA Coordinator)
Kennedy 37
GR-22100 TRIPOLIS-Arcadia
Tel./Fax: +30/71/22.50.72

Andreas Lentzos
President
Chamber of Commerce and Industry
Nikitara 24
GR-22100 TRIPOLIS
Tel.: +30/71/23.71.23
Fax: +30/71/23.37.38

George Katsinis
President
**Union of AgriculturalCooperatives of
Arcadia**
GR-22100 TRIPOLIS
Tel.: +30/71/22.24.17
Fax: +30/71/23.13.07

Nikos Katounis
Municipality of Istiea
Town Hall
GR-34200 ISTIEA-Evia
Tel.: +30/226/535.40
Fax: +30/226/543.84

Ilias Avramides
Local Union of Municipalities
26, G. Kapeta St.
GR-61100 KILKIS
Tel./Fax: +30/341/235.37

Anna Paraskevaidou
Prefecture of Kilkis
2, Metamorfoseos St.
GR-61100 KILKIS
Tel.: +30/341/229.69
Fax: +30/341/234.08

Nikos Petrakis
President
Sitia Development Organisation SA
M. Katapoti 44
GR-72300 SITIA-Crete
Tel.: +30/843/235.90
Fax: +30/843/253.14

Stefanos Xenikakis
Chairman
Union of Agricultural Co-operatives
Musunos 74
GR-72300 SITIA-Crete
Tel: +30/843/222.11

Mrs Tsouroufli
LEDA Forum Secretariät
Prefecture of Keffalonia
GR-28100 KEFALONIE
Tel.: +30/671/22.327
Fax: +30/671/28.462

Alexandra Ladou
Local Development Officer
Prefecture of Kefallonia
GR-28100 ARGOSTOLI
Tel.: +30/671/22.120
Fax: +30/671/28.462

ESPAÑA

Carlos Verdú Pons
Concejal de Economía y Hacienda
E-03800 ALCOY
Tel.: +34/6/554.52.11
Fax: +34/6/397.51.61

Enrique Masia
DATO association
Puente de San Jorge 3
E-03800 ALCOY
Tel.: +34/6/552.40.90

Carolina Orriols
**Area Desenvolupment Economic i
Social
Ajuntament de Barcelona**
Gran via 894
E-08018 BARCELONA
Tel.: +34/3/401.97.77
Fax: +34/3/300.97.52

Dr. Jesús María Rodríguez Román
Alcalde
Pl. del Carmen, 2
E-41560 ESTEPA
Tel.: +34/5/591.27.52
Fax: +34/5/591.24/79

Dr. Juan García Baena
Director
Joaquín Castro Rúiz
Unidad de Promoción de Empleo
c/Molinos, 1
Apartado 59
E-41560 ESTEPA
Tel.: +34/5/591.22.46
Fax: +34/5/591.22.41

Eugiono Guillén Torralba
Union of Agricultural Workers
La Roda Andalucía
E-41560 ESTEPA
Tel.: +30/5/482.06.04
Fax: +34/5/591.22.41

D. José Luis Cardenes Martín
Cabildo Insular de Gran Canaria
C/Bravo Murillo 23
LAS PALMAS DE GRAN CANARIA
E-ISLAS CANARIAS
Tel.: +34/28/36.45.73
Fax: +34/28/36.69.54

Antonio Lozano González
Ayuntamiento de la villa de Aguimes
C/Joaquín Artiles 1
E-35260 AGUMES (Las Palmas)
Tel.: +34/28/78.41.00
Fax: +34/28/78.36.63

Miguel Angel Molinero Espadas
Technicien en Développement Local
**Fundación Empresa Universidad de
Granada**
Cetti Merein
E-18010 GRANADA
Tel.: +34/58/29.27.23
Fax: +34/58/22.87.35

Jerónimo Arjona Luque
Sous-Directeur Provincial
Institut National de l'Emploi INEM
Complejo Administrativo LA CALETA
Calle Mirlo 4
E-18014 GRANADA
Tel.: +34/58/24.25.28
Fax: +34/58/24.25.06

FRANCE

Michel Grégoire
Président
**Syndicat d'Aménagement des
Baronnies**
BP 35
F-26170 BUIS-LES-BARONNIES
Tel.: +33/75/28.04.08
Fax: +33/75/26.03.45

Gilberte Brémond
Jean Pierre Dutruge
Chargés de Mission
**Syndicat d'Aménagement des
Baronnies**
BP 35
F-26170 BUIS-LES-BARONNIES
Tel.: +33/75/28.04.08
Fax: +33/75/28.11.32

Pierre Ferrier
Directeur de Développement
Ville de Bruay-la-Buissière
Place Cadot
F-62700 BRUAY-LA-BUISSIÈRE
Tel.: +33/21/64.56.00
Fax: +33/21/53.42.28

Jean-Luc Salmon
Directeur de la Formation
Communauté de Bruaysis
2, rue Hermant
F-62700 BRUAY-LA-BUISSIÈRE
Tel.: +33/21/62.13.04
Fax: +33/21/62.97.64

Michel Peyre
direction des actions de l'Etat
et de la vie économique
Préfecture de la Loire
Hôtel du Département de la Loire
F-42000 ST. ETIENNE
Tel.: +33/77/33.42.45
Fax: +33/77/41.72.22

257

Jacques Granger
Direction Départementale du Travail et de l'Emploi
11, rue Balay
F-42000 ST. ETIENNE
Tel;: +33/77/43.41.00
Fax: +33/77/43.41.80

Alain Fournier
ANPE
Délégation Departementale Loire
36, rue Balay
F-42026 ST. ETIENNE Cedex 1
Tel;: +33/77/33.02.69
Fax: +33/77/33.26.94

Bruno Roux
Chargé des Affaires Economiques
Ville de St. Etienne
6, rue Francis Garnier
F-4200 ST. ETIENNE
Tel.: +33/77/42.88.13
Fax: +33/77/41.61.81

Jean-François Guitton
Délégation au Dévéloppement
109 Centre République
B.P. 326
F-44615 ST. NAZAIRE Cedex
Tel.: +33/40/00.36.94
Fax: +33/40/66.50.05

Jean-Jacques Lhotellier
Cellule Economique
7, rue Etoile du Matin
F-44600 ST. NAZAIRE Cedex
Tel.: +33/40/09.08.27
Fax: +33/40/01.93.27

Sylvie Camus
Credit Formation Individualisé
Sous-Préfecture de St. Nazaire
Rue Vincent Auriol
F-44600 ST. NAZAIRE
Tel.: +33/40/01.84.32
Fax: +33/40/01.90.64

Alexandre Faidherbe, Président CBE
Véronique Falise, Permanente CBE
Eric Vanhuisse, CBE
88, rue du Haze
F-59200 TOURCOING
Tel.: +33/20/24.11.00
Fax: +33/20/70.48.16

J.D. Rey, Président
Hélène Hilaire
Comité de Bassin d'Emploi du Ventoux-la Grange
F-84570 VILLES SUR AUZON
Tel.: +33/90/61.91.03
Fax: +33/90/61.96.94

IRELAND

Mr. Ruan O'Bric
Chief Executive
Údarás na Gaeltachta na Forbacha
IRL-GALWAY
Tel.: +353/91/92.011
Fax: +359/91/92.037

Dr. Michaél Ó Cinnéide
Centre for Development Studies
Dr. Michael Keane
Department of Economics
University College Galway
IRL-GALWAY
Tel.: +353/91/24.411
Fax: +353/91/25.700

Tony Barrett
Regional Director F.A.S.
Island House, Cathedral Square
IRL-GALWAY
Tel.: +353/91/67.165
Fax: +353/91/62.718

Brendan Keating
Deputy Assistant City Manager
Cork Corporation
City Hall
IRL- CORK
Tel.: +353/21/96.62.22
　　　　96.60.17
Fax: +353/21/31.42.38

Joan Buckley
Dpt of Management and Marketing
Lee House
University College Cork
IRL-CORK
Tel.: +353/21/27.68.71 ext. 29.28
Fax: +353/21/27.26.42

Brian Callanan
Planning & Research Unit
Shannon Development, Shannon
IRL-COUNTY CLARE
Tel.: +353/61/36.15.55
Fax: +353/61/41.91.86

Richard Tobin
Planning Department
Limerick Corporation
The Granary
Michael St.
IRL-LIMERICK
Tel.: +353/61/41.57.99
Fax: +353/61/41.91.86

Professor David Coombes
Department of European Studies
Professor Donal Dineen
Head of Business Studies
University of Limerick
Plassey Technological Park
IRL-LIMERICK
Tel.: +353/61/33.36.44
Fax: +353/61/33.03.16

ITALIA

Dr. Giuseppe Drei
Assessore
Assessorato alla Formazione
Amministrazione provinciale di
Ravenna
Piazza dei Caduti per la Libertà 2/4
I-48100 RAVENNA
Tel.: +39/544/37.289
          35.635
Fax: +39/544/33.986

Mr. Vasco Errani
Assessore
Assessorato alle Attività Economiche
Comune di Ravenna
Via Gordini 27
I-48100 RAVENNA
Tel.: +39/544/22.613
Fax: +39/544/36.303

Dr. Maura Franchi
Assessorato Industria
Regione Emilia-Romagna
Via Aldo Moro 30
I-40127 BOLOGNA
Tel.: +39/51/28.36.35
Fax: +39/51/28.36.15

Prof. Giacomo Chiarelli
Presidente
Comunità Montana del Lago Negres
Via XXV Aprile
I-85045 LAURIA (Potenza)
Tel.: +39/973/82.39.09
          62.87.57
Fax: +39/973/82.21.30

Giuseppe Giura
Presidente
Comunità Montana
Medio Sinni-Pollino-Raparo
Via Don Sturzo
I-85038 SENISE (Potenza)
Tel.: +39/973/68.62.51
          68.63.98
Fax: +39/973/68.60.70

Mario Giuseppe Vitarelli
Presidente
Comunità Montana
Val Sarmento
Ctr Manche
I-85035 Noepoli
Tel.: +39/973/920.91
Fax: +39/973/920.91

Dr. Marianna Colangelo
Presidente
Società Cooperative APICE srl
Via Vallinoto 36
Fraz. S. Costantino
I-85040 RIVELLO (Potenza)
Tel.: +39/973/772.46
Fax: +39/973/772.50

Gesuino Salis
Assessore Provinciale al Turismo
I-ORISTANO
Tel./Fax: +39/783/793.305
Anna Paola Iacuzzi
Lori Manni
BIC Sardegna di Oristano
Via Canalis 11
I-09170 ORISTANO
Tel./Fax: +39/783/70.484

Franco Bertoglio
Rosalba La Grotteria
Assessore al Lavoro
Via Lagrange 2
I-10123 TORINO
Tel.: +39/11/5756.2505-2525
Fax: +39/11/5756.456

NEDERLAND

Dick Heesterbeek
Streekraad Oost-groningen
"Huis-te-wedde"
Hoofdweg 7
NL-9698 AA WEDDE
Tel.: +31/59/76.20.05
Fax: +31/59/76.24.10

259

Institut voor Service Management
Rengerslaan 8
Postbus 1298
9900 RG LEEUWARDEN
Tel: +31/58/33.05.50
Fax: +31/58/33.05.01

Jan Verhoef/Gerhard Hauser
Economic Affairs Department
City of Tilburg
P.O. Box 90155
NL-5000 LH TILBURG
Tel.: +31/13/42.94.63
Fax: +31/13/42.93.05

Dr. Frans Boekema
Department of Economics
Tilburg University
P.O. Box 90153
NL-5000 LE TILBURG
Tel.: 31/13/66.23.47
Fax: +31/13/66.27.64

PORTUGAL

Dr. Alexandre Chaves
Presidente da Câmara Municipal de Chaves
P-5400 CHAVES
Tel.: +351/76/33.29.66

Antonio Montalvão Machado
ADRAT
Av. Tenente Valadim 39, Escr 7
P-5400 CHAVES
Tel.: +351/76/33.35.97
Fax: +351/76/33.37.42

Nuno Almeidado
Comissão de Coordenação
da Região do Norte
Rua Rainha de Estafania 251
P-4100 PORTO
Tel.: +351/2/200.44.99
Fax: +351/2/600.20.40

Antonio Medeiros
Cooperativa Agrícola de Chaves
São Bento
P-5400 CHAVES
Tel.: +351/76/22.183

João Miguens
Presidente, Câmara Municipal de Portalegre
P-7300 PORTALEGRE
Tel.: +351/45/21.636
Fax: +351/45/24.235

José Manuel Samedo Basso
Presidente da Câmara Municipal de Nisa
P-6050 NISA
Tel.: +351/45/42.164
Fax: +351/45/42.799

António Andrade
Presidente da Câmara Municipal de Marvão
P-7330 MARVÃO
Tel.: +351/45/93.104
Fax: +351/45/24.570

António José Leitão
Presidente de Câmara Municipal de Crato
P-7430 CRATO
Tel.: +351/45/972.12

Fernando Soares
Presidente da Câmara Municipal de
Castelo de Vide
P-7320 CASTELO DE VIDE
Tel.: +351/45/91.350

Caçilda Trinidade
Chef des Services d'Etudes et Planification
**Instituto do Emprego e
Formação Profissional**
Rua Vasco de Gama 7
P-7000 EVORA
Tel.: +351/66/28.554
Fax: +351/66/24.637

Francisco Ramos
Universidade de Evora
Largo dos Colegiais
P-7000 EVORA
Tel.: +351/66/74.45.44
Fax: +351/66/74.45.44

Carolino Tapadejo
Director, ADT/NA
Rua da Boavista 8
P-7320 CASTELO DE VIDE
Tel.: +351/45/90.56.63
Fax: +351/45/90328

Eng˙ Orlando Gaspar de Almeida
Dr. Carlos Almeida
Dra Margarida M. Pinto Guimares
Dr. Francisco J. Guilherme Pereira
Câmara Municipal de Amadora
Ava MFA, 1
P-2700 AMADORA
Tel.: +351/1/492.38.43
Fax: +351/1/491.27.61

Dr. José M. Gaspar Bragança
Centro de Emprego de Amadora
Ava D. Nuno A. Pereira, 1
P-2700 AMADORA
Tel.: +351/1/554.22.0
Fax: +351/1/554.34.94

Câmara Municipal da Covilhã
Praça do Municipio
P-6200 COVILHÃ
Tel.: +351/75/32.21.06-7-8-9
Fax: +351/75/32.37.85

Dr. Alexandre Gomez de Oliveira
Director
**Delegação Local do Instituto de
Emprego e Formação Profissional**
Av. Marquês do Avila e Bolama 57
P-6200 COVILHÃ
Tel.: +351/75/327.208./403-608
Fax: +351/75/32.22.67

João José Barata Gomes
Director Serviços S.M.C.
Rua Marquês e Bolama 48
P-6200 COVILHÃ
Tel.: +351/75/32.20.01-2-3
Fax: +351/75/31.49.03

SUOMI-FINLAND

Ms. Helka linna
Provincial Government of Vaasa
Wolffintie 35, PL 200
SF-65101 VAASA
Tel.: +358/61/323.61.11
Fax: +358/61/37.48.17

SVERIGE

Mr. Lennart Andermo
Länsstyrelsen
S-62185 VISBY
Tel.: +46/498/29.21.00-3
Fax: +46/498/21.25.90
        24.86.50

Mr. Bo Frykenstam
Länsarbetsnämnden, AMI
Herkulesvägen 9
S-62141 VISBY
Tel.: +46/498/29.24.00-54
Fax: +46/498/21.08.59

Mr. Jan Björklund
County Administration
S-62185 VISBY
Tel.: +46/498/29.21.00
Fax: +46/498/21.25.90

Mr. Jan Bäckström
Utrecklingsfondon
Box 1647
S-62123 VISBY
Tel.: +46/498/21.54.30
Fax: +46/498/21.01.22

Ms. Lena Johanson
Municipality of Gotland
S-62181 VISBY
Tel.: +46/498/26.90.00
Fax: +46/498/21.27.25

Tage Levin
County Director
Deputy County Govonor
Länsstyrelsen
S-83186 ÖSTERSUND
Tel.: +46/63/14.62.52
Fax: +46/63/10.25.90

Anders Isaksson
Regional Policy Manager
Länsstyrelsen
S-83186 ÖSTERSUND
Tel;: +46/63/14.63.14
Fax: +46/63/10.25.90

UNITED KINGDOM

Mr. Alex Scott/Robert Pollack
Economic Development Department
City of Dundee District Council
City Square
UK-DUNDEE DD1 3RA
Tel.: +44/1382/23.141_42.12
Fax: +44/1382/20.33.02

Jack Searle/Tony Johnson
Planning Department
Tayside Regional Council
Tayside House
28 Crichton Street
UK-DUNDEE DD1
Tel.: +44/1382/30.36.10
Fax: +44/1382/30.30.13

261

Gillian Lochhead
Projects Executive
Scottish Enterprise Tayside
Enterprise House
45 North Lindsay Street
UK-Dundee DDI IHT
Tel.: +44/1382/23.100
Fax: +44/1382/20.13.19

Paul Burgess
Assistant Director
Training and Employment
Nottingham City Council
Exchange Buildings
Smithy Row
UK-NOTTINGHAM NG1 2BS
Tel.: +44/115/948.35.00
Fax: +44/115/941.03.33

Mr Malcolm Rose
Chief Executive's Policy Unit
Nottingham County Council
County Hall
West Bridgeford
UK-NOTTINGHAM NG2 7QP
Tel.: +44/115/977.34.72
Fax: +44/115/945.53.91

David Clarke
Fermanagh District Council
Wellington Road
ENNISKILLEN
Co. Fermanagh, BT4 7EF
Northern Ireland
Tel.: +44/365/32.31.10
Fax: +44/365/32.55.11

D. McCammick
Director od Corporate Services
Armagh Districy Council
The Palace Demesne
ARMAGH BT60 4EL
Northern Ireland
Tel.: +44/861/52.40.52
Fax: +44/861/52.42.46

Ian Lomas
European Development Officer
MERSEYSIDE TEC Ltd
Tithebarn House
TITHEBARN St.
UK-LIVERPOOL L2 2NZ
Tel.: +44/51/236.00.26
Fax: +44/51/236.40.13

262

Peter Houten
Employment Department
TEED North West Regional Office
Washington House
New Bailey Street
UK-MANCHESTER M3 5ER

**CENTRAL AND EASTERN EUROPEAN
ASSOCIATE AREAS:**

HONGRIE

Károly Fazekas
Deputy Director
Institute of Economics
Hungarian Academy od Sciences
Budapest XI, Budaörsi út 45
H-1052 BUDAPEST, P.O. Box 262
Tel.: +36/1/185.25.73
Fax: +36/1/185.11.58

Dávid János
(Sociologist)
**ELTE Szociológiai
és Szociálpolikai
Intézet**
H-1088 BUDAPEST
Pollack M. tér 10
Tel.: +36/1/266.56.86-02.21
Fax: +36/1/266.38.60

POLOGNE

Grazna Gesika
Uniwersytet Warszawski
Instytut Socjologii
WARSZAWA
ul. Karowa 18
POLOGNE
Tel.: +48/22/200.381 w. 711

Prof. Dr. Grzegorz Gorzelak
EUROREG
European Institute for Regional
and Local Development
Univesity of Warszawa
ul. Krakowskie Przedmie cie 30
WARSAW
POLOGNE
Tel./Fax: +48/22/26.16.54

SLOVAKIA

Dr. Miroslava Kopicová
Director
Labour Market Restructuring Programme
Project Management Unit
Restructuring Association
Palackého námestí 4
128 PRAGUE 2
CZECH REPUBLIC
Tel.: +42/2/21.18.23.84
Fax: +42/2/21.18.23.20

CZECH REPUBLIC

Dr. Alena Nesporovna
International Labour Office
Central and Eastern European Team
Mozsár utca 14
H-1066 BUDAPEST
Tel.: +36/1/153.35.20
                153.38.33
                153.34.57
Fax: +36/1/153.36.83

263

BULGARIA

Dr. Pobeda Loukanova
Institute of Economics
Bulgarian Academy of Sciences
3, Aksakov str.
1000 SOFIA
BULGARIA
Tel.: +359/2/84.121 ext. 853
Fax: +359/2/88.21.08

Antonina Stoyanovska
Help Desk Manager
Euroguichet
Union for Private Enterprise
54, DR G.M. Dimitrov BLVD
Business Centre, 4th floor
1797 SOFIA
BULGARIA
Tel.: +35/92/732.487-537
Fax: +35/92/730.435

Frauen

ILE
IRIS

Women

LEI
IRIS

Femmes

ILE
IRIS

ILE

> **Genaue Bezeichnung**

Lokale Beschäftigungsinitiativen für Frauen

> **Tätigkeitsbereich**

Aktionsprogramm für von Frauen betriebene Unternehmen.

> **Zielgruppe**

1. Frauen, die ein Unternehmen gründen möchten;
2. Frauenverbände, Handelskammern, Berufskammern, regionale und lokale Entwicklungsagenturen, Hilfsstrukturen für Unternehmensgründungen.

> **Wirkungskreis**

Ein europäischer Koordinator in Griechenland;
Koordinierung des Programms in Brüssel;
Netz mit einem Experten in jedem Mitgliedstaat.

> **Aktionen**

Finanzhilfe für Initiativbildung durch Frauen (Genossenschaften, KMU);
Einrichtung eines europäischen Netzes für die Förderung und
Unterstützung von Fraueninitiativen im
Beschäftigungsbereich.

> **Betreuung des Netzes und Kommunikationstechnik**
Information, Werbung, Beratung und Hilfe bei
Unternehmensgründungen;
Veröffentlichung von Leitfäden;
Unterstützung der Bewerber beim Erhalt eines Stipendiums;
Zusammenarbeit mit den nationalen und lokalen Institutionen zur
Förderung der Einleitung von Initiativvorhaben; Errichtung von
Partnerschaften und transnationalen Netzen.

> Europäische Kommission
Generaldirektion V
Referat V/A/3 - Chancengleichheit
200 Rue de la Loi
B - 1049 Brüssel
Tel. (+32-2) 295 20 93

LEI

> **Full title**

Local Employment Initiatives

> **Field of activity**

Action Programme for the encouragement of women to establish their own business or own employment.

> **Target public**

1. Women wishing to establish their own business;
2. Women's organisations, chambers of commerce, chambers of trade, regional and local development agencies, support facilities to the establishment of businesses.

> **Community coverage**

A European coordinator in Greece;
programme coordination in Brussels;
a network comprised of an expert in each Member State.

> **Actions**

Financial assistance awarded for initiatives taken by women (cooperatives, SMEs);
setting up a European network for the stimulation of and assistance to women's initiatives in the employment field.

> **Network animation and methods of communication**

Information, promotion, advice and assistance in the establishment of businesses;
publication of guides;
assistance to candidates in obtaining grants;
cooperation with national and local institutions to facilitate setting up project initiatives;
establishment of partnerships and transnational networks.

> European Commission
Directorate-General V
Unit V/A/3 - Equal opportunities
200 rue de la Loi
B - 1049 Brussels
Tel.: (+32.2) 295.20.93

ILE

➤ **Intitulé exact**

Initiatives locales d'emploi des femmes

➤ **Domaine d'activité**

Programme d'action en vue d'encourager les femmes à créer leur propre entreprise ou leur propre emploi.

➤ **Public cible**

1. Les femmes souhaitant créer leur entreprise;
2. les organisations féminines, chambres de commerce, chambres de métiers, agences de développement régional et local, structures d'appui à la création d'entreprises.

➤ **Rayonnement communautaire**

Un coordinateur européen en Grèce;
coordination du programme à Bruxelles;
réseau composé d'un expert dans chaque État membre.

➤ **Actions**

Aide financière accordée pour la création d'initiatives par les femmes (coopératives, PME);
mise en place d'un réseau européen pour la stimulation et l'aide aux initiatives féminines dans le domaine de l'emploi.

➤ **Animation du réseau et techniques de communication**

Information, promotion, conseil et aide à la création d'entreprises;
publication de guides;
assistance des candidates pour l'obtention d'une bourse;
coopération avec les institutions nationales et locales en vue de faciliter la mise en place de projets d'initiatives;
établissement de partenariats et réseaux transnationaux.

➤ Commission européenne
Direction générale V
Unité V/A/3 - Égalité des chances
200 rue de la Loi
B - 1049 Bruxelles
Tél.: (+32-2) 295.20.93

ASSISTANCE TECHNIQUE

Comitato Impresa Donna (CID)
Avenue de la Joyeuse Entrée, 1
B-1040 Bruxelles
Tél.: : +32/2/280.00.54
Fax: : +32/2/280.09.01

C.I.D./Head Office
Viale Aldo Moro, 22
I-40127 Bologna

RESEAU DES EXPERTS

COORDINATION EUROPEENNE

BREAKTHROUGH CONSULTANTS
Boulevard Clovis, 12a
B-1040 Bruxelles
Tel.: +32/2/732.51.19
Fax: +32/2/735.12.09

Head Office
Vas. Georgiou Street, 36
GR-54640 Thessaloniki
Tel.: +30/31/84.06.25
Fax: +30/31/86.11.00

EXPERTS NATIONAUX

BELGIQUE-BELGIË

Dominique RUELLE-CHARLEZ
Bernadette VINCKE
CERACTION ASBL
BP 87 - ETTERBEEK 1
B-1040 Bruxelles
Tél.: +32/2/646.53.31-32
Fax: +32/2/646.55.32

DANMARK

Leslie LARSEN
KVINFO
Nyhavn 22
DK-1051 København K
Tél.: +45/33/93.32.77
Fax: +45/33/14.11.56

DEUTSCHLAND

Angelika DIERKES
REA
Hermannstrasse 229
D-12049 Berlin
Tél.: +49/30/215.32.66
Fax: +49/30/217.05.42

ELLAS

Vassiliki KAZANA
EDIPAG
P.O. Box 16017
GR-54410 Thessaloniki
Tél.: +30/31/84.04.96
Fax: +30/31/86.11.00

ESPAÑA

Anna MERCADE
CTD
Via Laictana, 11
E-08003 Barcelona
Tél.: +34/3/268.12.55
Fax: +34/3/268.16.78

FRANCE

Véronique VALLEE
Chambre régionale des métiers Midi-Pyrénées
28, rue de Metz
F-31000 Toulouse
Tél.: +33/1/61.53.17.74
Fax: +33/1/61.25.38.96

IRELAND

Patricia BRAND
Contact International Ltd.
Equity House
16-17 Ormond Quay
IRL-Dublin 1
Tel.: +353/1/873.07.11
Fax: +353/1/873.04.74

ITALIA

Maria Pia Ponticelli
Associazione Donna & Sviluppo
c/o Fondazione IDID
ViaCoroglio, 104
I-80124 Napoli
Tél.: +39/81/230.23.11
Fax: +39/81/230.23.09-744.47.62

LUXEMBOURG

Angelika GEBHARDT-BERG
24. rue de Mersch
L-8293 Keispelt
Tél.: +352/30.70.06
Fax: +352/40.61.11

NEDERLAND

Engelien HENGEVELD
STEW (Steunpunt Elgen Werk)
Gebouw Oostenburg
Oostenburgervoorstraat, 172
NL-1018 MR Amsterdam
Tel.: +31/20/623.93.69
Fax: +31/20/420.08.04

PORTUGAL

Heloisa PERISTA
CESIS
Apartado 1159
P-1014 Lisboa Codex
Tél./Fax: +351/1/386.36.99

UNITED KINGDOM

Patricia RICHARDSON
Women's Enterprise Unit
Scottish Enterprise
Foundation University of Stirling
Stirling
UK-FK9 4LA Scotland
Tél.: +44/786/46.73.53 – 46.73.48
Fax: +44/786/45.02.01

CONSULTANT

Monique HALPERN
Rue Duvergier, 1
F-75019 Paris
Tél.: +33/1/40.34.01.19
Fax: +33/1/42.05.35.47

269

IRIS

> **Genaue Bezeichnung**

Europäisches Netzwerk von Ausbildungsmaßnahmen für Frauen

> **Tätigkeitsbereich**

Berufsausbildung für Frauen

> **Zielgruppe**

Insbesondere arbeitslose Frauen, berufsbildende Einrichtungen und Sozialpartner.

> **Wirkungskreis**

Ein europäisches Koordinierungsbüro;
eine Arbeitsgruppe bei der Kommission für die Berufsbildung von Frauen;
ein Netz mit Organisationen für Berufsausbildung von Frauen.

> **Aktionen**

Bildung von nationalen und transnationalen Verbindungen zwischen den Berufsbildungsprogrammen für Frauen, Engagement der Sozialpartner,
Förderung von innovativen Berufsbildungsaktionen, Sensibilisierung und Informationsverbreitung.

> **Betreuung des Netzes und Kommunikationstechnik**

Veröffentlichungen
IRIS-Bulletin (4/Jahr, FR-EN)
IRIS-Verzeichnis (Beschreibung der Programme)
IRIS-Dossiers / Methodologische Instrumente
Datenbank und elektronische Post
Sitzungen, IRIS-Seminar über Themen bezüglich der Berufsbildung von Frauen, programmübergreifende Austauschbesuche, Partnerschaften.

> Europäische Kommission
> Generaldirektion V
> Referat V/A/3
> Nathalie DAVIES
> 200 Rue de la Loi
> B - 1049 Brüssel
> Tel. (+32-2) 296 49 33 - Fax: (+32-2) 296 35 62

IRIS

➤ **Full title**

European Network of Training Projects for Women.

➤ **Field of activity**

Professional training for women.

➤ **Target public**

Women, particularly the unemployed, professional training bodies and employers' and employees' organizations.

➤ **Community coverage**

A European coordination office;
a working group with the Commission on the professional training of women;
a network of organisations concerned with the professional training of women.

➤ **Actions**

The setting up of national and transnational links between programmes of professional training for women,
commitment of the two sides of industry and public authorities,
promotion of innovative actions for professional training,
awareness and dissemination of information.

➤ **Network animation and methods of communication**

Publications
IRIS Bulletin (4/yr, FR-EN)
IRIS directory (description of programmes)
IRIS Files / methodological tools
Database and electronic mail
Meetings
IRIS Seminar on subjects relative to the vocational training of women,
interprogramme exchange visits, partnerships.

➤ European Commission
Directorate-General V
Unit V/A/3
Nathalie DAVIES
200 rue de la Loi
B - 1049 Brussels
Tel.: (+32.2) 296.49.33 - Fax: (+32.2) 296.35.62

IRIS

➤ **Intitulé exact**

Réseau Européen de développement d'actions de formation professionnelle pour les femmes

➤ **Domaine d'activité**

Formation professionnelle pour les femmes

➤ **Public cible**

Les femmes, particulièrement les chômeuses, les organismes de formation professionnelle et les partenaires sociaux.

➤ **Rayonnement communautaire**

Un bureau de coordination européenne;
un groupe de travail auprès de la Commission sur la formation professionnelle des femmes;
un réseau d'organisations qui font de la formation professionnelle pour les femmes.

➤ **Actions**

La création de liens nationaux et transnationaux entre les programmes de formation professionnelle des femmes,
l'engagement des partenaires sociaux et des pouvoirs publics,
la promotion d'actions de formation professionnelle innovantes,
la sensibilisation et la diffusion d'information.

273

➤ **Animation du réseau et techniques de communication**

Publications
Bulletin IRIS (4/an, FR-EN)
Répertoire IRIS (description des programmes)
Dossiers IRIS / outils méthodologiques
Base de données et courrier électronique
Réunions
Séminaire IRIS sur des sujets relatifs à la formation professionnelle des femmes,
visites d'échanges interprogrammes, partenariats.

➤ Commission européenne
Direction générale V
Unité V/A/3
Nathalie DAVIES
200 rue de la Loi
B - 1049 Bruxelles
Tél.: (+32-2) 296.49.33 - Fax: (+32-2) 296.35.62

BELGIQUE-BELGIË

Mevr. Julie Dhoore-Standaert
Emanciepatieraad
Reinpadstraat, 90
B - 3600 GENK
Tél.: +32/89/35.33.48
Fax: +32/89/35.33.48

Mme Patricia Bird
Office communautaire et régional de la formation et de l'emploi
Rue du Progrès 5
B - 1400 NIVELLES
Tél.: +32/67/217996
Fax: +32/67/840264

M. Jef Hostyn
V.D.A.B
Keizerslaan 11
B - 1000 BRUXELLES
Tel: (+32-02) 502.60.10
Fax: (+32-02) 502.54.74

DANMARK

Fru Inga Thaysen/Annet Bang
Arbejdsmarkedssty relsen
Blagdamsvej 56
DK - 2100 KOBENHAVN
Tél.: +45/35/288100
Fax: +45/35/362411

Fru Brigitte Simonsen / Fru Ann Dahlberg
Undervisningsministeriet
Ehrverusskoleafdelingen
43 H.C. Andersens Boulevard
DK - 1553 KOBENHAVN
Tél.: +45/33/925696
Fax: +45/33/925666

DEUTSCHLAND

Helga Ebeling
Bundesministerium für Bildung und Wissenschaft
Referat II B 6
Heinemannstrasse 2
D - 53175 BONN
Tél.: +49/228/572863
Fax: +49/228/572096

Frau Brigitte Wolf
Bundesinstitut für Berufsbildung
Fehrberlinerplatz 3
D - 1000 BERLIN 31
Tél.: +49/30/86432297
Fax: +49/30/86432455

ELLAS

Efi Synefopoulou
Organisme d'Emploi de la Main-d'Oeuvre
O.A.E.D.
Direction des Relations Internationales
P.O. Box 70017
GR - 16610 GLYFADA
Tél.: +30/1/9924352
Fax: +30/1/9921524

Savatou Tsolakidou
Secrétariat d'Etat pour l'Egalité des chances
Place Kannigos 20
GR - 10677 ATHENES
Tél.: +30/1/3302713/5
Fax: +30/1/3302718

ESPAÑA

Mme José Marti Jorge
Subdirectora General de Programas
Instituto de la Mujer
C/Almagro 336
E - 28016 MADRID
Tél.: +34/1/3478028
Fax: +34/1/3478073

Mme Pilar Martinez Diz
Subdirectora General de Programas
Instituto de la Mujer
Jefa de Servicio de Programas
C/Almagro 36
E- MADRID
Tel: +34/1/3477960
Fax: 34/1/3478073

Mme Térésa Martin Sanchez
Ministerio de Educacion y Ciencia
C/Los Madrazo, 17
E - 28071 MADRID
Tél.: +34/1/5221100 ext. 4123
Fax: +34/1/5213775

Mme Belen Rebollo Moral
Instituto Nacional de Empleo (INEM)
Servicio de Formacion de Formadores
C/ Josefa Valcarcel, 40 Duplicado 2° planta
E - 28027 MADRID
Tél.: +34/1/5852074
Fax: +34/1/5852912

FRANCE

Mme Claudine Brocard
Service des Droits des Femmes
**Ministère des Affaires Sociales
de la Santé et de la Ville**
31, rue Le Peletier
F - 75009 PARIS
Tél.: +33/1/47704158
Fax: +33/1/42469969

Mme Françoise Gouin
**Délégation à la Formation
Professionnelle**
Immeuble Mercure 1
31 Quai de Grenelle
F - 75015 PARIS
Tél.: +33/1/45784539
Fax: +33/1/45784500

IRELAND

Ms Mary Beggan
F.A.S.
Manager Programme Development
27-33 Upper Baggot Street
IRL - DUBLIN 4
Tél.: +353/1/6685777
Fax: +353/1/6600071

Ms Bernadette Forde/Mr Brian Merriman
Employment Equality Agency
Upper Mount Street 36
IRL - DUBLIN 2
Tél.: +353/1/6605966
Fax: +353/1/6605813

ITALIA

Sig.ra Alba Dini Martino
**Commissione Nazionale Parità
Presidenza Consiglio Ministri**
Palazzo Chigi
Piazza Colonna
I - 00187 ROMA
Tél.: +39/6/6793412
Fax: +39/6/6794720

Sig.ra Lea Battistoni
I.S.F.O.L.
33 via Morgani
I - 00161 ROMA
Tél.: +39/6/445901
Fax: +39/6/8845883

LUXEMBOURG

Mme Chantal Fandel
Ministère de l'Education Nationale
Service de Formation Professionnelle
29 rue Aldringen
L - 2926 LUXEMBOURG
Tél.: +352/4785251
+352/4785235
Fax: +352/474116

NEDERLAND

Mme Drs M.J. Mooren
**Ministerie van Onderwys en
Wetenschappen**
Europaweg 4
Postbus 25000
NL - 2700 LZ ZOETERMEER
Tél.:+31/79/533598
Fax:+31/79/531953

Mme Mirjam Hommes
C/O Emancipatieraad
Anna van Hannoverstraat 4
NL - 2594 BJ DEN HAAG
Tél.: +31/70/3334782 (privé
020/6767689)
Fax: +31/70/3334014

PORTUGAL

**Instituto do Emprego
e Formaçao Profissional**
Av. José Malhoa 11
P - 1100 LISBOA
Tél.: +351/1/7275755
Fax: +351/1/7264458

Mme Bonina Brandao Pedro
Commissao para a Igualdade e para os Direitos das Mulheres
Rua Fereira Borges 69, 2° centro
P - 4000 PORTO
Tél.: +351/2/2004396 ou
+351/2/2001996
Fax:+351/2/2003848

SUOMI-FINLAND

Pirjo Heikkila
Direction Nationale de l'Enseignement
Hakaniemenkatu 2
P.O. Box 380
FL - 00531 HELSINKI
Tel: +358/0/774775
Fax: +358/0/7777865

UNITED KINGDOM

Mr John Sharman
Equal Opportunities Commission
Overseas House
Qauty Street
UK - MANCHESTER M3 3HN
Tél.: +44/61/8338360
Fax: +44/61/8351657

Mr Lesley Robson
Employment Department
C/O Moorfoot
UK - SHEFFIELD S1 4PQ
Tél.: +44/742/593872
Fax:.+44/742/594984

276

COORDINATEUR DU RESEAU IRIS

CETEC
Mme Rebecca Franceskides/
Colette De Troy
Rue de la Tourelle, 21
B - 1040 BRUXELLES
Tél.: +32/2/2305158
Fax: +32/2/2306230

COMMISSION EUROPEENNE

Mme Agnès Hubert
Chef d'Unité
DG V/A/3
200 rue de la Loi
B - 1049 BRUXELLES
Tel: +32/2/2952093
Fax: +32/2/2963562

Mme Nathalie Davies
Unité pour l'Egalité des Chances
200 rue de la Loi
B - 1049 BRUXELLES
Tel: +32/2/2962767
    (Secrétariat, Marcelle Exner)
    2964933
Fax : +32/2/2963252

Mme Frances Smith
DG XXII/B/2
200 rue de la Loi
B - 1049 BRUXELLES
Tel: +32/2/2953795
Fax: +32/2/2955699

Mme Micheline Kocak
DG XXII/B/2
200 rue de la Loi
B - 1049 BRUXELLES
Tel: +32/2/2960385
Fax: +32/2/2955699

OBSERVATEURS

REPRESENTANTS CES (CONFEDERATION EUROPEENNE DES SYNDICATS)

Penny Clarke
Boulevard Emile Jacqmain 155
B - 1210 BRUXELLES
Tél.: +32/2/2240446
Fax: +32/2/2240454

**REPRESENTANT CEDEFOP
(CENTRE EUROPEEN DE FORMATION
PROFESSIONNELLE)**

Mme Marie Pierret
Bundesallee 22
D - 1000 BERLIN 15
Tél.: +49/30/884120
Fax: +49/30/88412222

**REPRESENTANT RACINE
(RESEAU D'APPUI ET DE
CAPITALISATION DES INNOVATIONS
EUROPEENNES)**

Mme Mora Fernanda/Fabienne Baumelou
Rue Friant 18
F - 75014 PARIS
Tél.: +33/1/40448020
Fax: +33/1/40447972

Soziales

Helios II
Missoc
Beobachtungsstelle für Familienpolitik

Social

Helios II
Missoc
Observatory for the Family

Social

Helios II
Missoc
Observatoire de la Famille

HELIOS II

> **Genaue Bezeichnung**

Handicapped People in the European Community Living Independently
in an Open Society

> **Tätigkeitsbereich**

Funktionelle Rehabilitation, schulische Eingliederung, berufliche
Rehabilitation und Berufsausbildung, wirtschaftliche Eingliederung,
soziale Eingliederung und selbständige Lebensführung.

> **Zielgruppe**

Behinderte Menschen und ihre Organisationen
Behörden und Sozialpartner; die breite Öffentlichkeit (Sensibilisierung).

> **Wirkungskreis**

Hunderte von Projekten und Initiativen in den Mitgliedstaaten;
Beratender Ausschuß mit den Vertretern der Mitgliedstaaten;
Europäisches Forum der behinderten Menschen mit 27 NSO und
Gewerkschafts- und Arbeitgebervertretern.

> **Aktionen**

Austausch- und Informationsaktivitäten, Austausch von erfolgreichen
Erfahrungen mit den Projektpartnern des Programms und den NSO.

> **Betreuung des Netzes und Kommunikationstechnik**

HANDYNET: Datenbank in neun Sprachen auf CD-ROM, elektronische
Nachrichtenzeitung und elektronische Post;
Zeitschriften: HELIOS FLASH (alle zwei Monate), HELIOS MAGAZINE
(vierteljährlich), Bibliothek.

> Europäische Kommission
Generaldirektion V
Referat V E.3 - Beschäftigung, Arbeitsbeziehungen und soziale
Angelegenheiten
Abteilung "Integration behinderter Menschen"
B. WEHRENS
200 Rue de la Loi
B - 1049 Brüssel
Tel. (+32-2) 296.05.61 - Fax: (+32-2) 295.10.12

> HELIOS-Expertenteam
79 Avenue de Cortenberg
B - 1040 Brüssel
Tel. (+32-2) 735.41.05 - Fax: (+32-2) 735.16.71

N.B. Briefsendungen zum HELIOS-Programm sind an Herrn B. WEHRENS,
Abteilungsleiter V E.3, zu richten

HELIOS II

➤ **Full title**

Handicapped People in the European Community Living Independently in an Open Society

➤ **Field of activity**

Functional rehabilitation, school integration, readjustment and professional training, integration in the economy, social integration and independent life.

➤ **Target public**

Handicapped people and their organisations;
public authorities and the two sides of industry;
the general public (public awareness).

➤ **Community coverage**

Several hundred projects and initiatives in the Member States;
Consultative Committee with the representatives of Member States;
European forum for handicapped people with 27 NGOs and representatives of the trades unions and employers.

➤ **Actions**

Information and exchange activities, transfer of fruitful experiences with projects allied to the programme and with the NGOs.

➤ **Network animation and methods of communication**

HANDYNET: database in nine languages on CD-ROM, newsletter and electronic mail;
Periodicals: HELIOS FLASH (bimonthly), HELIOS MAGAZINE (quarterly), library.

➤ European Commission
Directorate-General V
Unit V/E/3 - Employment, industrial relations and social affairs
Division "Integration of handicapped people"
B. WEHRENS
200 rue de la Loi
B - 1049 Brussels
Tel.: (+32.2) 296.05.61 - Fax: (+32.2) 295.10.12

➤ HELIOS Team of experts
79 Avenue de Cortenberg
B - 1040 Brussels
Tel.: (+32.2) 735.41.05 - Fax: (+32.2) 735.16.71

N.B. All mail relative to the HELIOS programme should be addressed to M. B. WEHRENS, Head of division V/E/3

HELIOS II

> **Intitulé exact**

Handicapped People in the European Community Living Independently
in an Open Society

> **Domaine d'activité**

Réadaptation fonctionnelle, intégration scolaire, réadaptation et
formation professionnelles, intégration économique, intégration
sociale et vie autonome.

> **Public cible**

Les personnes handicapées et leurs organisations;
les pouvoirs publics et les partenaires sociaux;
le grand public (sensibilisation).

> **Rayonnement communautaire**

Plusieurs centaines de projets et initiatives dans les États membres;
Comité consultatif avec les représentants des États membres;
Forum européen des personnes handicapées avec 27 ONG et les
représentants des syndicats et des employeurs.

> **Actions**

Activités d'échange et d'information, transfert d'expériences
fructueuses avec les projets partenaires du programme et avec les
ONG.

> **Animation du réseau et techniques de communication**

HANDYNET: base de données en neuf langues sur CD-ROM,
journal et courrier électronique;
Périodiques: HELIOS FLASH (bimestriel), HELIOS MAGAZINE (trimestriel);
bibliothèque.

> Commission européenne
Direction générale V
Unité V E.3 - Emploi, relations industrielles et affaires sociales
Division "Intégration des personnes handicapées"
B. WEHRENS
200 rue de la Loi
B - 1049 Bruxelles
Tél.: (+32-2) 296.05.61 - Fax: (+32-2) 295.10.12

> Équipe d'experts HELIOS
79 Avenue de Cortenberg
B - 1040 Bruxelles
Tél.: (+32-2) 735.41.05 - Fax: (+32-2) 735.16.71

N.B. Tout courrier relatif au programme HELIOS doit être adressé à M. B.
WEHRENS, Chef de division V E.3

MISSOC

> **Genaue Bezeichnung**

System zur gegenseitigen Information über sozialen Schutz

> **Tätigkeitsbereich**

Systeme der sozialen Sicherheit und Sozialhilfe:
Organisation, Finanzierung, Leistungen, Voraussetzungen.

> **Zielgruppe**

Gemeinschafts- und nationale Verwaltungen, Sozialpartner, Forscher.

> **Wirkungskreis**

Ein Koordinierungsbüro;
Nationales Koorespondentennetz.

> **Aktionen**

Bildung eines Expertensystems zur Förderung der gegenseitigen
Unterrichtung über die Systeme und Maßnahmen für sozialen Schutz
und Sozialhilfe in den Mitgliedstaaten.

> **Betreuung des Netzes und Kommunikationstechnik**

Veröffentlichung von Vergleichstabellen über die nationalen Systeme
für sozialen Schutz und Analysen über die Entwicklung dieser Systeme.

> Europäische Kommission
Generaldirektion V
Referat V/E/2
John Fabrice RAMARO JAONA
200 Rue de la Loi
B - 1049 Brüssel
Tel. (+32-2) 299 04 71

MISSOC

> **Full title**

Mutual Information System on Social Protection.

> **Field of activity**

Social security systems and social assistance/welfare:
organisation, financing, loans, conditions for assistance.

> **Target public**

Community and national administrations, the two sides of industry,
researchers.

> **Community coverage**

A coordination office;
Network of national correspondents.

> **Actions**

Establishment of a network of experts for the promotion of mutual
information on welfare policies and systems and social welfare in the
Member States.

> **Network animation and methods of communication**
Publication of comparative tables describing national social welfare
systems and analyses of the trends in these systems.

> European Commission
Directorate-General V
Unit V/E/2
John Fabrice RAMARO JAONA
200 rue de la Loi
B - 1049 Brussels
Tel.: (+32.2) 299.04.71

MISSOC

> **Intitulé exact**

Mutual Information System on Social Protection

> **Domaine d'activité**

Systèmes de sécurité sociale et d'assistance/aide sociale:
organisation, financement, prestations, conditions d'octroi.

> **Public cible**

Administrations communautaires et nationales, partenaires sociaux,
chercheurs.

> **Rayonnement communautaire**

Un bureau de coordination;
Réseau de correspondants nationaux.

> **Actions**

Création d'un réseau d'experts en vue de promouvoir l'information
mutuelle sur les systèmes et les politiques de protection et d'assistance
sociale dans les États membres.

> **Animation du réseau et techniques de communication**

Publication de tableaux comparatifs décrivant les systèmes nationaux
de protection sociale et d'analyse sur l'évolution de ces systèmes.

> Commission européenne
Direction générale V
Unité V/E/2
John Fabrice RAMARO JAONA
200 rue de la Loi
B - 1049 Bruxelles
Tél.: (+32-2) 299.04.71

COMMISSION

M. Yves CHASSARD
Commission des Communautés
Européennes
DG V/E/2
Bureau J27 1/
Rue de la Loi 200
B-1049 BRUXELLES
Tél.: +32/2/299.04.75
Fax: +32/2/299.05.09

BELGIQUE-BELGIË

M. Jacques DONIS
Ministère de la Prévoyance Sociale
Service des Relations Internationales
Rue de la Vierge Noire, 3C
B-1000 BRUXELLES
Tél.: +32/2/509.82.34
Fax: +32/2/509.85.30

M. Mathieu ROBERT
Ministère de la Prévoyance Sociale
Direction Générale de la Sécurité Sociale
Rue de la Vierge Noire, 3C
B-1000 BRUXELLES
Tél. : +32/2/509.81.91
Fax : +32/2/509.85.34

M. Friedrich VON HEUSINGER
Informationsbüro des Freistaates
Bayern
18, Boulevard Clovis
B - 1040 BRUXELLES
Tél.: +32/2/732.26.41
Fax: +32/2/732.32.25

DANMARK

Mme K. SÖDERBLOM, Kirsten
Socialministeriet
International Relations Division
Slotsholmsgade 6
DK-1216 KØBENHAVN K
Tél.: +45/33/92.47.00
Fax: +45/33/93.25.18

Mme MÖHL LARSEN, Karin
Socialministeriet
International Relations Division
Slotsholmsgade 6
DK - 1216 KØBENHAVN K
Tél. : +45/33/92.33.77
Fax : +45/33/93.25.18

Mme BANKE, Anni
Direktoratet for
Social Sicring og Bistand
Ny Kongensgade 9
DK - 1472 KOBENHAVN K
Tél. : +45/33/91.26.22
Fax : +45/33/91.56.54

DEUTSCHLAND

M. Rainer PRITZER
Internationale und Europäische
Sozialpolitik
Bundesministerium für Arbeit und
Sozialordnung
Rochusstrasse 1
Postfach 140280
D-53123 BONN
Tel.: +49/228/527.16.31
Fax: +49/228/527.11.76

Dr. Axel WEBER
Rosenstrasse 3
D- 51427 BERGISCH GLADBACH
Tél. : +49/2204/64.098
Fax : +49/2204/64.451

ELLAS

M. Nikos GRYLLIS
Ministère de le Santé, Prévoyance et
Sécurité Sociale
Direction des Conventions Internationales
Stadiou 29
EL-10110 ATHÈNES
Tél.: +30/1/322.56.60
Fax: +30/1/324.03.26

Mme Patouna, Despina
Ministère de la Santé, Prévoyance et
Sécurité Sociale
Direction des Conventions Internationales
Stadiou 29
EL-10110 ATHENES
Tél. : +30/1/323.92.70
Fax : +30/1/324.03.26

286

ESPAÑA

GARCÍA-CASILLAS DÍAZ, Jose Maria
Subdirector General de Servicios Técnicos
**Instituto Nacional
de la Seguridad Social**
Calle Padre Damián 4
E - 28036 MADRID
Tél.: +34/1/564.90.03
Fax: +34/1/563.29.76

DEL CAMINO CANALS PARETS, Maria
**Instituto Nacional
de la Seguridad Social**
Subdirección General de Servicios Técnicos
Jefe del Servicio de Informes Juridicos y
Documentación
Calle Padre Damián 4
E - 28036 MADRID
Tél. : +34/1/564.90.09
Fax : +34/1/563.29.76

FRANCE

Mme Nicole DELETANG
**Centre de Sécurité Sociale des
Travailleurs Migrants**
Rue de la Tour des Dames, 11
F-75436 PARIS CEDEX
Tél.: +33/1/45.26.80.25
Fax: +33/1/49.95.06.50
Centrale :
Tél. : +33/1/45.26.33.41

Mme Françoise TUROCHE
**Ministère des Affaires Sociales
de la Santé et de la Ville**
Direction de la Sécurité Sociale
Division des Conventions Internationales
1, Place de Fontenoy
F-75700 PARIS
Tél.: +33/1/40.56.70.18
Fax: +33/1/40.56.72.05
Centrale :
Tél.: +33/1/40.56.60.00

IRELAND

Doyle, Aodhnait
Department of Social Welfare
EU/International Division
Store Street
IRL-DUBLIN1
Tél.: +353/1/704.38.48
Fax: +353/1/704.38.68

Smith, Claire
**Department of Social Welfare
Planning Unit**
Store Street
IRL - DUBLIN 1
Tél. : +353/1/704.38.33
Fax : +353/1/704.38.68

ITALIA

Mantero, Gioia
Ministero dell'Interno
Direzione Generale dei Servizi Civili
Ufficio Studi e Cooperazione
Internazionale:
Settore Programmazione Servizi Sociali
e Sistema Informativo Socio-Assistenziale
Via Sforza 14
I-00184 ROMA
Tél.: +39/6/488.23.97
Fax : +39/6/482.72.62

Mme Cordialina COPPOLA
**Ministero del Lavoro e della
Previdenza Sociale**
Direzione Generale della Previdenza ed
Assistenza Sociale
Divisione II
Via Flavia 6
I-00187 ROMA
Tél.: +39/6/46.83.25.25
Fax: +39/6/47.88.72.12

Mme Laura CRESCENTINI
**Ministero del Lavoro e della
Previdenza Sociale**
Direzione Generale della Previdenza ed
Assistenza Sociale
Divisione VIII
Via Flavia 6
I-00187 ROMA
Tél. : +39/6/46.83.23.77
Fax : +39/6/47.88.71.74
474.16.77

287

LUXEMBOURG

M. Claude EWEN
Inspection Générale de la Sécurité Sociale
Ministère de la Sécurité Sociale
Bureaux :
26, rue Zithe
L-2763 LUXEMBOURG
Adresse postale :
Boîte postale 1308
L - 1013 LUXEMBOURG
Tél.: +352/478.63.38
Fax: +352/478.62.25

NEDERLAND

Mme Renée BRONSGEEST
Directoraat-Generaal Sociale Zekerheid
Ministerie van Sociale Zaken en Werkgelegenheid
Hoofdafdeling Verdragen
Postbus 90802
Anna van Hannoverstraat 4
NL-2509 LV DEN HAAG
Tél.: +31/70/333.58.83
Fax : +31/70/333.40.11

M. Ivo VAN DER STEEN
Ministerie van Sociale Zaken en Werkgelegenheid
Hoofdafdeling Verdragen
Directoraat-Generaal Sociale Zekerheid
Postbus 90802
NL - 2509 LV DEN HAAG
Tél. : +31/70/333.58.86
Fax : +31/70/333.40.11

ÖSTERREICH

SPIEGEL, Bernhard
Bundesministerium für Arbeit und Soziales
Abteilung II/B/4
Stubenring 1
A -1010 WIEN
Tél. : +43/1/711.00.63.40
Fax : +43/1/715.82.56

PRAMHAS, Christoph
Bundesministerium für Arbeit und Soziales
Sektion II
Stubenring 1
A - 1010 WIEN
Tél. : +43/1/711.00.63.40
Fax : +43/1/715.82.56

PORTUGAL

Mme Sara CARDIGOS
Ministerio do trabalho e Segurança Social
Direcção-Geral dos Regimes de Segurança Social
Largo do Rato, 1
P - 1296 LISBOA CODEX
Tél.: +351/1/65.03.01
       +351/1/69.35.70
Fax: +351/1/388.95.17

SUOMI-FINLAND

MÄKIRANTA, Marja-Terttu
Ministry of Social Affairs and Health
Insurance Department
P.O. Box 267
SF- 00171 HELSINKI
Tél. : +358/0/160.38.77
Fax : +358/0/160.41.68

SVERIGE

SIBBMARK, Bengt
Socialdepartementet
Ministry of Health and Social Affairs
S - 103 33 STOCKHOLM
Tél.: +46/8/405.34.29
Fax : +46/8/723.11.91

UNITED KINGDOM

Mr. Mike BRADLEY
Department of Social Security
International Relations
The Adelphi
Room 09/10, 9th Floor
1-11 John Adam Street
UK-LONDON WC2N 6HT
Tél.: +44/71/962.85.19
Fax: +44/71/962.86.47

Mr. Kevin DENCH
Department of Social Security
International Relations
The Adelphi
9th Floor
1-11 John Adam Street
UK-LONDON WC2N 6HT
Tél. : +44/71/962.87.19
Fax : +44/71/962.86.47

SUISSE

SIGG, Roland
**Association Internationale de la
Sécurité Sociale (AISS)**
Service de Recherche et Documentation
Case Postale 1
CH - 1211 GENEVE 22
Tél. : +41/22/799.80.11
Fax : +41/22/798.63.85

BEOBACHTUNGSSTELLE FÜR FAMILIENPOLITIK

➢ **Genaue Bezeichnung**

Europäische Beobachtungsstelle für Familienpolitik

➢ **Tätigkeitsbereich**

Familienpolitik in der EG

➢ **Zielgruppe**

Nationale, regionale und lokale Verwaltungen, Hochschul- und Verbandsbereich sowie Sozialpartner.

➢ **Wirkungskreis**

Ein im Familienbereich spezialisierter Experte in jedem Mitgliedstaat (z. B. Soziologen, Juristen, Statistiker, Demographen).

➢ **Aktionen**

Regelmäßige Sammlung, Erstellung und Präsentation von Informationen über die Bevölkerungsentwicklung und familienspezifische Maßnahmen (Struktur der Haushalte, Frauenerwerbstätigkeit, Geburtenentwicklung); Veröffentlichung eines zusammenfassenden Jahresberichts über die nationale Familienpolitik in den Mitgliedstaaten und die für ein bestimmtes Jahr verzeichneten Tendenzen und Veränderungen;

➢ **Betreuung des Netzes und Kommunikationstechnik**

Expertensitzungen in Brüssel (2 x jährlich); Durchführung von Fachstudien über die Lage der Familien in der EG.

➢ Europäische Kommission
Generaldirektion V
Referat V/E/1
Michèle THOZET-TEIRLINCK
200 Rue de la Loi
B - 1049 Brüssel
Tel. (+32-2) 299 2279

OBSERVATORY FOR THE FAMILY

> **Full title**

European Family Policy Observatory.

> **Field of activity**

Family policies in the European Community.

> **Target public**

National, regional and local administrations, the academic world, communities and social partners.

> **Community coverage**

A private expert in each Member State specialised in an activity concerning the family
(ex. sociologists, lawyers, statisticians, demographers).

> **Actions**

Collection, production and presentation of regular information on demographics and the data concerning families
(household structures, women's activities, trends in the birth rate); publication of an annual report on national family policies in the Member States and the trends and changes recorded for each given year;
Preparation, updating and publication of comparative tables on specific themes (ex. structures, benefits, housing).

> **Network animation and methods of communication**

Experts meeting in Brussels (2 x yr) and an annual seminar for the final elaboration of the summary report;
Carrying out theme studies on the status of the family in the Community.

> European Commission
Directorate-General V
Unit V/E/1
Michèle THOZET-TEIRLINCK
200 rue de la Loi
B - 1049 Brussels
Tel.: (+32.2) 299.22.79

OBSERVATOIRE DE LA FAMILLE

➤ **Intitulé exact**

Observatoire européen des politiques familiales nationales

➤ **Domaine d'activité**

Les politiques familiales dans la CE

➤ **Public cible**

Administrations nationales, régionales et locales, milieux académiques, associatifs et partenaires sociaux.

➤ **Rayonnement communautaire**

Un expert privé dans chaque État membre spécialisé dans un domaine concernant la famille (ex. sociologues, juristes, statisticiens, démographes).

➤ **Actions**

Collecte, production et présentation d'informations régulières sur la démographie et sur les mesures concernant les familles (structure des ménages, activités féminines, évolution de la natalité); publication d'un rapport annuel de synthèse sur les politiques familiales nationales dans les États membres et les tendances et changements enregistrés pour une année donnée.

➤ **Animation du réseau et techniques de communication**

Réunions des experts à Bruxelles (2 x l'an) et un séminaire par an pour l'élaboration finale du rapport de synthèse; Réalisation d'études thématiques sur la situation de la famille dans l'UE.

➤ Commission européenne
Direction générale V
Unité V/E/1
Michèle THOZET-TEIRLINCK
200 rue de la Loi
B - 1049 Bruxelles
Tél.: (+32-2) 299.22.79

OBSERVATOIRE EUROPEEN DES POLITIQUES FAMILIALES NATIONALES

COORDINATEUR

Mr. John DITCH
Dept. of Social Policy and Social Work
University of York
Heslington
UK-YORK YO1 5DD1
Tel.: +44/1904/433.612
           432.629
Fax: +44/1904/433.475

DIRECTEURS ADJOINTS

Prof. Jonathan BRADSHAW
IRISS
University of York
Heslington
UK-YORK YO1 5 DD1
Tel.: +44/1904/433.608
           433.480
Fax: +44/1904/433.618

Prof. Dr. Jacques COMMAILLE
C E V I P O F
10, rue de la Chaise
F- 75007 PARIS2
Tel.: +33/1/45.49.50.25
           45.48.63.18
Fax: +33/1/45.49.50.25

RAPPORTEUR

Mr. Tony EARDLEY
Social Policy Research Unit-S P R U
University of York
Heslington
UK-YORK YO1 5DD1
Tel.: +44/1904/433.608
           433.702
Fax: +44/1904/433.618

SECRETAIRE ADMINISTRATIVE

Hazel PARKER
S P R U (c/o SPSW)
University of York
Heslington
UK - YORK YO1 5DD
Tel: +44/1904/432.629
Fax: +44/1904/433.475
CONSEILLER JURIDIQUE

294

Prof. Dr Marie-Thérèse MEULDERS
Directeur du Centre de Droit de la Famille
UCL
place Montesquieu 2
B-1348 LOUVAIN-LA-NEUVE2
Tel.: +32/2/10.47.47.30
Fax: +32/2/10.47.48.01

BELGIQUE-BELGIË

Prof. Dr Bea CANTILLON
Universiteit Antwerpen
Centre for Social Policy
UFSIA
Prinsstraat 13
B-2000 ANTWERPEN1
Tel.: +32/3/220.41.11
Fax: +32/3/220.43.25

DANMARK

Dr Vita PRUZAN
Danish Institute of Social Affairs
Borgergade, 28
DK-1300 KOPENHAGEN1
Tél.: +45/33/13.98.11
Fax: +45/33/13.89.92

DEUTSCHLAND

Mr. Thomas BAHLE
Mannheim Centre for European Social Research
Research Unit 1
PO BOX 10 34 62
D-68131 MANNHEIM1
Tel.: +49/621/292.85.89
Fax: +49/621/292.84.35

ELLAS

Prof. Loukia M. MOUSSOUROU
Panteion University
Department of Social Policy
and Social Anthropology
136. leof. Syngrou
GR-176 71 ATHENS
Tel.: +30/1/923.88.41
           923.80.83
Fax: +30/1/923.82.90

ESPAÑA

Dr Juan Antonio FERNÁNDEZ CORDÓN
Director
Consejo Superior de Investigationes
Científicas
Instituto de Demografía
Calle Amaniel 2
E-28015 MADRID
Tél.: +34/1/522.25.58
522.83.55
521.67.09
Fax: +34/1/521.05.19

FRANCE

Dr Jeanne FAGNANI
CNRS
39, rue d'Estienne d'Orves
F - 92260 FONTENAY-AUX-ROSES
Tel: +33/45.65.57.00
Fax: +33/1/45.65.53.77

Dr Pierre STROBEL
Responsable du Bureau de Recherches
CNAF
23, rue Daviel
F-75634 PARIS Cedex 132
Tél.: +33/1/45.65.52.62
45.65.54.96
Fax: +33/1/45.65.53.77

IRELAND

Dr. Gabriel KIELY
Director of the Family Studies Unit
Department of Social Sciences
University College
Belfield Campus
IRL-DUBLIN 41
Tél.: +353/1/706.85.10
706.84.19
Fax: +353/1/706.11.97

Prof. Valérie RICHARDSON
Family Studies Centre
Department of Social Sciences
University College
IRL-DUBLIN 4
Tél.: +353/1/706.85.10
706.84.19
Fax: +353/1/706.11.97

ITALIA

Prof. Dr Giovanni B. SGRITTA
Università degli Studi di Roma
"La Sapienza"
Dipartimento di Scienze Demografiche
Via Nomentana, 41
I-00161 ROMA
Tél.: +39/6/44.25.02.56
44.25.03.15
44.25.03.05
Fax: +39/6/85.30.33.74

Prof. Dr Anna Laura ZANATTA
Università degli Studi di Roma
"La Sapienza"
Dipartimento di Scienze Demografiche
Via Nomentana, 41
I-00161 ROMA
Tél.: +39/6/44.25.03.15
25.02.56
25.03.05
Fax: +39/6/85.30.33.74

LUXEMBOURG

Dr Pierre HAUSMANN
C E P S-INSTFAD
BP 65
L-7201 WALFERDANGE1
Tél.: +352/333.233.241
Fax: +352/332.705

NEDERLAND

Prof. Dr Hans-Joachim SCHULZE
Faculteit der Psychologische
Wetenschappen
Van der Boechorststraat 1
NL-1081 BT AMSTERDAM1
Tel.: +31/20/444.88.84
444.89.00
Fax: +31/20/444.87.45

ÖSTERREICH

Prof. Dr Christoph BADELT
Department of Social Policy
Vienna University of Economics and Business
Administration
Reithlegasse 16
A - 1190 VIENNA
Tel: +43/1-36.92.355.72
Fax: 43/1-36.92.355.79

PORTUGAL

Dr Karin Elisabeth WALL
Universidade de Lisboa
Instituto de Ciencias Sociais
av. das Forças Armadas
P-1600 LISBOA1
Tél.: +351/1/793.22.72
Fax: +351/1/796.49.53

SUOMI-FINLAND

Dr Sirpa TASKINEN
Development Manager
National Research Centre for Welfare and Health
Siltasaarenkatu 8C
P.O. Box 220
SF - 00531 HELSINKI
Tel: +358/0/3967.2148
Fax: +358/0/3967.2201

SVERIGE

Dr Ulla BJORNBERG
Associate Professor of Sociology
Göteborgs Universitet
Department of Sociology
Skanstorget 18
S - 411 22 GÖTEBORG
Tel: +46.31.773.47.89
Fax: +46.31.773.47.64

UNITED KINGDOM

Prof. Dr Jane MILLAR
School of Social Sciences
University of Bath
Claverton Down
UK-BATH BA2 7AY
Tel.: +44/1225/82.68.141
Fax: +44/1225/82.63.81

FONCTIONNAIRE RESPONSABLE DE L'OBSERVATOIRE

Mme Michèle THOZET-TEIRLINCK
Administrateur principal
DG V/E/1
rue Joseph II 27 - bureau 0/240
B-1049 BRUXELLES
Tél.: +32/2/299.22.79
Fax: +32/2/299.38.90

FONCTIONNAIRE RESPONSABLE DES STATISTIQUES CONCERNANT LA FAMILLE

M. François BEGEOT
EUROSTAT
DG 34/E/1
bureau: JMO C3/094
rue Alcide De Gasperi
L-2920 LUXEMBOURG
Tel.: +352/430.13.49.05
Fax: +352/430.13.44.15

Zusammenarbeit

B.C. Net
Euro-Partnerschaft
Service Eurotech Data
Service EuroJOPP Data

Cooperation

BC-Net
Europartenariat
Eurotech Data Service
EuroJOPP Data Service

Coopération

B.C. Net
Europartenariat
Service Eurotech Data
Service EuroJOPP Data

B.C. NET

➤ **Genaue Bezeichnung**

Business Cooperation Network

➤ **Tätigkeitsbereich**

Unterstützung der Unternehmen bei ihrer Partnersuche durch ein Netz von Beratern und mit EDV-Träger.

➤ **Zielgruppe**

Unternehmen, vor allem KMU (kleine und mittlere Unternehmen).

➤ **Wirkungskreis**

Netz mit über 400 Einrichtungen (private oder öffentliche Unternehmensberater) im gesamten Gemeinschaftsgebiet und in zwanzig Drittländern.

➤ **Aktionen**

Bildung und Betreuung eines Netzes mit Unternehmensberatern, die an einer Zusammenarbeit interessierte Unternehmen zusammenbringen. Die Partnersuche wird je nach den Bedürfnissen des Kunden vertraulich behandelt.

➤ **Betreuung des Netzes und Kommunikationstechnik**
- Info-Schreiben, Sitzungen und Arbeitsgruppen;
- BC NET-Datenbank mit allen Unternehmensprofilen;
- E-Mail zwischen den Mitgliedern des Netzes.

➤ Europäische Kommission
Referat XXIII/B/2
Patricia DE SMET
200 Rue de la Loi
B - 1049 Brüssel
Tel. (+32-2) 295 94 21 / 296 04 53
Fax (+32-2) 296 25 72

B.C. NET

➢ **Full title**

Business Cooperation Network

➢ **Field of activity**

Assist companies in their search for partners through a network of consultants and a computerised information system.

➢ **Target public**

Companies and particularly SMEs (small and medium-sized enterprises).

➢ **Community coverage**

Network comprised of more than 400 bodies (private or public business consultants) over the whole Community and in some twenty non-EC countries.

➢ **Actions**

Creation and animation of a network of business consultants who assist and bring together companies interested in cooperating among themselves.
Confidentiality of partner searches is adapted to the client's needs.

➢ **Network animation and methods of communication**
- Newsletters, meetings and working group;
- BC-Net database capturing all cooperation profiles;
- E-mail communication among network members.

➢ European Commission
Directorate-General XXIII
Unit XXIII/B/2
Patricia DE SMET
200 rue de la Loi
B - 1049 Brussels
Tel.: (+32.2) 295.94.21 / 296.04.53
Fax: (+32.2) 296.25.72

300

B.C. NET

➤ **Intitulé exact**

Business Cooperation Network

➤ **Domaine d'activité**

Assister les entreprises dans leur recherche de partenaires par un réseau de consultants et avec un support informatique.

➤ **Public cible**

Les entreprises, et surtout les PME (petites et moyennes entreprises).

➤ **Rayonnement communautaire**

Réseau composé de plus de 400 organismes (conseillers d'entreprises privées ou publiques) sur l'ensemble du territoire de la Communauté et dans une vingtaine de pays tiers.

➤ **Actions**

Création et animation d'un réseau de conseillers d'entreprises qui assistent et mettent en relation les entreprises intéressées à coopérer entre elles.
La confidentialité de la recherche de partenaires est adaptée aux besoins du client.

301

➤ **Animation du réseau et techniques de communication**
- Infolettres, réunions et groupe de travail;
- Base de données BC NET reprenant l'ensemble des "Cooperation profiles";
- Messageries électroniques entre les membres du réseau.

➤ Commission européenne
Direction générale XXIII
Unité XXIII/B/2
Patricia DE SMET
200 rue de la Loi
B - 1049 Bruxelles
Tél.: (+32-2) 295.94.21 / 296.04.53
Fax: (+32-2) 296.25.72

EUROPARTNERSCHAFT

➤ **Genaue Bezeichnung**

Regionale Entwicklung durch transnationale Zusammenarbeit der KMU

➤ **Tätigkeitsbereich**

Transregionale Zusammenarbeit von förderfähigen Unternehmen einer Region mit Unternehmen anderer Regionen der Gemeinschaft, Mitteleuropas und den Drittländern im Mittelmeerraum.

➤ **Zielgruppe**

Unternehmen, Handelskammern, Berater und Entwicklungsagenturen.

➤ **Wirkungskreis**

Außenstelle in jedem Mitgliedstaat.

➤ **Aktionen**

Auswahl einer Region der Gemeinschaft: '88; Irland; '89: Andalusien; '90: Wales; '91: Portugal und Ostdeutschland; '92: 22.-23. Juni, Thessaloniki, Griechenland, 3.-4. Dezember, Bari, Italien; '93: Frankreich, 17.-18. Juni; Schottland, Glasgow, 13.-14. Dezember; '94: Polen, Gdansk, 9.-10. Juni; Spanien, Bilbao, 22.-22. November; '95: Deutschland, Dortmund, 20.-21. März.

303

➤ **Betreuung des Netzes und Kommunikationstechnik**

- Erstellung eines mehrsprachigen Katalogs mit allen Unternehmen, die eine grenzübergreifende Zusammenarbeit anstreben;
- Versand des Katalogs an die Unternehmen und an 2.000 Industrie- und Berufsverbände;
- zweimal pro Jahr Veranstaltung von zweitägigen direkten Kontakttreffen in den ausgewählten Regionen mit den Vertretern der Geschäftswelt.

➤ Europäische Kommission
Generaldirektionen XVI und XXIII
200 Rue de la Loi
B - 1049 Brüssel
Tel. (GD XVI): (+32-2) 295 88 92 - (GD XXIII): (+32-2) 295 12 85

EUROPARTENARIAT

➤ **Full title**

Regional development for transnational cooperation between small and medium-sized enterprises.

➤ **Field of activity**

Transregional cooperation between businesses of a region eligible for regional policies with businesses from other regions of the Community, Central and Eastern European- and Mediterranean Basin countries.

➤ **Target public**

Companies, chambers of commerce, consultants and development agencies.

➤ **Community coverage**

Relay in each Member State.

➤ **Actions**

Selection of a region of the Community: '88: Ireland; '89: Andalusia; '90: Wales; '91: Portugal and East Germany; '92: 22-23 June, Thessaloniki, Greece; 3-4 December, Bari, Italy; '93: 17-18 June, France; 13-14 December, Glasgow, Scotland; '94: 9-10 June, Gdansk, Poland; 21-22 November, Bilbao, Spain; '95: 20-21 March, Dortmund, Germany.

➤ **Network animation and methods of communication**

- Setting-up a multilingual directory covering all the companies interested in cross-border cooperation;
- despatch of the directory to companies and to 2,000 industrial and professional bodies;
- biannual organisation of direct contacts over two days, in the selected regions, with representatives of the business community.

➤ European Commission
Directorates-General XVI and XXIII
200 rue de la Loi
B - 1049 Brussels
Tel.: (DG XVI): (+32.2) 295.88.92 - (DG XXIII): (+32.2) 295.12.85

EUROPARTENARIAT

➤ **Intitulé exact**

Le développement régional par la coopération transnationale entre PME

➤ **Domaine d'activité**

Coopération transrégionale entre les entreprises d'une région éligible aux politiques régionales avec des entreprises d'autres régions de la Communauté, de l'Europe centrale et orientale et des pays tiers méditerranéens.

➤ **Public cible**

Entreprises, chambres de commerce, consultants et agences de développement.

➤ **Rayonnement communautaire**

Relais dans chaque État membre.

➤ **Actions**

Sélection d'une région de la Communauté:
88: Irlande; 89: Andalousie; 90: Pays de Galles; 91: Portugal et Allemagne de l'Est;
92: 22-23 juin, Thessaloniki, Grèce, 3-4 décembre, Bari, Italie;
93: France, 17-18 juin; Écosse, Glasgow, 13-14 décembre;
94: Pologne, Gdansk, 9-10 juin; Espagne, Bilbao, 21-22 novembre;
95: Allemagne, Dortmund, 20-21 mars.

➤ **Animation du réseau et techniques de communication**

- Constitution d'un catalogue multilingue reprenant l'ensemble des entreprises désirant une collaboration transfrontalière;
- envoi du catalogue aux entreprises et à 2.000 organismes industriels et professionnels;
- organisation, deux fois par an, de contacts directs pendant deux jours, dans les régions sélectionnées, avec des représentants des milieux d'affaires.

➤ Commission européenne
Directions générales XVI et XXIII
200 rue de la Loi
B - 1049 Bruxelles
Tél.: (DG XVI): (+32-2) 295.88.92 - (DG XXIII): (+32-2) 295.12.85

BELGIQUE-BELGIË

Mr J. HELSEN
GOM Vlaams-Brabant,
Toekomststraat 36-38
B - 1800 VILVOORDE
Tél.: +32/2/2515171 – 2514479
Fax: +32/2/2524594

Mrs Corinne DE RYCKER
SOCRAN
Parc Scientifique du Sart-Tilman
Avenue Pré-Aily
B - 4031 ANGLEUR (LIEGE)
Tél.: +32/41/678333
Fax: +32/41/678300

DANMARK

Mr Per SONDERGAARD
Danish Chamber of Commerce
Borsen
DK - 1217 KOBENHAVN K
Tél.: +45/33/950500
Fax: +45/33/325216
Télex 19520 chamco dk

DEUTSCHLAND

Mr Y. NEOPHYTOU
**IHK- Gesellschaft zur Förderung der
Aussenwirschaft und der
Unternehmensführung mbh**
Adenaueralle, 148
D - 53113 BONN
Tél.: +49/228/104165
Fax: +49/228/104238
Télex 885509 auwig d

Mrs Katrin RUH
**IHK- Gesellschaft zur Förderung der
Aussenwirschaft und der
Unternehmensführung mbh**
Schönholzer Strasse 10/11
D-13187 BERLIN
Tél.: +49/30/48806130
Fax: +49/30/48806333

ELLAS

Mr Babis FILADARLIS
Exporters Association of Northern Greece
1, Morihovou Square
GR-54625 THESSALONIKI
Tél.: +30/31/515196 - 546103 - 547312
Fax: +30/31/546102 - 543232
Télex 418193 SEVE GR

ESPAÑA

Mr Daniel GONZALEZ DE LA RIVERA
Mme Elena MORENO FERNANDEZ DE HEREDIA
I.M.P.I.
**Instituto de la Pequena y Mediana
Empresa Industrial**
Paseo de la Castellana, 141
E - 28046 MADRID
Tél.: +34/1/5829300 - 4829317 - 5829346
Fax: +34/1/5829399

FRANCE

Mme Anne SIBILLE
A.C.F.C.I.
**Assemblée des Chambres Françaises
de Commerce et d'Industrie**
45, Av. de léna
BP 448.16
F - 75769 PARIS CEDEX 16
Tél.: +33/1/40693796
Fax: +33/1/40693808
Télex ACFCI 645 396 F

IRELAND

Mr Charlie Kelly
An Bord Trachtala/ The Irish Trade Board
Merrion Hall Strand Road
Sandymount
IRL-DUBLIN 4
PO Box 203
Tél.: +353/1/2695011
Fax: +353/1/2695820

ITALIA

Mr Flavio Burlizzi
Mondimpresa
Via di Porta Pinciana 36
I - 00187 ROMA
Tél.: +39/6/4884055 - 4880727 - 4814912
Fax: +39/6/4882034

Mr Giovanni DE BIASE
Confindustria
Viale dell'Astronomia 30
I - 00144 ROMA
Tél.: +39/6/5903487
Fax: +39/6/5910629

LUXEMBOURG

Mr. L. Siebelaner
EMDA Institute
Dorfstrasse 15
L - 9766 LUXEMBOURG
Tél.: +352/926750
Fax: +352/929747

NEDERLAND

Mme Henriette VAN DER POLDER-SLINGENBERG
Mr Ruud MC GEENE
N.C.H.
Netherlands Council for Trade Promotion
Bezuidenhoutseweg 181
PO Box 10
ND-2501 CA DEN HAAG
Tél.: +31/70/3441544
Fax: +31/70/3853531

ÖSTERREICH

Mr. Heinz Hundertpfund
Wirtschaftskammer Österreich Abteilung
für Aussenwirtschaft
Referat KMU-Betreuung
Wiedner Haupstrasse, 63
postfach 150
A - 1045 WIEN
Tél.: +43/1/501054308
Fax: +43/1/50206255
Télex 111871

PORTUGAL

Mr. Manuel FERREIRA LINO
Bando do Fomento e Exterior
Av. Casal Ribeiro 59
P - 1000 LISBOA
Tél.: +351/1/3561071 - 352021
Fax: +351/1/3521540 - 548571
Télex 64752 FOBANC

Mr Mariano DOS SANTOS
I.A.P.M.E.I.
Instituto de Apoio às Pequenas e
Medias Empresas e ao Investimento
Rua Rodriga da Fonseca, 73
P - 1297 LISBOA CODEX
Tél.: +351/1/3864333
Fax: +351/1/3863161
Télex 15657 IAPMEL

SUOMI-FINLAND

Mr Timo KARISTO
The Finnish Foreign Trade Association
Arkadiankatu 2
PO Box 908
FIN - 00101 HELSINKI
Tél.: +358/0/6959388
Fax: +358/0/6851573
Télex 121696 trade sf

SVERIGE

Mme Birgitta SVENSSON
NUTEK
Swedish National Board fon Industrial
and Technical Development
S - 11786 STOCKHOLM
Tél.: +46/8/6819466
Fax: +46/8/7444045
Télex 10840 nutek s

UNITED KINGDOM

England and Wales

Mr Robin BUSSEL
British Chamber of Commerce
4 Westwood House
Westwood Business Park
UK - COVENTRY CV4 8HS
Tél.: +44/203/694484 - 694492
Fax: +44/203/694690

307

Northern Ireland

Mr. Gerry McCONNELL/ Mr Mike PARR
**Industrial Development Board for
Northern Ireland**
I.D.B. House
64 Chichester Street
UK - BELFAST BT1 4 JX
Tél.: +44/232/233233
Fax: +44/232/231328
Télex 747025

Scotland

Mme A. Barclay
Strathclyde Innovation Center
62, Templeton Street
UK - GLASGOW G40 1DA
Tél.: +44/41/5545995
Fax: +44/41/5566320

ASSOCIATION EUROPEENNE DE LIBRE ECHANGE (AELE)

ISLANDE

Mr Ingvar KRISTINSSON
Technological Institute of Iceland
Kelnaholt
IS - 112 REYKJAVIK
Tél.: +354/1/687000
Fax: +354/1/687409

NORVEGE

Mr Geir HJELLE
Norwegian Trade Council
Drammensvein, 40
N - 0243 OSLO
Tél.: +47/2/2926300
Fax: +47/2/2926400

SUISSE

Mme Verena WABER
Schweizerische Zentrale für
Handelsförderung
Stampfenbachstrasse 85
CH - 8035 ZÜRICH
Tél.: +41/1/3655214
Fax: +41/1/3655221

Mr Jacques ANSERMET
Association Info-Chambres
47, avenue d'Ouchy
Case Postale 205
CH - 1000 LAUSANNE 13
Tél.: +41/21/6177291
Fax: +41/21/6177303

EUROPE CENTRALE ET ORIENTALE

ALBANIE

Mr Zenel HOXHA / Mr Arben SHEHI
**Chamber of Commerce of Republic of
Albania**
Konferenca e Pezes st 6
TIRANA
Tél.: +355/42/27997
Fax: +355/42/27997-Télex 2179 DHOMA
AB

BULGARIE

Mr Vassili DJAROV
Infocenter
N 37, Vazrajdane blvd.
International Fair
Pavillon 27
PLOVDIV
Tél.: +359/32/562825 - 563781
Fax: +359/32/562428

REPUBLIQUE TCHEQUE

Mr Vladimir PROKOP
**Czech Chamber of Commerce and
Industry**
Argentiskà 38
17005 PRAHA 7
Tél.: +42/2/875344
Fax: +42/2/879134

HONGRIE

Doctor Miklos BENE
Chamber of Commerce and Industry of
Ungarian Entrepreneurs
Munkàcsy Mihàly U. 16
H - 1063 BUDAPEST
Tél.: +36/1/1323068 - 1323730 - 1323770
Ext. 68, 30
Fax: +36/1/1320211

POLOGNE

Mme Ewa MACIATEK
Polish Chamber of Commerce
ul. Trebaka 4
PL - 00074 WARSZAWA
Tél.: +48/22/260221
Fax: +48/22/274673
Télex 814361

Mme Jagoda Szonert
Euro Info Correspondance Centre
Ul. Zurawia 6/12
PL - 00503 WARSZAWA
Tél.: +48/2/6251319 - 6251426 - 6252466
Fax: +48/2/6251290

ROUMANIE

Mme Liliana DEAC
Camera de Comert si Industrie a
Romaniei
Bd. N. Balcescu nr.22
79502 BUCURESTI
Tél.: +40/0/6135271 - 6143965 - 6140448
Fax: +40/0/3123830
Télex 11374 AB

SLOVAQUIE

Mme Eva MICOVA
Slovak National Agency fo Foreign
Investment and Development
Manesovo nam.2
CSFR - 85101 BRATISLAVA
Tél.: +42/7/846225 - 847219
Fax: +42/7/849806

SLOVENIE

Mr Matevz PIRNAT
Chamber of Economy of Slovenia
Foreign Economic Relations Department
Slovenska 41
61000 LJUBLJANA
Tél.: +38/61/150122
Fax: +38/61/219536
Télex 31138

CONFEDERATION DES ETATS
INDEPENDANTS (CIS)

RUSSIE

Mr IAFFE
Moscow Foundation for Devolpment
of Small and Medium Business
PO Box 370
123242 MOSCOW
Tél.: +7/095/9247000 - 9257702
Fax: +7/095/2290179

UKRAINE

Mr Yuri P. ZANUDA
The Ukrainian Chamber of Commerce
and Industry
33 vul.Velyka Zhytomyrska
KIEV 254601
Tél.:+70/44/2122901
Fax: +70/44/2123353
Télex 131379 TOPAL SU

REPUBLIQUES BALTES

ESTONIE

Mr Peeter TAMMOJA
Estonian Chamber of Commerce and
industry
Eesti Vabarik
Toom-Kooli, 17
EE-200106 TALLINN
Tél.: +372/2/443859
Fax: +372/2/443656
Télex 173254 KODA SU

309

LETTONIE

Mr Henriks SILENIEKS
Latvian Chamber of Commerce and Industry
21, Britvibas Blvd.
LV - 1849 RIGA
Tél.: +371/2/225558
Fax: +371/8/220092
Télex 161100 PKP SU FOR 1145 RASA

LITUANIE

Mr Mindaugas CERNIAUSKAS
Lietuvos Tarptautiniu Organizaciju Komitetas
(Lithuanian International Organizations Committee)
18V. Kurdikos str.
2600 VILNIUS
Tél.:+370/2/222630
Fax: +370/2/222621
Télex 261137 LUVLN SU

310

MEDITERRANEE

ALGERIE

Mr Christian WEETS
FINALEP
(Financière Algero-Européenne de Participation)
Route National No 11
SATOUELI (W. TIPAZA)
Tél.: +213/2/393496 - 393494
Fax: +213/2/392020

CHYPRE

Mr.Phidias KARIS / Mme Maria FTELLEHA
Cyprus Chamber of Commerce and Industry
Chamber Building
38, Grivas, Dhigenis ave. & 3 Deligiorgis Str.
PO Box 1455
NICOSIE
Tél.: +357/2/449500 - 462312
Fax: +357/2/465685
Télex 2077 CHAMBER CY

EGYPTE

Doctor Adel GAZARIN
Industrial Consultation Office
46 Syria Street
Mohandisteen
LE CAIRE
Tél.: +202/348/0248 - 2404
Télex 20916

ISRAEL

MR Michael ADMON
Israel Export Institute
29 Hamered Street
TEL AVIV 68125
Tél.: +972/3/5142830 - 5142809
Fax: +972/3/5142881 - 5142959
Télex 35613 MEMEX IL

JORDANIE

Mr Hanni AL AZAB
Jordan Investment Corporation
PO Box 3294
HKJ - AMMAN
Tél.: +96/26/816181-5
Fax: +96/26/816915
Télex 21716

MALTE

Mr Bernard AGIUS
Malta Export Trade Corporatio Trade Limited
Research & trade Information Divisione
PO Box 44
GZIRA GZR 01
Tél.: +356/44/6186 - 6187 -6188
Fax: +356/49/6687
Télex 1956 EXPORT MW

MAROC

Doctor Alexander MOLL
British Chamber of Commerce for Morocco
Holiday Inn Crowne Plaza
Suite 201
Rond Point Hassan II
CASABLANCA
Tél.: +212/2/271519
Fax: +212/2/269744
Télex 24994 M

TERRITOIRES OCCUPES

Mr Hanna S SINIORA
**European Palestinian Chamber of
Commerce**
19 Nablus Road
PO Box 20185
JERUSALEM EST
Tél.: +972/2/894883 - 273293
Fax: +972/2/894975

SYRIE

Doctor Abdul Hamid MALAKANI
Damascus Chamber of Commerce
PO Box 1305
DAMAS
Tél.: +963/11/215042 - 213475 - 222205
Fax: +963/11/245981
Télex INCHAD 411280 SY

TUNISIE

Mr Monchef ABID
**Agence pour la Promotion de
l'Industrie (API)**
63, Rue de Syrie
1002 TUNIS BELVEDERE
Tél.: +21/61/792144
Fax: +21/61/782482
Télex 14166 TN

TURQUIE

Mme Sebnem KARAUCAT
Iktisadi Kalkinma Vakfi
Rumell Caddesi No. 85/7
80220 Osmanbey
ISTANBUL
Tél.: +90/1/2307637 - 2469437 - 2463657
Fax: +90/1/2477587

AMERIQUE DU NORD

ETATS-UNIS

Mr David LIGHTBODY
Lomond Inc.
1250 Northwest Highway
Suite 501
Palatine
ILLINOIS IL 60067
Tél.: +1/708/7055400
Fax: +1/708/7055406

Mr Glenn S MACNAUGHT
Economic Innovation Center
28 Jacome Way
Aquidneck Industrial PArk
Middletown
Rhode Island
PROVIDENCE 02840
Tél.: +1/401/8499889
Fax: +1/401/8490815

311

SERVICE EUROTECH DATA

➤ **Tätigkeitsbereich**

Service im Rahmen von Eurotech Capital, Aktionsprogramm zur
Förderung der Finanzierung von transnationalen Spitzentechnologie-
Projekten durch privates Kapital.

➤ **Zielgruppe**

Kleine und mittlere Unternehmen, die im Spitzentechnologiesektor
angesiedelt sind

➤ **Wirkungskreis**

Das Netz Eurotech Capital :
13 Mitglieder, auf fast alle Mitgliedstaaten verteilt.

➤ **Aktion**

Verbreitung eines Dossiers an die Mitglieder des Netzes Eurotech
Capital, das Informationen über ein bestimmtes Spitzentechnologie-
Produkt, den technologischen Entwicklungsstand, die Märkte und die
Struktur des jeweiligen Sektors enthält.

➤ **Betreuung des Netzes und Kommunikationstechnik**

Der Service Eurotech Data wird den Mitgliedern des Netzes
Eurotech Capital zur Verfügung gestellt.

313

Die Mitglieder des Netzes tagen zweimal pro Jahr in einem der
Mitgliedstaaten.

➤ Europäische Kommission
Generaldirektion XVIII
Referat A.4.
Giorgio CHIARION CASONI
Bâtiment Wagner
Rue Alcide de Gasperi
L-2920 Luxemburg
Tel. (+352) 4301-36404

EUROTECH DATA SERVICE

➤ **Field of activity**

Service developed in the framework of Eurotech Capital, an action programme for encouraging financing of high-technology transnational projects through private funds.

➤ **Target public**

Small and medium-sized enterprises in the high-technology sector.

➤ **Community coverage**

The Eurotech Capital network:
13 Members spread over nearly every Member State.

➤ **Action**

Distribution to Members of the Eurotech Capital network of documents containing information on a particular high-technology product, including the level of technology, the markets and the structure of the sector of industry in question.

➤ **Network animation and methods of communication**

The Eurotech Data services are available to Members of the Eurotech Capital network.

Network Members meet biannually in one of the Member States.

➤ European Commission
Directorate-General XVIII
Unit A/4
Georgio CHIARION CASONI
Wagner Building
Rue Alcide de Gasperi
L - 2920 Luxembourg
Tel.: (+352) 4301.36404

SERVICE EUROTECH DATA

➣ **Domaine d'activité**

Service développé dans le cadre d'Eurotech Capital, programme d'action pour encourager le financement de projets transnationaux de haute technologie par des capitaux privés.

➣ **Public cible**

Petites et moyennes entreprises situées dans le secteur de la haute technologie.

➣ **Rayonnement communautaire**

Le réseau Eurotech Capital :
13 Membres répartis sur la presque totalité des Etats membres.

➣ **Action**

Diffusion aux Membres du réseau Eurotech Capital, d'un dossier comprenant,sur un produit de haute technologie déterminé, des informations sur le niveau technologique, sur les marchés et sur la structure du secteur concerné.

➣ **Animation du réseau et techniques de communication**

Le service Eurotech Data est mis à disposition des Membres du réseau Eurotech Capital.

Les Membres du réseau se réunissent deux fois par an dans un des Etats membres.

➣ Commission européenne
Direction générale XVIII
Unité A.4.
Giorgio CHIARION CASONI
Bâtiment Wagner
Rue Alcide de Gasperi
L-2920 Luxembourg
Tél. (+352) 4301-36404

SERVICE EuroJOPP DATA

➤ **Tätigkeitsbereich**

Service im Rahmen von JOPP "Joint Venture Phare Programme",
Aktion zur Förderung der Gründung und Entwicklung von
Gemeinschaftsunterenehmen in den mittel- und osteuropäischen
Ländern (MOL).

➤ **Zielgruppe**

Kleine und mittlere Unternehmen, die die Gründung eines
Gemeinschaftsunternehmens in einem MOL anstreben.

➤ **Wirkungskreis**

56 zwischengeschaltete Finanzinstitute in 15 Mitgliedstaaten.

➤ **Aktionen**

Verbreitung eines Dossiers mit Informationen über die MOL an die
KMU.

➤ **Betreuung des Netzes und Kommunikationstechnik**

Anträge der KMU werden an den Service EuroJOPP Data
über die zwischengeschalteten Finanzinstitute gerichtet.
Diese führen ihre eigenen Kommunikationsaktionen durch, um die
Zielgruppe zu erreichen.

➤ Europäische Kommission
Generaldirektion XVIII
Referat A.4
Joêl BERGER
Bâtiment Wagner
Rue Alcide de Gasperi
L-2920 Luxembourg
Tel. (+352) 4301-36246

EuroJOPP DATA SERVICE

➤ **Field of activity**

Service developed in the framework of JOPP, "Joint Venture Phare Programme", a programme aimed at facilitating the creation and development of joint-ventures in countries of Central and Eastern Europe (CEE).

➤ **Target public**

Small and medium-sized enterprises contemplating the creation of a joint-venture in a CEE country.

➤ **Community coverage**

56 Financial Intermediaries in 15 Member States.

➤ **Action**

Distribution of documents containing information on a CEE to SMEs.

➤ **Network animation and methods of communication**

SME requests are addressed to the EuroJOPP Data Service via the Financial Intermediaries, which establish their own methods of diffusing information with a view to reaching the target public.

➤ European Commission
Directorate-General XVIII
Joêl BERGER
Wagner Building
Rue Alcide de Gasperi
L - 2920 Luxembourg
Tel.: (+352) 4301.36246

SERVICE EuroJOPP DATA

➤ **Domaine d'activité**

Service développé dans le cadre de JOPP "Joint Venture Phare Programme",
action pour faciliter la création et le développement d'entreprises conjointes dans les pays d'Europe Centrale et Orientale (PECO).

➤ **Public cible**

Petites et moyennes entreprises envisageant la création d'une entreprise conjointe dans un PECO.

➤ **Rayonnement communautaire**

56 Intermédiaires Financiers répartis sur les 15 Etats membres.

➤ **Action**

Diffusion aux PME d'un dossier comprenant des informations sur un PECO.

➤ **Animation du réseau et techniques de communication**

Les demandes des PME sont adressées au service EuroJOPP Data via les Intermédiaires Financiers.Ceux-ci mettent en oeuvre leurs propres actions de communication en vue d'atteindre le public cible.

319

➤ Commission européenne
Direction générale XVIII
Unité A.4
Joël BERGER
Bâtiment Wagner
Rue Alcide de Gasperi
L-2920 Luxembourg
Tél. (+352) 4301-36246

Energie, Forschung und Entwicklung

Opet
Value

Energy, Research and Development

OPET
Value

Energie, Recherche et développement

OPET
Value

OPET

> **Genaue Bezeichnung**

Stützpunkt für die Förderung der Energietechnologien.

> **Tätigkeitsbereich**

Im Rahmen des Programms THERMIE bilden die OPET ein Netz, das sich mit der Förderung der Energietechnologien in Europa befaßt.

> **Zielgruppe**

Unternehmen, lokale Behörden oder Einzelpersonen, die um Hilfe oder Informationen im Energiebereich ersuchen, insbesondere in den Bereichen Energieeinsparung, erneuerbare Energien, feste Brennstoffe und Öl.

> **Anmerkung**

Das Netz OPET befindet sich in einer Übergangsphase. Dies läßt sich dadurch erklären, daß das erste Programm THERMIE Ende 1994 auslief und die ersten Aktionen des neuen Programms THERMIE (Demo-Phase des Sonderprogramms FTE JOULE THERMIE) erst Mitte 1995 beginnen. Für genauere Auskünfte wenden Sie sich bitte an die GD XVII der Europäischen Kommission oder an OPET CS.

> Europäische Kommission
> Generaldirektion XVII - Energie
> 200 Rue de la Loi
> B - 1049 Brüssel

> OPET CS
> Avenuer R. Vandendriessche 18
> B-1150 Brüssel
> Tel. 02-778 28 11
> Fax 02-771 56 11

OPET

> **Full title**

Organisation for the Promotion of Energy Technologies.

> **Field of activity**

In the framework of the THERMIE programme, OPETs form a network working for the promotion of energy technologies in Europe.

> **Target public**

Companies, local authorities or individuals, seeking help or information on energy, in particular in the field of energy efficiency, renewable energy, combustible solids and hydrocarbons.

> **Note**

The OPET network is currently in a transitional phase. This is because the first THERMIE programme ended in late 1994 and the new THERMIE programme's first activities (demonstration phase of the specific programme RTD JOULE THERMIE) will not begin until mid-1995. For further information, please contact DG XVII of the European Commission or OPET CS.

> European Commission
  Directorate-General XVII - Energy
  200 rue de la Loi
  B - 1049 Brussels

> OPET CS
  Avenue R. Vandendriessche 18
  B - 1150 Brussels
  Tel.: (+32.2) 778.28.11
  Fax: (+32.2) 771.56.11

OPET

> **Intitulé exact**

Organisation pour la Promotion des Technologies Énergétiques.

> **Domaine d'activité**

Dans le cadre du programme THERMIE, les OPET forment un réseau travaillant pour la promotion des technologies énergétiques en Europe.

> **Public cible**

Les sociétés, autorités locales ou individus, recherchant une aide ou une information en matière d'énergie, en particulier dans les domaines de l'efficacité énergétique, des énergies renouvelables, des combustibles solides et des hydrocarbures.

> **Note**

Le réseau OPET se trouve dans une période de transition. Cela s'explique par le fait que le premier programme THERMIE s'est terminé fin 1994 et que les premières actions du nouveau programme THERMIE (phase de démonstration du programme spécifique RTD JOULE THERMIE) ne commencent que mi-1995.
Pour les informations plus précises, adressez-vous à la DG XVII de la Commission Européenne ou à l'OPET CS.

323

> Commission européenne
Direction générale XVII - Energie
200 rue de la Loi
B - 1049 Bruxelles

OPET CS
Avenue R. Vandendriessche 18
B-1150 Bruxelles
Tél. 02-778.28.11
Fax. 02-771.56.11

BELGIQUE-BELGIË

INSTITUT WALLON
ENERGIUM 2000
10, Bld Baron Huart
B-5000 NAMUR
Tél.: +32/81/23.04.52
Fax: +32/81/23.07.42

ETM Consortium
Euro-Technology Marketing
51, avenue Colonel Picquart
B-1030 BRUXELLES
Tel.: +32/2/539.00.15
Fax: +32/2/534.86.30

VLAAMSE THERMIE COORDINATIE
Boeretang 200
B-2400 MOL
Tel.: +32/14/33.27.16
Fax: +32/14/32.11.85

DANMARK

ENERGY CENTRE DENMARK
Suhmsgade 3
DK-1125 KØBENHAVN K
Tél.: +45/33/11.83.00
Fax: +45/33/11.83.33

COWIconsult
Engineers and Planners AS
Parallelvej 15
DK-2800 LYNGBY
Tel.: +45/45/97.22.11
Fax: +45/45/97.22.12

DEUTSCHLAND

CORA c/o SEA_
Cooperation of Regional Agencies
Saarländische Energie-Agentur GmbH
Altenkesselerstr. 17
D-66115 SAARBRÜCKEN
Tel.: +49/681/976.21.74
Fax: +49/681/976.21.75

EAB
Enregie-Anlagen Berlin
Flottwellstr. 4-5
D-10785 BERLIN
Tél.: +49/30/25.49.60
Fax: +49/30/25.49.62.30

KFA/FIZ
FIZ-Karlsruhe
Fachinformationszentrum-Karlsruhe
Gesellschaft für wissenschaftlich-
technische Information mbH
Postfach 24 65
D-76012 KARLSRUHE
Tél.: +49/7247/80.83.51
Fax: +49/7247/80.81.34

KFA Jülich
Projektträger BEO
Postfach
D-52425 JÜLICH
Tel.: +49/2461/61.37.29
　　　　　61.59.28
Fax: +49/2461/61.69.99

Friedemann & Johnson-Consultants
GmbH
Pestalozzistr. 88
D-10625 BERLIN
Tel.: +49/30/312.26.84
Fax: +49/30/313.26.71

GOPA-Consultants
Gesellschaft für Organisation,
Planung un Ausbildung mbH
Hindenburgring 18
D-61348 BAD HOMBURG
Tél.: +49/6172/93.00
Fax: +49/6172/35.046

ICEU
Internationales Zentrum für Energie
und Umwelttechnologie Leipzig GmbH
Auenstr. 25
D-04105 LEIPZIG
Tél.: +49/341/29.46.02
　　　　　29.43.50
Fax: +49/341/29.09.04

INNOTEC
Systemanalyse GmbH
Kurfüstendamm 199
D-10719 BERLIN
Tel.: +49/30/882.3251-3432
Fax: +49/30/885.44.33

TÜV RHEINLAND
Insitut für Umweltschutz
und Energietechnik
(KST 931)
Am Grauen Stein
D-51105 KÖLN
Tél.: +49/221/80.60
Fax: +49/221/80.61.350

ZrE
Zweckverband Regionale
Entwicklung und Energie
Wieshuberstrasse 3
D-93059 REGENSBURG
Tél.: +49/941/420.04
Fax: +49/941/446.91

ELLAS

CRES - Centre for Renewable Energy
Sources
19 km-Marathon Avenue
GR-19009 PIKERMI
Tel.: +30/1/603.99.00
Fax; +30/1/603.99.04-11

LDK Consultants,
Engineers & Planners
7 Sp. Traintafyllou Str.
GR-113 61 ATHENES
Tél.: +30/1/862.96.60
Fax: +30/1/861.76.81

SYNERGIA
Apollon Tower
64, Louise Riencourt Street
GR-11523 ATHENS
Tel.: +30/1/64.96.185
Fax: +30/1/64.96.186

ESPAÑA

EVE - Ente Vasco de la Energía
Edificio Albia 1
San Vicente, 8 - Planta 14
E-48001 BILBAO
Tél.: +34/4/423.50.50
Fax: +34/4/424.97.33

ICAEN-Insitut Catalá d'Energía
Departament d'Industria i Energia
Generalitat de Catalunya
Avgda. Diagonal 453 Bis, Atic
E-08036 BARCELONA
Tél.: +34/3/439.28.00
Fax: +34/3/419.72.53

IDAE
Instituto para la Diversificación y
Ahorro de la Energía
P. de la Castellana, 95 - P. 21
E-28046 MADRID
Tél.: 34/1/556.84.15
Fax: +34/1/555.13.89

IMPIVA
Institut de la Mediana y Pequeña
Industria Valenciana
Avellanas 14-3° F
E-46003 VALENCIA
Tél.: +34/6/392.00.03-04-05
Fax: +34/6/391.44.60

OCICARBON
Asociación Gestora para la
Investigación y Desarrollo
Tecnológico del Carbón
C/ Augustín de Foxá 29, 4 A
E-28036 MADRID
Tél.: +34/1/733.86.62
Fax: +34/1/314.32.96

SODEAN
Sociedad para el Desarrollo
Energético de Andalucía
Bolivia, 11
E-41012 SEVILLA
Tel.: +34/5/462.60.01-11
Fax: +34/5/462.63.01

FRANCE

325

ADEME
Agence de l'Environnement et
de la Maîtrise de l'Energie
27, rue Louis Vicat
F-75015 PARIS
Tél.: +33/1/47.65.20.21-56
Fax: +33/1/46.45.52.36

GEP-Groupement des Entreprises
Parapétrolières et Paragazières
rue Louis Blanc 45
Cédex 72
F-92038 PARIS LA DEFENSE
Tel.: +33/1/47.17.61.39
Fax: +33/1/47.17.67.47

RARE c/o RHONALPENERGIE_
Réseeau des Agences Régionales de
l'Energie
69 rue de la République
F-69002 LYON
Tél.: +33/78/37.29.14
Fax: +33/78/37.64.91

BCEOM
Société Française d'Ingéniérie
Place des Frères Montgolfier
F-78286 GUYANCOURT Cédex
Tel.: +33/1/30.12.49.90
Fax: +33/1/30.12.10.95

EUROPLAN
Euro-Consultant Technology
Energy Environement
CHORUS
2203 Chemin de Saint Claude
Nova Antipolis
F-06600 ANTIBES
Tel.: +33/93.74.31.00
Fax: +33/93.74.31.31

IRELAND

FORBAIRT
Enterprise-Innovation-Investement-Growth
Glasnevin
IRL-DUBLIN 9
Tél.: +353/1/837.01.01
Fax: +353/1/837.28.48

UNIVERSITY COLLEGE DUBLIN
Energy Research Group
School of Architecture
Richview, Clonskeagh
IRL-DUBLIN 14
Tél.: +353/1/269.27.50
Fax: +353/1/283.89.08

ITALIA

ASTER Srl
Agenzia per lo sviluppo tecnologico
dell'Emilia Romagna
Via Morgagni 4
I-40122 BOLOGNA
Tél.: +39/51/23.62.42
Fax: +39/51/22.78.03

FAST
Federazione delle Associazioni
Scientifice e Tecniche
Piazzale Rodolfo Morandi 2
I-20121 MILANO
Tél.: +39/2/76.01.56.72
Fax: +39/2/78.24.85

ICIE
Istituto Cooperativo per l'Innovazione
Via Nomentana,133
I-00161 ROMA
Tél.: +39/6/884.58.48
          854.91.41
Fax: +39/6/855.02.50

ENEA
National Agency for New Technology,
Energy and Environment
ERG-PROM CRE-Casaccia
Via Anguillarese 301
I-00060 S. MARIA DI GALERIA (Roma)
Tel.: +39/6/30.48.41.18-36.86
Fax: +39/6/30.48.64.49

CESEN S.p.A.
Viale Brigata Bisagno 2
I-16129 GENOVA
Tel.: +39/10/550.46.70
Fax: +39/10/550.46.18

SOGES S.p.A.
Organizzazione e Gestione
Corso Turati 49
I-10128 TORINO
Tel.: +39/11/319.08.33
Fax: +39/11/319.02.92

LUXEMBOURG

LUXCONTROL
Avenue des Terres Rouges, 1
L-4004 ESCH-SUR-ALZETTE
Tel;: +352/54.77.111
Fax: +352/54.79.30

NEDERLAND

NOVEM
The Netherlands Agency for Energy
and Environment
PO Box 17
Swentiboldstraat 21
NL-6130 AA SITTARD
Tél.: +31/46/59.52.39
Fax: +31/46/52.82.60

IRO
Branchevereniging voor de
Nederlandse
Toeleveranciers in de Olie-en Gasindustrie
P.O. Box 7261
NL-2701 AG ZOETERMEER
Engelanlaan 330
NL-2711 DZ ZOETERMEER
Tel.: +31/79/41.19.81
Fax: +31/79/41.97.64

326

KEMA Nederland B.V.
P.O. Box 9035
NL-6800 ET ARNHEM
Utrechtseweg 310
NL-6812 AR ARNHEM
Tel. +31/85/56.24.77
Fax: +31/85/56.20.11

PORTUGAL

CCE
Centro para a Conservação de Energia
Estrada de Alfragide
Praceta 1 - Alfragide
P-2700 AMADORA
Tél.: 351/1/471.1454-8110-8210
Fax: +351/1/471.13.16

CEEETA-PARTEX Cps
Centro de Estudos em Economia da
Energia, dos Transportes e do Ambiente
Companhia Portuguesa de Serviços
Calçada de Estrela, 82-1° DT°
P-1200 LISBOA
Tel.: +351/1/395.56.08
Fax: +351/1/395.24.90

INETI/ITE
Instituto Nacional de Engenharia e
Tecnologia Indusrtial
Instituto das Tecnologias Energéticas
Edificio J,
Azinhaga dos Lameiros à Estrada
do Paço do Lumiar
P-1699 LISBOA Codex
Tel.: +351/1/716.5141-2750-2761
Fax: +351/1/716.65.69

UNITED KINGDOM

BRECSU
Building Research Energy
Conservation
Support Unit
Garston, WATFORD
Hertfordshire
UK-WD2 7JR
Tél.: +44/923/66.47.56
Fax: +44/923/66.40.97

ECOTEC
Research and Consulting Ltd.
Priestley House
28-34 Albert Street
UK-BIRMINGHAM B4 7UD
Tel.: +44/21/616.10.10
Fax: +44/21/616.10.99

ETSU–Energy Technology Support Unit
Harwell
Oxfordshire
UK-OX11 0RA
Tél.: +44/235/43.33.27
Fax: +44/235/43.20.50

MARCH Consulting Group
Telegraphic House
Waterfront 2000
Salford Quays
UK-MANCHESTER M5 2XW
Tel.: +44/61/872.36.76
Fax: +44/61/848.01.81

NIFES
National Industrial Fuel Efficiency
Service Ltd.
8 Woodside Terrace
UK-GLASGOW G3 7UY
Tel.: +44/41/332.41.40
Fax: +44/41/332.42.55

PSTI
THE PETROLEUM SCIENCE AND
TECHNOLOGY INSTITUTE
Offshore Technology Park
Exploration Drive
UK-ABERDEEN AB23 8GX
Tel.: +44/22/470.66.00
Fax: +44/22/470.66.01

RARE

RARE-APCEDE
6 rue de l'Ancienne Comédie
BP 452
F-86021 POITIERS CEDEX
Tel.: +33/49/50.12.12
Fax: +33/49/41.61.11

RARE-AQUITAINERGIE
Hôtel De Région
14 rue François de Sourdis
F-33077 BORDEAUX CEDEX
Tel.: +33/56/90.53.90
Fax: +33/56/24.73.66

327

RARE-ARE Nord-Pas de Calais
50 rue Gustave Delory
F-59800 LILLE
Tel;: +33/20/88.64.30
Fax: +33/20/88.64.40

RARE-ARENE Provence-Alpes-
Côte d'Azur
C.M.C.I.
2 rue Henri Barbusse
F-13241 MARSEILLE CEDEX 1
Tel.: +33/91/91.53.00
Fax: +33/91/91.94.36

RARE-RHONALPENERGIE
69 rue de la République
F-69002 LYON
Tel.: +33/78/37.29.14
Fax: +33/78/37.64.91

CORA

CORA-BEA
Brandenburgische Energiespar-Agentur
GmbH
Feuerbachstr. 24-25
D-14471 POSTDAM
Tel.: +49/331/96.45.02
Fax: +49/331/96.45.92

CORA-hE
hessenENERGIE GmbH
Mainzer Str. 98-102
D-65189 WIESBADEN
Tel.: +49/611/74.62.30
Fax: +49/611/71.82.24

CORA SEA
Saarländische Energie-Agentur GmbH
Altenkesseler Str. 17
D-66115 SAARBRÜCKEN
Tel.: +49/681/976.21.70-74
Fax: +49/681/976.21.75

CORA-ZENIT
Zentrum für innovation und Technik GmbH
Dohne 54
D- 45468 MÜHLHEIM
Tel.: +49/208/300.04-23
Fax: +49/208/300.04-29

VALUE

➤ Das **Netz der Value-Relais** ist ein spezialisiertes Netz, das sich aus nationalen und regionalen Zentren zusammensetzt, deren Ziel die Annäherung der Gemeinschaftsaktivitäten für Forschung und technologische Entwicklung ihrer potentiellen Kunden in Europa ist.

➤ Ihr Mandat soll dafür sorgen, daß die FTE-Gemeinschaftsprogramme (ESPRIT, BRITE/EURAM, Bridge usw.) wirksam eingesetzt werden, damit die Unternehmen und Forschungsinstitute wettbewerbsfähiger werden.

➤ Die Value-Relais werden dieser Mission durch die Förderung der Verbreitung und Auswertung von Ergebnissen gerecht, die durch die Forschungsprogramme der Europäischen Gemeinschaft erzielt werden, sowie durch die Erleichterung der Teilnahme an diesen Programmen.

➤ Die Einrichtungen, die diese Relais beherbergen, wurden aufgrund ihrer Kompetenzen bei der Verbreitung und Valorisierung der Forschungsaktivitäten auf europäischer Ebene ausgesucht.

➤ Die Relais arbeiten eng zusammen, um aktuelle Informationen und starken Mehrwert sowie Hilfsdienste anzubieten, die über öffentliche Kanäle schwer verfügbar sind.

➤ Diese Dienste sind während des gesamten Forschungs- und Valorisierungsprozesses verfügbar, da sie sich sowohl auf die Beteiligung an diesen Programmen als auch auf die Nutzung ihrer Ergebnisse beziehen..

329

➤ Europäische Kommission
Generaldirektion XIII
Referat XIII/D/3
Bâtiment Jean Monnet - Plateau du Kirchberg
L-2920 Luxemburg
Tel.: (+35-2) 4301.34008
Fax: (+35-2) 4301.34009

VALUE

- The **network of Value relay** centres is a specialised network made up of national and regional centres whose goal is to bring Community activities in research and technological development closer to their potential clients in Europe.

- Its purpose is to ensure that Community RTD programmes (ESPRIT, BRITE/EURAM, Bridge, etc.) are used efficiently so that companies and research institutes may become more competitive.

- The Value relay centres fulfil that mission by promoting the diffusion and use of the results generated by European Community research programmes and by facilitating participation in such programmes.

- The host bodies of the relay centres have been chosen according to their position to diffuse and exploit the value of research activities on a European level.

- The relay centres work in close collaboration among themselves, in order to provide up-to-date and enhanced-value information in addition to assistance services not widely available through public bodies.

- These services are available at every phase of the research and exploitation process as they might just as well involve the participation in the programmes as the use of the programme results.

330

- European Commission
Directorate-General XIII
Unit XIII/D/3
Jean Monnet Building - Plateau du Kirchberg
L - 2920 Luxembourg
Tel.: (+352) 4301.34008
Fax: (+352) 4301.34009

VALUE

- Le **réseau des centres relais Value** est un réseau spécialisé constitué par des centres nationaux et régionaux dont le but est de rapprocher les activités communautaires de recherche et de développement technologique de leur clients potentiels en Europe.

- Son mandat consiste à faire en sorte que les programmes communautaires de RDT (ESPRIT, BRITE/EURAM, Bridge, etc.) soient utilisés efficacement de façon à rendre les entreprises et instituts de recherche plus concurrentiels.

- Les centres relais Value répondent à cette mission en promouvant la diffusion et l'exploitation des résultats générés par les programmes de recherche de la Communauté européenne ainsi qu'en facilitant la participation à ces programmes.

- Les organismes hébergeant les centres relais ont été choisis en fonction de leurs compétences dans les domaines de la diffusion et de la valorisation des activités de recherche au niveau européen.

- Les centres relais travaillent en étroite coopération, afin de fournir des informations à jour et à forte valeur ajoutée ainsi que des services d'assistance qui peuvent difficilement être disponibles par le biais de canaux publiques.

- Ces services sont disponibles tout au long du processus de recherche et de valorisation puisqu'ils peuvent porter sur la participation à ces programmes aussi bien que sur l'utilisation de leurs résultats.

331

- Commission européenne
  Direction générale XIII
  Unité XIII/D/3
  Bâtiment Jean Monnet - Plateau du Kirchberg
  L-2920 Luxembourg
  Tél.: (+35-2) 4301.34008
  Fax: (+35-2) 4301.34009

BELGIQUE-BELGIË

Walloon Region
Ministère de la Région Wallonne
Direction Générale des Technologies, de la
Recherche et de l'Energie
Avenue Prince de Liège 7
B - 5100 NAMUR
Mr. J.C. DISNEUR
Tél. : +32/81/32.15.52
Fax : +32/81/30.66.00

Flemish Region
**Ministerie van de Vlaamse
Gemeenschap**
Dept. Coördinatie Adm. Programmatie van
het Wetenschapsbeleid
Boudewijnlaan 30
B- 1210 BRUSSEL
Mr. Freddy COLSON
Tél.:+32/2/507.60.08
Fax : +32/2/507.59.81

Brussels Region
Technopol Brussel-Bruxelles A.S.B.L
Rue Gabrielle Petit 4
Bte 12
B-1210 BRUXELLES
Mr. J. EVRARD
Tél. : +32/2/422.00.25
Fax : +32/2/422.00.43

DANMARK

Whole Country

PUF - DTI Innovation
Gregersenvej
Postbox 141
DK-2630 TAASTRUP
Mr. T. RITZAU
Tél. : +45/43/50.43.50
Fax : +45/43/50.48.88

Whole Country

PUF Erhvervsfremme Styrelsen
Gregersenvej
Postbox 141
DK-2630 TAASTRUP
Mrs. M. BOELSKOV
Tél. : +45/43/71.09.66
Fax : +45/43/71.63.60

Whole Country

PUF Forskningsministeriet
HC Andersens Boulevard 40
DK - 1553 COPENHAGEN V
Mrs. A. FONNESBECH
Tél. : +45/33/11.43.00
Fax : +45/33/32.35.01

DEUTSCHLAND

South-Eastern Germany

**Agentur für Innovationsförderung &
Technologietransfer GmbH**
LEIPZIG (AGIL GmbH)
Prager Straße 28
D-04103 LEIPZIG
Mr. H.J. WEIDNER
Tél.:+49/341/967.26.10
Fax : +49/341/967.26.12

South-Western Germany

Steinbeis-Europa-Zentrum
Haus der Wirtschaft
Willi-Bleicher-Str. 19
D-70174 STUTTGART
Mr. H.J. TÜMMERS
Tél. : +49/711/123.13.20
Fax : +49/711/123.13.22

North-Eastern Germany

**VDI/VDE - Technologiezentrum
Informationstechnik GmbH**
Rheinstr. 10 B
D-14513 TELTOW/BERLIN
Mr. W. GESSNER
Tél. : +49/3328/43.51.73
Fax : +49/3328/43.52.16

North-Western Germany

**Zentrum für Innovation & Technik in
Nordrhein-Westfalen GmbH**
ZENIT
Dohne 54
D-45468 MUELHEIM AN DER RUHR
Mr. Peter WOLFMEYER
Tél. +49/208/300.04.31
Fax : +49/208/300.04.29

ELLAS

Whole Country

National Documentation Centre (NHRF)
Hellenic Value Relay Centre
48 Vas. Konstantinou Ave
GR-11635 ATHENS
Mrs. L.POULAKAKI
Tél. : +30/1/724.21.72
Fax : +30/1/724.68.24

ESPAÑA

Whole Country

CDTI
Paseo de la Castellana 141
E-28046 MADRID
Mr. Luis DEL POZO
Tél. : +34/1/581.55.86
Fax : +34/1/581.55.94

Whole Country

SGPN I+D
6a Planta
Rosario Pino 14-16
E-28020 MADRID
Mr. Julio GUZMAN
Tél. : +34/1/336.04.10
Fax : +34/1/336.04.35

FRANCE

Whole Country

Assemblée des Chambres Françaises de
Commerce
et d'Industrie (Réseau ARIST)
Service Industrie
37, rue Galilée
F-75016 PARIS
Mr. A. VASSY
Tél. : +33/1/40.69.38.32
Fax : +33/1/40.70.93.62

Pic.-Nord-Champ., Normandie, Ile de France

Association Inter-Régionale sur la Recherche Européenne
7, rue Anne Frank
F-80136 RIVERY
Ms. N. GERARD
Tél. : +33/22/80.92.10
Fax : +33/22/91.14.99

Whole Country

Association Nationale de la Recherche Technique
ANRT Europe
16, Avenue Bugeaud
F-75116 PARIS
Mrs. F. GIRAULT
Tél. : +33/1/53.70.10.70
Fax : +33/1/47.04.25.20

Côte d'Azur, Languedoc Provence

Association Route des Hautes Technologies
Espace Colbert
8, rue Sainte Barbe
F-13231 MARSEILLE CEDEX 01
Mr. C. DUBARRY
Tél. : +33/91/14.05.60
Fax : +33/91/14.05.70

Whole Country

France Innovation Scientifique et Transfert
FIST S.A.
135, bd. Saint Michel
F-75005 PARIS
Mrs. A.C. JOUANNEAU
Tél. : +33/1/40.51.00.90
Fax : +33/1/40.51.78.58

IRELAND

Whole Country

FORBAIRT
Irish Value Relay Centre
GLASNEVIN
IE DUBLIN 9
Ms. Dorothy TIMMONS
Tél. : +353/1/837.01.01
Fax : +353/1/837.90.82

333

ITALIA

Whole Country

ARC (APRE Relay Centre)
Lung. Thaon di Revel 76
I-00196 ROMA
Ms. R. ZOBBI
Tél. : +39/6/323.43.59
Fax : +39/6/323.26.18

North East and Central Italy

CRENEST (Centro Relay Nord Est)
ENEA C.R.E. CASACCIA, Inn-Diff. sp. 124
Santa Maria di Galeria
I-00060 ROMA
Ms. A. G. GANDINI
Tél. : +39/6/30.48.41.47
Fax : +39/6/30.48.38.25

Southern Italy and Islands

IRIDE (Interfaccia Ricerca Industria Diffusione Europea)
Tecnopolis CSATA Novus Ortus
S.P. per Casamassima Km3
I-70010 VALENZANO (Ba)
Ms. M. SASSO
Tél. : +39/80/877.02.38
Fax : +39/80/877.02.60

North West Italy

**RECNOVA
(Relay Centre Nord Ovest Value)**
Consorzio Genova Ricerche
Via dell'Acciaio 139
I-16152 GENOVA
Mr. G. BERTUCCI
Tél. : +39/10/650.76.76
Fax : +39/10/650.38.01
LUXEMBOURG

Whole Country

LUXINNOVATION
7, rue Alcide de Gasperi
L-1615 LUXEMBOURG-KIRCHBERG
Mr. S. POMMERELL
Tél. : +352/43.62.63
Fax : +352/43.83.26

NEDERLAND

Whole Country

EG-LIAISON
Grote Marktstraat 43
Postbus 13766
NL-2501 ET DEN HAAG
Mr. A. VAN PAASSEN
Tél. : +31/70/346.72.00
Fax : +31/70/356.28.11

Whole Country

SENTER
Grote Marktstraat 43
Postbus 30732
NL-2501 GS DEN HAAG
Mr. H. HOUF
Tél. : +31/70/361.04.26
Fax : +31/70/361.44.30

ÖSTERREICH

Whole Country

Bureau for International Research &Technology Cooperation (BIT)
Wiedner Haupstrasse 76
A - 1040 WIEN
Mr. Manfred HORVAT
Tél. : +43/1/58.11.61.60
Fax : +43/1/581.16.16.16

PORTUGAL

Whole Country

Agência de Inovaçäo S.A.
Centro Value Portugal
Av. dos Combattentes 43-10° C/D
Edificio Greenpark
P-1600 LISBOA
Mr. J.C. PERDIGOTO
Tél. : +351/1/727.13.65
Fax : +351/1/727.17.33

SUOMI-FINLAND

Whole Country

Finnish Secretariat for EC E&D Technology
Development Centre (TEKES)
Malminkatu 34
P.O. Box 69
SF- 00101 HELSINKI
Mr. H. JÄRVINEN
Tél. : +358/0/69.36.91
Fax : +358/0/694.91.96

SVERIGE

Whole Country

NUTEK
The Swedish VRC (NUTEK)
Liljeholmsvaegen 32
S-11786 STOCKHOLM
Mr. Thomas LILJEMARK
Tél. : +46/8/681.94.32
Fax : +46/8/681.96.25

Whole Country

The Swedish EC/R&D Council
The Swedish VRC
(The Swedish EC/R&D Council)
Liljeholmsvaegen 32
S-11786 STOCKHOLM
Ms. K. BRYNER
Tél. : +46/8/681.94.22
Fax : +46/818.43.29

UNITED KINGDOM

Scotland and Northern England

Euro Info Centre Ltd. (EIC)
Atrium Court
50 Waterloo Street
UK-G2 6HQ GLASGOW
Mr. David CRANSTON
Tél. : +44/41/221.09.99
Fax : +44/41/221.65.39

Northern Ireland

Northern Ireland Value Relay Centre
LEDU House
Upper Galwally
UK-BT8 4TB BELFAST
Ms. L.W.B. EMERSON
Tél. : +44/232/49.10.31
Fax : +44/232/69.14.32

Central and Southern England

The Technology Broker Ltd.
Station Road, LONGSTANTON
UK-CB4 5DS CAMBRIDGE
Ms. Maureen FIRLEJ
Tél. : +44/954/26.11.99
Fax : +44/954/26.02.91

WALES

Welsh Development Agency (WDA)
Pearl House - Greyfriars Rd.
UK-CF1 3XX CARDIFF
Mr. Anthony ARMITAGE
Tél. : +44/222/82.87.39
Fax : +44/222/64.00.30

ISLAND

Whole Country

Icelandic Research Council
Laugavegi 13
IS-101 REYKJAVIK
Mr. T. FINNBJÖRNSSON
Tél. : +354/1/62.13.20
Fax : +354/1/29.814

NORWAY

Whole Country

The Norwegian EC R&D
Information Centre/
The Research Council of Norway
Pb. 2700 St. Hanshaugen
Stensberggata 26
N-0131 OSLO
Mr. T. GRONNINGSAETER
Tél. : +47/22/03.71.78
Fax : +47/22/03.70.01

335

Ländliche Entwicklung

Leader II

Rural development

Leader II

Développement rural

Leader II

LEADER II

➤ Im Rahmen der Umsetzung der Europäischen Beobachtungsstelle für Innovation und ländliche Entwicklung wird die Kommission von einem Organismus unterstützt, der sich mit einer Reihe von Verwaltungs- und Betreuungsaufgaben befaßt, die mit der Funktionsweise des **Europäischen Netzes für ländliche Entwicklung** verbunden sind, das Teil der Initiative LEADER II ist.

Von diesem Organismus werden folgende Leistungen erbracht:

• Sammlung, Erfassung und Verbreitung von Informationen bezüglich der gesamten Gemeinschaftsaktionen zugunsten der ländlichen Entwicklung einerseits und andererseits der innovativen Modell-Aktionen, die von der Initiative LEADER II oder von anderen Quellen finanziert werden;

• Verwertung und Abfassung der Bewertungsarbeit, die mit jedem regionalen oder nationalen Programm LEADER II einhergeht;

• Betreuung des Europäischen Netzes für ländliche Entwicklung durch fortschrittliche Kommunikationstechniken (E-Mail), verschiedene Veröffentlichungen, Treffen und Veranstaltungen, sowie durch die fachliche Unterstützung der nationalen Netze und nichtstaatlichen Organisationen, die für die gute Funktionsweise von LEADER II notwendig sind;

• fachliche Unterstützung der Verwaltungen und Gebietskörperschaften im Bereich der ländlichen Entwicklung;

• fachliche Unterstützung zur Förderung von transnationalen Kooperationsaktionen im Rahmen von LEADER II.

➤ **AEIDL**
260 Chaussée de St Pierre
1040 Brüssel
Tel. (+32-2) 736 49 60
Fax: (+32-2) 736 04 34

337

LEADER II

➤ In the framework of the implementation of the European Innovation and Rural Development Observatory, the Commission is assisted by a structure which is responsible for a series of administrative duties in addition to activities tied to the operation of the **European Network for Rural Development,** around which the entire LEADER II Initiative is structured.

The structure provides the following services:

- the collection, documentation and diffusion of information concerning, on the one hand, all Community programmes favouring rural development and, on the other hand, the innovative and demonstrative activities financed by the regional or national LEADER II Initiatives;

- the exploitation and documentation of the evaluation work attached to each national or regional LEADER II programme;

- the promotion of the European Network for Rural Development, through advanced communication techniques (electronic mail), various publications, meetings and events, and through technical support offered to the national networks and non-governmental organizations which are essential to the efficient operation of LEADER II;

- technical assistance to administrations and local communities in the field of rural development;

- technical assistance in facilitating the setting up of transnational, rural cooperation activities in the framework of LEADER II.

➤ **IAEIDL**
260 chaussée de St Pierre
B - 1040 Brussels
Tel.: (+32.2) 736.49.60
Fax: (+32.2) 736.04.34

LEADER II

> Dans le cadre de la mise en oeuvre de l'Observatoire Européen de l'Innovation et du Développement Rural, la Commission est assistée par un organisme qui assure une série de tâches administratives et d'animation liées au fonctionnement du Réseau Européen du Développement Rural autour duquel s'articule l'ensemble de l'Initiative LEADER II.

Les prestations fournies par cet organisme sont les suivantes:

- recueil, mise en forme et diffusion d'informations concernant, d'une part, l'ensemble des actions communautaires en faveur du développement rural et, d'autre part, les actions innovantes et démonstratives financées par l'Initiative LEADER II ou par d'autres sources;

- exploitation et mise en forme du travail d'évaluation attaché à chaque programme LEADER II régional ou national;

- animation du Réseau Européen du Développement Rural, par des techniques de communication avancées (courrier électronique), différentes publications, des rencontres et manifestations, et par l'appui technique à des réseaux nationaux et d'organisations non gouvernementales nécessaires au bon fonctionnement de LEADER II;

- assistance technique aux administrations et aux collectivités territoriales dans le domaine du développement rural;

- assistance technique pour faciliter le montage des actions de coopération rurale transnationale dans le cadre de LEADER II.

> **AEIDL**
260 chaussée de St Pierre
1040 Bruxelles
Tél.: (+32-2) 736.49.60
Fax: (+32-2) 736.04.34

Katastrophenschutz

Katastrophenschutz
Unfallbedingte Meeresverschmutzung

Civil Protection

Civil protection
Civil protection at sea

Protection Civile

Protection Civile
Protection Civile en mer

KATASTROPHENSCHUTZ

> **Genaue Bezeichnung**
Ständiges Netz nationaler Korrespondenten im Bereich des
Katastrophenschutzes

> **Tätigkeitsbereich**
Gemeinschaftskooperation im Bereich des Schutzes, der Prävention
und Bekämpfung von Natur- oder vom Menschen verursachten
Katastrophen in der Gemeinschaft.

> **Zielgruppe**
Nationale, regionale oder lokale Behörden

> **Wirkungskreis**
Ein EG-Verantwortlicher in der Kommission;
ein nationaler hoher Beamter, der die allgemeine Politik im
Katastrophenschutzbereich in jedem Mitgliedstaat verwaltet.

> **Ziele**
Das erste Ziel dieser Zusammenarbeit ist die Unterstützung der auf
nationaler, regionaler und lokaler Ebene getroffenen Maßnahmen;
das zweite Ziel ist die Erstellung eines ständigen
Gemeinschaftsrahmens in Zusammenarbeit mit der Kommission, eine
wirksame und schnelle Zusammenarbeit der Mitgliedstaaten;
langfristig ist die Schaffung von Bedingungen geplant, um die
Interventionen der Gemeinschaft und ihrer Mitgliedstaaten in
Drittländern wirksamer und sichtbarer zu gestalten.

341

> **Betreuung des Netzes und Aktionen**
A. Bezüglich der Vorbereitung:
1. Technische Instrumente
• Kommunikations- und Informationssystem, Vademekum des
Katastrophenschutzes, Pilotprojekte;
2. Menschliche Faktoren
• Ausbildung, Simulierungsübungen, System für den Austausch von
Experten.

B. Bezüglich der Intervention:
1. Operationelle Zelle rund um die Uhr in den Dienststellen der
Kommission
2. Interventionsteams: Task Force "Meeresverschmutzung",
Verbindungsoffizier für Waldbrände, Bewertungs- und
Verbindungsexperten, Umwelt- und chemisches Gutachten.

> Europäische Kommission
Generaldirektion XI
Referat XI/C/5 - Katastrophenschutz
200 Rue de la Loi
B - 1049 Brüssel
Tel. (+32-2) 299 22 48 -
Fax: (+32-2) 299 0314

CIVIL PROTECTION

> **Full title**
Advisory Committee of national correspondents for civil protection.

> **Field of activity**
Community cooperation in the protection, prevention and the combat of natural or man-made disasters in the Community.

> **Target public**
National, regional or local authorities.

> **Community coverage**
A Community official in the Commission;
a high level national government official managing the general policy for civil protection in each Member State.

> **Objectives**
The first objective of this cooperation is to sustain efforts undertaken at national, regional and local level;
the second objective is to establish a Community framework, in collaboration with the Commission, of an effective and speedy cooperation between Member States;
the final objective, in the longer term, is to create conditions for interventions by the Community and its Member States in non-EC countries, to do so in the most effective and visible manner.

> **Network animation and actions**
A. As far as preparation is concerned:
1. Technical tools
• Information communication system, Pocketbook of Civil Protection, Pilot projects;
2. Human factors
• Training, simulation exercises, experts exchange system.

B. As far as intervention is concerned:
1. 24 hour operational unit within the Commission services
2. Intervention teams: Task Force marine Pollution, Officers for cooperation on forest fires, Evaluation and liaison Experts, Environmental and chemical expertise.

> European Commission
Directorate-General XI
Unit XI/C/4 - Civil Protection
200 rue de la Loi
B - 1049 Brussels
Tel.: (+32.2) 299.22.48 -
Fax: (+32.2) 299.03.14

PROTECTION CIVILE

> **Intitulé exact**
Réseau permanent de correspondants nationaux en matière de protection civile

> **Domaine d'activité**
Coopération communautaire en matière de protection, de prévention et de lutte contre les catastrophes naturelles ou d'origine humaine dans la Communauté.

> **Public cible**
Pouvoirs publics nationaux, régionaux ou locaux.

> **Rayonnement communautaire**
Un responsable communautaire à la Commission;
un haut fonctionnaire national gérant la politique générale en matière de protection civile dans chaque État membre.

> **Objectifs**
Le premier objectif de cette coopération est de soutenir les efforts entrepris à cet effet au niveau national, régional et local;
le deuxième objectif est d'établir un cadre communautaire permettant, en collaboration avec la Commission, une coopération efficace et rapide entre les États membres;
le dernier objectif, à plus long terme, est de créer les conditions pour que les interventions de la Communauté et de ses États membres en pays tiers se fassent de manière plus efficace et visible.

> **Animation du réseau et actions**
A. En ce qui concerne la préparation:
1. Outils techniques
- Système information de communication et d'information, Vade-mecum de la Protection civile, Projets pilotes;
2. Facteurs humains
- La formation, Les exercices de simulation, Le système d'échange d'experts.

B. En ce qui concerne l'intervention:
1. Cellule opérationnelle 24h/24h au sein des services de la Commission
2. Équipes d'intervention: Task Force Pollution marine, Officiers de coopération incendies forêts, Experts d'évaluation et de liaison, Expertise environnementale et chimique.

> Commission européenne
Direction générale XI
Unité XI/C/4 - Protection civile
200 rue de la Loi
B - 1049 Bruxelles
Tél.: (+32-2) 299.22.48 -
Fax: (+32-2) 299.03.14

BELGIQUE-BELGIË

Mme C. BREYNE-DEVOS
Directeur Général de la protection civile
**Ministère de l'Intérieur et de la
Fonction Publique**
Rue Royale, 66
B- 1000 BRUXELLES
Tél.: +32/2/5002385
Fax: +32/2/5002365
Télex 046/25610 pcbbel b

DANMARK

Brigade Chef F.L. ARPE
Emergency Management Agency
16 Datavej
DK - 3460 BIRKEROD
Tél.: +45/45/825400
Fax: +45/45/826565
Télex 05/27410 brs dk

DEUTSCHLAND

Mr. Hermann AHRENS
Bundesministerium des Innern
Abteilung O/Referat O III 2
Graurheindorfer Str. 198
D - 53117 BONN
Tél.: +49/228/6812318
Fax:. +49/228/6812155
Télex 041/886896 dmi d

ELLAS

Mr. D. PAPANIKOLAOU
President
**Earthquake Planning and Protection
Organization**
226, Messogion Avenue
GR - 15561 CHOLARGOS-ATHENS
Tél.: +30/1/7242743 ou 7284403
Fax: +30/1/6519899

ESPAÑA

M. Juan Pedro LAHORE LACOSTE-
PEDELABORDE
**Direccion general
de la Proteccion civil**
Calle Quintiliano, 21
E - 28002 MADRID
Tél.: +34/1/5373305/4
Fax: +34/1/5628941/ 5628926
Telex: 47446/49767

FRANCE

M. Benoît BROCART
Directeur de Cabinet
Direction de la Sécurité Civile
Ministère de l'Intérieur
Place Beauvau, 1
F - 75008 PARIS
Tél.: +33/1/40877427
Fax:. +33/1/47578267

IRELAND

Mr. R. DOLLARD
Principal Officer
Emergency Planning Section
Department of the Environment
Custom House
IRL - DUBLIN 1
Tél.: +353/1/6793377 (ext. 2364)
Fax: +353/1/8742710
Télex: 0500-31014 env ei

ITALIA

Ministre Salvatore ZOTTA
Département de la Protection Civile
Via Ulpiano 11
I - 00193 ROME
Tél.: +39/6/6820290 – 6820299 –
6820495
Fax: +39/6/6875531 / 6820360
Télex 043-613675 prociv i

344

LUXEMBOURG

M. Jean-Mathias GOERENS
Premier Conseiller de Gouvernment
Ministère de l'Intérieur
Rue Beaumont 19
L - 2933 LUXEMBOURG
Tél.: +352/4784617
Fax: +352/41846
Telex: 0402-2929 prociv lu

NEDERLAND

Mme Drs. A.V.M. SMIT
Ministry of the Interior
Fire Services Department
Postbus 20011
NL - 2511 EZ 's-GRAVENHAGE
Tél.: +31/70/3027426
Fax: +31/70/3639153
Télex: 31225 hi gv nl
ÖSTERREICH

Mr Robert FUNIOK
Ministry of the Interior
Herrengasse 7
Postfach 100
Tel: 43/1/531262781
Fax: 43/1/531262706
Telex : 47-11 40 95 bmi fe a
A-1014 WIEN

PORTUGAL

Mr. Armando P.M. TABORDA
Serviço Nacional de Protecçao Civil
Av. da Republica, 2-5
P - 1050 LISBOA
Tél.: +351/1/547313
Fax: +351/1/521809
Télex 14395 snpc p

SUOMI-FINLAND

Mr. Pentii PARTANEN
Director General
Rescue Services
Ministry of the Interior
Kirkkokatu 12
Tel: 358/0/1602960
Fax : 358/0/1604672
Telex: 123275
SF-00171 HELSINKI

SVERIGE

Mr. U. BJURMAN
Deputy Assistant Under-Secretary
Swedish Rescue Services Agency
Karolinen
Tel: 46/8/7631000
Fax: 46/8/7231189
S-10333 STOCKHOLM

UNITED KINGDOM

Mr. N.M. CLOWES
Emergency Planning Division
Home Office
Queen Anne's Gate, 50
UK - LONDON SW1H 9AT
Tél.: +44/171/2733221
Fax: +44/171/2733900
Télex 051-24986 hohqa

345

KATASTROPHENSCHUTZ
(UNFALLBEDINGTE MEERESVERSCHMUTZUNG)

➢ **Genaue Bezeichnung**
Beratender Ausschuß für Kontrolle und Verringerung der durch
Ableitung von Ölen und anderen gefährlichen Stoffen verursachten
Meeresverschmutzung.

➢ **Tätigkeitsbereich**
Aktionsplan der Gemeinschaft zur Unterstützung der Bemühungen der
Mitgliedstaaten bei der Verbesserung ihrer Reaktionsfähigkeit auf
größere Unfälle mit Ölen oder anderen gefährlichen Stoffen sowie
Schaffung von Voraussetzungen für eine wirksame gegenseitige
Unterstützung.

➢ **Zielgruppe**
Nationale, regionale oder lokale Behörden

➢ **Wirkungskreis**
Ein EG-Verantwortlicher in der Kommission;
ein hoher Beamter, der für die allgemeine Politik bei unfallbedingter
Meeresverschmutzung in jedem Mitgliedstaat zuständig ist.

➢ **Ziele**
- Koordinierung der Information und ihre Verbreitung in den
  Mitgliedstaaten mit dem SCI - Gemeinschaftliches Informationssystem;
- Operationelle Unterstützung der Mitgliedstaaten, die mit bedeutenden
  unfallbedingten Verschmutzungen konfrontiert sind, mit Hilfe der Task
  Force "Meeresverschmutzung";
- Koordinierung der Unterstützung mit den internationalen
  Kooperationsabkommen (bei unfallbedingter Umweltverschmutzung);
- Förderung der Technologieentwicklung zur Bekämpfung der
  Umweltverschmutzung.

➢ **Betreuung des Netzes und Aktionen**
- Bezüglich des Informationssystems der Gemeinschaft: Verzeichnis der
  Mittel zur Bekämpfung, Zusammenfassung der Eigenschaften und des
  Verhaltens von Kohlenwasserstoffen, Auswirkungen der
  Kohlenwasserstoffe auf Flora und Fauna, Überblick über Datenbanken
  und Modelle, nationale Organisationen;
- Bezüglich der berufsbildenden Programme: Allgemeine Kurse über die
  Bekämpfung der Meeresverschmutzung durch Kohlenwasserstoffe und
  andere gefährliche Stoffe, Spezialkurse;
- Bezüglich der Studien und Pilotprojekte: Über 70 Studien &
  Pilotprojekte zur Verbesserung des Reaktionsvermögens der
  Mitgliedstaaten.

➢ Europäische Kommission
Generaldirektion XI
Referat XI/C/5 - Katastrophenschutz
200 Rue de la Loi
B - 1049 Brüssel
Tel. (+32-2) 299 22 48 - Fax: (+32-2) 299 03 14

CIVIL PROTECTION
(ACCIDENTAL POLLUTION AT SEA)

➤ **Full title**
Advisory Committee on the control and reduction of pollution caused by oil and other harmful substances discharged at sea.

➤ **Field of activity**
Community Action Plan to support the efforts of Member States and help them to improve their reaction capacity in the event of major accidents involving hydrocarbons and other dangerous substances, and for creating the conditions required for effective mutual aid.

➤ **Target public**
National, regional and local authorities.

➤ **Community coverage**
A Community official in the Commission;
A high level government official in each Member State administering general policy on the subject of accidental marine pollution.

➤ **Objectives**
- Coordinate information and disseminate it to Member States and CIS - Community Information System;
- provide an operational support to Member States faced with significant accidental pollution through the agency of the Marine Pollution Task Force;
- within international cooperation agreements, coordinate assistance (in the case of accidental pollution);
- encourage development of the required technology to combat pollution.

➤ **Network animation and actions**
- As far as the Community Information System is concerned: Inventory of control methods, Catalogue of control methods, Summary of the properties and behaviour of hydrocarbons, Impact of hydrocarbons on fauna and flora, an insight into databases and models, National organisations;
- As far as training programmes are concerned: General courses on fighting marine pollution caused by hydrocarbons and other dangerous substances, specialised courses;
- As far as studies and pilot projects are concerned: More than 70 studies and pilot projects aiming at improving the reaction capacity of Member States.

➤ European Commission
Directorate-General XI
Unit XI/A/5 - Civil Protection
200 rue de la Loi
B - 1049 Brussels
Tel.: (+32.2) 299.22.48 - Fax: (+32.2) 299.03.14

PROTECTION CIVILE
(POLLUTION ACCIDENTELLE EN MER)

➢ **Intitulé exact**
Comité consultatif en matière de contrôle et de réduction de la pollution causée par le déversement en mer d'hydrocarbures et d'autres substances dangereuses.

➢ **Domaine d'activité**
Plan d'Action Communautaire pour soutenir les efforts des États membres et les aider à améliorer leur capacité de réaction en cas d'accidents majeurs impliquant des hydrocarbures ou d'autres substances dangereuses, et pour créer les conditions nécessaires à une assistance mutuelle efficace.

➢ **Public cible**
Pouvoirs publics nationaux, régionaux ou locaux

➢ **Rayonnement communautaire**
Un responsable communautaire à la Commission;
un haut fonctionnaire gérant la politique générale en matière de pollution accidentelle en mer dans chaque État membre.

➢ **Objectifs**
- Coordonner l'information et la diffuser aux États membres grâce au SCI - Système Communautaire d'Information;
- fournir un appui opérationnel aux États membres confrontés à des pollutions accidentelles importantes par l'intermédiaire de la Task Force Pollution marine;
- avec les accords de coopération internationale, coordonner l'assistance (en cas de pollutions accidentelles);
- encourager l'évolution de la technologie nécessaire pour combattre les pollutions.

349

➢ **Animation du réseau et actions**
- En ce qui concerne le système communautaire d'information:
Inventaire des moyens de lutte, Catalogue des moyens de lutte, Résumé des propriétés et du comportement des hydrocarbures, Impact des hydrocarbures sur la faune et la flore, Aperçu des bases de données et des modèles, Organisations nationales;
- En ce qui concerne les programmes de formation:
Cours généraux sur la lutte contre la pollution en mer, par les hydrocarbures et autres substances dangereuses, Cours spécialisés;
- En ce qui concerne les études et projets pilotes:
Plus de 70 études & projets pilotes visant à améliorer les capacités de réaction des États membres.

➢ Commission européenne
Direction générale XI
Unité XI/A/5 - Protection civile
200 rue de la Loi
B - 1049 Bruxelles
Tél.: (+32-2) 299.22.48 - Fax: (+32-2) 299.03.14

BELGIQUE-BELGIË

MEMBRES OFFICIELS/ OFFICIAL MEMBERS :

M. Th. JACQUES
Unité de Gestion du Modèle Mathématique
Mer du Nord et Estuaire de L'Escaut
Ministère de la Santé Publique et de l'Environnement
Gulledelle 100
B-1200 BRUXELLES
Tél.: +32/2/773.21.24 - +32/2/773.21.11
(standard)
Fax: +32/2/770.69.72

Officier N3/POL
Ministère de la Défense nationale
COMOPSNAV
Graaf Jansdijk 1
8380 ZEEBRUGGE
Tél.: +050/54.53.85
Fax: +050/55.01.04

SUPPLÉANT/REPLACEMENT :

M. G. PICHOT
Directeur
Unité de Gestion du Modèle mathématique
Mer du Nord et Estuaire de l'Escaut
Ministère de la Santé Publique et de l'Environnement
Gulledelle 100
B-1200 BRUXELLES
Tél.: +32/2/773.21.11 (standard)
Fax: +32/2/770.69.72

DANMARK

MEMBRES OFFICIELS/ OFFICIAL MEMBERS :

Mr. Preben S. STAMP
Ministry of the Environment
Environmental Protection Agency
29 Strandgade
DK-1401 COPENHAGEN K
Tél.: +45/32/66.01.00 - +45/32/ 66.04.44
(direct)
Fax: +45/32/66.04.78

350

SUPPLÉANT/REPLACEMENT :

Hr. Mogens RASMUSSEN
National Agency of Industry and Trade
Fuldmaegtig
Industriministeriet
Slotsholmsgade 12
DK-1216 COPENHAGEN K
Tél.: +45/31/92.33.50
Fax: +45/31/12.37.78

DEUTSCHLAND

MEMBRES OFFICIELS/ OFFICIAL MEMBERS :

Herrn Dipl. Ing. Dietrich SCHRÖDER
Bundesministerium für Verkehr
Referat BW 15
Rober Schumann Platz 1
D-53170 BONN
Tél.:   +49/228/300.41.50 (direct)
        +49/228/3000 (centrale)
Fax: +49/228/300.40.09
        +49/228/300.34.29

Captain H.J. ROOS
Hafenkapitain Bremen für Bundesrat
Hafenamt Bremen
Hafenkopf II nr. 2
D-28217 BREMEN
Tél.:+49/421/361.82.71
Fax: +49/421/361.83.87

Dr. Wilfried TEUBER
Bundesministerium für Umwelt,
Naturschutz und Reaktorsicherheit
Referat WA I 6 (M)
Postfach 120629
D-53048 BONN
Tél.: +49/228/305.25.27
Fax: +49/228/305.23.98-9

SUPPLÉANTS/REPLACEMENTS :

Herrn Sigbert ZESEWITZ
Bundesministerium für Verkehr
Referat BW 15
Rober Schumann Platz 1
D-53175 BONN
Tél.: +49/228/3000 (centrale)
Fax: +49/228/300.34.28-9

Herrn F. SCHWEE
Bundesministerium für Umwelt,
Naturschutz und Reaktorsicherheit
Referat WA I 6 (M)
Postfach 12.06.29
D-53048 BONN
Tél.: +49/228/305.25.27
Fax: +49/228/305.23.98-9

ELLAS

**MEMBRES OFFICIELS/
OFFICIAL MEMBERS :**

Cpt HCG J. TZAVARAS
Ministry of Mercantile Marine
Marine Environment Protection Division
109 Ipsilantou Street
GR-18532 PIRAEUS
Tel: +30/1/422.04.41
Fax: +30/1/422.04.41

SUPPLÉANT/REPLACEMENT :

Plus copy for information to :

Mr. Athena MOURMOURIS
Permanent Representation of Greece
71, avenue de Cortenberg
1040 BRUXELLES
Tél.: +32/2/739.56.11
　　　　739.56.39
Fax: +32/2/735.59.79

ESPAÑA

**MEMBRES OFFICIELS/
OFFICIAL MEMBERS :**

Sr. D. Emilio MARTÍN BAUZA
Subdirector General de Seguridad Marítima
y Contaminación
**Ministerio de Obras Públicas,
Transportes y Medio Ambiente**
Dirección General de la Marina Mercante
C/ Ruiz de Alarcón, 1
E-28010 MADRID
Tél.: +34/1/597.92.69/70
Fax: +34/1/597.92.87

D. Julio DE LA CUEVA ALEU
Dirección Técnica Puertos del Estado
C/Avenida del Partenón, 10
E-28042 MADRID
Tel.: +34/1/52.45.561
Fax: +34/1/52.45.506

SUPPLÉANT/REPLACEMENT :

Dna Ampara RAMBLA GIL
Dirección General de Medio Ambiente
Ministerio de Obras Públicas y Urbanismo
Paseo de la Castellana, 67
E-28071 MADRID
Tél.: +34/1/254.19.28
Fax: +34/1/253.29.74

FRANCE

**MEMBRES OFFICIELS/
OFFICIAL MEMBERS :**

M. le Commissaire en chef de la Marine
Xavier LA ROCHE
Mission Interministérielle de la Mer
3, Square Desaix
F-75015 PARIS
Tél.: +33/1/44.37.16.46 - 44.37.16.40
Fax: +33/1/40.58.10.50

M. Jean Marie MASSIN
Ministère de l'Environnement
Direction de l'Eau
100 avenue de Suffren
F-75015 PARIS
Tél.: +33/1/42.19.12.66
Fax: +33/1/42.19.12.69

Suppléants/Replacements :

M. Michel WEIZMANN
Secrétariat d'Etat à la Mer
3, Square Desaix
F-75015 PARIS
Tél.: +33/1/44.37.16.46
Fax: +33/1/40.58.10.50

Mme Marthe MELGUEN
Directeur du CEDRE
Technopole Brest
Iroise - BP 72
F-29280 PLOUZANE
Tél.: +33/98/49.12.66
Fax: +33/98/49.64.46

351

IRELAND

**MEMBRES OFFICIELS/
OFFICIAL MEMBERS :**

Mr. S. McLOUGHLIN
Deputy Chief Surveyor
Marine Survey Office
Department of the Marine
Eden Quay 27
IRL-DUBLIN 1
Tél.: +353/1/874.33.25
              874.49.00
              878.78.81
Fax: +353/1/872.44.91

Captain W.A. KIRWAN
Director
Irish Marine Emergency Service (IMES)
Department of the Marine
Leeson Lane
IRL-DUBLIN 2
Tél.: +353/1/678.54.44 ext. 671
Fax: +353/1/662.09.75

SUPPLÉANTS/REPLACEMENTS :

Capt. G. LIVINGSTONE
Chief of Operations
Irish Marine Emergency Service (IMES)
Department of the Marine
Leeson Lane
IRL-DUBLIN 2
Tél.: +353/1/678.54.44 ext. 672
Fax: +353/1/616.26.66

ITALIA

**MEMBRES OFFICIELS/
OFFICIAL MEMBERS :**

Cte Guido MATTEINI
Ministero dell'Ambiente
Ispettorato Centrale per la Difesa del Mare
Viale dell'Arte 16
I-00144 ROMA
Tél.: +39/6/590.84.767-39/6/638.52.91-
39/337/721.205
Fax: +39/6/590.84.111

Dott. BARADA
Direttore generale
Ministero dell'Ambiente
Ispettorato Centrale per la Difesa del Mare
Viale dell'Arte 16
I-00144 ROMA
Tél.: +39/6/592.36.77
Fax: (office hours) +39/6/59.08.41.11
Fax: (24h/24h) +39/6/592.27.37

SUPPLÉANTS/REPLACEMENTS:

Mr. CATTANEO
Ministero dell'Ambiente
Ispettorato Centrale per la Difesa del Mare
Viale dell'Arte 16
I-00144 ROMA
Tél.: +39/6/592.36.77
Fax: +39/6/59.08.41.11

Dipartimento Protezione civile
Procivilmare
Via Ulpiano, 11
I-00193 ROMA
Tél.: +39/6/682.02.73
Fax: +39/6/682.03.60

NEDERLAND

**MEMBRES OFFICIELS/
OFFICIAL MEMBERS :**

De Heer C. VELD
**Ministry of Transport, Public Works
and Water Management**
North Sea Directorate
P.O. Box 5807
NL-2280 HV RIJSWIJK
Tél.: +31/70/33.66.600
Fax: +31/70/39.00.691

Mrq K. PORTEGIES
**Ministry of Transport, Public Works
and Water Management**
Directorate-General for Shipping and
Maritime Affairs
P. O. Box 5817
NL-2280 HV RIJSWIJK
Tél.: +31/70/39.55.555
Fax: +31/70/39.96.2774

SUPPLÉANTS/REPLACEMENTS :

De Heer ir R.J. van DIJK
**Ministry of Transport, Public Works
and Water Management**
North Sea Directorate
P.O. Box 5807
NL-2280 HV RIJSWIJK
Tél.: +31/70/33.66.600
Fax: +31/70/39.00.691

De Heer P. BERGMEIJER
**Ministry of Transport, Public Works
and Water Management**
Directorate-General for Shipping and
Maritime Affairs
P.O. Box 5817
NL-2280 HV RIJSWIJK
Tél.: +31/70/39.55.555
Fax: +31/70/31.91.456

PORTUGAL

**MEMBRES OFFICIELS/
OFFICIAL MEMBERS :**

Enga Nelida MIGUENS
**Direcção Geral da Qualidade do
Ambiente**
Av. Almirante Gago Coutinho, 30 (2° Piso)
P-1000 LISBOA
Tél.: +351/1/84.70.096
Fax: +351/1/84.97.668

Vice-Almirante Lopes CARVALHEIRA
Direcção Geral de Marinha
Praça do Comércio
P-1188 LISBOA CODEX
Tél.: +351/1/34.69.221
Fax: +351/1/34.24.137

SUOMI-FINLAND

MEMBRE OFFICIEL/OFFICIAL MEMBER :

Mr. Olli PAKHALA
Ministry of the Environment
P.O. Box 399
FIN - 00121 HELSINKI
Tel: 358/0/1991.97.37
Fax : 358/0/1991.97.17

Mr. Kalervo JOLMA
**National Board of Waters and the
Environment**
P.O. Box 250
FIN - 00101 HELSINKI
Tel: 358/0/6951.353
Fax: 358/0/6951.326

UNITED KINGDOM

**MEMBRES OFFICIELS/
OFFICIAL MEMBERS :**

Mr. David BEDBOROUGH
Department of Transport
Coastguard Agency
Spring Place
105 Commercial Road
UK-SOUTHAMPTON-HAMPSHIRE S01 0ZD
Tél.: +44/1703/32.91.00
             32.94.09 (ligne directe)
Fax: +44/1703/32.94.46

Mr. D. PATTERSON
Department of Transport
Coastguard Agency
Spring Place
105 Commercial Road
UK-SOUTHAMPTON-HAMPSHIRE S01 0ZD
Tél.: +44/1703/32.91.00
             32.91.98 (direct line)
Fax: +44/1703/32.92.04

ABACUS Partnership
4 River's Edge
15 Ravenhill Road
Belfast BT6 8DN
Contact: Dr. Robert Bunn / Dr. Tom
Courtney
Tel.: +44/1232/46.15.33
Fax: +44/1232/46.15.34

353

Audiovisuelle Medien

Media II
Media Desks & Media Außenstellen

Audiovisual

Media II
Media Desks & Media Agencies

Audiovisuel

Media II
Media Desks & Media Antennes

PROGRAMM MEDIA II

> **Tätigkeitsbereich**

Das Programm MEDIA II hat eine Laufzeit von 5 Jahren (1996-2000) und ist insgesamt mit einem Haushalt von 310 Millionen ECU ausgestattet und soll ein wachstumsorientiertes Umfeld für die Unternehmen der europäischen Industrie für Film- und Fernsehprogramme schaffen.

> **Zielgruppe**

Europäische Unternehmen und Fachleute im Bereich "Audiovisuelle Medien".

> **Wirkungskreis**

Ein Programm, das allen europäischen Film- und Fernsehfachleuten der 15 Mitgliedstaaten offensteht und vorbehaltlich der Kooperationsabkommen auf die EWR-Länder, die MOL, Zypern und Malta ausgeweitet wird.

> **Aktionen**

Das Proramm MEDIA II entwickelt Aktionen in 3 prioritären Sektoren der Film- und Fernsehindustrie:

- Ausbildung von europäischen Fachleuten, in erster Linie für die Verwaltung und die neuen Technologien;

- Entwicklung von Produktionsprojekten, die für den europäischen und den Weltmarkt bestimmt sind;

- transnationaler Verleih von europäischen Filmen und Programmen.

355

Die Konzentrierung der Mittel auf diese 3 Bereiche sollte ermöglichen, beträchtliche Auswirkungen in einem Sektor zu erzielen, dessen kulturelle und wirtschaftliche Bedeutung heutzutage unbestreitbar ist.

Da die Finanzinterventionen von MEDIA II nur einen Teil der Kosten der geförderten Aktionen erfassen (im allgemeinen 50 %) sollte das Programm auch eine bedeutende Kapazität für das Freisetzen von Geldern für die Programmindustrie aufweisen.

> Europäische Kommission
> GD X D4 - Programm MEDIA
> Jacques DELMOLY
> 102, Rue de la Loi
> B - 1040 BRÜSSEL
> Tel : 32 2 295 84 06
> Fax : 32 2 299 92 14

MEDIA II PROGRAMME

➤ **Field of activity**
With a 5 year duration (1996-2000) and a global budget of 310 million ECU, the objective of the MEDIA II Programme is to create an environment favourable to the growth of companies in the European audiovisual programme industry.
MEDIA II is the sequel to MEDIA I which carried out activities from 1991 to 1995.

➤ **Target public**
European Companies and Professionals and of the audiovisual industry.

➤ **Community coverage**
Programme accessible to all European professionals in the sector from the 15 Member States, and by extension, subject to the existence of a cooperation agreement, to EEA and CEE countries and Cyprus and Malta.

➤ **Actions**
The MEDIA II Programme pursues its activities in the 3 priority sectors of the audiovisual industry:

• the training of European professionals, mainly in management and new technologies;

• the development of production projects for the European and international markets;

• the transnational distribution of European films and audiovisual programmes.

The pooling of funds in these three areas should allow for significant effects, in a sector with undeniable cultural and economic importance today.

Since MEDIA II's financial intervention only covers a part of the expenses of the activities being supported (50% generally speaking), the Programme should be significantly capable of generating support in favour of the programme industry.

➤ European Commission
DG X/D4 - MEDIA Programme
Jacques Delmoly
102 rue de la Loi
B - 1040 Brussels
Tel.: (+32.2) 295.84.06
Fax: (+32.2) 299.92.14

PROGRAMME MEDIA II

> **Domaine d'activité**
> S'étalant sur une durée de 5 ans (1996-2000), et doté d'un budget global
> de 310 millions d'ECU, le Programme MEDIA II a pour objectif de créer
> un environnement favorable à l'essor des entreprises de l'industrie
> européenne des programmes audiovisuels.
> MEDIA II succède à MEDIA I, qui a mené son action de 1991 à 1995.

> **Public cible**
> Entreprises et professionnels européens du secteur audiovisuel.

> **Rayonnement communautaire**
> Programme ouvert à l'ensemble des professionnels européens du
> secteur des 15 Etats Membres, et par extention sous réserve d'accords
> de coopération, aux pays EEE; PECO, Chypre et Malte.

> **Actions**
> Le Programme MEDIA II développe des actions dans 3 secteurs
> prioritaires de l'industrie audiovisuelle :

- la formation des professionnels européens, principalement à la gestion
  et aux nouvelles technologies;

- le développement de projets de production destinés aux marchés
  européen et mondial;

- la distribution transnationale des films et programmes audiovisuels
  européens.

357

La concentration des moyens dans ces 3 volets, devrait permettre
d'obtenir des effets significatifs, dans un secteur dont l'importance
culturelle et économique est aujourd'hui évidente.

Etant donné que l'intervention financière de MEDIA II ne couvre qu'une
partie des coûts des actions soutenues (50 % en règle générale), le
Programme devrait avoir une importante capacité de mobilisation en
faveur de l'industrie des programmes.

> Commission européenne
> DG X D4 - Programme MEDIA
> M. Jacques DELMOLY
> 102, Rue de la Loi
> B - 1040 BRUXELLES
> Tél : 32 2 295 84 06
> Fax : 32 2 299 92 14

> **Tätigkeitsbereich**
Unterrichtung der Film- und Fernsehfachleute über die audiovisuelle Politik der Europäischen Union und insbesondere über die Möglichkeiten, die das Programm MEDIA bietet. Dies ermöglicht ihnen somit voll und ganz an den verschiedenen Aktionen teilzunehmen, aus denen sich dieses Programm zusammensetzt.

> **Zielgruppe**
Fachleute und europäische Unternehmen im Bereich "audiovisuelle Medien".

> **Wirkungskreis**
Das Netz setzt sich aus 18 MEDIA-DESKS (nationale Vertretungen) und 9 MEDIA-AUSSENSTELLEN (regionale Vertretungen) zusammen, verteilt auf 15 Mitgliedstaaten, Norwegen und Island.
Diese Büros arbeiten ggf. mit den Vertretungen der Europäischen Kommission in den Mitgliedstaaten zusammen, sowie mit den EURO-INFO-ZENTREN.

> **Aktionen**
- Werktags wird ein ständiger Informationsdienst für alle Film- und Fernsehfachleute gewährleistet, die in dem Mitgliedstaat arbeiten, damit sie einen Zugang zu den Aktionen des MEDIA-Programms erhalten.

- Übersetzung, Adaptation und Herausgabe der verschiedenen Veröffentlichungen, die vom Programm MEDIA zur Verfügung gestellt werden.

- Bildung eines Dokumentationszentrums für die audiovisuelle Politik der Gemeinschaft und insbesondere das Programm MEDIA und seine unterschiedlichen Aktionen, Verteilung dieser Dokumentation an alle Film- und Fernsehfachleute, die hiefür anfragen.

- Auf nationaler, regionaler und lokaler Ebene eine aktive Verbreitung der Informationen für Film- und Fernsehfachleute über die audiovisuelle Medienpolitik der Gemeinschaft und insbesondere das Programm MEDIA durch geeignete Werbeaktionen, wie z. B. die Anwesenheit bei nationalen, regionalen oder lokalen Medienveranstaltungen, die Teilnahme an Aktionen, die von Berufsverbänden durchgeführt werden, Werbung in den Fachgremien usw.

- Auf nationaler, regionaler und lokaler Ebene die Sensibilisierung der wirtschaftlichen, industriellen und kulturellen Entscheidungsträger sowie der breiten Öffentlichkeit für die Gemeinschaftsaktivitäten im audiovisuellen Bereich und insbesondere für die vom Programm MEDIA angebotenen Möglichkeiten.

> Europäische Kommission
GD X D4 Programm MEDIA
Alvaro MASON
102, Rue de la Loi
B - 1040 BRÜSSEL
Tel : 32 2 299 91 51

359

➤ Field of activity

Inform the professionals of the audiovisual industry on the audiovisual policy of the European Union and, particularly, on the possibilities offered by the MEDIA Programme, and allow them to participate fully in the various activities included in the Programme.

➤ Target public

Professionals and European companies working in the audiovisual sector.

➤ Community coverage

Network composed of 18 MEDIA DESKS (national offices) and 9 MEDIA AGENCIES (regional offices) in the 15 Member States, Norway and Iceland.
The offices work, when necessary, in collaboration with the European Commission offices in the Member States and with EURO INFO CENTRES.

➤ Actions

Provide each working day information and assistance for all audiovisual professionals working in a Member State, in order to allow them access to the various activities offered by the MEDIA Programme.

- Provide translation, adaption as well as appropriate editing of the different publications put out by the MEDIA Programme.

- Set up a documentation centre on the Community audiovisual policy and, particularly, on the MEDIA Programme through adequate promotional activities such as its presence at national, regional or local audiovisual events, participation in actions taken by professional associations, publicity within professional bodies, etc.

- Heighten awareness of economic, industrial and cultural authorities as well as the general public on a national, regional and local level, as to Community actions in the audiovisual field and, more particularly, as to opportunities available through the MEDIA Programme.

➤ European Commission
DG X/D4 - MEDIA Programme
Alvaro MASON
102 rue de la Loi
B - 1040 Bruxelles
Tel.: (+32.2) 299.9151

360

➤ **Domaine d'activité**
Informer les professionnels du secteur audiovisuel sur la politique audiovisuelle de l'Union européenne et plus particulièrement sur les possibilités qu'offre le Programme MEDIA, et de leur permettre ainsi de participer pleinement aux diverses actions qui composent ce Programme

➤ **Public cible**
Les professionnels et entreprises européennes du secteur audiovisuel.

➤ **Rayonnement communautaire**
Réseau composé de 18 MEDIA DESKS (bureaux nationaux), et de 9 ANTENNES MEDIA (bureaux régionaux), répartis dans les 15 Etats Membres, la Norvège et l'Islande.
Ces bureaux travaillent, le cas échéant, en collaboration avec les Bureaux de la Commission européenne dans les Etats Membres, ainsi qu'avec les EURO INFO CENTRES.

➤ **Actions**
- Assurer pendant les jours ouvrables une permanence d'information et d'assistance pour tous les professionnels de l'audiovisuel travaillant dans un Etat Membre, afin de leur permettre d'accéder aux actions offertes par le Programme MEDIA.

- Assurer la traduction, l'adaptation ainsi que l'édition appropriée des diverses publications mises à disposition par le Programme MEDIA.

361

- Constituer un centre de documentation sur la politique audiovisuelle communautaire et en particulier sur le Programme MEDIA et ses différentes actions, et assurer la distribution de cette documentation à tous les professionnels de l'audiovisuel qui en font la demande.

- Promouvoir activement au niveau national, régional et local, l'information des professionnels de l'audiovisuel sur la politique audiovisuelle communautaire et en particulier sur le Programme MEDIA, par des actions de promotion adéquates, comme par exemple, sa présence lors d'événements audiovisuels nationaux, régionaux ou locaux, la participation à des actions menées par des associations professionnelles, la publicité dans des organes professionnels, etc.

- Sensibiliser au niveau national, régional et local les responsables économiques, industriels et culturels ainsi que le grand public aux réalisations communautaires en matière audiovisuelle,et plus particulièrement aux opportunités offertes par le Programme MEDIA.

➤ Commission européenne
DG X D4 Programme MEDIA
Alvaro MASON
102, Rue de la Loi
B - 1040 BRUXELLES
Tél : 32 2 2999151

BELGIQUE-BELGIË

**MEDIA DESK BELGIQUE -
COMMUNAUTE FRANCAISE**
M. Gilbert DUTRIEUX
44, Boulevard Léopold II
B 1080 BRUXELLES
Tél : 32 2 413 22 45
Fax : 32 2 413 20 68

**MEDIA DESK BELGIE -
VLAAMSE GEMEENSCHAP**
Mme Rita GOEGEBEUR
18, Quai du Commerce, Boîte 12
B 1000 BRUSSEL
Tél : 32 2 219 31 25
Fax : 32 2 219 31 53

DANMARK

MEDIA DESK DENMARK
M. Soren STEVNS
4, Store Sondervolstraede
DK 1419 KOBENHAVN
Tél : 45 31 576500
Fax : 45 31 576700

362

DEUTSCHLAND

MEDIA DESK DEUTSCHLAND
Mme Sigrid LOTZ
14-16 Friedensallee
D 22765 HAMBURG
Tél : 49 40 3906585
Fax : 49 40 3908632

ANTENNE MEDIA MÜNCHEN
Mme Carola ZIMMERER
30, Widenmayerstrasse
D 80538 MÜNCHEN
Tél : 49 89 21214884
Fax : 49 89 21214849

ANTENNE MEDIA DÜSSELDORF
Mme Anne MARBURGER
14, Kaistrasse
D 40221 DÜSSELDORF
Tél : 49 211 930500
Fax : 49 211 930505

ELLAS

MEDIA DESK ELLAS
M. Vassilis KAPETANYANNIS
44, Vassileos Konstantinou Street
GR 11635 ATHINAI
Tél : 30 1 7254056
Fax : 30 1 7254058

ESPAÑA

MEDIA DESK ESPAÑA
Mme Maria Cruz ALONSO
6, Plaza de la Independencia
E 28001 MADRID
Tél : 34 1 3300725
Fax : 34 1 3300675

MEDIA ANTENNA SEVILLA
M. Luis PEREZ TOLON
35, Ximenez de Enciso
E 41004 SEVILLA
Tél : 34 5 4213174
Fax : 34 5 4214397

MEDIA ANTENNA BARCELONA
Mme Aurora MORENO
279-283, Diputacio
E 80007 BARCELONA
Tél : 34 3 4881038
Fax : 34 3 4874192

MEDIA ANTENNA SAN SEBASTIAN
M. Miguel SAZATORNIL
3-6, Calle Bergara
E 20004 SAN SEBASTIAN
Tél : 34 43 429163
Fax : 34 43 430900

FRANCE

MEDIA DESK FRANCE
Mme Françoise MAUPIN
3, Rue Boissière
F 75016 PARIS
Tél : 33 1 47271277
Fax : 33 1 47270415

ANTENNE MEDIA STRASBOURG
Mme Catherine BURESI
1, Place de l'Etoile
F 67070 STRASBOURG
Tél : 33 88 609297
Fax : 33 88 609590

IRELAND

MEDIA DESK IRELAND
mme Siobhan O'DONOGHUE
6, Eustace Street
IRL DUBLIN 2
Tél : 353 1 6795744
Fax : 353 1 6799657

MEDIA ANTENNA GALWAY
Mme Eibhlin Ni MHUNGHAILE
Cluain Mhuire - Monivea Road
IRL GALWAY
Tél : 353 91 770728
Fax : 353 91 770746

ITALIA

MEDIA DESK ITALIA
Mme Pauline DE VITO
1055, Via Tuscolana
I 00173 ROMA
Tél : 39 6 7223444
Fax : 39 6 7223474

LUXEMBOURG

MEDIA DESK LUXEMBOURG
Mme Françoise POOS
Maison du Cassal
5, Rue Large
L 1917 LUXEMBOURG
Tél : 352 4782170
Fax : 352 467495

NEDERLAND

MEDIA DESK NEDERLAND
Mme Veroniek SCHAAFSMA
Post Box 256
NL 1200 HILVERSUM
Tél : 31 35 238641
Fax : 31 35 218541

ÖSTERREICH

MEDIA DESK AUSTRIA
Mme Iris HELLER
6, Stiftgasse
A 1070 WIEN
Tél : 43 1 526 9730
Fax : 43 1 526 97 330

PORTUGAL

MEDIA DESK PORTUGAL
Mme Amelia SOUSA TAVARES
45, Rua Sao Pedro Alcantara
P 1200 LISBOA
Tél : 351 1 3478644
Fax : 351 1 3478643

SUOMI-FINLAND

MEDIA DESK SUOMI
M. Kai SALMINEN
K 13, Kanavakatu, 12
SF 00160 HELSINKI
Tél : 35 80 62203029
Fax : 35 80 62203070

SVERIGE

MEDIA DESK SVERIGE
M. Lasse SVANBERG
5, Borgvagen
S 10252 STOCKHOLM
Tél : 46 86 651100
Fax : 46 86 622684

UNITED KINGDOM

MEDIA DESK UNITED KINGDOM
Mme Suzanne KNEPSCHER
21, Stephen Street
UK W1P 1PL LONDON
Tél : 44 171 2551444
Fax : 44 171 6366568

363

MEDIA ANTENNA CARDIFF
M. Robin HUGHES
Llantrisant Road - Llandaf
UK CF5 2PU CARDIFF
Tél : 44 1222 572307
Fax : 44 1222 578654

MEDIA ANTENNA GLASGOW
Mme Erica KING
74, Victoria Crescent Road
UK G12 9JN GLASGOW
Tél : 44 141 3344445
Fax : 44 141 3348132

ISLAND

MEDIA DESK ICELAND
Mme Sigridur VIGFUSDOTTIR
24, Laugavegi - Post Box 320
IS 101 REYKJAVIK
Tél : 354 5 626366
Fax : 354 5 627171

NORGE

MEDIA DESK NORGE
M. Nils KLEVJER AAS
Grev Wedels Plass - Post Box 482
N 0105 OSLO
Tél : 47 22 428740
Fax : 47 22 332277

3

EUR-OP

AMT FÜR AMTLICHE VERÖFFENTLICHUNGEN DER EUROPÄISCHEN GEMEINSCHAFTEN

Das Amt für amtliche Veröffentlichungen der Europäischen Gemeinschaften - bzw. EUR-OP - ist das Verlagshaus aller Institutionen der Europäischen Union: des Europäischen Parlaments, des Rats, der Kommission, des Gerichtshofs, des Rechnungshofs, des Wirtschafts- und Sozialausschusses, der Europäischen Investitionsbank und anderer Einrichtungen der Union.

EUR-OP veröffentlicht und verbreitet im Namen dieser Institutionen nicht nur das Amtsblatt der Europäischen Gemeinschaften, sondern auch durchschnittlich 5500 Monographien und rund 90 regelmäßig erscheinende Publikationen pro Jahr sowie eine bedeutende Anzahl von CD-ROM, Datenbanken, Videos usw.

EUR-OP veröffentlicht derzeit den Großteil seiner Texte regelmäßig in den elf Amtssprachen der Gemeinschaft: Spanisch, Dänisch, Deutsch, Griechisch, Englisch, Französisch, Italienisch, Niederländisch, Portugiesisch, Finnisch und Schwedisch. Um kundennah zu bleiben, hat EUR-OP ein Netz von 50 Verkaufsstellen (weltweit) für den Verkauf der Veröffentlichungen eingerichtet und verfügt über mehr als 100 Partner für den Verkauf seiner elektronischen Produkte. Aus diesem Grunde ist EUR-OP eines der wenigen Verlagshäuser, die in der ganzen Welt vertreten sind.

Alle bei EUR-OP erhältlichen Veröffentlichungen sowie die gesamte EU-Gesetzgebung sind nach Themen in den Katalogen und Verzeichnissen von EUR-OP aufgeführt. Eine andere bedeutende Informationsquelle ist die Zeitung **EUR-OP *News,*** die viermal jährlich erscheint und sowohl die jüngsten Veröffentlichungen von EUR-OP sowie alle Informationen über die aktuelle Politik der Europäischen Union im allgemeinen enthält.

Auf den folgenden Seiten finden Sie alles in bezug auf:

DEN KAUF VON PRINT- UND AUDIOVISUELLEN PRODUKTEN
- **Verkaufsstellen**
- **Euro-Buchhandlungen**
- **Document Delivery (Zugang zu den Rechtsakten der Europäischen Union)**

DATENBANKEN DER EUROPÄISCHEN UNION
- **Beschreibung**
- **Gateways**

DIE CD-ROM
- **Beschreibung**
- **Kauf der CD-Rom**

DEN ZUGANG ZU AUSSCHREIBUNGEN · TED ALERT

INFORMATIONEN FÜR STUDENTEN

EUR-OP

THE OFFICE FOR OFFICIAL PUBLICATIONS
OF THE EUROPEAN COMMUNITIES

The Office for Official Publications of the European Communities - or EUR-OP - is the publishing house for all the European institutions: the European Parliament, the Council, the Commission, the Court of Justice, the Court of Auditors, the Economic and Social Committee, the European Investment Bank and other organs of the Union.

In the name of these institutions, EUR-OP publishes and distributes not only the Official Journal of the European Communities but also an average of 5500 monographs and some 90 periodicals each year as well as a large number of CD-ROM's, databases, videos, etc.

EUR-OP at present publishes the majority of these texts systematically in the eleven community languages: Spanish, Danish, German, Greek, English, French, Italian, Dutch, Portuguese, Finnish and Swedish. In order to be readily accessible to the customer, EUR-OP has set up a network of 50 sales offices (throughout the world) for the sale of the publications and has more than 100 partners for the sale of its electronic products. As such, EUR-OP is one of the few publishing houses with a worldwide presence.

All available EUR-OP publications as also the complete community legislation are listed by subject in EUR-OP catalogues and indexes. Another important source of information is **EUR-OP *News*** which appears four times a year and covers both recent EUR-OP publications as well as full information on the current policies of the European Union in general.

In the following pages full information is provided on:

THE PURCHASE OF BOTH PRINTED AND AUDIO-VISUAL MATERIAL
- **sales offices**
- **European Bookshops**
- **document delivery (access to legislative acts of the European Union)**

EUROPEAN UNION DATABASES
- **description**
- **gateways**

CD-ROMs
- **description**
- **purchase of CD-ROMs**

ACCESS TO CALLS FOR TENDER - TED ALERT

INFORMATION FOR STUDENTS

EUR-OP

L'OFFICE DES PUBLICATIONS OFFICIELLES DES COMMUNAUTES EUROPEENNES

L'Office des publications officielles des Communautés européennes - ou EUR-OP est la maison d'édition de toutes les institutions de l'Union européenne: le Parlement européen, le Conseil, la Commission, la Cour de justice, la Cour des comptes, le Comité économique et social, la Banque Européenne d'Investissement et autres organes de l'Union.

Au nom de ces institutions, l'EUR-OP publie et diffuse non seulement le Journal officiel des Communautés européennes mais aussi en moyenne 5500 monographies et quelques 90 périodiques par an ainsi qu'un nombre important de CD-ROM, de bases de données, de vidéos, etc.

L'EUR-OP publie actuellement la plupart de ses textes systématiquement dans les onze langues communautaires: espagnol, danois, allemand, grec, anglais, français, italien, néerlandais, portugais, finlandais et suédois. Afin de rester proche du client, l'EUR-OP a érigé un réseau de 50 bureaux de vente (répartis dans le monde entier) pour la vente des publications et possède plus de 100 partenaires pour la vente de ses produits électroniques. De ce fait, l'EUR-OP est une des rares maisons d'édition présente dans le monde entier.

Toutes les publications disponibles de l'EUR-OP ainsi que la totalité de la législation communautaire sont répertoriées par thème dans les catalogues et répertoires de l'EUR-OP. Une autre source d'information importante est le journal **EUR-OP** *News* qui paraît quatre fois par an et qui présente à la fois les publications récentes de l'EUR-OP ainsi que toute information sur la politique actuelle de l'Union européenne en général.

Vous trouverez dans les pages suivantes tout ce qui concerne:

L'ACHAT DES PRODUITS IMPRIMES ET AUDIO-VISUELS
- **bureaux de vente**
- **eurolibrairies**
- **document delivery (accès aux actes législatifs de l'Union européenne)**

LES BASES DE DONNEES DE L'UNION EUROPEENNE
- **description**
- **gateways**

LES CD-ROM
- **description**
- **achat des CD-Rom**

L'ACCES AUX APPELS D'OFFRE - TED ALERT

L'INFORMATION AUX ETUDIANTS

1. VERKAUFSSTELLEN
(AMT FÜR AMTLICHE VERÖFFENTLICHUNGEN DER EUROPÄISCHEN GEMEINSCHAFTEN)

> **Tätigkeitsbereich**

Offizielles EUR-OP-Netz für den Vertrieb seiner Produkte (Veröffentlichungen, Videos, Zeitungen) gemäß dem Subsidiaritätsprinzip (EUR-OP verkauft seine Produkte nicht direkt).

> **Zielgruppe**

Breite Öffentlichkeit

> **Wirkungskreis**

15 Mitgliedstaaten, plus 30 Verkaufsstellen weltweit (5 in den östlichen Ländern, Japan, Australien, den Vereinigten Staaten, Kanada usw.)

> **Aktionen**
- Verkauf (und Versand) von Zeitungen, regelmäßig erscheinenden Publikationen, Monographien und Videos;
- oft: Verkauf (und Versand) von Rechtstexten (Versand von Dokumenten);
- allgemeine Informationen über die Politik der Gemeinschaft im Rahmen der Verkaufspolitik.

369

> **Betreuung des Netzes und Kommunikationstechnik**
Ein Förder-, Betreuungs- und Kooperationsprogramm wird von EUR-OP durchgeführt: Sitzungen, Dokumentarfilme, Rundschreiben usw.

> **Verantwortliche Stelle**

EUR-OP
(Amt für amtliche Veröffentlichungen der Europäischen Gemeinschaften)
OP/4 - Verkauf und Buchführung

1. EUR-OP-SALES OFFICES

(THE OFFICE FOR OFFICIAL PUBLICATIONS OF THE EUROPEAN COMMUNITIES)

➢ Field of Activity

Official EUR-OP network for the distribution of its products (publications, videos, periodicals) according to the principal of subsidiarity (EUR-OP does not sell its products directly).

➢ Target Public

The general public.

➢ Presence in the Community

15 Member States, more than 30 sales offices in the rest of the world (5 in East European countries, Japan, Australia, the United States, Canada, etc.).

➢ Actions

- Sale (and despatch) of newspapers, periodicals, monographs and videos;
- often: sale (and despatch) of legislative documents (document delivery);
- general information on Community policy in the context of sales policy.

➢ Network animation and methods of communication

A support, animation and cooperation programme led by EUR-OP: meetings, documentaries, circulars, etc.

➢ Responsible office

EUR-OP
(The Office for Official Publications of the European Communities)
OP/4 - Sales and Accounts.

1. BUREAUX DE VENTE
(OFFICE DES PUBLICATIONS OFFICIELLES DES COMMUNAUTES EUROPEENNES)

➤ **Domaine d'activité**

Réseau officiel d'EUR-OP pour la distribution, de ses produits (publications, vidéos, journaux) selon le principe de subsidiarité (l'EUR-OP ne vend pas ses produits directement).

➤ **Public cible**

Grand public

➤ **Rayonnement communautaire**

15 Etats membres, plus de 30 bureaux de vente dans le reste du monde (5 dans les pays de l'Est, le Japon, l'Australie, les Etats-Unis, le Canada, etc.)

➤ **Actions**

- Vente (et expédition) de journaux, périodiques, monographies et vidéos;
- souvent: vente (et expédition) de documents législatifs (document delivery);
- information générale sur la politique de la Communauté dans le cadre de la politique de vente.

➤ **Animation du réseau et techniques de communication**

Un programme d'appui, d'animation et de coopération est mené par l'EUR-OP:
réunions, documentaires, circulaires, etc.

➤ **Bureau responsable**

EUR-OP
(Office des Publications Officielles des Communautés européennes)
OP/4 - Vente et Comptabilité

371

2. EURO-BUCHHANDLUNGEN

> **Tätigkeitsbereich**

Verkauf der Veröffentlichungen von EUR-OP

> **Träger-Struktur**

Buchhandlungen

> **Zielgruppe**

Breite Öffentlichkeit

> **Wirkungskreis**

Über 60 Buchhandlungen in den Mitgliedstaaten

> **Ziele**

Bereitstellung eines qualifizierten Personals, das die Kundschaft über die Dossiers der Europäischen Union und die geeigneten Veröffentlichungen beraten und an maßgebliche Institutionen und Ad-hoc-Informationsquellen verweisen kann.

> **Aktionen**

- Darstellung der Veröffentlichungen von EUR-OP in einem dafür vorgesehenen Raum oder Schaufenster;
- Besitz eines ständigen Lagerbestands an Veröffentlichungen von EUR-OP;
- schnelle Lieferung der nicht im Lager verfügbaren Veröffentlichungen.

> **Betreuung des Netzes und Kommunikationstechnik**

Ein Förder-, Betreuungs- und Kooperationsprogramm wird von EUR-OP durchgeführt: Ausbildung von Verkäufern, Sitzungen, Dokumentarfilme, Rundschreiben usw

> **Verantwortliche Stelle**

EUR-OP
(Amt für amtliche Veröffentlichungen der Europäischen Gemeinschaften)
OP/4 - Verkauf und Buchführung

2. EUROPEAN BOOKSHOPS

➤ **Field of Activity**

Sale of EUR-OP publications.

➤ **Host Structure**

Bookshops.

➤ **Target Public**

The general public.

➤ **Presence in the Community**

More than 60 bookshops in the Member States.

➤ **Objectives**

Provide qualified personnel to be able to advise the customer on European Union documents and the appropriate publications and direct them towards relevant institutions and to ad hoc information sources.

➤ **Actions**

- Display of EUR-OP publications in a dedicated shop or sales window;
- holding of a permanent stock of EUR-OP publications;
- speedy supply of all publications not available from stock.

➤ **Network animation and methods of communication**

A support, animation and cooperation programme led by EUR-OP: training of sales assistants, meetings, documentaries, circulars, etc.

➤ **Responsible office**

EUR-OP
(The Office for Official Publications of the European Communities)
OP/4 - Sales and Accounts

2. EUROLIBRAIRIES

➤ **Domaine d'activité**

Vente des publications de l'EUR-OP

➤ **Structure hôte**

Librairies

➤ **Public cible**

Grand public

➤ **Rayonnement communautaire**

Plus de 60 librairies dans les Etats membres

➤ **Objectifs**

Offir un personnel qualifié qui peut conseiller la clientèle sur les dossiers de l'Union européenne et les publications appropriées et l'orienter vers les institutions compétentes et les sources d'information ad hoc.

➤ **Actions**

- Présentation des publications de l'EUR-OP dans un local ou une vitrine distincts;
- possession d'un stock permanent de publications de l'EUR-OP;
- fourniture rapide de toute publication non disponible en stock.

➤ **Animation du réseau et techniques de communication**

Un programme d'appui, d'animation et de coopération est mené par l'EUR-OP:
formation des vendeurs, réunions, documentaires, circulaires, etc.

➤ **Bureau responsable**

EUR-OP
(Office des Publications Officielles des Communautés européennes)
OP/4 - Vente et Comptabilité

3. DOKUMENTENDIENST AUF ANFRAGE

ZUGANG ZU ALLEN RECHTSAKTEN DER EUROPÄISCHEN UNION

➤ **Träger-Struktur**

Vertriebshändler von EUR-OP

➤ **Zielgruppe**

Jede an besonderen Dokumenten interessierte Person (Rechtstexte ...)

➤ **Wirkungskreis**

15 Mitgliedstaaten, plus 30 Verkaufsstellen weltweit (5 in den östlichen Ländern, Japan, Australien, den Vereinigten Staaten, Kanada usw.)

➤ **Ziele**

Der Dienst *Document Delivery* gibt interessierten Personen die Möglichkeit, nur spezifische Dokumente eines für sie interessanten Bereichs zu bestellen (z. B. im Amtsblatt veröffentlichte Richtlinien oder KOM-Dokumente). Abonnenten können genau angeben, ob sie die angeforderten Dokumente per Fax oder Post erhalten möchten.

Das Heraussuchen und die Lieferung aller Gesetzestexte der europäischen Institutionen werden für folgende Bereiche angeboten: Institutionelle Fragen, Zollunion und Handelspolitik, Landwirtschaft, Forstwirtschaft und Fischfang, Beschäftigung und Arbeitskräfte, Soziales, Gesetze und Verfahren, Verkehr, Wettbewerb und Unternehmen, Finanzierung, Wirtschaftsthemen - Verbraucherschutz, Auswärtige Beziehungen, Energie, Regionalpolitik, Umwelt - wissenschaftliche und technologische Forschung, Information, Bildung und Kultur - Statistiken.

377

➤ **Verantwortliche Stelle**

EUR-OP
(Amt für amtliche Veröffentlichungen der Europäischen Gemeinschaft)
OP/4 - Verkauf und Buchführung

3. DOCUMENT DELIVERY
ACCESS TO ALL THE LEGISLATIVE ACTS OF THE EUROPEAN UNION

➢ **Host Structure**

EUR-OP sales agents.

➢ **Target Public**

Everyone interested in specific community documents (legislative texts ...).

➢ **Presence in the Community**

15 Member States, more than 30 sales offices in the rest of the world (5 in the East European countries, Japan, Australia, the United States, Canada, etc.).

➢ **Objectives**

The *Document Delivery* service provides to interested parties the possibility of ordering specific documents only in a field which is of interest to them (e.g. directives published in the Official Journal or COM documents). Subscribers can specify if they want to take delivery of the required documents by fax or mail.

Research and provision of all legislative texts of the European Institutions affecting the following fields are offered: Institutional questions, Customs and commercial policy, Agriculture, forestry and fishing, Employment and labour, Social questions, Laws and procedures, Transport, Competition and companies, Financing, Economic issues, Consumer protection, External relations, Energy, Regional policy, Environment, Scientific and technical research, Information, Education and culture, Statistics.

➢ **Responsible office**

EUR-OP
(The Office for Official Publications of the European Communities)
OP/4 - Sales and Accounts.

3. SERVICE DES DOCUMENTS À LA DEMANDE

ACCES A TOUS LES ACTES LEGISLATIFS DE L'UNION EUROPEENNE

> **Structure hôte**

Agents de vente de l'EUR-OP

> **Public cible**

Toute personne intéressée par des documents communautaires spécifiques (textes législatifs ...)

> **Rayonnement communautaire**

15 États membres, plus de 30 bureaux de vente dans le reste du monde (5 dans les pays de l'Est, le Japon, l'Australie, les Etats-Unis, le Canada, etc.)

> **Objectifs**

Le service *Document Delivery* donne la possibilité aux parties intéressées de ne commander que des documents spécifiques d'un domaine qui les intéresse (p. ex. des directives publiées dans le Journal Officiel ou des documents COM). Les abonnés peurvent spécifier s'ils désirent prendre livraison des documents requis par fax ou par courrier.

Recherche et fourniture de tous les textes législatifs des Institutions européennes concernant les domaines suivants sont offerts: Questions institutionelles, Union douanière et politique commerciale, Agriculture, sylviculture et pêche, Emploi et main-d'oeuvre, Questions sociales, Lois et procédures, Transports, Concurrence et entreprises, Financement, Questions économiques - protection des consommateurs, Relations extérieures, Énergie, Politique régionale-
Environnement- Recherche scientifique et technique- Information, éducation et culture- Statistiques.

> **Bureau responsable**

EUR-OP
(Office des Publications Officielles des Communautés européennes)
OP/4 - Vente et Comptabilité

ELEKTRONISCHE PRODUKTE

EU in Ihrer Sprache – Zahlung in Ihrer Währung
EUROPE ELECTRONIC – EUR-OP_S NEW NETWORK OF
GATEWAYS

Das Interesse an Informationen über die EU, ihre Institutionen und ihre Politiken nimmt immer mehr zu. EUR-OP bietet eine Reihe von Datenbanken an, um Ihnen dabei zu helfen, Informationen aller Art – schnell, leicht und in der Sprache Ihrer Wahl - zu erlangen: EU-Recht, Pressemitteilungen, Bezugnahmen auf EU-Politik, öffentliche Ausschreibungen, Statistiken usw. (siehe *EUR-OP-Datenbanken* und *EU-Informationen auf CD-ROM,* unten).

Um den Zugang zu diesen On-line-Diensten zu erleichtern, wurde das neue System der nationalen Gateway-Vertriebshändler von EURO-OP im Januar 1995 in Betrieb genommen. Diese Gateways ermöglichen den Zugang zu allen Informationen über die Datenbank Eurobases der Europäischen Kommission und zu TED (Tenders Electronic Daily). Die Benutzer müssen jetzt nicht länger verschiedene Script-Dateien handhaben, da der Zugang jetzt über eine einzige Zugangsstelle erfolgt.

Durch die Übertragung der Verwaltungsfragen in bezug auf Abkommen und Unterstützung der Benutzer auf die Mitgliedstaaten, wendet EUR-OP das EU-Subsidiaritätsprinzip auf seine kommerziellen Datenbanken an. Gleichzeitig wird die Interaktion zwischen dem Informationslieferant und dem Benutzer leichter gestaltet.

Benutzer müssen eine Teilnahmegebühr zahlen, die in Landeswährung erfolgen kann (in Übereinstimmung mit der Referenz-Preisliste von EUR-OP).

ELECTRONIC PRODUCTS

The EU in your language – Payment in your currency
EUROPE ELECTRONIC – EUR-OP'S NEW NETWORK OF GATEWAYS

The interest in information on the EU, its institutions and their policies is ever-increasing. EUR-OP offers a series of databases to help obtain whatever information you need – quickly, easily and in the language of your choice: EU law, press releases, references to EU policy, public tenders, statistics, etc. (see *EUR-OP's databases* and *EU information on CD-ROMs*, below).

In order to further facilitate access to these on-line services, EUR-OP's new system of national gateway distributors became operational in January 1995. These gateways allow access to all information services on the European Commission database Eurobases and to TED (Tenders Electronic Daily). Users will no longer have to manage numerous script files as all can now be accessed through one single entry point.

By transferring the administrative matters related to the agreements and the user support to the Member States, EUR-OP applies the EU principle of subsidiarity to its commercial databases. At the same time, the interaction between the information supplier and user is made easier.

It will be necessary for users to conclude a subscription contract which can be paid in national currency (conforming to EUR-OP's reference price list).

PRODUITS ELECTRONIQUES

L'UE dans votre langue - Le paiement dans votre devise
**EUROPE ELECTRONIC – LE NOUVEAU RESEAU D'AGENTS DE
LIAISON DE L'EUR-OP**

L'intérêt pour les informations sur l'UE, ses institutions et leurs politiques ne
cesse de croître. L'EUR-OP propose une série de bases de données pour vous
permettre d'obtenir rapidement, facilement et dans la langue de votre choix,
toute information nécessaire: droit de l'UE, communiqués de presse,
références à la politique de l'UE, appels d'offres publics, statistiques, etc. (voir
bases de données de l'EUR-OP et *informations de l'UE sur CD-ROM*, ci-après).
Afin de faciliter davantage l'accès à ces services on-line, le nouveau
système des agents de distribution nationaux de l'EUR-OP est devenu
opérationnel en janvier 1995. Ces agents de liaison donnent accès à tous
les services d'information repris sur Eurobases, la base de données de la
Commission européenne, et à TED (Tenders Electronic Daily). Les
utilisateurs ne devront plus gérer de nombreux fichiers de textes car tous
sont désormais accessibles par un seul point d'entrée.
En transférant aux Etats membres les questions administratives portant
sur les conventions et l'assistance à l'utilisateur, l'EUR-OP applique le
principe de subsidiarité de l'UE à ses bases de données commerciales. Par
la même occasion, l'interaction entre le fournisseur et l'utilisateur des
informations est rendue plus facile.
Les utilisateurs devront souscrire un abonnement qui peut être payé dans
la devise nationale (conformément aux tarifs de référence de l'EUR-OP).

EUR-OP-Gateway-Vertriebshändler bieten folgende Datenbanken an:

ABEL: Ein Dokument-Versandsystem ermöglicht Ihnen on-line alle jüngsten EU-Richtlinien per Fax oder Post zu bestellen.

CELEX: Dies enthält das gesamte Regelwerk des EU-Rechts (siehe unten – CD-ROM).

ECLAS: Eine Datenbank der Zentralbibliothek der Europäschen Kommission mit Quellenangaben für alle Aspekte der europäischen Integration.

EUROCRON: Drei statistische Datenreihen, die die wichtigsten Bereiche des sozialen und wirtschaftlichen Klimas in der EU, regionale und Agrarstatistiken umfassen.

INFO 92: Erfaßt den aktuellen Stand der Verwirklichung des Binnenmarkts und die Sozial-Charta (Beschreibung der maßgeblichen Richtlinien), einschließlich der Eingliederung dieser Richtlinien in die nationale Gesetzgebung der Mitgliedstaaten.

OIL: Eine wöchentliche Angabe der Preise für Erdölprodukte ohne Zölle und Steuern.

RAPID: Der tägliche Presseinformations-Dienst gibt eine Auswahl von Pressemitteilungen und Hintergrundinformationen binnen zwei Stunden nach mittäglichen Briefings in Brüssel heraus.

SCAD: Bibliographische Datenbank mit mehr als 190 000 Dokumententiteln über EU-Politik.

SESAME: Eine Datenbank mit Beschreibungen der Forschungs- und Entwicklungsprojekte im Energiebereich auf EU-Ebene.

TED: Ausschreibungen für öffentliche Aufträge und Zulieferverträge, nicht nur der Mitgliedstaaten, sondern auch der AKP-Länder, der EFTA-Staaten, Japan und der USA. Windows-Softwarezugang zu TED: ECHO, PO Box 2373, L-1023 Luxemburg, Fax (352) 34 98 12 34.

IDEA: Eine neue, täglich aktualisierte Datenbank mit einer genauen Darstellung der verantwortlichen Personen in allen europäschen Institutionen (wird bald in Betrieb genommen siehe auch *Interinstitutioneller Leitfaden*, Seite 3);

EU information on-line
EUR-OP's DATABASES

EUR-OP's gateway distributors offer the following databanks:

ABEL: A document-delivery system. Enables you to order on-line all recent EU directives via fax or letter.

CELEX: This contains the complete body of EU law (see below – CD-ROMs).

ECLAS: A database run by the Central Library of the European Commission containing references to all aspects of European integration.

EUROCRON: Three statistical data sets covering the most important sectors of the social and economic climate in the EU, regional and agricultural statistics.

INFO 92: Covers the state of implementation of the single market and the social charter (description of the relevant directives), including the incorporation of those directives into the national legislation of the Member States.

OIL: A weekly indicative of prices of petroleum products without duties and taxes.

RAPID: The daily press information service giving a selection of press releases and background information notes within two hours of daily midday Brussels briefings.

SCAD: Bibliographical database containing more than 190 000 titles of documents on EU policy.

SESAME: A database containing descriptions of research and development projects in the energy sector at EU level.

TED: Invitations to tender for public works and supply contracts not only from the Member States but also from the ACP countries, the EFTA States, Japan and the USA. Windows software access to **TED:** ECHO, PO Box 2373, L-1023 Luxembourg, Fax (352) 34 98 12 34.

IDEA: A new daily updated database providing an accurate presentation of all the persons in charge of all European institutions (soon to be released; see also *Inter-Institutional Guide*, page 3).

Les agents de distribution de l'EUR-OP proposent les banques de données suivantes:

ABEL: Système de livraison de documents. Vous permet de commander on-line toutes les directives récentes de l'UE par fax ou courrier.

CELEX: Elle contient la totalité de la législation de l'UE (voir ci-après – CD-ROM).

ECLAS: Base de données gérée par la Bibliothèque Centrale de la Commission européenne contenant des références à tous les aspects de l'intégration européenne.

EUROCRON: Trois ensembles de données statistiques couvrant les secteurs les plus importants du paysage socio-économique de l'UE, des statistiques régionales et agricoles.

INFO 92: Compte rendu du degré de réalisation du marché unique et de la charte sociale européenne (description des directives ad hoc), y compris l'incorporation de ces directives dans la législation nationale des Etats membres.

OIL: Indicatif hebdomadaire des prix des produits pétroliers sans droits ni taxes.

RAPID: Service quotidien d'information de presse offrant une sélection de communiqués de presse et de notes d'information de fond dans un délai de deux heures après les séances d'information quotidiennes tenues à Bruxelles à la mi-journée.

SCAD: Base de donnée bibliographique contenant plus de 190 000 titres de documents relatifs à la politique de l'UE.

SESAME: Base de données contenant des descriptions de projets de recherche et développement dans le secteur énergétique au niveau de l'UE.

TED: Appels d'offres portant sur les marchés publics de fournitures et de services en provenance non seulement des Etats membres mais aussi des pays ACP, des Etats de l'AELE, du Japon et des Etats-Unis. Accès à TED par logiciel Windows: ECHO, PO Box 2373, L-1023 Luxembourg, Fax (352) 34 98 12 34.

IDEA: Nouvelle base de données mise à jour quotidiennement et qui donne une présentation exacte de tous les responsables de toutes les institutions européennes (à paraître prochainement);

EUR-OP-Gateways
EUR-OP-Passerelles

DEUTSCHLAND

Outlaw Informationssysteme GmbH
Ursulinergasse 1
D-97070 Würzburg
Tel. (49-931) 35 31 24-0
Fax (49-931) 35 31 24-1

ESPAÑA

Spritel
Parque Tecnológico, Edificio 103
E-48016 Zamudio (Vizcaya)
Tel. (34-4) 42 09 470
Fax (34-4) 42 09 465

ICELAND

Skyrr
Háaleitisbraut, 9
IS-108 Reykjavík
Tel. (354-1) 69 51 00
Fax (354-1) 69 52 51

IRELAND

InterGate
71 Talbot Street
IRL-Dublin 1
Tel. (353-1) 83 64 903
Fax (353-1) 85 51 509

ISRAEL

Trendline
12 Yad-Harutzim St.
Tel-Aviv 67778
Tel. (972-3) 63 88 822
Fax (972-3) 63 88 288

ITALIA

Cerved SpA
Via Staderini, 93
I-00155 Roma
Tel. (39-6) 22 59 11
Fax (39-6) 22 59 13 09

NORGE

Vestlandsforsking
Fossetunet 3
N-5800 Sogndal
Tel. (47-57) 67 60 00
Fax (47-57) 67 61 90

ÖSTERREICH

EDV-Elektronische Datenverarbeitung Gesellschaft
Hofmühlgasse 3-5
A-1060 Wien
Tel. (43-1) 59 90 72 77
Fax (43-1) 59 90 72 50

PORTUGAL

Telepac
Rua Dr. António Loureiro Borges 1
Arquiparque – Miraflores
P-1495 Lisboa
Tel. (351-1) 79 07 000
Fax (351-1) 79 07 043

SCHWEIZ/SUISSE/SVIZZERA

Schweizerische Zentrale für Handelsförderung (OSEC)
Stampfenbachstrasse 85
CH-8035 Zürich

SUOMI/FINLAND

VTKK Information Service Ltd
Espoontori B
SF-02770 Espoo
Tel. (358-0) 45 72 332
Fax (358-0) 45 73 756

SVERIGE

Sema Group InfoData AB
PO Box 34 101
Fyrverkarbacken 34-36
S-100 26 Stockholm
Tel. (46-8) 73 85 000
Fax (46-8) 61 89 778

UNITED KINGDOM

Context – Electronic Publishers
Grand Union House
20 Kentish Town Road
UK-London NW1 9NR
Tel. (44-71) 26 78 989
Fax (44-71) 26 71 133

Alle anderen Länder:

M. John Mortier
EUR-OP
2, Rue Mercier
I-2985 Luxembourg
Tel.: (352) 29 29 42563
Fax: (352) 29 29 42758

All other countries:

M. John Mortier
EUR-OP
2, rue Mercier
L-2985 Luxembourg
Tel.: (352) 29 29 42563
Fax: (352) 29 29 42758

All other countries:

M. John Mortier
EUR-OP
2, rue Mercier
L-2985 Luxembourg
Tel.: (352) 29 29 42563
Fax: (352) 29 29 42758

Informationen über die Tätigkeit des Europäschen Parlaments

EPOQUE:
EPOQUE ist eine dokumentarische Datenbank des Europäischen
Parlaments. Die Datenbank EPOQUE ermöglicht den Mitgliedern und ihren
Assistenten, politischen Fraktionen und dem Personal des Europäischen
Parlaments über eine Datenbank den Zugang zu für sie und ihre Arbeit
nützlichen Dokumentationen. Das zweite Ziel ist, Informationen über die
Tätigkeit des Europäischen Parlaments an die Außenwelt zu geben. Die in
EPOQUE verfügbare Dokumentation beinhaltet:

- gesetzgebende Verfahren (seit dem Inkrafttreten der Einheitlichen Akte),
- Sitzungsdokumente (Berichte, Entschließungsanträge...),
- Parlamentsfragen (schriftliche und mündliche Fragen),
- Datenbanken, Petitionen, Studien,den Bibliothekskatalog usw.

EPOQUE gibt derzeit Zugang zu 93 000 Dokumenten und 2 900
gesetzgebenden Verfahren.

Kontaktadresse:
Dokumentarische Datenbanken,
Datenverarbeitung, Anwendungen &
Indexe der Abteilung Debatten (GD IV),
Europäisches Parlament,
Bâtiment Schuman 3/73,
L-2929 Luxemburg
Fax (352) 43 93 17

Information on European Parliament activities

EPOQUE:
EPOQUE is a documentary database produced by the European Parliament. The EPOQUE database enables Members and their assistants, political groups and European Parliament staff to have access, via a database, to documentation useful to them in their work. Its second objective is to provide information on the activities of the European Parliament to the outside world. Documentation available in EPOQUE includes:

* legislative procedures (since the entry into force of the Single Act),
* session documents (reports, motions for resolutions...),
* parliamentary questions (written and oral questions),
* dabates, petitions, studies,
* the library catalogue, etc.

EPOQUE currently gives access to 93 000 documents and 2 900 legislative procedures.

Contact address:
    Documentary databases,
    Data-processing, Applications &
    Indexes of Debates Division (DG IV),
    European Parliament,
    Bâtiment Schuman 3/73,
    L-2929 Luxembourg,
    Fax (352) 43 93 17

Informations sur les activités du Parlement européen

EPOQUE:
EPOQUE est une base de données documentaire produite par le Parlement européen. La base de données EPOQUE permet aux Membres et à leurs assistants, aux groupes politiques et au personnel du Parlement européen d'accéder, au moyen d'une base de données, à la documentation qui leur est utile dans leur travail. Son second objectif est de fournir au monde extérieur des informations sur les activités du Parlement européen. La documentation disponible dans EPOQUE comprend:

* les procédures législatives (depuis l'entrée en vigueur de l'Acte Unique),
* les documents de séances (rapports, propositions de résolutions...),
* les questions parlementaires (questions écrites et orales),
* les débats, les requêtes, les études,
* le catalogue de la bibliothèque, etc

EPOQUE donne actuellement accès à 93 000 documents et 2900 procédures législatives.

Adresse de contact:
    Bases de données documentaires,
    Traitement des données,
    Division des Demandes & Index des Débats
    (DG IV), Parlement européen,
    Bâtiment Schuman 3/73,
    L-2929 Luxembourg
    Fax (352) 43 93 17

EU-INFORMATIONEN AUF CD-ROM

Einige der EUR-OP-Datenbanken sind auf CD-ROM erhältlich. Sie stimmen zwar nicht zu 100 % mit den jeweiligen On-line-Datenbanken überein, doch häufig sind sie benutzerfreundlicher und - wenn es viele Benutzer gibt ` (z. B. in Bibliotheken) - billiger, da hohe Telekom-Kosten verringert werden können. Andererseits haben sie den Nachteil, daß sie nur vier- oder zweimal pro Jahr aktualisiert werden, während Datenbanken ggf. täglich aktualisiert werden können:

1. **CD-ROM CORDIS** (Community R&D information service) gibt schnellen und leichten Zugang zu Informationen über Forschungsprogramme.

2. **Panorama der EU-Industrie** gibt einen umfassenden Überblick über die Lage der verarbeitenden und Dienstleistungsindustrie in der EU. Es enthält Analysen der Industriestruktur, die gegenwärtige Situation, Trends bei Produktion, Beschäftigung und Handel, Ländervergleiche der EU-Zahlen mit den USA und Japan, sowie Zahlen von 1983 bis 1993 mit Prognosen für die wichtigsten Sektoren bis 1997.

3. **Comext** ist auf CD-ROM erhältlich und enthält Außenhandelsstatistiken der EU und ihrer Mitgliedstaaten.

4. **Eurostat CD** enthält wirtschaftliche und soziale Statistiken, regionale Daten, Außenhandelsdaten, das Produktionsniveau sowie die Nomenklaturen zur Klassfizierung der unterschiedlichen Daten.

5. **Eurofarm:** Statistiken über Farmstrukturn, Weinanbau und Obstbäume. Die CD-ROM der historischen Ergebnisse ist eine einmalige Veröffentlichung und enthält methodologische Erläuterungen, Tabellen und ein mehrsprachiges Glossar.

EUR-OP richtet derzeit ein Netz der Vertriebshändler für die CD-ROM ein. Zwischenzeitlich sind Informationen erhältlich bei:
Jacques Phlypo,
MER 01/132,
2, Rue Mercier,
L-2985 Luxemburg,
Tel. (352) 29 29-420 17,
Fax (352) 29 29-420 27.

Kompletter Katalog der EU-Veröffentlichungen
EUROCAT CD-ROM

Diese CD-ROM enthält über 450 000 Quellenangaben für europäische Veröffentlichungen, die besonders nützlich für Personen sind, die an EG-Gesetzgebung, -Politik und -Tätigkeit interessier sind. Sie wird gemeinsam von Chadwyck-Healey, Ellis Publications und EUR-OP herausgegeben: Info:
Chadwyck-Healey Ltd.,
Cambridge Place,
UK-Cambridge CB2 1NR,
Tel. (44-1223) 31 14 79,
Fax (44-1223) 30 12 78/66 440,
und Ellis Publications,
EPMS BV,
Postbus 1059,
NL-6201 BB Maastricht,
Tel. (31-44) 57 22 75,
Fax (31-44) 57 22 99.

EU INFORMATION ON CD-ROMs

Some of the EUR-OP databanks are available on CD-ROM. They are not 100% identical to the corresponding on-line databanks but often they are more user-friendly and, if there are many users (e.g. in libraries), cheaper, as high Telecom costs can be reduced. On the other hand they have the disadvantage of being amended and updated only four or two times per year, while databanks can be updated daily, if necessary:

1. **CD-ROM CORDIS** (Community R&D information service) gives quick and easy access to information on research programmes.

2. **Panorama of EU industry** is an extensive review of the situation of the manufacturing industries and services in the EU. It provides analyses of industry structure, the current situation, trends in production, employment and trade, country comparisons of EU figures with the USA and Japan, and figures from 1983 to 1993 with forecasts for major sectors up to 1997.

3. **Comext** is available on CD-ROM and provides external trade statistics of the EU and its Member States.

4. **Eurostat CD** contains economic and social statistics, regional data, external trade data at product level and the nomenclatures used to classify the different data.

5. **Eurofarm:** statistics on farm structure, wine-growing and orchard fruit. The CD-ROM of historical results is a one-off publication comprising methodological notes, tabular results and a multilingual glossary.

391

EUR-OP is currently setting up a network of Sales agents for CD-ROMs. For the time being information can be obtained from:
Jacques Phlypo,
MER 01/132,
2, rue Mercier,
L-2985 Luxembourg,
Tel. (352) 29 29-420 17,
Fax (352) 29 29-420 27.

Complete catalogue of EU publications
EUROCAT CD-ROM

This CD-ROM gives more than 450 000 references for European publications especially useful for people inquiring about EC legislation, policies and activities. It is co-published by Chadwyck-Healey, Ellis Publications and EUR-OP: Info:
Chadwyck-Healey Ltd,
Cambridge Place,
UK-Cambridge CB2 1NR,
Tel. (44-1223) 31 14 79,
Fax (44-1223) 30 12 78/66 440,
and Ellis Publications,
EPMS BV, Postbus 1059,
NL-6201 BB Maastricht,
Tel. (31-44) 57 22 75,
Fax (31-44) 57 22 99.

INFORMATIONS DE L'UE SUR CD-ROM

Certaines banques de données de l'EUR-OP sont disponibles sur CD-ROM. Elles ne sont pas identiques à 100% aux banques de données on-line correspondantes mais elles sont souvent plus conviviales et lorsqu'il y a plusieurs utilisateurs (par ex. dans les bibliothèques), elles sont moins chères car les frais de télécommunication peuvent être réduits. D'autre part, elles présentent l'inconvénient de n'être corrigées et mises à jour que deux ou quatre fois par an alors que les banques de données on-line peuvent être mises à jour quotidiennement, si nécessaire:

1. **CD-ROM CORDIS** (Service d'information R&D communautaire) donne un accès rapide et facile aux informations sur les programmes de recherche.

2. **Panorama de l'industrie de l'UE** est un compte rendu détaillé de la situation des services et des industries de fabrication dans l'UE. Il propose des analyses du tissu industriel, de la situation actuelle, des tendances dans la production, l'emploi et le commerce, des comparaisons par pays des chiffres de l'UE avec les Etats-Unis et le Japon, et des chiffres de 1983 à 1993 avec des prévisions pour les secteurs les plus importants jusqu'à 1997.

3. **Comext** est disponible sur CD-ROM et fournit des statistiques sur le commerce extérieur de l'UE et de ses Etats membres.

4. **Eurostat CD** contient des statistiques économiques et sociales, des données régionales, des données sur le commerce extérieur au niveau des produits et les nomenclatures utilisées pour classer les différentes données.

5. **Eurofarm:** statistiques sur le tissu agricole, la viticulture et la culture fruitière. Le CD-ROM des résultats marquants est une publication à tirage limité comprenant des notes méthodologiques, des résultats sous forme de tableaux et un glossaire multilingue.

EUR-OP établit actuellement un réseau d'Agents de ventes pour les CD-ROM. Il est possible d'obtenir pour le moment des informations auprès de: Jacques Phlypo, MER 01/132, 2, rue Mercier, L-2985 Luxembourg, Tel. (352) 29 29-420 17, Fax (352) 29 29-420 27.

Catalogue complet des publications de l'UE
EUROCAT CD-ROM

Ce CD-ROM donne plus de 450 000 références de publications européennes particulièrement utiles pour les personnes qui font des recherches sur la législation, les politiques et les activités communautaires. Il est publié conjointement par Chadwyck-Healey, Ellis Publications et EUR-OP: Info:
Chadwyck-Healey Ltd,
Cambridge Place,
UK-Cambridge CB2 1NR,
Tél. (44-1223) 31 14 79,
Fax (44-1223) 30 12 78/66 440,
et Ellis Publications,
EPMS BV, Postbus 1059,
NL-6201 BB Maastricht,
Tél. (31-44) 57 22 75,
Fax (31-44) 57 22 99.

CD-ROM ÜBER EUROPÄISCHES RECHT

CELEX, die Datenbank mit dem gesamten Regelwerk des geltenden EU-Rechts, wie z. B. Unionsgesetzgebung, Fallrecht, vorbereitende Rechtsakte, Parlamentsfragen und nationale Bestimmungen zur Umsetzung von Richtlinien, ist jetzt auf CD-ROM erhältlich. Mit der Zusammenarbeit und Förderung von EUR-OP hat eine Reihe privater Firmen CD-ROM-Versionen von CELEX entwickelt. Es sind zwei Systeme in Englisch, Französisch und Deutsch und eines in Italienisch erhältlich. Alle CD-ROM sind als Einzelkopien und als Abonnement mit regelmäßiger Aktualisierung erhältlich:

1. EUROLEX

➢ **Inhalt:** CELEX 1:1 (100%) auf Eurolex CD-ROM. 540 MB (über 130 000 Dokumente) von EU-Recht auf einer Diskette – Überkreuz-Suche (in allen Bereichen) – direkter Zugang zu andern Anwendungen ist möglich.

➢ **Hardware-Erfordernisse:** PC/AT (MS-DOS-Version 3.0 und aufwärts) mit einem CD-ROM- Laufwerk (Modus 2).

➢ **Software:** Standard-Rechtssoftware – Standard-Eingabefeld und Hilfssystem auf CD-ROM.

➢ **Verfügbare Sprachen:** Deutsch.

➢ Info: Bundesanzeiger Verlag, Postfach 10 80 06, Breite Strasse 78-80, D-50667 Köln 1, Tel. (49-221) 202 91 13, Fax (49-221) 202 92 88, oder Verlag Dr. Otto Schmidt KG, Unter den Ulmen 96-98, D-50968 Köln, Tel. (49-221) 937 38 01, Fax (49-221) 937 389 43.

2. JUSTIS

➢ **Inhalt:** Die Justis CELEX CD-ROM enthält die komplette CELEX-Datenbank. Darüber hinaus wurden einige fehlende Texte der in CELEX gespeicherten Dokumente hinzugefügt.

➢ **Hardware-Erfordernisse:** IBM PC/AT, PS/2 oder kompatibel (MS-DOS-Version 3.3 und aufwärts) mit einem CD-ROM-Laufwerk, Microsoft CD-ROM-Erweiterungen Versionen 2.1 und aufwärts. 530 K frei in RAM.

➢ **Software:** Context-Software ermöglicht die Austauschbarkeit der Reihe rechtlicher CD-ROM, die derzeit von Context herausgegeben werden.
➢ **Verfügbare Sprachen:** Englisch, Französisch und Deutsch, Dänisch soll bis zum Sommer verfügbar sein.

➢ Info: Context Limited, Grand Union House, 20 Kentish Town Road, UK-London NW1 9NR, Tel. (44-171) 267 89 89, Fax (44-171) 267 11 33. Context bietet auch CD-ROM mit SCAD, der EG-Bibliographischen Datenbank, an und mit Rapid, Pressemitteilungen der EU (siehe EUR-OP-Datenbanken, oben).

3. EUROLAW

Eurolaw entält den gesamten Text der EU-Gesetzgebung und der Rechtsvorschriften (Verträge, Sekundar- und vorbereitende Gesetzgebung, Fallrecht, nationale Umsetzung und Parlamentsfragen). Es enthält Briefings über die UK-Umsetzung, die von DTI vorbereitet wird. Gewinner des Europäischen Informationspreises 1995!
Info: ILI – Infonorme London Information, Index House, Ascot, UK-Berks SL5 7EU, Tel. (44-1344)-874 343, Fax (44-1344) 29 11 94.

CD-ROM ON EUROPEAN LAW

CELEX, the database containing the complete body of EU law in force, such as Union legislation, case-law, preparatory acts, parliamentary questions and national provisions which implement directives is now available on CD-ROM. With the cooperation and encouragement of EUR-OP, a number of private firms have developed CD-ROM versions of CELEX. There are two systems available in English, French and German, and one in Italian. All CD-ROMs are available as single copies and on subscription with regular updates:

1. EUROLEX

➤ **Content:** CELEX 1:1 (100%) on Eurolex CD-ROM. 540 MB (more than 130 000 documents) of EU law on one disc – cross-searching (in all fields) – direct access to other applications is possible.

➤ **Hardware requirements:** PC/AT (MS-DOS version 3.0 and higher) with one CD-ROM drive (mode 2).

➤ **Software:** Standard legal software – Standard main input field and help-system on the CD-ROM.

➤ **Languages available:** German.

➤ Info: Bundesanzeiger Verlag, Postfach 10 80 06, Breite Strasse 78-80, D-50667 Köln 1, Tel. (49-221) 202 91 13, Fax (49-221) 202 92 88, or Verlag Dr Otto Schmidt KG, Unter den Ulmen 96-98, D-50968 Köln, Tel. (49-221) 937 38 01, Fax (49-221) 937 389 43.

2. JUSTIS

➤ **Content:** The Justis CELEX CD-ROM carries the complete CELEX database. In addition, certain missing texts of the documents stored on CELEX have been added.

➤ **Hardware requirements:** IBM PC/AT, PS/2 or compatible (MS-DOS version 3.3 and higher) with one CD-ROM drive, Microsoft CD-ROM extensions versions 2.1 and higher. 530 K free RAM.

➤ **Software:** Context software allowing for interchangeability between the range of legal CD-ROMs actually published by Context.

➤ **Languages available:** English, French and German, with Danish being due this summer.

➤ Info: Context Limited, Grand Union House, 20 Kentish Town Road, UK-London NW1 9NR, Tel. (44-171) 267 89 89, Fax (44-171) 267 11 33. Context also offers CD-ROMs with SCAD, the EC bibliographical database, and with Rapid, press releases of the EU (see EUR-OP_s databases, above).

3. EUROLAW

Eurolaw contains the full text of EU legislation and law (treaties, secondary and proposed legislation, case-law, national implemenation and parliamentry questions). It includes briefings on the UK implementation prepared by the DTI. Winner of the European Information Award 1995!
Info: ILI – Infonorme London Information, Index House, Ascot, UK-Berks SL5 7EU, Tel. (44-1344)-874 343, Fax (44-1344) 29 11 94.

CD-ROM SUR LE DROIT EUROPEEN

CELEX, la base de données contenant l'intégralité du droit de l'UE en vigueur, entre autres la législation de l'Union, le droit jurisprudentiel, les actes préparatoires, les questions parlementaires et les dispositions nationales qui appliquent les directives, est à présent disponible sur CD-ROM. Avec la coopération et les encouragements de l'EUR-OP, un certain nombre d'entreprises privées ont élaboré des versions CD-ROM de CELEX. Il y a deux systèmes disponibles en anglais, français et allemand et un en italien. Tous les CD-ROM sont disponibles en exemplaires uniques et sur souscription avec des mises à jour régulières:

1. EUROLEX

➢ **Contenu:** CELEX 1:1 (100%) sur CD-ROM Eurolex. Un disque de 540 MB (plus de 130 000 documents) sur le droit de l'UE – recherche croisée (dans tous les champs) – l'accès direct à d'autres applications est possible.

➢ **Equipement machine** requis: PC/AT (version 3.0 et supérieure de MS-DOS) avec une unité CD-ROM (mode 2).

➢ **Logiciel:** Logiciel standard autorisé – Champ de saisie principal standard et système d'aide sur le CD-ROM.

➢ **Langues disponibles:** allemand.

➢ Info: Bundesanzeiger Verlag, Postfach 10 80 06, Breite Strasse 78-80, D-50667 Köln 1, Tél. (49-221) 202 91 13, Fax (49-221) 202 92 88, ou Verlag Dr Otto Schmidt KG, Unter den Ulmen 96-98, D-50968 Köln, Tél. (49-221) 937 38 01, Fax (49-221) 937 389 43.

2. JUSTIS

➢ **Contenu:** Le CD-ROM Justis CELEX comporte la base de données CELEX dans son intégralité. En outre, certains textes manquants dans les documents mémorisés sur CELEX ont été ajoutés.

➢ **Equipement machine requis:** IBM PC/AT, PS/2 ou compatible (version 3.3 et supérieure de MS-DOS) avec une unité CD-ROM, extensions CD-ROM Microsoft versions 2.1 et supérieures. 530 K RAM libres.

➢ **Logiciel:** Logiciel Context permettant l'interchangeabilité dans la gamme des CD-ROM autorisés réellement publiés par Context.

➢ **Langues disponibles:** anglais, français et allemand, la version en danois devant paraître cet été.

➢ **Info:** Context Limited, Grand Union House, 20 Kentish Town Road, UK-London NW1 9NR, Tél. (44-171) 267 89 89, Fax (44-171) 267 11 33. Context propose également des CD-ROMs avec SCAD, la base de données bibliographique communautaire, et avec Rapid, communiqués de presse de l'UE (voir bases de données de l'EUR-OP, ci-avant).

3. EUROLAW

Eurolaw contient le texte intégral de la législation et du droit de l'UE (traités, législation annexe et proposée, droit jurisprudentiel, mise en application au niveau national et questions parlementaires). Il comporte des instructions sur la mise en application en Grande-Bretagne préparées par le Ministère du Commerce et de l'Industrie. A remporté le Prix européen de l'Information 1995! Info: ILI – Infonorme London Information, Index House, Ascot, UK-Berks SL5 7EU, Tél. (44-1344)-874 343, Fax (44-1344) 29 11 94.

ZUGANG ZU AUSSCHREIBUNGEN (TED-ALERT)

➤ **Genaue Bezeichnung**

Tenders Electronic Daily

➤ **Tätigkeitsbereich**

On-line-Version der *Supplements zum Amtsblatt der EG*, die die öffentlichen Ausschreibungen für öffentliche Aufträge und Dienstleistungen veröffentlichen

➤ **Träger-Struktur**

TED-ALERT-Vertriebshändler

➤ **Zielgruppe**

Erbringer von Dienstleistungen und Zulieferer

➤ **Wirkungskreis**

Mitgliedstaaten, Drittländer

➤ **Ziele**

Der *TED-alert*-Dienst ist über Vertriebshändler in verschiedenen Ländern innerhalb und außerhalb der EU erhältlich. Dieser Dienst bietet die Schaffung eines Unternehmensprofils in den neun Sprachen der EU an und erfaßt die Aktivitäten und Interessensbereiche eines Unternehmens, das dann in seiner eigenen Benutzersparte gespeichert wird. Alle Angebote werden täglich mit diesem Unternehmensprofil verglichen und bei Übereinstimmung werden die entsprechenden Dokumente an das jeweilige Unternehmen in einem vorher vereinbarten Format weitergeleitet (kurz, Standard, lang)

➤ **Verantwortliche Stelle**

EUR-OP
(Amt für amtliche Veröffentlichungen der Europäischen Gemeinschaften)
OP/4 - Verkauf und Buchführung

TENDERS ON-LINE DAILY
TED-ALERT

➤ **Precise Title**

Tenders Electronic Daily

➤ **Field of Activity**

On-line version of the *Supplement to the Official Journal of the EC*
which publishes public calls for tender for the procurement of supplies
and services

➤ **Host Structure**

TED-ALERT Agents

➤ **Target Public**

Providers of supplies and services

➤ **Presence in the Community**

Member States, non-EC countries

➤ **Objectives**

The *TED-alert* service is available through the intermediary of agents
established in various countries, both within and outside the EU.
This service offers the creation of a profile in the nine languages of the
EU (→ 1994), covering the activities and centres of interest of a
company, which is then stored under its own user schedule. All the
offers are compared with this profile on a daily basis and in the case of
conformity, the corresponding documents are sent to the company
concerned in a prior agreed format (short, standard, long)

397

➤ **Responsible Office**

EUR-OP
(The Office for Official Publications of the European Communities)
OP/4 - Sales and Accounts

ACCES AUX APPELS D'OFFRE
(TED-ALERT)

➤ **Intitulé exact**

Tenders Electronic Daily

➤ **Domaine d'activité**

Version on-line du Supplément au Journal officiel de la CE qui publie les appels d'offres publics portant sur les marchés publics de fournitures et services

➤ **Structure hôte**

Agents TED-ALERT

➤ **Public cible**

Prestateurs de fournitures et de services

➤ **Ravonnement communautaire**

Etats membres, pays tiers

➤ **Objectifs**

Le service TED-alert est disponible par l'intermédiaire d'agents établis dans divers pays, à l'intérieur et à l'extérieur de l'UE. Ce service offre la création d'un profil dans les neuf langues de l'UE (→ 1994), couvrant les activités et centres d'intérêt d'une entreprise, qui est alors stocké sous sa propre grille d'utilisateur. Toutes les offres sont comparées avec ce profil de façon quotidienne et en cas de concordance, les documents correspondants sont transmis à l'entreprise concernée dans un format préalablement convenu (court, standard, long)

➤ **Bureau responsable**

EUR-OP
(Office des Publications Officielles des Communautés européennes)
OP/4 - Vente et Comptabilité

FREIER ZUGANG ZU EUR-OP-VERÖFFENTLICHUNGEN

WOLLEN SIE MEHR ÜBER EUROPA WISSEN?

Schreiben Sie gerade ein Referat, eine Diplom-Arbeit, Doktorarbeit usw. über die Europäische Union? Brauchen Sie sachdienliche Informationen?

Falls ja, wird Ihnen diese kurze Information bei der Suche nach Literatur und anderen für Ihre Arbeit unerläßlichen Informationen helfen.

Was ist EUR-OP?

EUR-OP ist der offizielle Herausgeber für alle EU-Institutionen (Kommission, Rat, Parlament, Wirtschafts- und Sozialausschuß, Gerichtshof, Rechnungshof, Investitionsbank usw.). Aus diesem Grunde sind wir gezwungen, für unsere Produkte ebenso wie andere Verlagshäuser Gebühren zu erheben und wir bedauern, daß keine Ausnahmen gemacht werden können.

Unsere Produkte

Weiter unten finden Sie einen Überblick über unsere Produkte (Bücher, regelmäßig erscheinende Zeitschriften, Datenbanken, CD-ROM, Videos usw.):

➤ unsere kostenlose Zeitung, EUR-OP News, die vierteljährlich über alle neuen, wichtigen Veröffentlichungen berichtet

➤ unser jährlicher Katalog mit Publikationen (Auszüge aus Veröffentlichungen der letzten fünf Jahre)

➤ der "Mini-Katalog", der die wichtigsten aktuellen EUR-OP-Veröffentlichungen enthält

➤ verschiedene themenspezifische Kataloge (Eurostat, Videos, Datenbanken und eine Reihe von einzelnen Prospekten)

➤ CATEL, unser elektronischer Katalog, der über die meisten unserer Verkaufsstellen zugänglich ist (für mehr Auskünfte wenden Sie sich bitte an unsere Verkaufsstellen - siehe beiliegende Liste).

Für mehr Informationen über EUR-OP-Produkte bzw. für die Bestellung der o. g. Kataloge oder EUR-OP News, wenden Sie sich bitte an:
EUR-OP, OP/4 Promotion,
2 Rue Mercier,
L-2985 Luxemburg,
Fax (352) 48 85 73

Wenn Sie an einem Abonnement interessiert sind oder einzelne Bücher bestellen möchten, wenden Sie sich bitte direkt an einen guten Buchhandel oder EUR-OP-Verkaufsstellen in Ihrem Land (siehe Liste im Anhang).

FREE ACCESS TO EUR-OP PUBLICATIONS

DO YOU NEED TO KNOW MORE ABOUT EUROPE?

Are you writing a paper, a dissertation, a thesis etc. on the European Union? Do you need relevant information?

If so, this brief information will help you obtain the literature and other information necessary for your work.

What is EUR-OP?

EUR-OP is the official publisher for all the EU institutions (Commission, Council, Parliament, Economic and Social Committee, Court of Justice, Court of Auditors, European Investment Bank etc.). In this capacity we are obliged to charge for our products like any commercial publisher and we regret that no exceptions can be made.

Our Products

Any of the following will give you an idea of our products (books, periodicals, databanks, CD-ROM, videos etc.):

- ➤ our free newspaper, EUR-OP News, which reports quarterly on all important new publications;

- ➤ our annual publications catalogue (extracts from publications over the last five years);

- ➤ the "Mini-Catalogue", which contains the most important current EUR-OP publications;

- ➤ various thematic catalogues (Eurostat, videos, databanks and a series of individual leaflets);

- ➤ CATEL, our electronic catalogue which can be accessed through most of our sales offices (for details, please contact our sales offices - see the enclosed list).

For further information on EUR-OP products, or to order the above catalogues or EUR-OP News, please contact:
EUR-OP, OP/4 Promotion,
2 rue Mercier,
L - 2985 Luxembourg,
Fax (+352) 48.85.73

If you are interested in taking out a subscription or ordering individual books, please apply directly to a good bookshop or EUR-OP sales office in your country (see the enclosed list).

LIBRE ACCES AUX PUBLICATIONS DE L'EUR-OP

VOUS FAUT-IL EN SAVOIR DAVANTAGE SUR L'EUROPE?

Etes-vous en train de rédiger un article, un mémoire, une thèse, etc. sur l'Union européenne? Avez-vous besoin d'informations appropriées?

Si tel est le cas, ces brèves informations vous aideront à obtenir la documentation et autres renseignements nécessaires pour votre travail.

Qu'est-ce que l'EUR-OP?

EUR-OP est la maison d'édition officielle de toutes les institutions de l'Union européenne (Commission, Conseil, Parlement, Comité économique et social, Cour de justice, Cour des comptes, Banque Européenne d'Investissement, etc.). En cette qualité, nous sommes obligés de faire payer nos produits comme toute maison d'édition commerciale et regrettons de ne pouvoir faire aucune exception.

Nos Produits

Toutes les publications suivantes vous donneront une idée de nos produits (livres, périodiques, banques de données, CD-ROM, vidéos etc.):

- ➤ notre journal gratuit, EUR-OP News, qui paraît quatre fois par an et qui présente toutes les nouvelles publications importantes;

- ➤ notre catalogue annuel des publications (extraits des publications parues au cours des cinq dernières années);

401

- ➤ le "Mini-Catalogue", qui contient les publications actuelles les plus importantes de l'EUR-OP;

- ➤ divers catalogues thématiques (Eurostat, vidéos, banques de données et une série de prospectus individuels);

- ➤ CATEL, notre catalogue électronique qui est accessible par l'intermédiaire de la plupart de nos bureaux de vente (pour plus de détails, veuillez contacter nos bureaux de vente - voir liste ci-jointe).

Pour tout complément d'information sur les produits EUR-OP, ou pour commander les catalogues susmentionnés, ou EUR-OP News, veuillez contacter un des agents de vente de l'EUR-OP (....)

Si vous êtes intéressé par un abonnement ou des ouvrages particuliers, veuillez vous adresser directement à une bonne librairie ou au bureau de vente de l'EUR-OP dans votre pays (voir liste ci-jointe).

EUROPÄISCHE DOKUMENTATIONSZENTREN:
Ein Fenster zu allen EUR-OP-Vëröffentlichungen

Siehe auch Kapitel 1, EDZ S.31

Es wird Sie sicherlich interessieren, daß all unsere Veröffentlichungen gebührenfrei in jedem Europäischen Dokumentationszentrum (EDC) in einer der über 700 Universitätsbibliotheken eingesehen werden können. EDC sind normalerweise in akademischen Einreichtungen zu finden, deren Unterrichts- und Forschungsprograme als Schwerpunktbereich Studien über europäische Integration beinhalten. Die Veröffentlichungen in diesen Zentren sind der Öffentlichkeit zugänglich und können gemäß den Verleihbedingungen der jeweiligen Bibliothek ausgeliehen oder konsultiert werden.

EURISTOTE: 4 000 Abhandlungen über Europa

Die Euristote-Datenbank interessiert Sie vielleicht auch. Sie enthält detaillierte Erklärungen zu allen 4 000 Abhandlungen über Europa, die seit 1987 geschrieben wurden und andere seit 1989 laufende Forschungsarbeiten über europäische Integration, zusammen mit Adressen der Universitäten und eine Liste der Autoren und Forscher.

Kontaktadresse:
Europäisches Hochschulinstitut (EHI),
CP Nr. 2230,
I-50100 Firenze,
Tel. (39-55) 509 23 73,
Fax (39-55) 509 24 44

Ausdruck von Euristote:
CAT: CC-74-92-605-2A-C (Englisch/Französisch),
730 S., ECU 20; erhältlich in unseren Verkaufsstellen (siehe Anhang).

EUROPEAN DOCUMENTATION CENTRES:
A window on all EUR-OP publications

See also Chapter 1, page 32

It will certainly interest you that all of our publications can be viewed free of charge at any European Documentation Centre (EDC) in one of over 700 university libraries. EDCs are usually to be found in academic establishments which have made the study of European integration a permanent part of their teaching and research programmes. The publications at these centres are available to the public and can be borrowed or consulted, depending on the arrangements at the library concerned.

EURISTOTE: 4 000 dissertations on Europe

The Euristote databank may also interest you. It contains details of all 4 000 dissertations on Europe completed since 1987, other studies of European integration and studies in progress since 1989, together with the addresses of the universities and a list of authors and researchers.

Contact:
Europäisches Hochschulinstitut (EHI),
CP Nr. 2230,
I-50100 Firenze,
Tel. (39-55) 509 23 73,
Fax (39-55) 509 24 44

Printout of Euristote:
Cat.: CC-74-92-605-2A-C (English/French),
730 pp., ECU 20; obtainable from our sales office (see annex).

CENTRES EUROPEENS DE DOCUMENTATION:
Une fenêtre ouverte sur toutes les publications de l'EUR-OP

Voir aussi le chapitre 1, page 33

Vous serez sûrement intéressé par le fait que toutes nos publications peuvent être consultées gratuitement dans tout Centre Européen de Documentation (CED) existant dans plus de 700 bibliothèques universitaires. Les CED se trouvent généralement dans les établissements universitaires qui ont fait de l'étude de l'intégration européenne un élément permanent de leurs programmes d'enseignement et de recherche. Dans ces centres, les publications sont accessibles au public qui peut les emprunter ou les consulter suivant les dispositions en vigueur dans la bibliothèque concernée.

EURISTOTE: 4 000 mémoires sur l'Europe

La banque de données Euristote est également susceptible de vous intéresser. Elle contient des précisions sur les 4 000 mémoires réalisés sur l'Europe depuis 1987, sur d'autres études relatives à l'intégration européenne et des études en cours depuis 1989, ainsi que les adresses des universités et une liste des auteurs et des chercheurs.

Contact:
Europäisches Hochschulinstitut
(EHI), CP Nr. 2230,
I-50100 Firenze,
Tél. (39-55) 509 23 73,
Fax (39-55) 509 24 44

404

4

EUROPA PER SATELLIT

➤ **Tätigkeitsbereich**

Informationen der Unionsbürger über Verfahren des Parlaments, der Kommission

➤ **Träger-Struktur**

Fernsehprogramm übertragen über EUTELSAT II, von Montag bis Freitag, zweimal täglich (vor und nach 12h.)

➤ **Zielgruppe**

Breite Öffentlichkeit, Journalisten

➤ **Wirkungskreis**

Von EUTELSAT II-Übertragungen erfaßte Länder

➤ **Aktionen**

Live-Übertragungen von:
- Informationen über Pressekonferenzen
- Zusammenfassungen von Sitzungen und Besuchen der Kommissare, Minister und Staatschefs
- Tätigkeit des Parlaments in Straßburg und Brüssel
- alle Plenartagungen des Parlaments
- aktuelle Veranstaltungen der Kommission über die Union.

➤ **Kommunikationstechnik**

EUTELSAT II F2 10° E. Transponder 21. Frequenz down-link 11 080 000 MHz. Horizontale Polarität 19 Hhz/Volt. Audio: 6.60 MHz. Ïs pre-emphasis Wegener Panda 1. Subcarriers 7.02, 7.20, 7.38, 7.56 MHz. Audio-Abweichung: 150 KHz + 9dbm.

➤ Europäische Kommission
Generaldirektion X
Referat X/A T120 01/61

EUROPE BY SATELLITE

➤ **Field of Activity**

Information for citizens of the Union on the procedures of the
European Parliament, and of the Commission

➤ **Host Structure**

Television programme transmitted on EUTELSAT II, from Monday to
Friday, twice daily (morning and afternoon)

➤ **Target Public**

General public, journalists

➤ **Presence in the Community**

Countries receiving EUTELSAT II transmissions

➤ **Actions**

Direct transmission of:
* information on press conferences;
* summaries of meetings between Commissioners, Ministers and Heads
  of state;
* Parliamentary activities in Strasbourg and Brussels;
* all plenary sessions of the Parliament;
* current events of the Commission on the Union.

➤ **Communication techniques**

EUTELSAT II F2 at 10° E. Transponder 21. Frequence down-link 11 080
000 MHz. Horizontal polarity 19 Hhz/Volt. Audio: 6.60 MHz. Ïs pre-
emphasis Wegener Panda 1. Subcarriers 7.02, 7.20, 7.38, 7.56 MHz.
Deviation audio: 150 KHz + 9dbm.

➤ European Commission
Directorate-General X
Unit X/A T120 01/61

L'EUROPE PAR SATELLITE

> **Domaine d'activité**

Information des citoyens de l'Union sur les procédures du Parlement européen et de la Commission

> **Structure hôte**

Programme de télévision transmis sur EUTELSAT II, du lundi au vendredi, deux fois par jour (avant et après 12h.)

> **Public cible**

Grand public, journalistes

> **Rayonnement communautaire**

Pays couverts par les transmissions d'EUTELSAT II

> **Actions**

Transmission en direct de:
* information sur les conférences de presse;
* sommaires de réunions et visites entre Commissaires, Ministres et Chefs d'État;
* activités du Parlement à Strasbourg et Bruxelles,
* toutes les sessions plénaires du Parlement;
* événements d'actualité de la Commission sur l'Union.

> **Techniques de communication**

EUTELSAT II F2 à 10° E. Transponder 21. Fréquence down-link 11 080 000 MHz. Polarité horizontale 19 Hhz/Volt. Audio: 6.60 MHz. Is pre-emphasis Wegener Panda 1. Subcarriers 7.02, 7.20, 7.38, 7.56 MHz. Déviation audio: 150 KHz + 9dbm.

> Commission européenne
> Direction générale X
> Unité X/A T120 01/61

EUROPA AUF INTERNET

> **Tätigkeitsbereich**

Allgemeine Informationen über die EU

> **Träger-Struktur**

Der Serveur World Wide Web (WWW) der Kommission (EUROPA)

> **Zielgruppe**

Breite Öffentlichkeit

> **Wirkungskreis**

Weltweit. Jede Person mit Zugang zu Internet hat Zugang zum Serveur *EUROPA*

> **Ziele**

Dieses Pilotprojekt soll klare, vollständige und aktuelle Informationen über die Institutionen, Politiken, Ziele und Dienstleistungen der EG geben. Und dies auf leicht zugängliche Weise für die Unionsbürger und interessierte Personen weltweit.

> **Aktionen**

Gibt Zugang zu:
- Dokumenten allgemeinen Interesses des Parlaments und der Kommission
- Dokumenten über die Verfahren des Parlaments und der Kommission
- Informationen über die Datenbanken der Kommission
- Informationen über EUR-OP (und demnächst zu Auszügen aus seiner Zeitung *EUR-OP News*)
- Informationen für Studenten und Forscher.

411

> **Kommunikationstechnik**

> Es ist ein Internet-Zugang und WWW-Software erforderlich (für IBM-kompatible PC oder Macintosh: *NCSA Mosaic* oder *Netscape*; für die Systeme UNIX oder VAX: *Lynx*). Die Zugangsadresse für den Serveur *EUROPA* ist: http://www.cec.lu.

> Europäische Kommission
> Generaldirektion X
> Referat B/1
> Fax (+32-2) 299 92 96

EUROPE ON INTERNET

> **Field of Activity**

General information on the EU

> **Host Structure**

World Wide Web (WWW) server of the Commission (EUROPA)

> **Target Public**

General public.

> **Presence in the Community**

Worldwide. Everyone having access to Internet can access the server *EUROPA*

> **Objectives**

This pilot project endeavours to supply clear, precise, complete and current information on the institutions, policies, objectives and services of the EU, in a way that it is easily accessible to citizens of the Union and to interested parties worldwide

> **Actions**

Provide access to:
- general interest documents of the Parliament and the Commission;
- procedural documents of the Parliament and the Commission;
- information on Commission databases;
- information on EUR-OP (and, shortly, extracts of its journal *EUR-OP News*);
- information intended for students and researchers.

> **Communication techniques**

An Internet access and WWW software is required (for IBM or Macintosh compatible PCs: *NCSA Mosaic* or *Netscape*; for UNIX or VAX systems: *Lynx*). The access address for the *EUROPA* server is: http://www.cec.lu.

> European Commission
> Directorate-General X
> Unit B1
> Fax (+32.2) 299.92.96

LE SERVEUR EUROPA SUR L'INTERNET

➣ **Domaine d'activité**

Information générale sur l'UE

➣ **Structure hôte**

Le serveur World Wide Web (WWW) de la Commission (EUROPA)

➣ **Public cible**
Grand public

➣ **Rayonnement communautaire**

Mondial. Toute personne ayant accès a l'internet peut accéder au serveur *EUROPA*

➣ **Objectifs**

Ce projet pilote tâche de fournir des informations claires, complètes et actuelles sur les institutions, politiques, objectifs et services de l'UE, d'une manière facilement accessible aux citoyens de l'Union et aux parties intéressées dans le monde entier

➣ **Actions**

Donne accès à:
- des documents d'intérèt général du Parlement et de la Commission;
- des documents sur les procédures du Parlement et de la Commission;
- des informations sur les banques de données de la Commission;
- des informations sur l'EUR-OP (et, prochainement, des extraits de son journal *EUR-OP News*);
- des informations destinées aux étudiants et chercheurs.

➣ **Techniques de communication**

Il faut disposer d'un accès internet et d'un logiciel WWW (pour PC compatible IBM ou Macintosh: *NCSA Mosaic* ou *Netscape*; pour systèmes UNIX ou VAX: *Lynx*).
L'adresse d'accès pour le serveur *EUROPA* est: http://www.cec.lu.

Commission européenne
Direction générale X
Fax (+32-2) 299 92 96

IDA ON-LINE

➢ **Genaue Bezeichnung**

Interchange of Data between Administrations

➢ **Tätigkeitsbereich**

Schnelle Informationsübertragung (elektronische Post) zwischen den Verwaltungen der Mitgliedstaaten und den europäischen Institutionen

➢ **Träger-Struktur**

Netz X.400 (NSPP-12MS) der europäischen Institutionen

➢ **Wirkungskreis**

15 Mitgliedstaaten

➢ **Ziele**
Der IDA-Dienst ist um die Vereinfachung und Verbesserung der Kommunikation zwischen den europäischen Institutionen und Regierungsorganen der Mitgliedstaaten über interpersonelle elektronische Post bemüht, die schneller und zuverlässiger ist als die traditionelle Post. IDA stellt seinen Benutzern ebenfalls verschiedene telematische Dienste zur Verfügung.

➢ **Aktionen**
- Elektronische Post
- EIONET (Europäisches Netz für Umweltinformationen und -beobachtung)
- Netz für den Informationsaustausch über Pharmaprodukte in Europa
- TESS/SOSNET (Telematisches Netz für soziale Sicherheit)
- ANIMO (Informationsnetz für den Transport von Schlachtvieh)
- REITOX (Europäisches Informationsnetz über Drogenabhängigkeit)
- SIMAP (Informationssystem für öffentliche Aufträge)
- SHIFT (Hilfssystem für Hygienekontrollen an den Grenzposten zu Drittländern)
- PHYSAN (Pflanzenschutzkontrollen)
- DSIS (Informationssystem für Statistiken)
- SIGL (Integriertes Lizenzverwaltungssytem)
- QUOTA (Kontrollsystem für die Einfuhr von Waren aus Drittländern, die Mengenbeschränkungen unterliegen)
- TARIC (Integrierter Gemeinschaftszoll)
- EBTI
- TRANSIT (Automatisches Verzollungssystem für Waren im Transitverkehr zwischen der EU und EFTA-Staaten)
- VIES (Austauschsystem für Informationen über MwSt)

➢ Europäische Kommission
   Generaldirektion III

IDA ON-LINE

> **Precise Title**

Interchange of Data between Administrations

> **Field of Activity**

Rapid information transfer (electronic mail) between the
administrations of the Member States and the European Institutions.

> **Host Structure**

X.400 (NSPP-12MS) network of the European Institutions

> **Presence in the Community**

15 Member States.

> **Objectives**

The IDA service endeavours to simplify and improve communication
between the European Institutions and the governmental organisations
of the Member States by means of electronic mail, quicker and more
reliable than traditional mail. At the same time ZIDA makes various
telecommunications information services available to its users.

> **Actions**
- Electronic mail
- EIONET (European network for information on and observation of the
  environment)
- Network for information exchange on pharmaceutical products in
  Europe
- TESS/SOSNET (Telecommunications network on social security)
- ANIMO (Information network on the transportation of live animals)
- REITOX (European information network on drug addiction)
- SIMAP (Information system on public markets)
- SHIFT (System for assistance to health inspectors at border posts with
  non-EC countries)
- PHYSAN (Phytosanitary controls)
- DSIS (Distribution service for statistical information)
- SIGL (Integral system for licence administration)
- QUOTA (Control system for the importation of goods from non-EC
  countries subject to quantity restrictions)
- TARIC (Integrated community tariffs)
- EBTI
- TRANSIT (System of automatic customs clearance for goods in transit
  between the EU and EFTA countries)
- VIS (VAT Exchange Information System)

> European Commission
> Directorate-General III

IDA ON-LINE

> **Intitulé exact**

Interchange of Data between Administrations

> **Domaine d'activité**

Transfert d'information rapide (courrier électronique) entre les
administrations des Etats membres et les Institutions européennes

> **Structure hôte**

Réseau X.400 (NSPP-12MS) des Institutions européennes

> **Rayonnement communautaire**
15 Pays membres

> **Objectifs**

Le service IDA s'efforce de simplifier et d'améliorer la communication
entre les Institutions européennes et les organes gouvernementaux des
Etats membres par le moyen du courrier électronique interpersonnel,
plus rapide et fiable que le courrier traditionnel. IDA mettra également
divers services d'information télématiques à la disposition de ses
utilisateurs.

> **Actions**

- Courrier électronique
- EIONET (Réseau européen d'information et observation de
l'environnement)
- Réseau pour l'échange d'information sur les produits pharmaceutiques
en Europe
- TESS/SOSNET (Réseau télématique de la sécurité sociale)
- ANIMO (Réseau d'information sur le transport d'animaux vivants)
- REITOX (Réseau européen d'information sur les toxicomanies)
- SIMAP (Système d'information sur les marchés publics)
- SHIFT (Système d'assistance pour les contrôleurs sanitaires aux postes
de frontière avec des pays tiers)
- PHYSAN (Contrôles phytosanitaires)
- DSIS (Service d'information statistique distribué)
- SIGL (Système intégré de gestion de licences)
- QUOTA (Système de contrôle de l'importation de marchandises de pays
tiers soumis à des restrictions quantitatives)
- TARIC (Tarif intégré communautaire)
- EBTI
- TRANSIT (Système de dédouanement automatique pour les
marchandises en transit entre l'EU et les pays AELE)
- VIES (Système d'échange d'information sur la TVA)

> **Commission européenne**
Direction générale III

5

BELGIQUE / BELGÏE

**Commission Européenne -
Europese Commissie**
Bureau in België- Bureau en Belgique
rue Archimède 73 , Archimedesstraat 73
1040 Brussel-Bruxelles
Belgique-België

**Bureau d'information du Parlement
européen / Europees Parlement**
97-113 rue Belliard, Belliardstraat, 97-113
1047 Bruxelles-Brussel
Belgique-België

DANMARK

Europa-Kommissionen
Repraesentation i Danmark
Højbrohus, Østergade 61 - Postbox 144
1004 København K
Danmark

Information Kontor
Børsen
P.O. Box
1217 København
Danmark

DEUTSCHLAND

Europäische Kommission
Vertretung in der Bundesrepublik
Deutschland
Zitelmannstrasse 22
53113 Bonn
Deutschland

Vertretung in Berlin
Kurfürstendamm 102
10711 Berlin
Deutschland

Vertretung in München
Erhardtstrasse 27
80331 München
Deutschland

**Informationsbüro des Europäischen
Parlaments in Bonn**
Bonn-Center
Bundeskanzlerplatz
53113 Bonn
Deutschland

**Informationsbüro des Europäischen
Parlaments in Berlin (Außenstelle)**
Kurfürstendamm 102
10711 Berlin
Deutschland

ELLAS

Commission Européenne
Representation en Grèce
Vassilissis Sofias, 2 - T.K. 30 284
106 74 Athina
Ellas

**Bureau d'information du Parlement
Européen**
Leof. Amalias, 8
10557 Athens
Ellas

ESPAÑA

Comisión Europea
Representación en España
Paseo de la Castellana, 46
28046 Madrid
España

Representación en Barcelona
Av. Diagonal, 407 bis, Planta 18
08008 Barcelona
España

**Oficina de Información del Parlamento
Europeo**
Calle Fernanflor 4-7
28 4 Madrid
España

FRANCE

Commission Européenne
Représentation en France
288, boulevard Saint-Germain
75007 Paris
France

Représentation à Marseille
2, rue Henri Barbusse
13241 Marseille Cedex
France

421

Bureau d'information du Parlement Européen
288, boulevard Saint-Germain
75341 Paris Cédex 07
France

Bureau d'information du Parlement Européen
Boîte postale 1024
67070 Strasbourg Cédex
France

IRELAND

European Commission
Representation in Ireland
Jean Monnet Centre
39, Molesworth Street
Dublin 2
Ireland

European Parliament
Information Office
43, Molesworth Street
Dublin 2
Ireland

ITALIA

Commissione Europea
Rappresentanza in Italia
Via Poli, 29
00187 Roma
Italia

Rappresentanza a Milano
Corso Magenta, 59
20123 Milano
Italia

Officio Informazione del Parlamento Europeo
Via IV Novembre, 149
00187 Roma
Italia

LUXEMBOURG

Commission européenne
Représentation au Luxembourg
Bâtiment Jean Monnet
Rue Alcide de Gasperi
2920 Luxembourg
Luxembourg

Bureau d'information du Parlement européen
1, rue du Fort Thüngen
2929 Luxembourg
Luxembourg

NEDERLAND

Europese Commissie
Bureau in Nederland
Korte Vijverberg 5
2513 AB Den Haag
Nederland

Voorlichtingsbureau van het Europese Parlement
Korte Vijverberg, 6
2513 AB Den Haag
Nederland

ÖSTERREICH

Europäische Kommission
Vertretung in Österreich
Hoyosgasse 5
1040 Wien
Österreich

Informationsbüro des Europäischen Parlaments in Wien
Hoyosgasse 5
1040 Wien
Österreich

PORTUGAL

Comissão Europeia
Gabinete em Portugal
Centro Europeu Jean Monnet
Largo Jean Monnet, 1-10°
1200 Lisboa
Portugal

Gabinete de Informação do Parlamento Europeu
Largo Jean Monnet, 1-6°
1200 Lisboa
Portugal

SUOMI / FINLAND

Euroopan komission Suomen edustusto
Pohjoisesplanadi 31
00131 Helsinki
Suomi/Finland

Euroopan Parlamentti
Suomen tiedotustoimisto
Pohjoisesplanadi 31
00131 Helsinki
Suomi/Finland

SVERIGE

Europeiska kommissionen
Representation i Sverige
Hamngatan 6
10390 Stockholm
Sverige

Riksdagens Förvaltningskontor F5-41
10012 Stockholm
Sverige

UNITED KINGDOM

European Commission
Representation in the United Kingdom
Jean Monnet House, 8 Storey's Gate
London SW1 P3 AT
United Kingdom

Representation in Northern Ireland
Windsor House, 9/15 Bedford Street
Belfast BT2 7EG
United Kingdom

Representation in Wales
4 Cathedral Road
Cardiff CF1 9SG
United Kingdom

Representation in Scotland
9 Alva Street
Edinburgh EH2 4PH
United Kingdom

European Parliament
Information Office
2 Queen Anne's Gate
London SW1H 9AA
United Kingdom

423

Europäische Kommission
European Commission
Commission européenne

Europe Info – Verzeichnis wichtiger Informationsquellen der Europäischen Union
Europe Info – Directory of important information sources on the European Union
Europe Info – Répertoire des principales sources d'information de l'Union européenne

Luxemburg: Amt für amtliche Veröffentlichungen der Europäischen Gemeinschaften
Luxembourg: Office for Official Publications of the European Communities
Luxembourg: Office des publications officielles des Communautés européennes

1995 - 426 p. - 17,6 X 25 cm

ISBN 92-827-4950-9

CC-88-95-767-3A-C

Preis in Luxemburg (ohne MwSt.):
Price (excluding VAT) in Luxembourg: ECU 8
Prix au Luxembourg, TVA exclue:

424

EUROPE INFO dient als Leitfaden für diejenigen, die Informationen über die Europäische
Union suchen. Er enthält wichtige Informationsquellen in Europa und weltweit.

EUROPE INFO is designed as a concise reference guide for those seeking information on the
European Union. It lists the principal information sources both within Europe and worldwide.

EUROPE INFO sert de guide de référence concis pour les personnes à la recherche
d'informations sur l'Union européenne. Il donne la liste des principales sources
d'information en Europe et dans le reste du monde.